Assembly Modeling with SolidWorks 2006

For the Intermediate SolidWorks User

David C. Planchard & Marie P. Planchard

ISBN: 1-58503-280-8

SDC

PUBLICATIONS

Schroff Development Corporation

www.schroff.com
www.schroff-europe.com

Trademarks and Disclaimer

SolidWorks and its family of products are registered trademarks of the SolidWorks Corporation. Microsoft Windows, Microsoft Office and its family of products are registered trademarks of the Microsoft Corporation. Other software applications and parts described in this book are trademarks or registered trademarks of their respective owners.

Dimensions of parts are modified for illustration purposes. Every effort is made to provide an accurate text. The authors and the manufacturers shall not be held liable for any parts or drawings developed or designed with this book or any responsibility for inaccuracies that appear in the book. World Wide Web and company information was valid at the time of this printing.

About the cover:

The assembly illustrated in this book is created with components provided by the following companies:

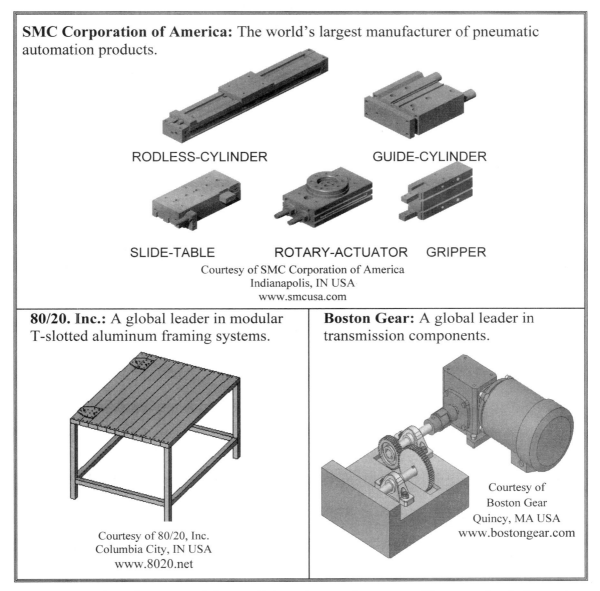

SMC Corporation of America: The world's largest manufacturer of pneumatic automation products.

RODLESS-CYLINDER   GUIDE-CYLINDER

SLIDE-TABLE   ROTARY-ACTUATOR   GRIPPER

Courtesy of SMC Corporation of America
Indianapolis, IN USA
www.smcusa.com

80/20. Inc.: A global leader in modular T-slotted aluminum framing systems.

Courtesy of 80/20, Inc.
Columbia City, IN USA
www.8020.net

Boston Gear: A global leader in transmission components.

Courtesy of
Boston Gear
Quincy, MA USA
www.bostongear.com

Designers and engineers work in a collaborative environment. They receive information from internal departments such as marketing, sales and purchasing. They supply information to external sources such as vendors and customers.

Collaborative information translates into numerous formats such as paper drawings, electronic files, rendered images and animations. On-line intelligent catalogs guide engineers to the product that meets both their geometric requirements and functional performance characteristics.

INTRODUCTION

Assembly Modeling with SolidWorks is written to assist the *intermediate* SolidWorks user who desires to enhance their skill sets in assembly modeling. The book provides a solid foundation in assembly modeling using competency-based projects. In step-by-step instructions, you perform the following tasks:

- Explore top-level assemblies that contain hundreds of features, parts, and sub-assemblies.

- Design, create, and modify assemblies, parts, and drawings based on geometric and functional requirements.

- Develop assemblies from a Bottom-up design modeling approach utilizing components from global suppliers.

- Develop a Top-down design modeling approach incorporating a Layout sketch and in-context features.

- Incorporate Configurations, Design tables, Bill of Materials, and Custom properties to represent multiple design options in the part, assembly and drawing.

- Understand external references and features developed In-Context of an assembly; edit and redefine references, features, and components.

- Exercise Shortcut keys, Customize toolbars, and Pop-up menus to build modeling speed.

- Maximize geometric relationships in the part sketch, build symmetry in the part, and reuse components in the assembly.

- Manage files through SolidWorks Explorer.

Each project begins with the desired outcomes and usage competencies. You know the templates, components, drawing and tables you need to create. You review a complete list of SolidWorks tools and commands up front.

Explore assembly modeling techniques through a series of design situations, industry scenarios, projects and objectives. The book compliments and enhances the **SolidWorks Reference Guide** and **SolidWorks Tutorials**. Although over 150 SolidWorks tools and commands are utilized in **Assembly Modeling with SolidWorks,** the book is not a commands guide. The book is a self-paced tutorial in a realistic design setting. Complex models expose you to large assembly modeling techniques. You focus on the design process while learning the commands relative to assemblies.

To obtain the most from this text, you should be familiar with the SolidWorks User Interface or other parametric modeling software application. Your skill sets should include the ability to create parts, assemblies, and drawings and manipulate documents through the Windows operating system.

The authors developed the industry scenarios by combining their own industry experience with the knowledge of engineers, department managers, vendors and manufacturers. These professionals are directly involved with SolidWorks everyday. They create assemblies with thousands of components and drawings with hundreds of sheets. Their responsibilities go far beyond the creation of just a 3D model.

About the Authors

Marie Planchard is the Director of Education Marketing at SolidWorks Corporation. Before she joined SolidWorks, Marie spent over 10 years as an engineering professor at Mass Bay College in Wellesley Hills, MA. She has 13 plus years of industry software experience and held a variety of management and engineering positions including Beta Test Manager for CAD software at Computervision Corporation. As a Certified SolidWorks Professional (CSWP), she presented at SolidWorks World 2003 & 2004. Marie was the founder and coordinator of the New England SolidWorks Users Group.

David Planchard is the President of D&M Education, LLC. Before starting D&M Education LLC, he spent over 23 years in industry and academia holding various Engineering and Marketing positions and degrees. He has five U.S. patents and one International patent. He has published and authored numerous papers on equipment design. David is also a technical editor for Cisco Press. He is a member of the New England Pro/Users Group, New England SolidWorks Users Group and the Cisco Regional Academy Users Group. David Planchard is an active industry and education consultant. David is a SolidWorks Research Partner and SolidWorks Solution Partner.

David and Marie are co-authors of the following books:

- **Engineering Design with SolidWorks 1999, 2000, 2001, 2001Plus, 2003, 2004, 2005, and 2006.**

- **SolidWorks Tutorial with Multimedia CD 2001/2001Plus, 2003, 2004, 2005, and 2006.**

- **SolidWorks The Basics, with Multimedia CD 2004, 2005, and 2006.**

- **Assembly Modeling with SolidWorks 2001Plus, 2003, 2004-2005, and 2006.**

- **Drawing and Detailing with SolidWorks 2001/2001Plus, 2002, 2003, 2004, 2005, and 2006.**

- **Applications in Sheet Metal Using Pro/SHEETMETAL & Pro/ENGINEER.**

- **An Introduction to Pro/SHEETMETAL.**

Acknowledgements

The authors would like to acknowledge the following professionals for their contribution to the design and content of this book. Their assistance has been invaluable.

Wayne Tiffany, CSWP, Automatic Systems Inc.

SMC Corp. of America.

Richard Barber and the EPT Team, Emerson-EPT Corporation.

The SolidWorks Educational Team.

Dave Pancoast and the SolidWorks Training Team.

Computer Aided Products Application Engineers: Jason Pancoast, Keith Pederson, Adam Snow and Joe St Cyr.

SolidWorks professionals: Mike J. Wilson, Devon Sowell, Scott Baugh, Paul Salvador, Gene Dimonte and Matt Lombard.

Ivette Rodriguez, ASME International.

Leonard Connor, American Welding Society.

For this 4th edition of **Assembly Modeling with SolidWorks**, we realize that keeping software application books up to date remains important to our customers. We value the hundreds of professors, students, designers and engineers that have provided us input to enhance our books. We also value your suggestions and comments.

Please contact us with any comments, questions or suggestions on this book or any of our other SolidWorks SDC Publications.

Please contact us with any comments, questions or suggestions on this book or any of our other SolidWorks SDC Publications at dplanchard@msn.com.

References:

References used in this text:

- <u>SolidWorks Users Guide</u>, SolidWorks Corporation, 2006.
- <u>SolidWorks Reference Guide</u>[1], SolidWorks Corporations, 2006.
- COSMOS/Works On-line help 2006.
- ASME Y14 <u>Engineering Drawing and Related Documentation Practices</u>.
- Gradin, Hartley, Fundamentals of the Finite Element Method, Macmillan, NY 1986.
- Jensen, Cecil, <u>Interpreting Engineering Drawings</u>, Glencoe 2002.
- Norton, Robert, <u>Design of Machinery</u>, 2ed. McGraw Hill, Boston, MA.
- Hibbler, R. C. <u>Engineering Mechanics Statics and Dynamics</u>, 8th ed. Prentice Hall, Saddle River, NJ.
- Beer & Johnson, <u>Vector Mechanics for Engineers</u>, 6th ed. McGraw Hill, Boston, MA.
- Planchard & Planchard, <u>Drawing and Detailing with SolidWorks</u>, SDC Pub., Mission, KS 2002.
- 80/20 Product Manual, 80/20, Inc., Columbia City, IN, 2006.
- Reid Tool Supply Product Manual, Reid Tool Supply Co., Muskegon, MI, 2006.
- SMC Corporation of America, Product Manuals, Indiana, USA, 2006.
- DE-STA-CO Industries, On-line Catalog, 2006.
- Boston Gear, On-line Catalog, 2006.

[1] The <u>SolidWorks Reference Guide 2006</u> is a .pdf document available to subscription users to download from the SolidWorks website.

TABLE OF CONTENTS

Index

Design Intent

SolidWorks defines design intent as the process in which the model is developed to accept future changes.

Models behave differently when design changes occur. Design for change. Utilize geometry for symmetry, reuse common features and reuse common parts.

Build change into the following areas:

1. Sketch.

2. Feature.

3. Part.

4. Assembly.

5. Drawing.

1. Design Intent in the Sketch.

Build the design intent in the sketch as you create the profile.

A profile is determined from the sketch tools, Example: rectangle, circle and arc.

Build symmetry into the profile through a sketch centerline, mirror entity and position about the reference planes and Origin.

Build design intent as you sketch with automatic relationships.

A rectangle contains horizontal, vertical and perpendicular automatic relations. Build design intent using added geometric relations. Example: horizontal, vertical, coincident, midpoint, intersection, tangent and perpendicular.

Example A: Develop a square profile.

Build the design intent to create a square profile.

Sketch a rectangle with the Origin approximately in the center. Insert a centerline. Add a midpoint relation. Add an equal relation between the two perpendicular lines. Insert a dimension to define the exact width of the square.

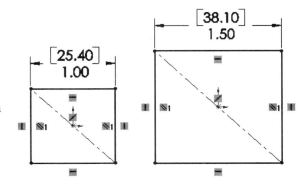

Example B: Develop a rectangular profile.

Position the bottom horizontal midpoint of the rectangular profile at the Origin.

Sketch a rectangle. Add a midpoint relation between the horizontal edge of the rectangle and the Origin. Insert two dimensions to define the width and height of the rectangle.

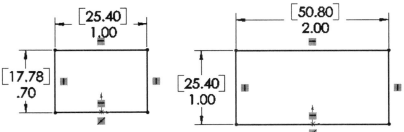

2. Design Intent in the Feature.

Build design intent into a feature by addressing symmetry, feature selection and the order of feature creations.

Example A: Extruded feature remains symmetric about a plane.

Utilize the Mid Plane Depth option. Change the depth and the feature remains symmetric about the Front Plane.

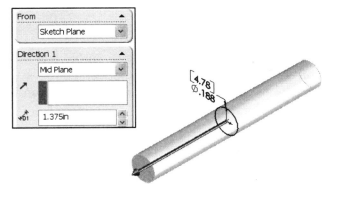

Example B: Part manufactured utilizing an injection-molded process.

Plastic parts require draft to remove the part from the mold. Utilize the Draft feature. Change the draft angle as determined by the manufacturer.

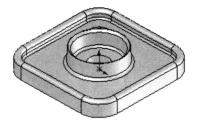

Example C: Six holes for a bolt circle.

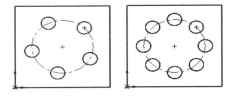

Do you create six separate Extruded Cuts? No. Create one hole with the Hole Wizard. Insert a Circular Pattern. Change the number of holes from five to eight. The holes remain centered on the bolt circle.

3. Design Intent in the Part.

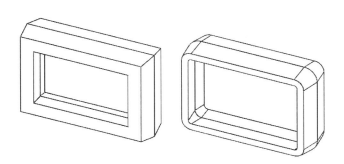

Utilize symmetry, feature order and reuse common features to build design intent into the part.

Example A: Feature Order.

Is the entire part symmetric?

Feature order affects the part. Apply the Shell feature before the Fillet feature and the inside corners remain perpendicular.

4. Design Intent in the Assembly.

Utilize symmetry, reuse common parts and use the Mate relationship between parts to build the design intent into an assembly.

Example A: Reuse Geometry in the PLATE-TUBE assembly.

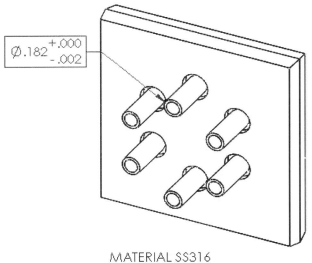

The PLATE part contains a Circular Pattern of six Holes. Insert one TUBE into the first Hole. Utilize Component Pattern to copy the TUBE to the other five holes.

MATERIAL SS316
LASER WELD ONLY, NO EPOXY

5. Design Intent in the Drawing.

Utilize dimensions, tolerances and notes in parts and assemblies to build the design intent into the Drawing.

Example A: Tolerance and material in the drawing.

Insert an outside diameter tolerance +.000/-.002 into the TUBE part. The tolerance propagates to the drawing.

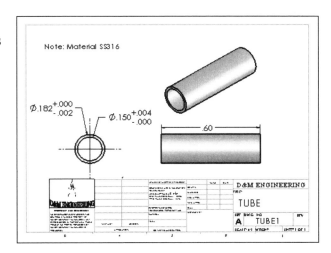

Example B: Utilize reference dimension in the drawing for manufacturing requirements.

Dimensions and geometric relations are created in a part to represent the symmetric design intent.

Add reference dimensions from the horizontal and vertical baseline for manufacturing.

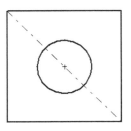

Part Sketch created with diagonal construction line and Midpoint geometric relation.

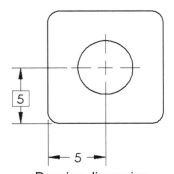

Drawing dimension scheme created from horizontal and vertical base line.

Overview of Projects:

Project 1: File Management

File management is a very important tool in the development process. In a large assembly, there could be hundreds or even thousands of parts. To facilitate time, parts and assemblies are organized and distributed between team members. The project manager develops an assembly layout to organize assemblies and parts.

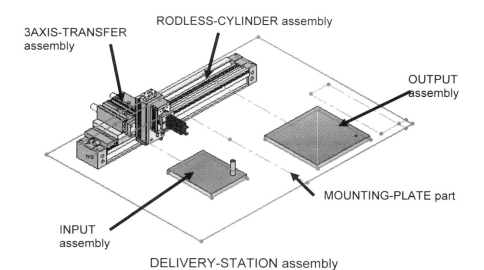

DELIVERY-STATION assembly

In Project 1 you review the customer's requirements and the pneumatic components specified by the senior engineer. Create the file folders, Assembly Template and Part Template required to organize the project. Qualify vendor components obtained from the World Wide Web. Utilize SolidWorks Explorer to preview and rename components.

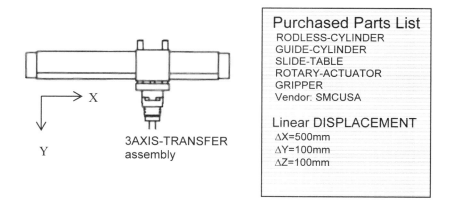

Rough Sketch -Top view and Purchased Parts List
3AXIS TRANSFER assembly (Your Task)

Project 2: Fundamentals of Assembly Modeling

Project 2 introduces the fundamentals of Assembly Modeling by creating the LINEAR-TRANSFER assembly. The first component of the 3AXIS-TRANSFER assembly is the LINEAR-TRANSFER assembly. Create the PLATE-A part based on the geometric and functional requirements of the RODLESS-CYLINDER assembly. Create configurations for the RODLESS-CYLINDER assembly to represent the various physical positions.

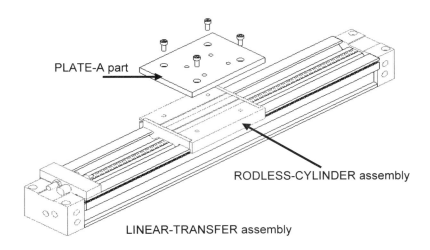

PLATE-A part

RODLESS-CYLINDER assembly

LINEAR-TRANSFER assembly

Project 3: Top-Down Design – In Context

The 2AXIS-TRANSFER assembly is the second sub-assembly for the 3AXIS-TRANSFER assembly. The 2AXIS-TRANSFER assembly combines the GUIDE-CYLINDER assembly and the SLIDE-TABLE assembly.

The SLIDE-TABLE assembly cannot be fastened directly to the GUIDE-CYLINDER assembly. Design the PLATE-B part as an interim part to address this issue. Create configurations for the GUIDE-CYLINDER, SLIDE-TABLE, and 2AXIS-TRANFER assemblies.

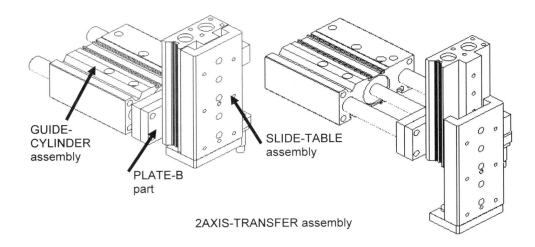

GUIDE-
CYLINDER
assembly

PLATE-B
part

SLIDE-TABLE
assembly

2AXIS-TRANSFER assembly

Project 4: Configurations, Properties, Design Tables, and References

The ROTARY-GRIPPER assembly is the third sub-assembly for the 3AXIS-TRANSFER assembly. The ROTARY assembly rotates the GRIPPER assembly.

The GRIPPER assembly cannot be directly fastened to the ROTARY assembly. Design PLATE-D as an interim part to address this issue. Create the PLATE-D configurations with a Design Table. Control the mass, material and description of PLATE-D through Custom Properties.

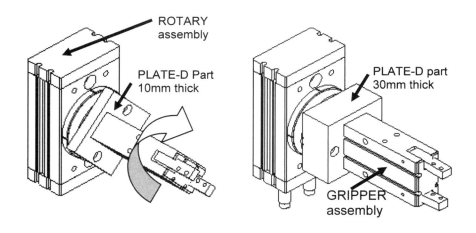

ROTARY-GRIPPER assembly

Project 5: Assembly Drawing

Create the 3AXIS-TRANSFER drawing. The 3AXIS-TRANSFER drawing utilizes different configurations of the 3AXIS-TRANSFER assembly. Add dimensions, Bill of Materials, and Custom Properties.

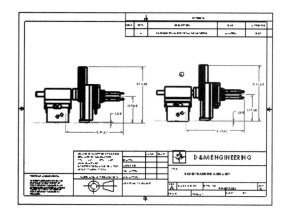
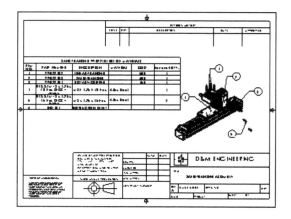

3AXIS-TRANSFER drawing

Project 6: Top-Down Design Assembly Modeling Techniques

Project 6 focuses on the Top-Down Design Assembly Modeling approach. Develop a Layout Sketch for the DELIVERY-STATION assembly. Create components and modify them in the context of the assembly. Reorder parts contained in different levels of the assembly. Utilize an Equation to control part and assembly dimensions. Import 3D and 2D Autocad geometry to create the FRAME assembly.

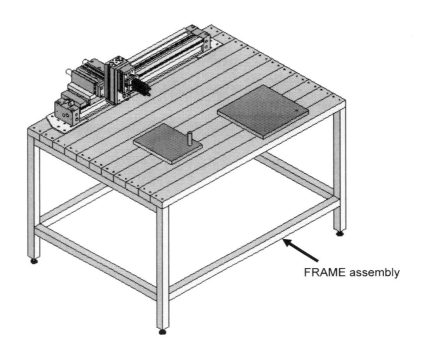

FRAME assembly

DELIVERY-STATION assembly

Command Syntax

The following command syntax is utilized throughout the text. Commands that require you to perform an action are displayed in **Bold** text.

Format:	Convention:	Example:
Bold	All commands actions. Selected icon button. Selected geometry: line, circle. Value entries.	Click **Tools**, **Options** from the Main menu. Click **Rectangle** ▭ from the Sketch toolbar. Select the **center point**. Enter **3.0** for Radius.
Capitalized	Filenames. First letter in a feature name.	Save the **LINEAR-TRANSFER** assembly. Click the **Fillet** feature.

Windows Terminology

The mouse buttons provide an integral role in executing SolidWorks commands.

The mouse buttons execute commands, select geometry, display Shortcut menus and provide information feedback. The table below contains a summary of mouse button terminology:

Item:	Description:
Click	Press and release the left mouse button.
Double-click	Double press and release the left mouse button.
Click inside	Press the left mouse button. Wait a second, and then press the left mouse button inside the text box.
	Use this technique to modify Feature names in the FeatureManager design tree.
Drag	Point to an object, press and hold the left mouse button down.
	Move the mouse pointer to a new location.
	Release the left mouse button.
Right-click	Press and release the right mouse button.
	A Shortcut menu is displayed. Use the left mouse button to select a menu command.
ToolTip	Position the mouse pointer over an Icon (button). The tool name is displayed below the mouse pointer.
Large ToolTip	Position the mouse pointer over an Icon (button). The mouse pointer displays the tool name and a description of its functionality below the Icon.
Mouse pointer feedback	Position the mouse pointer over various areas of the sketch, part, assembly or drawing. The cursor provides feedback depending on the geometry.
Window-select	To select multiple items, position the mouse pointer in an upper corner location. Drag the mouse pointer to the opposite corner. Release the mouse pointer. The bounding box contains the selected items.

A mouse with a center wheel provides additional functionality in SolidWorks.

Roll the center wheel downward to enlarge the model in the Graphics window.

Hold the center wheel down. Drag the mouse in the Graphics window to rotate the model.

Windows Shortcuts

The table below contains the pre-defined keyboard shortcuts in Microsoft Windows:

Action:	Keyboard Combination:
Open the Start menu	Windows Logo key
Open Windows Explorer	Windows Logo key + E
Minimize all open windows	Windows Logo key + M
Open a Search window	Windows Logo key + F
Open Windows Help	Windows Logo key + F1
Select multiple geometry items in a SolidWorks document	Ctrl key (Hold the Ctrl key down. Select items.) Release the Ctrl key.

Review various Windows terminology and the graphical user interface in SolidWorks.

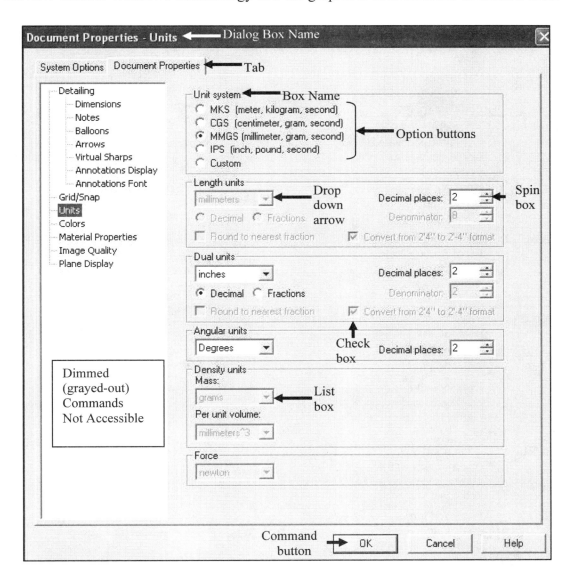

Item:	Description:
Property Manager/ Dialog box name	Name of a window in which to enter information.
Box name	Name of a sub-window area inside the dialog box.
Check box	A square box. Click to turn on/off an option.
Spin box	A box in which to type values or scroll by numerical increments.
Dimmed command	A menu command that is not currently available (light gray).
Tab	Dialog box sub-headings to simplify complex menus.
Option button	A small circle to activate/deactivate a single dialog box option.
Drop down arrow	Opens a cascading list containing additional options.
List box	A box containing a list of items. Click the list drop down arrow. Click the desired option.
Select box	A box containing select items such as edges and faces.
Text box	A box to type text.
OK	Executes the command and closes the dialog box.
CANCEL	Closes the dialog box and leaves the original dialog box settings.
APPLY	Executes the command. The dialog box remains open.

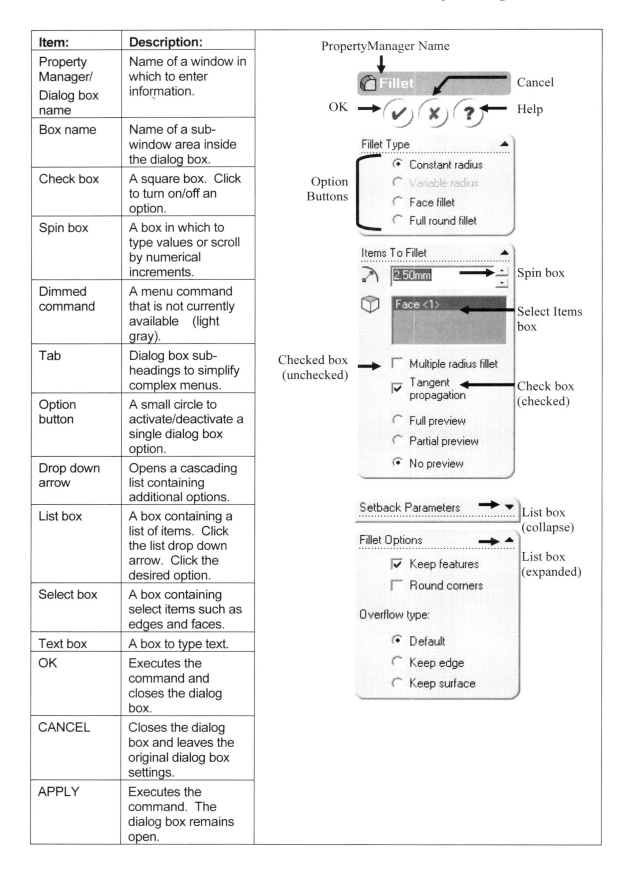

SolidWorks Keyboard Shortcuts

The table below lists the pre-defined keyboard shortcuts in SolidWorks:

Action:	Key Combination:
Model Views:	
Rotate the model horizontally or vertically:	**Arrow** keys
Rotate the model horizontally or vertically 90 degrees.	**Shift + Arrow** keys
Rotate the model clockwise or counterclockwise	**Alt** + left of right **Arrow** keys
Pan the model	**Ctrl + Arrow** keys
Zoom in	**Shift + z**
Zoom out	**z**
Zoom to fit	**f**
Previous view	**Ctrl + Shift + z**
View Orientation:	
View Orientation menu	**Spacebar**
Front view	**Ctrl + 1**
Back view	**Ctrl + 2**
Left view	**Ctrl + 3**
Right view	**Ctrl + 4**
Top view	**Ctrl + 5**
Bottom view	**Ctrl + 6**
Isometric view	**Ctrl + 7**
NormalTo view	**Ctrl + 8**
Selection Filters:	
Filter edges	**e**
Filter vertices	**v**
Filter faces	**x**
Toggle Selection Filter toolbar	**F5**
Toggle selection filters on/off	**F6**
File menu items:	
New SolidWorks document	**Ctrl + n**
Open document	**Ctrl + o**
Open From Web Folder	**Ctrl + w**
Make Drawing from Part	**Ctrl + d**
Make Assembly from Part	**Ctrl + a**
Save	**Ctrl +s**
Print	**Ctrl + p**
Additional shortcuts:	
Access online help inside of PropertyManager or dialog box	**F1**
Rename an item in the FeatureManager design tree	**F2**
Rebuild the model	**Ctrl + b**
Force rebuild – Rebuild the model and all its features	**Ctrl + q**
Redraw the screen	**Ctrl + r**
Cycle between open SolidWorks document	**Ctrl + Tab**
Line to arc/arc to line in the Sketch	**a**
Undo	**Ctrl + z**
Redo	**Ctrl + y**
Cut	**Ctrl + x**
Copy	**Ctrl + c**

Additional shortcuts:	
Paste	**Ctrl + v**
Delete	**Delete**
Next window	**Ctrl + F6**
Close window	**Ctrl + F4**
Selects all text inside an Annotations text box	**Ctrl + a**

In the Sketch, the Esc key unselects geometry items currently selected in the Properties box and Add Relations box. In the model, the Esc key closes the PropertyManager and cancels the selections. The text utilizes Shortcut keys in the step-by-step instructions.

Learning Method

The Learning Method utilized in this text follows an active learning approach.

- Read the description in the text to understand the actions to perform.
- Do the step-by-step instructions in each Activity.
- Perform the additional exercises.

The start of each activity begins with an Activity label.

Activity: LINEAR-TRANSFER Assembly

The steps you perform in SolidWorks contain a number. Execute commands are displayed in **bold**. Work through the steps in sequence.

Example: **34)** Click **OK** ✔.

Step 34 requires you to click the OK ✔ icon with the left mouse button.

Notes to Instructors:

Additional Information on utilizing Assembly Modeling with SolidWorks can be obtained from the SDC Corporation: (www.schroff.com). All models utilized in the DELIVERY STATION project were saved at SolidWorks 2006.

Performance:

The assemblies contain numerous components and features. System performance is best when the assemblies are loaded on the local hard drive and only the SolidWorks applications are opened.

Working across a network in a school environment is possible. Please contact the authors on utilizing this text in a classroom network environment for assistance.

Vendor Components:

Components are obtained from the vendor's web site and supplied on the enclosed CD. The components are representations of the actual parts and assemblies. They have been modified for instructional purposed.

Notes:

Project 1
File Management

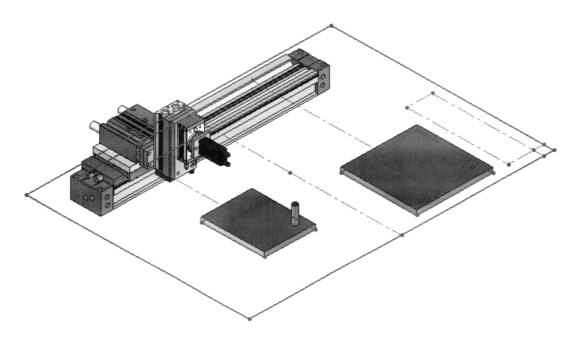

Below are the desired outcomes and usage competencies based on the completion of this Project.

Project Desired Outcomes:	Usage Competencies:
• ASM-MM-ANSI Assembly Template. • ASM-MM-ANSI-DESIGN-JOURNAL Assembly Template. • PART-MM-ANSI-AL6061 Part Template.	• Understanding of System Options and Document Properties as they are applied to an Assembly and an Assembly Template.
	• Skill to create project folders and to develop an understanding of SolidWorks file references.
• Review the purchased components that comprise the DELIVERY-STATION assembly.	• Ability to download components using 3D ContentCentral. • Aptitude to use SolidWorks Explorer.

Notes:

Project 1 – File Management

Project Objective

You will create the following documents in this project:

- ASM-MM-ANSI Assembly Template.

- ASM-MM-ANSI-DESIGN-JOURNAL Assembly Template.

- PART-MM-ANSI-AL6061 Part Template.

Download a SolidWorks assembly and review specification sheets from the World Wide Web for geometric and functional requirements. View and rename various SolidWorks assemblies using SolidWorks Explorer.

On the completion of this project, you will be able to:

- Set System Options as they relate to assemblies.

- Modify File Location references for the Templates, Referenced Documents, and the Design Library.

- Incorporate Document Properties and create an Assembly Template.

- Create a Part Template and apply material properties.

- Develop an Assembly Task List and Assembly Layout Diagram.

- Download components from the 3D ContentCentral website.

- Address the SolidWorks DWGEditor.

- View and rename sub-assemblies in SolidWorks Explorer required for the 3AXIS-TRANSFER assembly.

- Obtain and confirm geometric and functional requirements from the vendor's component specifications. Utilize the SolidWorks Measure tool.

In Project 1, utilize the following SolidWorks tools and commands.

SolidWorks Tools and Commands:				
Configurations	Hide/Show	Save As:	System Options:	SolidWorks Explorer:
Document Properties:		Assembly Template	External References	Open files in SolidWorks
Units	Lightweight		File Locations	
Dimensioning Standard	Materials Editor	Part Template	Assembly	Preview
File Locations:		States:	User Interface:	Rename
Document Templates	Measure	Lightweight	Main menu	Use Full Screen
Design Library		Resolved	Shortcut keys	
Referenced Documents	Help	Suppressed	Task bar	

Project Overview

You are part of a design team to develop the DELIVERY-STATION assembly for a customer's industrial application. The DELIVERY-STATION assembly contains hundreds of components.

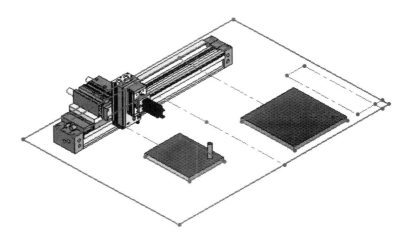

You attend a design review meeting to discuss the customer requirements with your colleagues.

DELIVERY-STATION assembly

The two fingers of the GRIPPER assembly obtain an object from the INPUT assembly.

The 3AXIS-TRANSFER assembly rotates the object 90 degrees and linearly translates 500mm along the RODLESS CYLINDER assembly.

The 3AXIS-TRANSFER assembly raises the object 100mm. The 3AXIS-TRANSFER assembly moves the object outward 100mm. The two fingers of the GRIPPER assembly places the object into the OUTPUT assembly.

A senior engineer on your project team provides a list of five purchased pneumatic parts for the program.

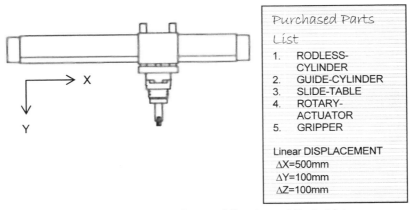

Rough Sketch - Top view and Purchased Parts List
3AXIS-TRANSFER Assembly (Your Task)

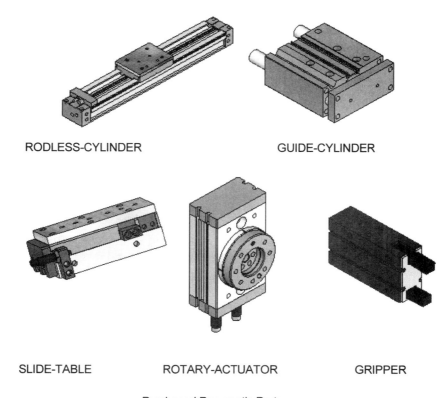

RODLESS-CYLINDER   GUIDE-CYLINDER

SLIDE-TABLE   ROTARY-ACTUATOR   GRIPPER

Purchased Pneumatic Parts
Courtesy of SMC Corporation of America

The senior engineer provides key dimensions for linear displacement and a rough sketch of the top view for the 3AXIS-TRANSFER assembly.

Your responsibilities include:

- Obtain the five component models from a manufacturer.

- Extract information required from each component.

- Model the 3AXIS-TRANSFER assembly.

Project 1 - 6 develops the 3AXIS-TRANSFER assembly utilizing SolidWorks features, tools, and commands.

Project 1 explores templates, system options, file locations, and file references. Review the file type definitions and extensions utilized in this project.

Definitions

File type:	Extension:	Definition:
Part	.sldprt	A part is a single 3D object that consists of various features.
Assembly	.sldasm	An assembly combines two or more parts. A part inserted into an assembly is called a component. A sub-assembly is a component contained within an assembly.
Part Template	.prtdot	The foundation for a SolidWorks part is the Part Template. Define part drawing standards, units and other properties in the Part Template.
Assembly Template	.asmdot	The foundation for a SolidWorks assembly is the Assembly Template. Define drawing standards, units and other properties in the Assembly Template.

Assembly Task List – Before you begin

You are required to perform numerous tasks before you create a SolidWorks assembly. Review the following list. Mark this page for future reference.

Assembly Task List – Before you Begin:		
Task:	Comments:	Complete:
Review the Assembly Layout Diagram with your colleagues. Group components into sub-assemblies.	My task – 3AXIS-TRANSFER assembly	✓
Comprehend the geometric and functional requirements of the purchased components. How do the components interact with other components in the assembly? Know the fit and function of each component. Obtain model files and data specifications from the vendors.		
Place yourself in the position of the machinist, manufacturing technician, field service engineer, or customer. Identify potential obstacles or design concerns.		

Task:	Comments:	Complete:
Plan and create the Assembly, Part, and Drawing Templates. Identify units, dimensioning standards, and other document properties.		
Organize documents into file folders. Place templates, vendor components, library components, parts, assemblies, and drawings in a specific location.		
Obtain unique part numbers for components. A unique part number avoids duplication problems in the assembly. Note: In this project, utilize a part description filename. In Project 5, rename part description filenames to your company's unique part number filename.		

DELIVERY STATION Assembly Layout Diagram

The project leader developed a layout diagram for the DELIVERY-STATION assembly structure. Review the DELIVERY-STATION assembly layout diagram.

Before you begin an assembly, organize the components. The DELIVERY-STATION assembly is comprised of the following components:

- 3AXIS-TRANSFER assembly.

- MOUNTING-PLATE component.

- INPUT assembly.

- OUTPUT assembly.

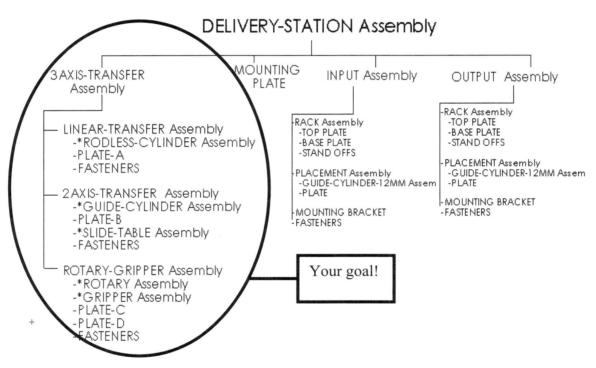

DELIVERY-STATION Assembly Layout Diagram

*Purchased SMC Components.

There are two key methods to document an assembly layout:

- Top-Down assembly modeling.

- Bottom-Up assembly modeling.

You will first address the Top-Down level approach.

Example 1: A Top-Down level assembly contains two sub-assemblies. Each sub-assembly contains five parts.

Action: Sketch a manual assembly layout diagram on paper.

Example 2: The Engine assembly contains hundreds of components.

Action: Utilize a Top-Down Assembly Modeling approach to design the assembly layout.

Define the names, grouping, and relationships between the major components.

The sub-assemblies contain the reference planes and Origin.

The Lifter-Rocker sub-assembly contains two additional sub-assemblies; the Lifter assembly and the Rocker assembly.

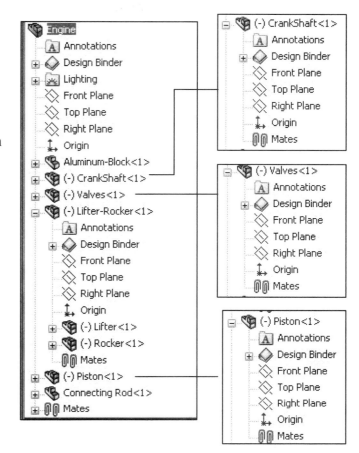

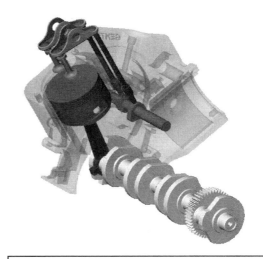

Valve-Cam-Follower Assembly
Courtesy of Keith Pedersen
Computer Aided Products, Peabody, MA

In a planning meeting, team members review the DELIVERY-STATION assembly layout diagram. Other members of the design team are concurrently developing the MOUNTING-PLATE part, INPUT assembly, and OUTPUT assembly.

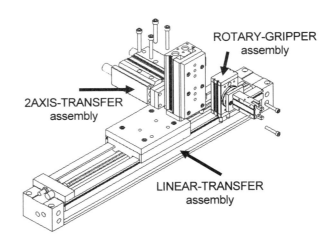

The goal is to create the 3AXIS-TRANSFER assembly. The 3AXIS-TRANSFER assembly consists of three sub-assemblies. They are:

- LINEAR-TRANSFER assembly.

- 2AXIS-TRANSFER assembly.

- ROTARY-GRIPPER assembly.

The three modular sub-assemblies provide different examples of SolidWorks assembly modeling techniques. Resource allocations change during the product development cycle. In an engineering environment, create modular sub-assemblies.

File Organization

File organization is essential to a successful design. A common file structure relates components in an assembly. Changes in the part affect the assembly and vice a versa. Managing assembly information is a complex undertaking and goes far beyond just creating SolidWorks parts, assemblies, and drawings.

Companies develop Engineering Change Orders, "ECO" and manufacturing procedures to document product revisions. Companies utilize Product Data Management (PDM) systems to control engineering documents.

The projects in this book focus on using SolidWorks parts, assemblies, and drawings along with SolidWorks Explorer. SolidWorks Explorer is a file management tool. SolidWorks Explorer assists in viewing, renaming, replacing, and copying SolidWorks files.

How do you organize components in an assembly? Answer: Before you begin an assembly, utilize file organization to create an assembly layout diagram. The following examples describe assembly layout structures.

Example 1:

Take a closer look at the 3AXIS–TRANSFER assembly. Why is this example a difficult layout structure? Answer: All of the sub-assemblies and parts are at the top level.

```
    3AXIS-TRANSFER
       ASSEMBLY
          |
  ┌───────┴
  ├ RODLESS-CYLINDER-500MM ASSEMBLY
  ├ GUIDE-CYLINDER-50MM ASSEMBLY
  ├ SLIDE-TABLE ASSEMBLY
  ├ ROTARY-ACTUATOR ASSEMBLY
  ├ GRIPPER ASSEMBLY
  ├ PLATE-A
  ├ PLATE-B
  ├ PLATE-C
  ├ PLATE-D
  ├ FASTENERS SHCS M6
  ├ FASTENERS SHCS M8
  └ FASTENERS SHCS M10
```

The 3AXIS-TRANSFER assembly consists of more parts than sub-assemblies. This structure can be difficult to create, modify, and resolve problems. Dividing a larger assembly into smaller sub-assemblies provides the ability to:

- Identify problems and address issues quicker.

- Provide and divide work between teammates.

☼ Maximize sub-assemblies at each assembly level. Minimize parts at the assembly level.

Example 2:

Create three sub-assemblies:

- LINEAR-TRANSFER assembly.

- 2AXIS-TRANSFER assembly.

- ROTARY-GRIPPER assembly.

Utilize three sub-assemblies to simplify the layout structure.

Each sub-assembly is self-contained.

```
         3AXIS-TRANSFER Assembly
                  |
  ┌───────────────┴
  ├LINEAR-TRANSFER-500MM Assembly
  │  -*RODLESS-CYLINDER-500MM Assembly
  │  -PLATE-A
  │  -FASTENERS
  │
  ├2AXIS-TRANSFER  Assembly
  │  -*GUIDE-CYLINDER-50MM Assembly
  │  -PLATE-B
  │  -*SLIDE-TABLE Assembly
  │  -FASTENERS
  │
  └ROTARY-GRIPPER Assembly
     -*ROTARY-ACTUATOR  Assembly
     -*GRIPPER Assembly
     -PLATE-C
     -PLATE-D
     -FASTENERS
```

You are responsible for the 3AXIS-TRANSFER assembly. You must be cognizant of your teammates working on the INPUT assembly and OUTPUT assembly. Both the INPUT assembly and OUTPUT assembly requires a TOP PLATE part, BOTTOM PLATE part, and a STAND OFFS part. The STAND OFFS part separates the TOP PLATE part from the BOTTOM PLATE part

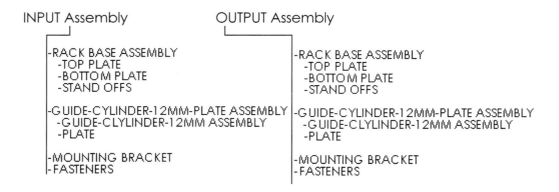

🔅 Reuse existing geometry. Design parts and assemblies to reuse and manipulate common information with Design Tables.

Review the 3AXIS-TRANSFER Assembly Layout diagram. Determine the required document templates.

🔅 Conserve design time. Develop Assembly Templates and Part Templates before you create new assemblies and parts.

Determine the required models to create in SolidWorks. Obtain purchased component models from the World Wide Web or directly from the vendor.

🔅 Conserve design time. A model obtained from another source is one you do not have to create.

3AXIS-TRANSFER Assembly

- LINEAR-TRANSFER-500MM Assembly
  - *RODLESS-CYLINDER-500MM Assembly
  - PLATE-A
  - FASTENERS
- 2AXIS-TRANSFER Assembly
  - *GUIDE-CYLINDER-50MM Assembly
  - PLATE-B
  - *SLIDE-TABLE Assembly
  - FASTENERS
- ROTARY-GRIPPER Assembly
  - *ROTARY-ACTUATOR Assembly
  - *GRIPPER Assembly
  - PLATE-C
  - PLATE-D
  - FASTENERS

File Management

Why do you require file management? In a large assembly, there could be hundreds or even thousands of parts. To facilitate time, distribute parts and sub-assemblies between team members. Design changes occur frequently in the development process. How do you manage and control these changes? Answer: Through file management. File management is a very important tool in the development process.

The DELIVERY-STATION assembly consists of multiple folders. Utilize folders for projects, vendor components, templates and libraries. Folders exist on your local hard drive, example C:\. Folders can also exist on a network drive, example Z:\.

The CD included in the book contains the following folders:
ASSEMBLY-SW-FILES-2006, EXERCISES, and
SOLUTIONS. Project 1 through Project 4 requires the
documents contained in the ASSEMBLY-SW-FILES-2006
folder. Copy the ASSEMBLY-SW-FILES-2006 folder to
your computer.

Review the documents contained in the ASSEMBLY-SW-FILES-2006 folder. In the next section, utilize the MY-TEMPLATES folder to store Assembly Templates and Part Templates for this project. The SMC folder contains five components obtained from the World Wide Web.

Activity: File Management

Copy the file folders.
1) Place the **CD** into the CD drive.

2) Click and drag the **ASSEMBLY-SW-FILES-2006** folder into the My Documents folder.

3) Remove and save the **CD**. The CD is required for future projects and exercises.

Modify the file attributes.
4) Right-click the **ASSEMBLY-SW-FILES-2006** folder.

5) Click **Properties**.

6) Uncheck the **Read-only** Attribute box.

7) Click **Apply**.

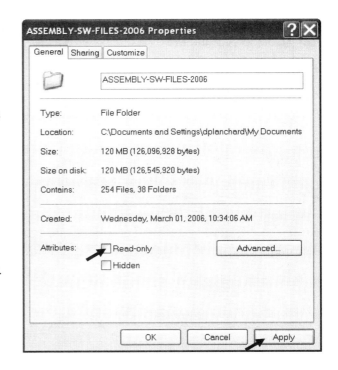

8) Check **Apply changes to this folder, subfolders and files**.

9) Click **OK** from the Confirm Attribute Changes box.

10) Click **OK** from the ASSEMBLY-SW-FILES-2006 Properties box.

Confirm Attribute Changes

You have chosen to make the following attribute changes:

unset read-only

Do you want to apply this change to this folder only, or do you want to apply it to all subfolders and files as well?

◯ Apply changes to this folder only

⦿ Apply changes to this folder, subfolders and files

[OK]   [Cancel]

Review the folder contents.
11) Expand the **ASSEMBLY-SW-FILES-2006** folder.

12) Expand the **DELIVERY-STATION** folder. The DELIVERY-STATION file folder is empty. Store the parts that you create in the DELIVERY-STATION file folder.

13) Click the **Back** ⬅ Back icon to return to the ASSEMBLY-SW-FILES-2006 folder.

⊟ 📁 ASSEMBLY-SW-FILES-2006
　　📁 DELIVERY-STATION
　　📁 MY-TEMPLATES
⊞ 📁 MY-TOOLBOX
⊞ 📁 Project5-2006
　　📁 Project6-2006
　　📁 project6-AdditionalModels2006
⊞ 📁 SMC
⊞ 📁 EXERCISES
⊞ 📁 SOLUTIONS

Review the MY-TEMPLATES file folder.
14) Double-click the **MY-TEMPLATES** file folder.

15) Click the **Back** ⬅ Back icon.

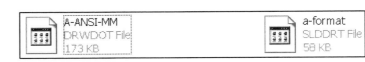

A-ANSI-MM
DRWDOT File
173 KB

a-format
SLDDRT File
58 KB

The MY-TEMPLATES file folder contains the A-ANSI-MM.drwdot Drawing Template and the a-format.slddrt Sheet Format.

Store the project Assembly Templates and Part Templates in the MY-TEMPLATES file folder.

Review the MY-TOOLBOX folder.
16)   Double-click the **MY-TOOLBOX** folder.

17)   Click the **Back**  Back icon.

Utilize the MY-TOOLBOX folder to store copies of the SolidWorks/Toolbox parts.

Review the SMC folder.
18)   Double-click
          the **SMC**
          folder.

Five folders
contain the SMC
assemblies and
parts that are
utilized later in this
project.

MGPM50-100

MHY2-20D

MSQB30R

MXS25L-100B

MY1M50G-500LS

Zip Models

DELIVERY STATION ORG CHART
SolidWorks Drawing Document
85 KB

DELIVERY-STATION-LAYOUT-DIAGR...
DWGeditor Drawing
30 KB

System Options – File Locations

System Options are stored in the registry of the computer. System Options are not part of the document. Changes to the System Options affect current and future documents.

Review and modify System Options in this project. If you work on a local drive, C:\, the System Options are stored on the computer.

If you work on a network drive, Z:\ and change computers during this project, the System Options will reset. Conserve modeling time. Set the System Options before you begin an assembly.

Add folder search pathnames to the Document Templates and Reference Documents options in the next activity.

File Locations, Document Templates

Each folder is listed under Tools, Options, System Options, File Locations, Folders.

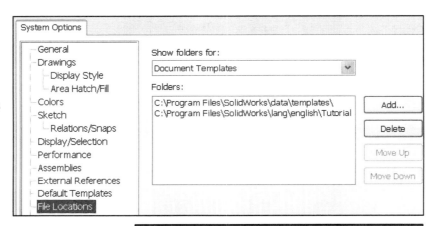

Each template produces a corresponding tab in the New SolidWorks Document dialog box.

The tab is visible when the folder contains one or more SolidWorks Part, Assembly, or Drawing Templates.

The order in the Folders list determines the tab order in the New SolidWorks Document box.

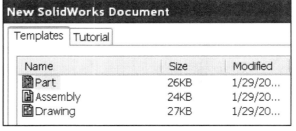

The default Template folder is called: \SolidWorks\data\templates.

Note: In a networked educational license installation, SolidWorks prompts the student to select a working folder for the Default Templates and a working folder for the SolidWorks\Toolbox.

File Locations, Reference Documents

SolidWorks utilizes a compound file structure that creates file references between documents. Example; when you open an assembly drawing, SolidWorks searches for the referenced assembly document. If the assembly document cannot be located, SolidWorks performs a search to locate the missing document. In the file open process, the search order is as follows:

- Documents loaded in memory.

- Optional user-defined search lists.

Utilize the first pathname under the Referenced Documents, Folders box. Example: \ASSEMBLY-SW-FILES-2006\DELIVERY-STATION.

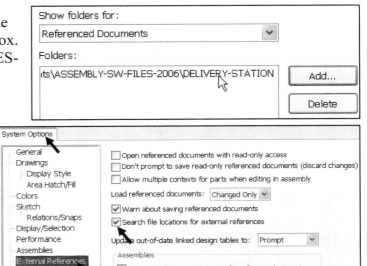

To activate a search, click System Options, External References. Check the Search file locations for the external references box.

- Current folder of the drawing or assembly documents.

- Same folder as the last found referenced.

- Stored pathname saved in the assembly document. SolidWorks searches the current drive and then the stored drive.

- Prompt the user to search for the file location.

A file reference differs from an external reference. A file reference is the file pathname. The File, Find References option lists the pathname of the referenced documents.

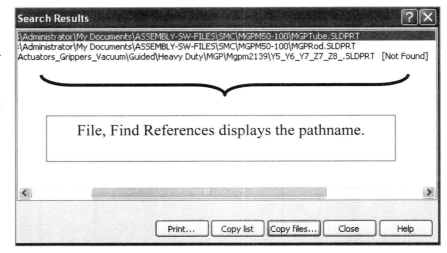

An external reference is geometry from one entity that is dependent on geometry in another component.

Utilize the List External References option in Project 3.

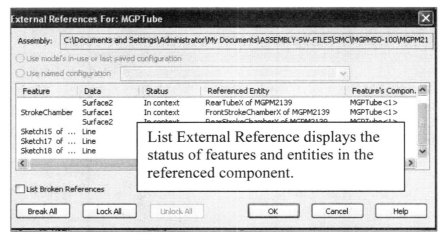

During the search process, SolidWorks uses an absolute pathname including drive letter, folder location, and filename.

Example:

Absolute pathname

D:\Project-A\Transmission\Gear-A-Assembly\p2357-21.sldprt.

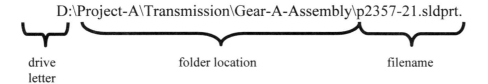

drive   folder location   filename
letter

Avoid problems with file references. Utilize a unique filename.

File Locations, Design Library

The Design Library contains reusable elements in the form of parts, assemblies, annotation favorites, blocks, library features, and DWG/DXF files.

The Design Library includes entries for the Design Library, Toolbox, and 3D ContentCentral. Add the MY-TOOLBOX and SMC folders to the Design Library.

Note: File management in SolidWorks incorporates the Design Library.

Activity: System Options, File Locations

Start a SolidWorks 2006 session.

19) Click **Start** from the Windows Taskbar

20) Click **All Programs.**

21) Click the **SolidWorks 2006** folder.

22) Click the **SolidWorks 2006** application. The SolidWorks program window opens. Note: Do not open a document.

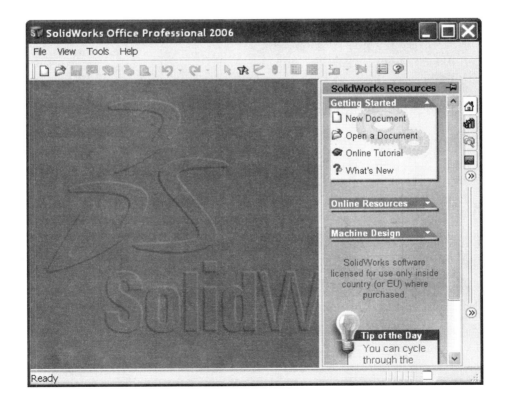

The SolidWorks 2006 Task Pane contains four options:

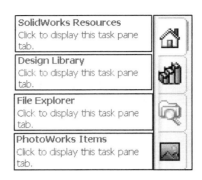

- SolidWorks Resources.

- Design Library.

- File Explorer.

- PhotoWorks Items. Note: If PhotoWorks Items is not displayed, click Tools, Add-Ins from the Main menu. Check PhotoWorks. Click OK.

Utilize the left/right arrows  to Expand or Collapse the Task Pane options.

SolidWorks Resources contains the Getting Started menu, the Online Resources menu, and the Tip of the Day.

The Design Library includes entries for the Design Library, Toolbox, and 3D ContentCentral. The Design Library contains the following folders: annotations, assemblies, features, forming tools, parts, routing, and smart components.

To access the Design Library folders, click Add File

Location  , enter: C\Programs Files\SolidWorks\data\design library. Click OK.

File Explorer duplicates Windows Explorer in functionality.

PhotoWorks Items create photo-realistic images of SolidWorks models. PhotoWorks provides many professional rendering effects. PhotoWorks is based on the mental ray® rendering engine.

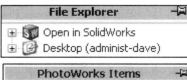

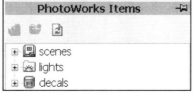

Explore the options in SolidWorks Resources, Design Library, and File Explorer as you use the book.

Set System Options.
23) Click **Tools**, **Options** from the Main menu.

Add a folder for the Document Templates.
24) Click **File Locations**.

25) Select **Document Templates** from the Show folders for: list box.

26) Click **Add**.

27) Browse and select the **ASSEMBLY-SW-FILES-2006\MY-TEMPLATES** folder. Click **OK** from the Browse for folder box.

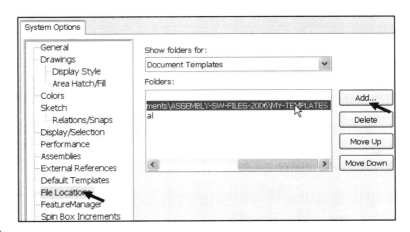

28) If required, click the **Move Down** button to position the MY-TEMPLATES folder at the bottom of the Folders list. Note: The MY-TEMPLATES folder is the third tab in the New dialog box.

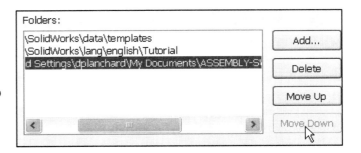

Add a folder for the Referenced Documents.
29) Select **Referenced Documents** in the Show folders for box.

30) Click **Add**.

31) Select the **ASSEMBLY-SW-FILES-2006\DELIVERY-STATION** folder.

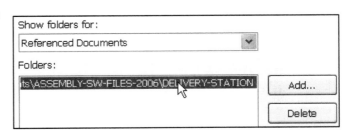

32) Click **OK** from the Browse for folder box.

Add two folders from the Design Library.
33) Select **Design Library** in the Show folders for list box. Click **Add**.

34) Select the **ASSEMBLY-SW-FILES-2006\MY-TOOLBOX folder**. Click **OK**.

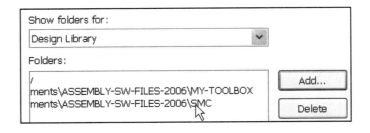

35) Click **Add**.

36) Select the **ASSEMBLY-SW-FILES-2006\SMC** folder. Click **OK** from the Browse for folder box.

System Options - Large Assembly Mode

Large Assembly Mode is a collection of options utilized to improve performance of large assemblies. Large Assembly Mode is active by default.

A lightweight component loads only a sub-set of its model data into memory. Lightweight components improve system performance. The remaining model data loads into memory when you edit the component in the assembly. The component automatically transforms from a lightweight state to a resolved state.

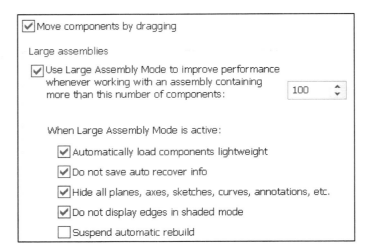

Review the Lightweight component state benefits table and the Resolved component state abilities table.

Lightweight component state benefits:	
Increase speed during loading, saving, and manipulating assemblies.	Select, move, or rotate lightweight components.
Maintain assembly mates, physical placement, and orientation.	Display Shaded, Hidden, or Wireframe modes.
Display mates between components.	Modify transparency, color, or texture.
Resolved component state abilities:	
Edit components.	Mate to selected faces, edge, vertices, or component planes.
Expand the list of features in the FeatureManager.	Calculate Mass Properties.
Modify configuration properties.	Determine Interference.
Select Save As, References option.	

Activate the Lightweight state for a single component. Check the Lightweight box in the Open dialog box of the assembly.

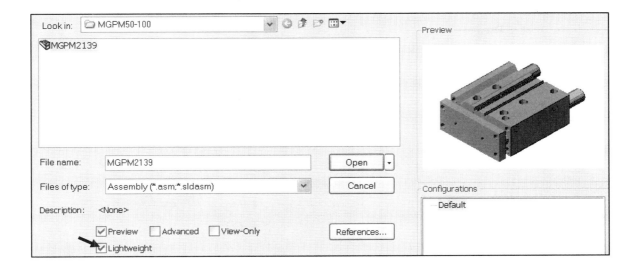

 Conserve design time. Utilize the Lightweight checkbox in the Open dialog box to open assemblies.

The Level of detail option affects performance. Drag the slider to the right for a faster display and a reduced level of detail.

The Large Assembly Mode by default hides all planes, axes, sketches, curves, and annotations.

Uncheck the Hide all planes, axes, sketches, curves, annotations, etc. option when working with Layout Sketches.

Incorporate Layout Sketches with the Top Down Design assembly modeling approach in Project 6.

Large Assembly Mode controls Drawing options:

- Automatic hiding of components on view creation.

- Default display style for new views: Hidden Lines Removed.

- Default display quality for new views.

Selected lightweight components in a drawing remain in a lightweight state.

Modify Display modes at any time in the assembly, part, or drawing.

☑ Automatically place dimensions inserted from model
☑ Automatically scale new drawing views
☑ Show contents while dragging drawing view
☑ Smooth dynamic motion of drawing views
☐ Display new detail circles as circles
☐ Select hidden entities
☑ Eliminate duplicate model dimensions on insert
☑ Allow auto-update when opening drawings
☑ Detail item snapping when dragging corner
☑ Detail item snapping when dragging center
☑ Print out-of-sync water mark
☐ Show reference geometry names in drawings
☐ Automatically hide components on view creation
☐ Display sketch arc centerpoints
☐ Display sketch entity points
☑ Save tessellated data for drawings with shaded and draft quality views
☑ Print breaklines in broken view

Wireframe   Hidden Lines Visible   Hidden Line Removed   Shaded with Edges   Shaded

Save models in the Shaded with Edges or Shaded display mode.

How large is a large assembly? Answer: There is no right or wrong answer. The goal is to develop sound assembly modeling techniques and to understand the various assembly options.

Activity: Set Large Assembly Mode

Set the Large Assembly Mode threshold.
37)   Click **Assemblies** from the System Options tab.

38)   Enter **100** for the Large assemblies mode.

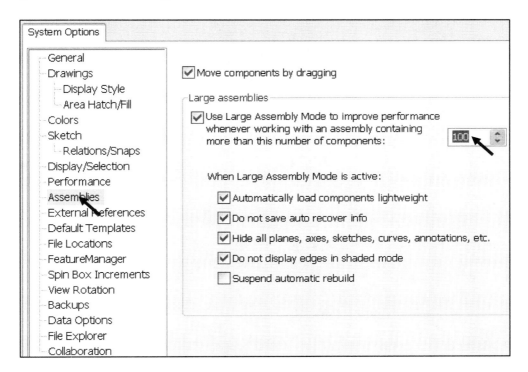

Set the System Options.
39)   Click **OK** from the System Options box.

Display the Desktop.
40) Click the **File Explorer** icon on the right side of the
Task pane.

41) Double-click **Desktop**.

42) Double-click the **ASSEMBLY-SW-FILES-2006**
folder. View the file folders.

43) Drag the left **Task Pane edge** to the right to resize
File Explorer.

Close File Explorer.
44) Click a **position** inside the Graphics window.

Note: The Collapsed arrow ⌕ also closes File
Explorer.

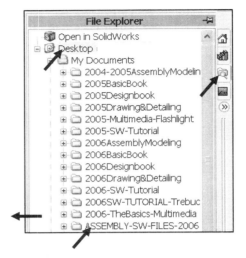

Assembly Template, Part Template, and Document Properties

Templates are the foundation for assemblies, parts, and drawings. Document Properties
address: dimensioning standards, units, text style, center marks, witness lines, arrow
styles, tolerance, precision, and other parameters. Document Properties apply only to the
current document.

The foundation of a SolidWorks assembly is the Assembly
Template. The custom Assembly Template begins with the
default Assembly Template.

Conserve modeling time. Store Document Properties
in the Assembly Template. Set the parameters for the
Dimensioning standard and Units. New documents that
utilize the same template contain the saved parameters.

The Dimensioning standard options are: ANSI, ISO, DIN,
JIS, BSI, GOST, and GB. The SMC engineers dimensioned
the components using the ISO standard. Display sub-
assemblies you create for the DELIVERY-STATION
assembly project in the ANSI standard.

Modify Document Properties, Annotations settings and the
document, Design Journal.doc. Save the custom Assembly
Template in the MY-TEMPLATES folder.

ASSEM1.sldasm is the default document name. Assembly documents end with the extension ".sldasm." Assembly Templates end with the extension, ".asmdot."

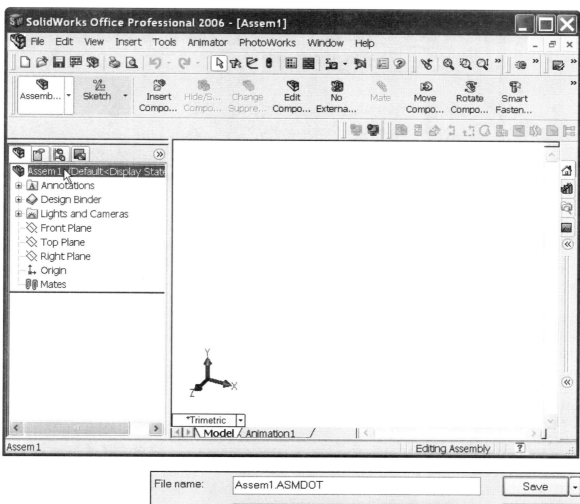

The Annotations, Details option contains the Annotation Properties. Store the Annotation Properties with the Assembly Template. Insert Annotations created in the assembly and part into the drawing.

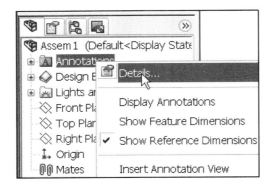

The Design Binder contains the embedded Microsoft Word document and the Design Journal.doc.

The document resembles an engineering journal. The default document contains the entries File Name, Description, Material, Revision, and embedded images of the model.

Utilize the Design Binder, Add Attachment option to insert the file, DELIVERY-STATION-LAYOUT-DIAGRAM.dwg.

The default Assembly Template contains the assembly Origin and three default assembly Reference planes:

- Front Plane.

- Top Plane.

- Right Plane.

New parts require a Part Template. The foundation for a SolidWorks part is a Part Template. Modify the Documentation Properties Units and Dimensioning standard. Templates store material properties.

Utilize the Materials Editor and select Aluminum, 6061 Alloy. The material parameters pass to the Mass Property calculations in the part and the Section view hatching in the drawing.

Reuse information. Create Assembly Templates and Part Templates before you begin a project!

The MY-TEMPLATES folder contains the Drawing Template, A-ANSI-MM. Text height, arrows, and line styles are defined in millimeter values according to the ASME Y14.2-1992(R1998) Line Conventions and Lettering standard. The Drawing Template contains a Sheet Format. A Sheet Format contains Title block, Company logo, and Custom Properties. The SolidWorks drawing combines the Drawing Template, Sheet Format, and views of a part or assembly. The Drawing file extension is ".slddrw."

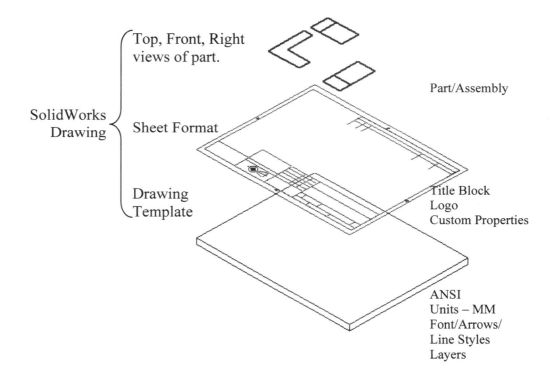

For additional information on Drawing Templates, see Planchard and Planchard, **Drawing and Detailing with SolidWorks 2006**, SDC Publications.

Activity: Assembly Template, Part Template, and Document Properties

---

Create a new assembly.

45) Click **File**, **New** from the Main menu.

46) Click the default **Templates** tab.

47) Double-click **Assembly** from the New SolidWorks Document dialog box. The Insert Component PropertyManager is displayed.

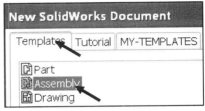

48) Click **Cancel** from the Insert Component PropertyManager.

Set document properties.

49) Click **Tools**, **Options**, **Document Properties** tab from the Main menu.

50) Select **ANSI** from the Dimensioning standard drop down list.

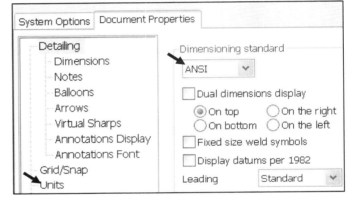

Set Linear units.

51) Click **Units** from the left text box.

52) Click **MMGS (millimeter, gram, second)** for Unit system.

53) Enter **2** for Length units Decimal places.

54) Click **OK**.

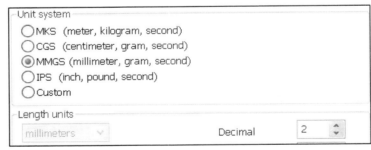

Display the Annotation Properties.

55) Right-click **Annotations** from the Assembly FeatureManager.

56) Click **Details**. Review the default settings.

57) Click **OK** from the Annotations Properties box.

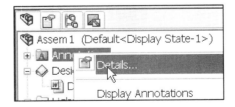

Save the Assembly Template.

58) Click **Save** 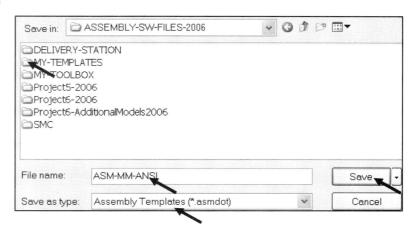 from the Main menu.

59) Select **Assembly Templates(*.asmdot)** for Save as type.

60) Select **ASSEMBLY-SW-FILES-2006\MY-TEMPLATES** from the Save in list.

61) Enter **ASM-MM-ANSI** for File name.

62) Click **Save**.

Close all files.

63) Click **Window, Close All** from the Main menu.

Create a new assembly.

64) Click **File, New** from the Main menu.

65) Click the **MY-TEMPLATES** tab.

66) Click the **List** icon.

67) Double-click **ASM-MM-ANSI**.

68) Click **Cancel**  from the Insert Component PropertyManager. The Assembly2 FeatureManager is displayed.

Edit the Design Journal.doc in Word.

69) Expand **Design Binder** from the Assembly FeatureManager.

70) Double-click **Design Journal.doc**.

71) Enter **Deliver Station Project** below the Design Journal text as illustrated.

72) Click **Close**.

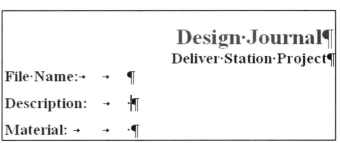

Insert a drawing file.

73) Right-click **Design Binder** from
       the FeatureManager.

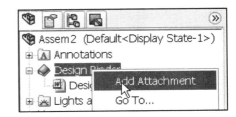

74) Click **Add Attachment**.

75) Click **Browse**.

76) Double-click **\ASSEMBLY-SW-
       FILE-2006\SMC\DELIVERY-
       STATION-LAYOUT-
       DIAGRAM**.

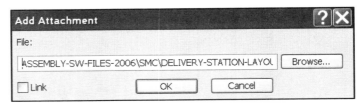

77) Click **OK** from the Add
       Attachment box.

Display the dwg file in the SolidWorks DWGEditor.

78) Double-click **DELVERY-STATION-LAYOUT-
       DIAGRAM.DWG** from the FeatureManager.

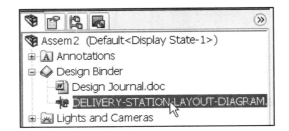

The SolidWorks DWGeditor displays the
AutoCAD dwg/dxf format. Review the entries
on the Main menu. The menus, toolbars, and
commands simulate the AutoCAD interface.

Close the
DWGeditor.

79) Click **Close**.

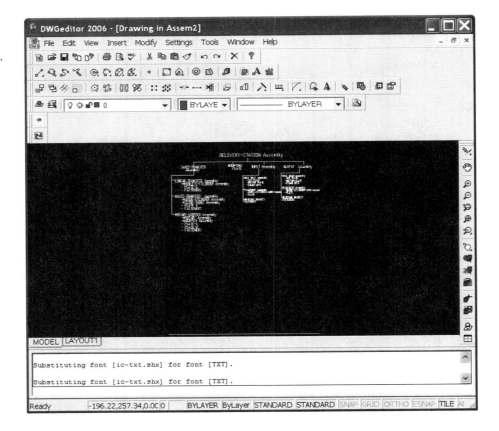

Save the second Assembly Template.

80) Click **Save**  from the Main menu.

81) Select **Assembly Templates(*.asmdot)** for Save as type.

82) Select **MY-TEMPLATES** from the Save in list.

83) Enter **ASM-MM-ANSI-DESIGN-JOURNAL** for File name.

84) Click **Save**.

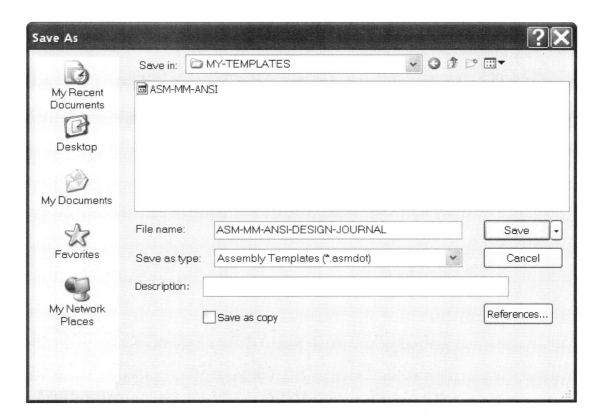

Close all files.
85) Click **Windows**, **Close All** from the Main menu. Do not exit SolidWorks.

Note: Embedded documents into the drawing Template increase file size.

Create a new Part Template.
86) Click **File**, **New** from the Main menu.

87) Click the default **Templates** tab.

88) Double-click **Part**. The Part1 FeatureManager is displayed.

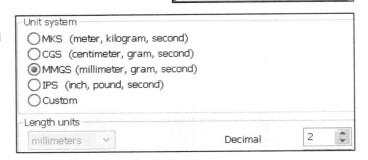

Set the document properties.
89) Click **Tools**, **Options**, **Document Properties** tab from the Main menu.

90) Select **ANSI** for Dimensioning standard.

Set Linear units.
91) Click **Units** from the left text box.

92) Click **MMGS (millimeter, gram, second)** for Unit system.

93) Enter **2** for Length units Decimal places.

94) Click **OK**.

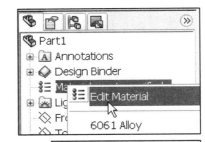

Apply material to the part template.

95) Right-click **Material** from the Part1 FeatureManager.

96) Click **Edit Material**.

97) Expand **Aluminum Alloys**.

98) Click **6061 Alloy**.

99) Click **OK** from the Materials Editor PropertyManager. 6061 Alloy is displayed in the Part1 FeatureManager.

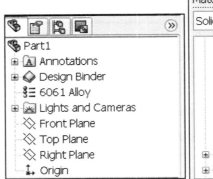

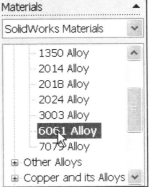

Applying material to a Part Template increases file size significantly. The Part FeatureManager contains a Design Binder with a new embedded Design Journal.doc. If the Design Journal is not activated, the file size does not increase.

Save the Part Template.

100) Click **Save** 💾 from the Main menu.

101) Click **Part Templates (*.prtdot)** from the Save As type list box.

102) Select **MY-TEMPLATES** from the Save in list box.

103) Enter **PART-MM-ANSI-AL6061** in the File name text box.

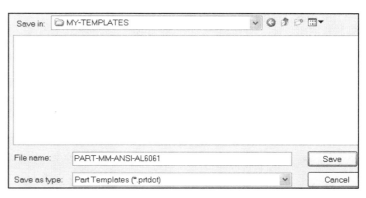

104) Click **Save**. The PART-MM-ANSI-AL6061 FeatureManager is displayed.

Close all documents.
105) Click **Windows**, **Close All** from the Main menu.

Create a new part.
106) Click **File**, **New** from the Main menu.

107) Click the **MY-TEMPLATES** tab.

108) Double **PART-MM-ANSI-AL6061**. The Part2 FeatureManager is displayed with the Part-MM-ANSI-AL6061 template.

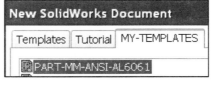

Close all documents.
109) Click **Windows**, **Close All** from the Main menu.

Download Components

The SMC folder contains the purchased components required for the DELIVERY STATION assembly project.

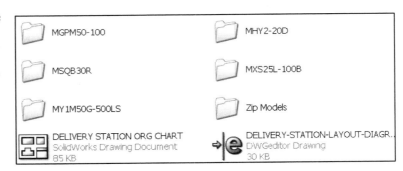

The senior engineer on the team specified the five SMC assemblies based on the application and loading conditions.

An additional SMC sub-assembly is required for the DELIVERY-STATION assembly. Download the sub-assembly from the World Wide Web. Utilize 3D ContentCentral to locate 3D models from SMC. View folders and documents with File Explorer.

Note: If you do not have access to the Internet, locate the folder, SMC\Zip Models from the CD in the book and unzip the files into the SMC folder.

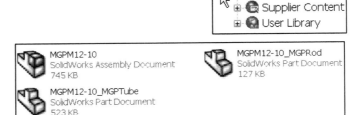

Activity: Download Components

Perform this next activity if you want to download the components from the web. If you un-ziped the components from the CD in the book, go to step 136.

Expand the SMC folder.
110) Click **Design Library** from the SolidWorks Task bar.

111) Double-click the **SMC** folder. There are five folders containing assemblies and parts.

Invoke the 3D ContentCentral.
112) Invoke a web **browser**.

113) Double-click **3D ContentCentral** from the Design Library.

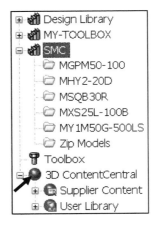

114) Double-click the **Supplier Content** icon.

115) Double-click the **Pneumatics** folder from the Supplier Content list.

116) Double-click **SMC Corporation of America**. The SMC E-TECH web site is displayed.

117) Click the **E-Tech** button.

118) **Register** if required to utilize the 3D Content Central web site.

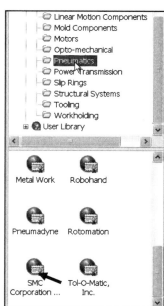

Size a sub-assembly for the DELIVERY-STATION assembly.

119) Click **Size Applications**.

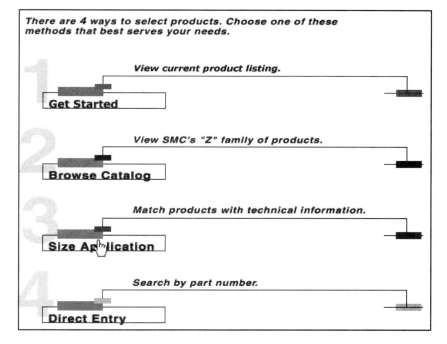

120) Click **Guided Actuators**.

121) Read and **accept** the Sizing Disclaimer.

Enter the design parameters.
122) Enter **10**mm for Stoke.

123) Enter **0.5**MPa for Supply Pressure.

124) Click the **Set Mass Load** button.

125) Enter **1**kg for Load. Note: There can be more than one solution without all of the specified variables.

Guided Actuators

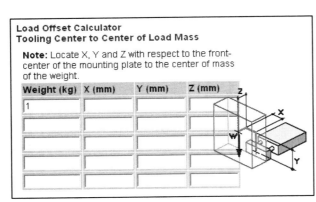

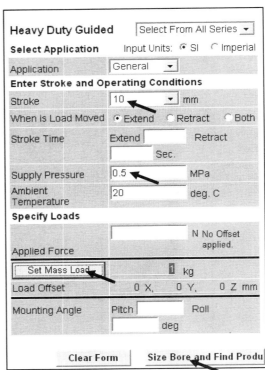

126) Click the **Size Bore and Find Products** button.

Select the Guide Cylinder.
127) Click the **MGPM, Compact Guide Cylinder, Slide Bearing** option.

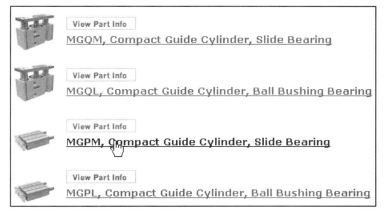

128) Select **10** for Stroke.

129) Click the **Download CAD File** button.

Download the zip file.
130) Select the **SolidWorks Part/Assembly (.sldpt)**.

131) Select **2006** for Version.

132) Click the **Download Files** button. The file MGPM-12-10.zip is downloaded to your computer. Extract the assembly and parts to the SMC folder.

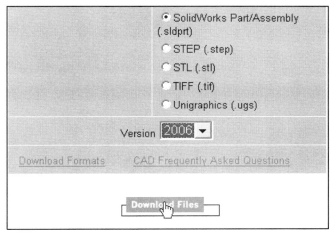

133) Double-click **MGPM12-10.zip**.

134) Click **Extract all files**.

135) Browse and select the **ASSEMBLY-SW-FILES-2006\SMC** folder.

Return to SolidWorks.
136) Click the **SMC** folder from the Design Library.

137) Position the mouse pointer on the **MGPM12-10** icon. The icon displays a large thumbnail of the assembly.

138) Click and drag the **MGPM12-10** icon into the Graphics window. The MGPM12-10 assembly is displayed in the Graphics window.

139) Click **OK** for update.

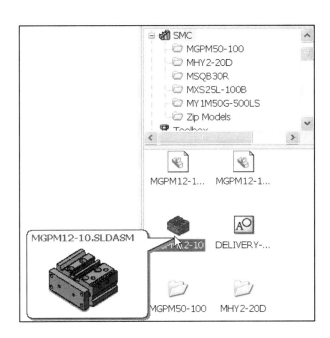

Review the FeatureManager component names.

140) Drag the FeatureManager **slider bar** downward to display the two part icons MGPM12-10_MGPTube and MGPM12-10_MGPRod.

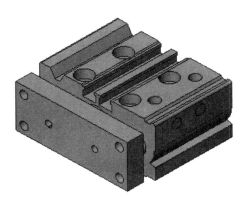

Close all documents.

141) Click **Save** 🔲 from the Main menu.

142) Click **Windows**, **Close All** from the Main menu.

How do you distinguish the difference between an assembly and a part in the FeatureManager? Answer: The assembly icon ⬛ contains a green square block and an upside down yellow "T" extrusion. The part icon ⬛ contains an upside down yellow "T" extrusion.

SolidWorks Explorer

SolidWorks Explorer is a file management tool designed to assist in viewing, renaming, replacing, and copying SolidWorks files. Execute SolidWorks Explorer within SolidWorks or directly from the desktop. The SolidWorks documents remain closed while manipulating names in SolidWorks Explorer.

The SMC engineers assign unique part numbers to the assemblies; MGPM50-10 and MGPM12-10. Your Engineering department requests a new part number for the two assemblies.

Assembly names are comprised of alphanumeric characters. Companies utilize part names, part numbers, or a combination of both. Utilize descriptive part names for the DELIVERY-STATION assembly. Do not use spaces in document names.

Utilize SolidWorks Explorer to rename the MGPM2139 assembly contained in the MGPM50-10 folder. Update the assembly and part references using SolidWorks Explorer.

Do not rename SolidWorks files through Windows Explorer. SolidWorks Explorer is not a PDM (Product Data Management) tool; however, it performs useful tasks and simplifies numerous file management processes.

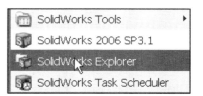

Activate SolidWorks Explorer from the SolidWorks Tools menu or from the Windows Start menu. The application is located on the SolidWorks installation CD's or on the SolidWorks website.

Activity: SolidWorks Explorer

Activate SolidWorks Explorer.
143) Click **Tools**, **SolidWorks Explorer** from the Main menu. SolidWorks Explorer is displayed.

Open the assembly.
144) Click **Browse** from the SolidWorks Explorer box.

145) Double-click the **ASSEMBLY-SW-FILES-2006\SMC\MGPM50-100** folder.

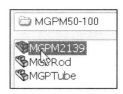

146) Double-click **MGPM2139**. The MGPM2139 assembly is displayed in the Main window.

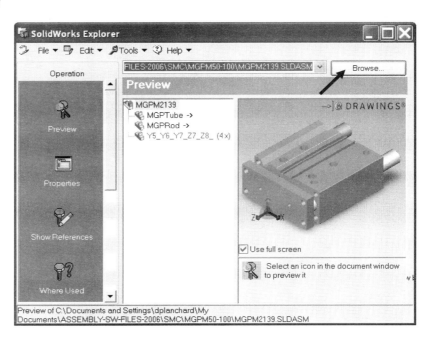

The MGPM2139 assembly contains the MGPTube part and MGPRod part. The MGPTube part and MGPRod part names are displayed in black. The MGPM50-100 folder contains the two parts on your system.

The Y5_Y6_Y7_Z7_Z8 part name is displayed in red. The Y5_Y6_Y7_Z7_Z8 part is not on your system. The part is a suppressed component in the MGPM2139 assembly. Suppressed components are not downloaded.

Display assembly references with the Show Reference option.

Display references for the MGPM2139 assembly.

147) Click **Show References** from the Operation box. The complete file name is displayed in the Main window.

148) Display the long file name. Click the **File name** entry in the Main window.

149) Click the **New name** entry in the Main window to display the short file name.

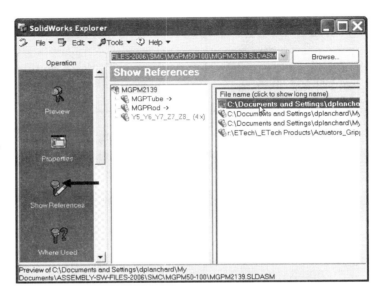

Rename the MGPM50-100M\ MGPM1239 assembly to GUIDE-CYLINDER.

150) Right-click **MGPM2139** as illustrated.

151) Click **Rename**.

152) Enter **GUIDE-CYLINDER. SLDASM**.

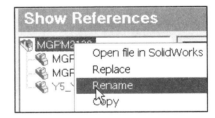

List the parts contained in the assembly.

153) Click **Find now**. The MGPRod and MGPTube parts are checked to be updated.

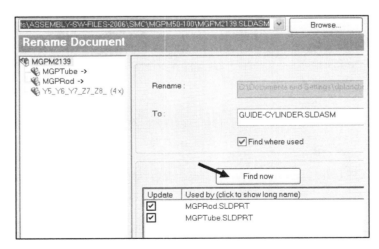

Apply the name change.
154) Click **Apply**.

SolidWorks Explorer displays the new GUIDE-
CYLINDER assembly name in the Main window.

Open the GUIDE-CYLINDER assembly in SolidWorks.
155) Right-click **GUIDE-CYLINDER**.

156) Click **Open File in SolidWorks**.

157) Return to **SolidWorks**. The GUIDE-CYLINDER
assembly is displayed in the SolidWorks Graphics
window.

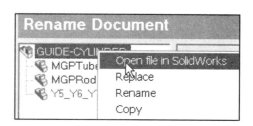

Save the model.
158) Click **Save** 🖫 from the Main menu.

Return to SolidWorks Explorer.
159) Return to **SolidWorks Explorer**.

Preview the parts and
assembly.
160) Click **Preview** from
the Operations box.

161) Uncheck **Use full
screen**.

162) Click the **GUIDE-
CLYINDER
assembly** name
icon.

163) Click **MGPTube**.

164) Click **MGPRod**.

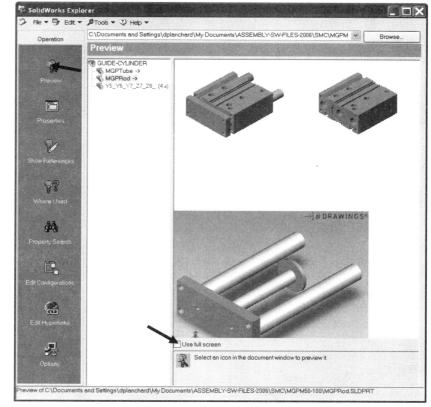

Return to SolidWorks and close all parts and assemblies to avoid reference name issues.

💡 Close a document to rename it. Rename the document with SolidWorks Explorer. SolidWorks Explorer updates file references and requires less work. Microsoft Windows Explorer does not update file references. You are required to locate individual file references.

Return to SolidWorks.
165) Return to **SolidWorks**.

Close all documents.
166) Click **Window, Close All** from the Main menu.

Return to SolidWorks Explorer.
167) Return to **SolidWorks Explorer**.

Preview the MGPM12-10 assembly.
168) Click **Browse**.

169) Double-click **ASSEMBLY-SW-FILES2006\SMC\ MGPM12-10**.

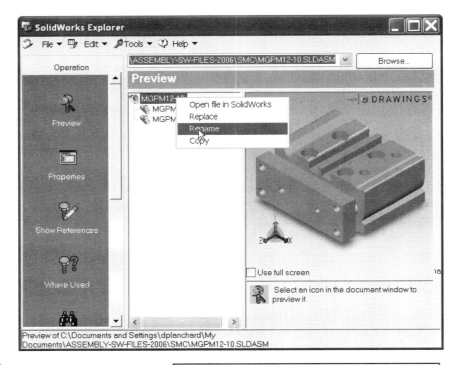

Rename the SolidWorks assembly.
170) Right-click **MGPM12-10**.

171) Click **Rename**.

172) Enter **GUIDE-CYLINDER-12MM.SLDASM**.

173) Click **Find now** to list the parts contained in the assembly.

174) Click **Apply**.

Note: The SolidWorks Explorer Preview uses the last saved image of the SolidWorks document. Display the entire model in the Graphics window before exiting SolidWorks. If SolidWorks Explorer displays no Preview image, open the document in SolidWorks. Fit the model to the screen. Save and Close the document.

Preview the GRIPPER assembly.
175) Click **Browse**.

176) If required, click **Up One Level** to return to the SMC folder.

177) Double-click **MHY2-20D**.

178) Double-click **GRIPPER**.

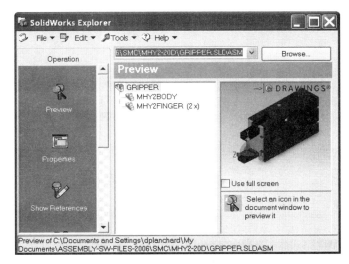

Preview the ROTARY assembly.
179) Click **Browse**.

180) Click **Up One Level** to return to the SMC folder.

181) Double-click **MSQB30R**.

182) Double-click **ROTARY**.

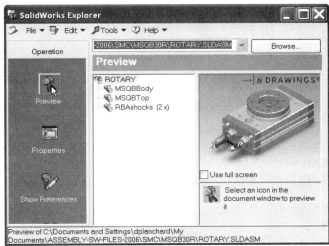

Preview the SLIDE-TABLE assembly.
183) Click **Browse**.

184) Click **Up One Level** to return to the SMC folder.

185) Double-click **MXS25L-100B**.

186) Double-click **SLIDE-TABLE**.

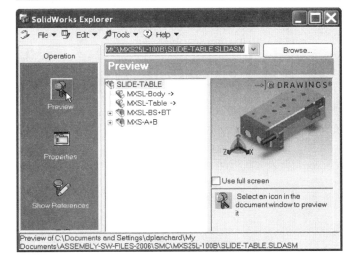

Preview the RODLESS-CYLINDER
assembly.

187) Click **Browse**.

188) Click **Up One Level** 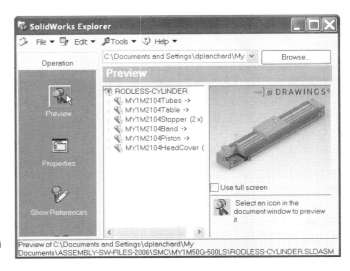 to return
to the SMC folder.

189) Double-click **MY1M50G-500LS**.

190) Double-click **RODLESS-
CYLINDER**.

Open the GUIDE-CYLINDER assembly in
SolidWorks Explorer.

191) Click **Browse**.

192) Click **Up One Level** to return
to the SMC folder.

193) Double-click **MGPM50-100**.

194) Double-click **GUIDE-CYLINDER**.

195) Right-click the **GUIDE-CYLINDER**
assembly icon.

196) Click **Open File in SolidWorks**.

Close SolidWorks Explorer.

197) Click **Close**.

Return to SolidWorks

198) Return to the **SolidWorks**. The
GUIDE-CYLINDER
FeatureManager is displayed.
The GUIDE-CYLINDER is
displayed in the Graphics window.

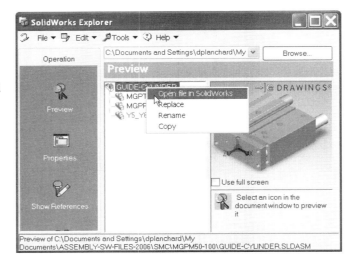

Note: The filename, MGPM2139 was modified to a descriptive name, GUIDE-
CYLINDER to improve name clarity in the DELIVERY-STATION project.

Summary of SMC Components

A summary of the SolidWorks Explorer document renaming convention is as follows:

Assembly Shaded Images: Note: Not to Scale.	New Assembly Name:	Folder Location: (SMC Part Number)	SMC Assembly Name:
	GUIDE-CYLINDER-12MM	MGPM12-10	MGPM2139
	GUIDE-CYLINDER	MGPM50-100	MGPM2139
	GRIPPER	MHY2-20D	MHY3141
	ROTARY	MSQB30R	MSQB4007
	SLIDE-TABLE	MXS25L-100B	MXSL3123A

Assembly Shaded Images: Note: Not to Scale.	New Assembly Name:	Folder Location: (SMC Part Number)	SMC Assembly Name:
	RODLESS-CYLINDER	MY1M50G-500LS	MY1M2104

FeatureManager and Component States

Entries in the FeatureManager design tree have specific definitions. Understanding syntax and states saves time when creating and modifying assemblies. Review the columns of the MGPTube part syntax in the FeatureManager.

Column 1: A resolved component (not in lightweight state) displays a plus ⊞ icon. The plus icon indicates that additional feature information is available. A minus ⊟ icon displays the fully expanded feature list.

Component States:	
Symbol:	**State:**
	Resolved part. A yellow part icon indicates a resolved state. A blue part icon indicates a selected, resolved part.
	Lightweight part. A blue feather on the part icon indicates a lightweight state.
	Out-of-Date Lightweight. A red feather on the part icon indicates out-of-date references.
	Suppressed. A gray icon indicates the part is not resolved in the active configuration.
	Hidden. A clear icon indicates the part is resolved but invisible.
	Hidden Lightweight. A clear feather over a clear part icon indicates the part is hidden and lightweight.
	Hidden, Out-of-Date, Lightweight. A red feather over a clear part icon indicates the part is hidden, out-of-date, and lightweight.
	Rebuild required.
	Resolved assembly. The part states also apply to an assembly.

Column 2: Identifies a component's (part or assembly) relationship with other components in the assembly.

Column 3: The MGPTube part is fixed (f). Review other relations between components in an assembly:

Component relationship with other components in the assembly:	
Symbol:	**Relationship:**
(-)	A minus sign (–) indicates that the part or assembly is under-defined and requires additional information.
(+)	A plus sign (+) indicates that the part or assembly is over-defined.
(f)	A fixed symbol (f) indicates that the part or assembly does not move.
(?)	A question mark (?) indicates that additional information is required on the part or assembly.

Column 4: MGPTube - Name of the part.

Column 5: The symbol <#> indicates the particular inserted instance of a component. The symbol <1> indicates the first inserted instance of a component, "MGPTube" in the assembly. If you delete a component and reinsert the same component again, the <#> symbol increments by one.

Column 6: The Resolved state displays the MGPTube icon with an additional external reference symbol, "- >".

There are modeling situations in which unresolved components create rebuild errors. In these situations, issue the forced rebuild, Ctrl+Q. The Ctrl+Q option rebuilds the model and all its features. If the mates still contain rebuild errors, resolve all the components below the entry in the FeatureManager that contains the first error.

Comparison of Component States

A complete list of component suppression states is displayed in: SolidWorks Help Topics \ Lightweight\Comparison of Components Suppression.

	Resolved	Lightweight	Suppressed	Hidden
Loaded in memory	Yes	Partially	No	Yes
Visible	Yes	Yes	No	No
Features available in FeatureManager design tree	Yes	No	No	No
Faces and edges accessible for adding mates	Yes	Yes	No	No
Mates solved	Yes	Yes	No	Yes
In-context features solved	Yes 1	Yes	No	Yes
Assembly features solved	Yes	Yes	No	Yes
Considered in global operations 2	Yes	Yes 3	No	Yes
May be edited in-context	Yes	Yes 4	No	No
Load and rebuild speed	Normal	Faster	Faster	Normal
Display speed	Normal	Normal	Faster	Faster

Geometric and Functional Requirements

The senior engineer on the design team specified the geometric and functional requirements for the GUIDE-CYLINDER assembly.

Geometric Requirements:

The GUIDE-CYLINDER assembly mounts to the RODLESS-CYLINDER assembly. The RODLESS-CYLINDER assembly contains a table with the following dimensions: 200mm x 144mm x 30mm.

Functional Requirements:

The GUIDE-CYLINDER assembly Stroke distance is 100mm. The force and pressure conditions determine the Bore diameter of the GUIDE-CYLINDER assembly. The Bore diameter is 50mm.

Conserve time. Validate that a vendor component meets both your geometric and functional requirements. Review the model configuration parameters and key dimensions.

The SMC components are modeled using part and assembly configurations. Configurations are different variations of a component based on a series of parameters. Review the configuration information for Bore size and Stroke parameters for the GUIDE-CYLINDER assembly. Measure key features and compare dimensions with the specification data sheets.

Review the Configuration Properties of the GUIDE-CYLINDER assembly. The Configuration Properties dialog box displays the Configuration Name. The Custom button contains configuration specific information.

Record the Stroke distance 100mm and the Bore Size 50mm in the Configuration Specific Properties.

Measure the overall dimensions of the MGPTube. The depth is 144mm, the width is 148mm and the height is 64mm.

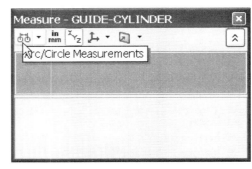

These dimensions meet the geometric requirements for the 3-AXIS-TRANSFER assembly. Common measurements appear in the Status bar in the lower right corner of the Graphics window.

Additional measure options are available from the Tools, Measure toolbar.

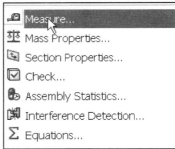

Activity: Geometric and Functional Requirements

Review the GUIDE-CYLINDER Configuration Properties.

199) Click the
ConfigurationManager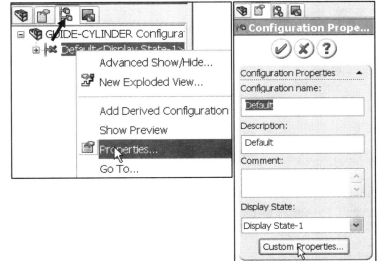
icon.

200) Right-click **Default**.

201) Click **Properties**.

202) Click **Custom Properties**
from the Configuration
Properties
PropertyManager. The
Summary Information box is
displayed.

203) Click the
**Configuration
Specific** tab.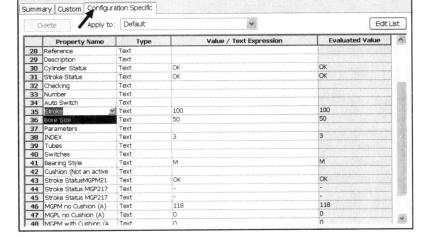

204) Drag the Properties
scroll bar downward
in the table to display
the values for the
Stroke (100) and Bore
Size (50).

205) Click **OK** from the
Summary Information
box.

206) Click **OK** 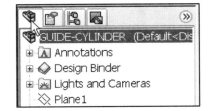 from
the Configuration
Properties
PropertyManager.

Return to the Assembly FeatureManager.
207) Click the **FeatureManager** icon.

Measure the feature geometry.

208) Click **Top** 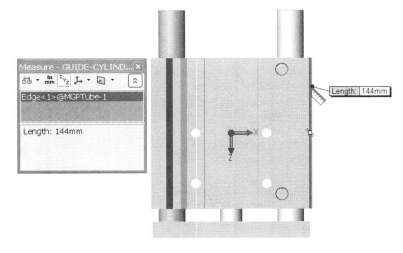 view.

209) Click **Tools**, **Measure**
Measure... from the
Main menu.

210) Click the **vertical left edge** of the MGPTube part. The Status bar displays Length: 144mm.

Clear the vertical left edge selection from the Measure box.
211) Right-click in the **highlighted red** box.

212) Click **Clear Selection**.

Display an Isometric view.
213) Click **Isometric** view .

Measure the overall width.
214) Click the **right face**. Face<1> is displayed.

215) Rotate the **model 90°**.

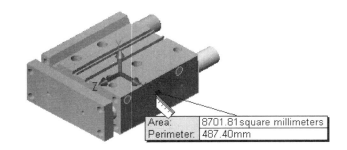

216) Click the **left face as** illustrated. Face<2> is displayed. The Status bar displays: Normal Distance: 148.00mm.

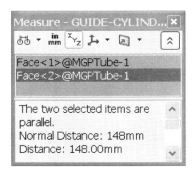

Clear the overall width selection from the Measure box.
217) Right-click in the **highlighted red** box.

218) Click **Clear Selection**.

Measure the overall height.
219) Click **Isometric** view.

220) Click the **top face**. Face <3> is displayed.

221) Rotate the **model 90°**.

222) Click the **bottom face**. Face<4> is
displayed. The Status bar displays: Normal
Distance: 64mm.

223) Click **Close** from the
Measure box.

Display an Isometric view and
save the model.
224) Click **Isometric** view.

225) Click **Shaded With
Edges** 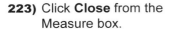.

226) Click **Save** .

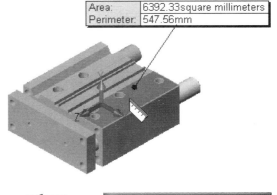

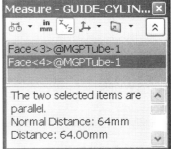

☼ View Thumbnails easily.
Before you exit SolidWorks, save
assemblies in their Isometric
view, Shaded With Edges
display.

The Isometric view option
enlarges the model to fit the
Graphics window.

As an exercise, measure the
distance between the two sets of
Counterbore faces.

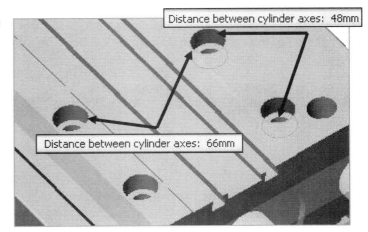

The Status area displays the Distance between cylindrical axes.

SolidWorks Toolbox Configuration

The SolidWorks Toolbox is a library of feature based design automation tools for SolidWorks. The SolidWorks Toolbox uses the Microsoft Window's click, drag, and drop functionality.

There are three options to apply fasteners in the 3AXIS-TRANSFER assembly.

- Utilize SolidWorks Toolbox for fasteners.

- Utilize the Socket Head Cap Screw part file that is located in the MY-TOOLBOX folder.

- Utilize your own fasteners.

This book utilizes the SolidWorks Toolbox fasteners.

Configure the SolidWorks Toolbox to create a copy of the library part. Store the SolidWorks Toolbox parts in the ASSEMBLY-SW-FILES-2006\MY-TOOLBOX folder.

Activity: SolidWorks Toolbox

Add SolidWorks Toolbox to the Main Menu.
227) Click **Tools**, **Add-Ins** from the Main menu.

228) Click **SolidWorks Toolbox**.

229) Click **Toolbox Browser**.

230) Click **OK**. Toolbox is added to the Main menu.

Configure the SolidWorks Toolbox Browser.
231) Click **Toolbox**, **Browser Configuration** from the Main menu.

Set the Storage folder to copy the Toolbox parts.
232) Click **Document Properties** from the Browser Tab.

233) Check **Always create copy**.

234) Click **Browse**.

235) Select the **ASSEMBLY-SW-FILES-2006\MY-TOOLBOX** folder for Copy Directory.

236) Click **OK** from the Select Directory box.

237) Click **Apply** from the Configure Browser box.

Configure Browser

Browser | Smart Fasteners

Document Properties
Colors
Part Numbers
Custom Properties

Copy Part File
○ No copy (always use master part file)
◉ Always create copy
○ Create copy on ctrl-drag

Copy Directory:

My Documents\ASSEMBLY-SW-FILES-2006\MY-TOOLBOX   [Browse...]

Writing to read-only documents
○ Error when writing to a read-only document
◉ Always change read-only status of document before writing

238) Click **OK** from the Configure Browser box.

Close all models.
239) Click **Windows**, **Close All** from the Main menu.

Vendor Information

Vendors supply information through Online intelligent catalogs. The below specification was obtained from the SMC website: (www.smcworld.com).

SMC provides drawings and tables on their components. The depth and width dimensions are required for the GUIDE-CYLINDER assembly. What two letters in the table below represent the depth and width dimensions? Answer: C and H, respectively.

What are the values for C and H?

C = 44 + Stroke Length = 44 + 100 mm = 144mm.

H = 148mm.

The GUIDE-CYLINDER depth is 144mm and the width is 148mm.

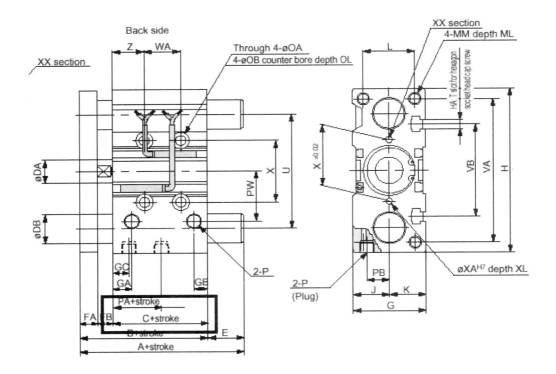

MGPM, MGPL/Common Dimensions

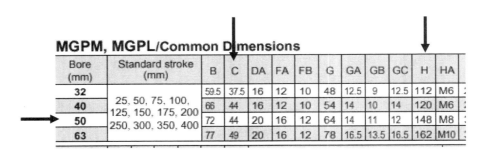

Bore (mm)	Standard stroke (mm)	B	C	DA	FA	FB	G	GA	GB	GC	H	HA	
32	25, 50, 75, 100, 125, 150, 175, 200 250, 300, 350, 400	59.5	37.5	16	12	10	48	12.5	9	12.5	112	M6	
40		66	44	16	12	10	54	14	10	14	120	M6	
50		72	44	20	16	12	64	14	11	12	148	M8	
63		77	49	20	16	12	78	16.5	13.5	16.5	162	M10	

Companies utilize On-line intelligent catalogs, digitized photographs, electronic drawings, and engineering professionals to support their customers.

Companies control hundreds or even thousands of parts. They must also manage the design changes that occur frequently in the development process.

Digital photographs of
SMC GUIDE CYLINDERS

Project Summary

You reviewed the DELIVERY-STATION assembly layout diagram and the 3AXIS-TRANSFER assembly. The 3AXIS-TRANSFER assembly contains three separate sub-assemblies:

- LINEAR-TRANSFER.

- 2AXIS-TRANSFER.

- ROTARY-GRIPPER.

The MGPM-12mm GUIDE-CYLINDER assembly was either downloaded from the SMC website based on engineering criteria: pressure, stroke, and load or copied from the CD in the book.

You created a custom Assembly Template, ASM-MM-ANSI and Part Template, PART-MM-ANSI-AL6061. The Templates are stored in the MY-TEMPLATES folder.

You viewed and renamed assemblies using SolidWorks Explorer. You obtained and confirmed geometric and functional requirements utilizing Tool, Measure from the Main menu and component specification sheets from the SMC website.

Develop the LINEAR-TRANSFER assembly in Project 2. Utilize the Bottom Up Design Assembly modeling approach. Develop the 2AXIS-TRANSFER assembly in Project 3. Utilize a Top Down Design Assembly modeling approach.

Develop the ROTARY-GRIPPER assembly in Project 4. Utilize both the Top Down and Bottom Up Design Assembly modeling techniques. Note: Be prepared for a few design changes along the way.

Review the project questions and exercises before developing new parts, assemblies, drawings, and configurations in the next Projects.

Questions

1. Why is file management critical in the design and development process?

2. Identify the document that is the foundation for a SolidWorks assembly.

3. Describe the difference between an assembly and a part.

4. Describe the difference between a component and a part.

5. List the three SolidWorks default Templates in the New dialog box.

6. Why should you use unique part numbers and assembly filenames? Provide an example.

7. True or False. Maximize the amount of parts at the top level of the assembly. Explain.

8. True or False. Design parts and assemblies to reuse information. Explain.

9. An Assembly Template file extension is _____, a Part Template file extension is _____.

10. True or False. System Options are stored with the current SolidWorks document. Explain.

11. Utilize _____ Explorer to rename parts and assemblies.

12. Provide an example of a geometric requirement for the GUIDE-CYLINDER assembly. Provide an example of a functional requirement.

13. Identify the symbol used to represent the Lightweight State in the FeatureManager.

14. Identify the following component states for the FeatureManager.

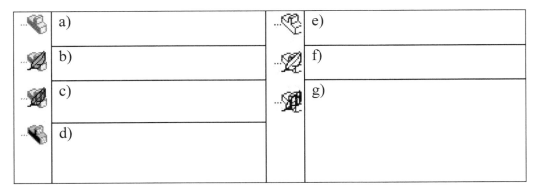

	a)		e)
	b)		f)
	c)		g)
	d)		

Exercises

Exercise 1-1: Create an Assembly Template, ASSEMBLY-INCH-ANSI. Select inch for units. Select ANSI for the Dimensioning Standard. Save the ASSEMBLY-INCH-ANSI Template to the MY-TEMPLATES folder.

Exercise 1-2: Create an Assembly Template, ASSEMBLY-MM-ISO. Select mm for units. Select ISO for the Dimensioning Standard. Save the ASSEMBLY-MM-ISO Template to the MY-TEMPLATES folder.

Exercise 1-3: Create a Part Template, PART-INCH-ANSI. Select inch for units. Select ANSI for the Dimensioning Standard. Save the PART-INCH-ANSI Template to the MY-TEMPLATES folder. Create a second inch Part Template, PART-INCH-ANSI-IRON. Utilize the Materials Editor and select Cast Gray Iron.

Exercise 1-4: Create a PART Template, PART-MM-ISO. Select mm for units. Select ISO for the Dimensioning Standard. Save the PART-MM-ISO Template to the MY-TEMPLATES folder. Create a second metric Part Template, PART-MM-ANSI-SS304. Utilize the Materials Editor and select AISI 304 Stainless Steel.

Exercise 1-5: Measure the ROD diameter in millimeters for the MPGRod part in the GUIDE-CYLINDER assembly. Determine the Rod diameter for a 50mm Bore size on the Theoretical Force table.

Theoretical Force (N)

Bore size (mm)	Rod diameter (mm)	Operating direction	Piston area (mm²)	0.2	0.3	0.4	0.5	0.6	0.7	0.8	0.9	1.0
12	6	OUT	113	23	34	45	57	68	79	90	102	113
		IN	85	17	26	34	43	51	60	68	77	85
16	8	OUT	201	40	60	80	101	121	141	161	181	201
		IN	151	30	45	60	76	91	106	121	136	151
20	10	OUT	314	63	94	126	157	188	220	251	283	314
		IN	236	47	71	94	118	142	165	189	212	236
25	12	OUT	491	98	147	196	246	295	344	393	442	491
		IN	378	76	113	151	189	227	265	302	340	378
32	16	OUT	804	161	241	322	402	482	563	643	724	804
		IN	603	121	181	241	302	362	422	482	543	603
40	16	OUT	1257	251	377	503	629	754	880	1006	1131	1257
		IN	1056	211	317	422	528	634	739	845	950	1056
50	20	OUT	1963	393	589	785	982	1178	1374	1570	1767	1963
		IN	1649	330	495	660	825	990	1154	1319	1484	1649

Exercise 1-6: Identify the dimensions required to locate the four Counterbores in the Top view for a 50mm Bore size. See Exercise Figure1-1.

Series *MGP*

MGPM, MGPL Ø32 to Ø63

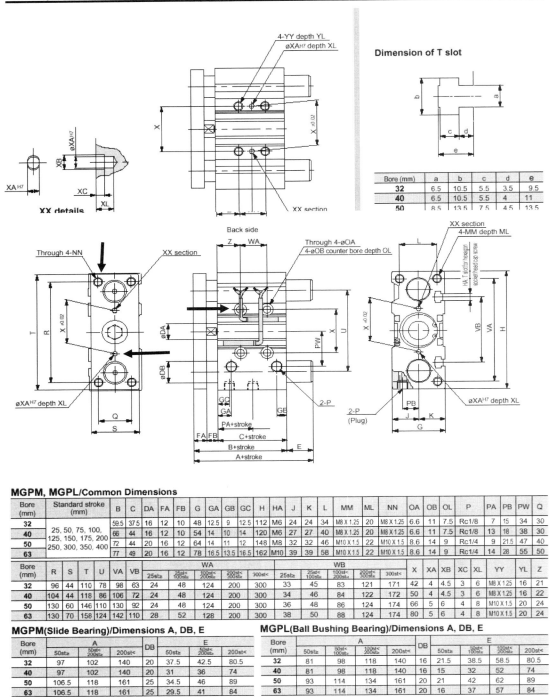

Dimension of T slot

Bore (mm)	a	b	c	d	e
32	6.5	10.5	5.5	3.5	9.5
40	6.5	10.5	5.5	4	11
50	8.5	13.5	7.5	4.5	13.5

MGPM, MGPL/Common Dimensions

Bore (mm)	Standard stroke (mm)	B	C	DA	FA	FB	G	GA	GB	GC	H	HA	J	K	L	MM	ML	NN	OA	OB	OL	P	PA	PB	PW	Q
32	25, 50, 75, 100, 125, 150, 175, 200 250, 300, 350, 400	59.5	37.5	16	12	10	48	12.5	9	12.5	112	M6	24	24	34	M8 X 1.25	20	M8 X 1.25	6.6	11	7.5	Rc1/8	7	15	34	30
40		66	44	16	12	10	54	14	10	14	120	M6	27	27	40	M8 X 1.25	20	M8 X 1.25	6.6	11	7.5	Rc1/8	13	18	38	30
50		72	44	20	16	12	64	14	11	12	148	M8	32	32	46	M10 X 1.5	22	M10 X 1.5	8.6	14	9	Rc1/4	14	21.5	47	40
63		77	49	20	16	12	78	16.5	13.5	16.5	162	M10	39	39	58	M10 X 1.5	22	M10 X 1.5	8.6	14	9	Rc1/4	14	28	55	50

Bore (mm)	R	S	T	U	VA	VB	WA 25st≥	WA 25st< 100st≥	WA 100st< 200st≥	WA 200st< 300st≥	WA 300st<	WB 25st≥	WB 25st< 100st≥	WB 100st< 200st≥	WB 200st< 300st≥	WB 300st<	X	XA	XB	XC	XL	YY	YL	Z
32	96	44	110	78	98	63	24	48	124	200	300	33	45	83	121	171	42	4	4.5	3	6	M8 X 1.25	16	21
40	104	44	118	86	106	72	24	48	124	200	300	34	46	84	122	172	50	4	4.5	3	6	M8 X 1.25	16	22
50	130	60	146	110	130	92	24	48	124	200	300	36	48	86	124	174	66	5	6	4	8	M10 X 1.5	20	24
63	130	70	158	124	142	110	28	52	128	200	300	38	50	88	124	174	80	5	6	4	8	M10 X 1.5	20	24

MGPM(Slide Bearing)/Dimensions A, DB, E

Bore (mm)	A 50st≥	A 50st< 200st≥	A 200st<	DB	E 50st≥	E 50st< 200st≥	E 200st<
32	97	102	140	20	37.5	42.5	80.5
40	97	102	140	20	31	36	74
50	106.5	118	161	25	34.5	46	89
63	106.5	118	161	25	29.5	41	84

MGPL(Ball Bushing Bearing)/Dimensions A, DB, E

Bore (mm)	A 50st≥	A 50st< 100st≥	A 100st< 200st≥	A 200st<	DB	E 50st≥	E 50st< 100st≥	E 100st< 200st≥	E 200st<
32	81	98	118	140	16	21.5	38.5	58.5	80.5
40	81	98	118	140	16	15	32	52	74
50	93	114	134	161	20	21	42	62	89
63	93	114	134	161	20	16	37	57	84

3.17-14   Exercise Figure 1-1

Exercise 1-7: Manually sketch the four Counterbore position in the Top view. Use a simple rectangle to represent the MGPTube part. See Exercise Figure1-1.

Exercise 1-8: There are two sets of holes in the MGPRod part Front view. Manually sketch the positions and diameters in a Front view. Use a simple rectangle to represent the MGPRod part. See Exercise Figure1-1.

Exercise 1-9: Determine the width, height and depth of the GUIDE-CYLINDER-12MM assembly. There are two sets of holes in the MGPRod-12MM part Front view. Manually sketch the positions and diameters in a Front view.

Determine the locations of the four Counterbores in the MGPTube-12MM part Top view. Manually sketch the Counterbore positions and diameters in a Top view sketch.

Exercise 1-10: Develop a layout assembly diagram for the following household items:

a. Blender.

b. Toaster.

c. Coffee Pot.

d. Gas Grill.

e. Table.

f. Bicycle.

g. Speaker.

Exercise 1-11: Review the Web Site, 3DContentCentral. List the major categories of components available from this site.

Notes:

Project 2

Assembly Modeling – Bottom-Up Design Approach

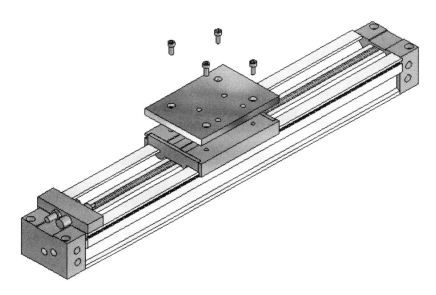

Below are the desired outcomes and usage competencies based on the completion of this Project.

Project Desired Outcomes:	Usage Competencies:
• PLATE-A part.	• Knowledge to create new parts based on component features utilizing the Bottom-Up Design Approach.
• LINEAR-TRANSFER assembly.	• Increase skill and speed using SmartMate tools.
• RODLESS-CYLINDER configuration.	• An appreciation of engineering mechanics to simulate the physical assembly process.
• LINEAR-TRANSFER configuration.	• Aptitude to manage components and to create configurations at various levels of the assembly.
• Socket Head Cap Screw.	• Ability to identify and determine the correct fastener specifications.

Notes:

Project 2 – Assembly Modeling – Bottom-Up Design Approach

Project Objective

Develop the LINEAR-TRANSFER assembly. The LINEAR-TRANSFER assembly is the first assembly in the 3AXIS-TRANSFER assembly.

Create the following models in this project:

- PLATE-A part.

- LINEAR-TRANSFER assembly.

On the completion of this project, you will be able to:

- Apply a Bottom-Up Design Assembly Modeling Approach.

- Identify Standard and Advanced Mate types.

- Utilize SmartMates to assemble the PLATE-A part to the RODLESS-CYLINDER assembly.

- Obtain the required dimensions, and identify the required features in mating components.

- Insert components into an assembly.

- Modify a Distance Mate.

- Address Suppress/Un-suppress states and Rigid/Flexible Mates in a configuration.

- Work with the SolidWorks Design Library.

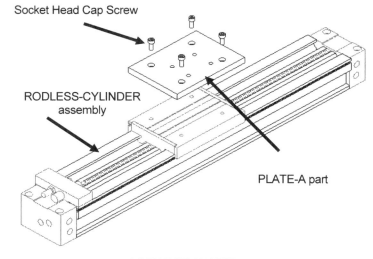

Socket Head Cap Screw

RODLESS-CYLINDER assembly

PLATE-A part

LINEAR-TRANSFER assembly

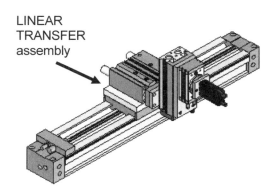

LINEAR TRANSFER assembly

3AXIS-TRANSFER assembly

SolidWorks Tools and Commands

In Project 2, utilize the following SolidWorks tools and commands.

SolidWorks Tools and Commands:		
Add Configuration	Hide	Rigid
Coincident Mate	Hole Wizard	Rotate Component
Collision Detection	Insert Component	Section view
Component Properties	Linear Pattern	Select Other
Concentric Mate	Make assembly from part/assembly	Shortcut keys
Configurations	Mate	Show
Customize keyboard, menu	Mate Reference	Sketch tools: Rectangle, Centerline, Dimension, Midpoint
Derived Component Pattern	Mate Types	SmartMate
Design Library	Measure	SolidWorks Toolbox
Distance Mate	Move Component	Suppress
Edit color	Move with Triad	Unsuppress
Extrude Base	Open part, Open assembly	View Planes, Origins, Temporary Axis
Feature Palette	Parallel Mate	Zoom tools
Flexible	Rename	

Build modeling skill and speed.
Project 2 primarily utilizes Pop-up
menus to execute the tools in the
Assembly toolbar.

Project Overview

A Bottom-Up Design Approach is an assembly modeling technique that combines individual components. Based on design criteria, the components are developed independently.

The three major steps in a Bottom-Up Design Approach are as follows:

1. Create each component independent of any other component in the assembly.

2. Insert the components into the assembly.

3. Mate the components in the assembly as they relate to the physical constraints of the design.

The geometry and functionality of the PLATE-A part depends on the GUIDE-CYLINDER assembly and the RODLESS-CYLINDER assembly.

The mounting holes in the GUIDE-CYLINDER are not aligned to the mounting holes of the RODLESS-CYLINDER.

The new PLATE-A part utilizes design criteria from the two assemblies to locate two sets of holes.

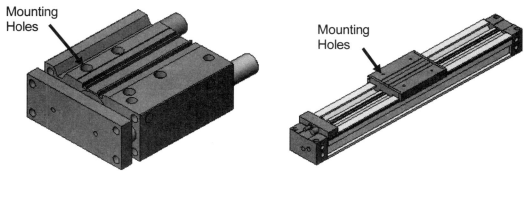

GUIDE-CYLINDER assembly   RODLESS-CYLINDER assembly

Utilize a Bottom-Up Design Approach to develop the LINEAR-TRANSFER assembly. The LINEAR-TRANSFER assembly consists of the following:

- RODLESS-CYLINDER assembly, (located in the SMC file folder).
- PLATE-A part, (create the new part in SolidWorks).
- Four M8 x 1.25 Socket Head Cap Screws, (SolidWorks Toolbox).
- Identify the design components.
- Identify the purchased components.
- Identify the library components.

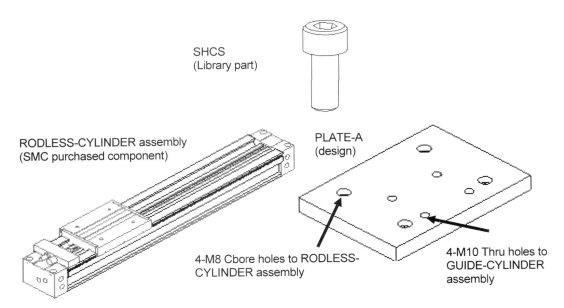

Components for the LINEAR-TRANSFER assembly
(Not to scale)

Create the PLATE-A part. Assemble PLATE-A to the RODLESS-CYLINDER assembly.

Use four, M8 x 1.25 Socket Head Cap Screw (SHCS) to fasten the PLATE-A part to the RODLESS-CYLINDER assembly.

Determine the required length of the SHCS by analyzing the components in the LINEAR-TRANSFER assembly.

The M8 x 1.25 SHCS is defined as follows:

- M8 represents a metric screw: 8mm major outside diameter.
- 1.25 thread pitch (mm per thread).

Develop the configurations for the
RODLESS-CYLINDER assembly.
The RODLESS-CYLINDER
configurations are named:

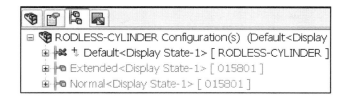

- Default.

- Normal.

- Extended.

Default   Normal   Extended

Create three configurations for the LINEAR-TRANSFER assembly.

The LINEAR-TRANSFER configurations are named Normal, Extended, and Fastener.

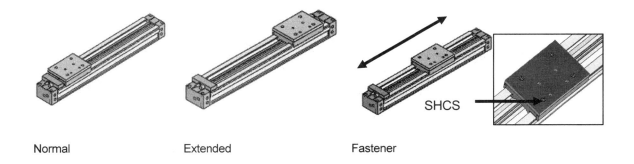

Normal   Extended   Fastener

Geometric and Functional Requirements of the PLATE-A part

The PLATE-A part contains five features. Determine the geometric and functional requirements for PLATE-A.

Obtain the requirements from the parts and reference geometry in the GUIDE-CYLINDER assembly, and the RODLESS-CYLINDER assembly.

The project contains thousands of assemblies, parts, features, Mate types, and sketches. Know your location.

Example 1: The PLATE-A part is contained in the LINEAR-TRANSFER assembly. The FeatureManager full name of the PLATE-A part is: LINEAR-TRANSFER\PLATE-A.

- LINEAR-TRANSFER is the assembly name.

- PLATE-A is the part name.

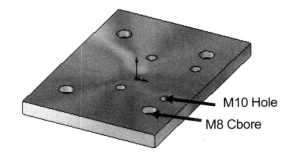

PLATE-A

Example 2: Sketch3 is the sketch name of the M8 Cbore Hole. The FeatureManager full name of Sketch3 is LINEAR-TRANSFER\PLATE-A\CBORE for M8 SHCS1\Sketch3. CBORE is the abbreviation for Counterbore.

- LINEAR-TRANSFER is the assembly name.

- PLATE-A is the part name.

- CBORE for M8 SHCS1 is the feature name.

- Sketch3 is the sketch name.

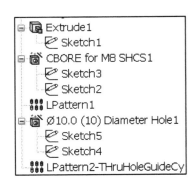

Before you begin a part, review the following New Part Task List.

New Part Task List – Before you begin:		
Task:	**Comments:**	**Complete:**
Identify the part function.	PLATE-A combines the RODLESS-CYLINDER with the GUIDE-CYLINDER in the LINEAR-TRANSFER assembly.	✓
Identify the components that directly affect the part.	RODLESS-CYLINDER, GUIDE-CYLINDER, and M8 SHCS parts	✓
Research the company component database. Identify if PLATE-A, or a similar part exists.	No. Always verify that the existing part does not exist. Copy similar parts to save model time.	✓
Identify the Mate references in the assembly.	Utilize 2 Concentric Mates between mating holes. Utilize a Coincident Mate between the bottom face of PLATE-A and the top face of the RODLESS-CYLINDER.	✓
Define the material, units, tolerance and precision. Utilize the Custom Part Template.	Aluminum. Use company default standard tolerance and precision values for all machined parts.	✓
Identify the geometric requirements of the part; width, height, depth, hole locations, etc.	Utilize Tools, Measure	partial
Is the part symmetrical? Yes, design with symmetry in the sketch of the base feature.		
Design for changes.		
Identify Features and Mates with descriptive names.		
Group Fillets, Draft, and Patterns together. Reuse geometry. Locate the seed feature in a pattern to be utilized in a component pattern.		
Will this part be used in another assembly? Design for multiple configurations. Create a simplified version with no Fillets, no Draft or on unnecessary features.		
Utilize patterns to be referenced in the assembly and suppressed.		
Obtain a unique filename.	PLATE-A (45-63421). Utilize PLATE-A assigned part number in Project 5.	✓

Six of the new part tasks are completed. You have some work to do! Determine the Geometric requirements for the PLATE-A part from the size and shape of the following features:

- GUIDE-CYLINDER\MGPTube\Cbores.
- GUIDE-CYLINDER\MGPTube\ThruHoles.
- RODLESS-CYLINDER\MY1M2104Table\Table.
- RODLESS-CYLINDER\MY1M2104Table\Table_Holes.

In the first activity, determine the location of the MGPTube\Cbores and MGPTube\ThruHoles.

In the second activity, determine the proper overall size of the RODLESS-CYLINDER\MY1M2104Table\Table and the location of the Table_Holes.

Quickly locate entries in the FeatureManager. Rename Features, Mates, and Reference Geometry with descriptive names.

The ThruHoles feature defines the Thru Hole position and diameter. Record the dimensions for the CBORES and ThruHoles features. Avoid precision and tolerance stack-up issues. Perform the following tasks:

- Set the precision to the appropriate number of decimal places.
- Mate two diagonal holes between PLATE-A and the MGPTube\ThruHoles.

In modeling, utilize Concentric Mates with any two sets of holes. Mating the diagonal holes simulates the shop floor practice to utilize diagonal holes for the best stability and clamping.

Note: The SMC components utilize an ISO dimensions standard. Additional Delivery Station components utilize AutoCAD and Imported geometry. Large assemblies contain models with legacy data (inherited older models).

Activity: Geometric and Functional Requirements – PLATE-A and GUIDE-CYLINDER

Open the GUIDE-CYLINDER assembly.

1)   Click the **Design Library** 📚 icon.

2)   Expand **SMC**.

3)   Double-click **MGPM50-100**.

4)   Click and drag the **GUIDE-CYLINDER** icon into the Graphic window. The GUIDE-CYLINDER assembly is displayed.

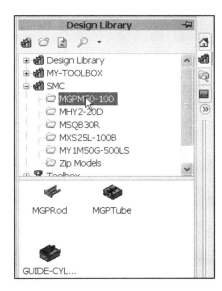

Open the MGPTube part.
5)   Right-click **MGPTube** from the FeatureManager.

6)   Click **Open Part**. The MGPTube is displayed in the Graphics window.

Locate the Cbores and ThruHoles features.
7)   Drag the **slider** downward in the MGPTube FeatureManager. The Extruded Cut icon is displayed before the ThruHoles and Cbores features.

Expand the features.
8)   Expand **ThruHoles** and **Cbores**. Sketch15 and Sketch16 are fully defined. Sketch15 contains External References as indicated by the '->' symbol.

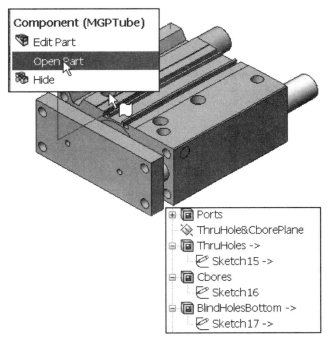

Know the default SW colors. Avoid the color green for a component. A selected feature in the Graphics window is displayed in green. The corresponding feature entry in the FeatureManager is displayed in blue. Fully defined sketched dimensions are displayed in black. Extruded depth dimensions are displayed in blue. Modify default colors in Tools, Options, System Options, Colors, System colors.

Display feature dimensions.
9) Double-click **Cbores** and **ThruHole** from the MGPTube FeatureManager. View the dimensions.

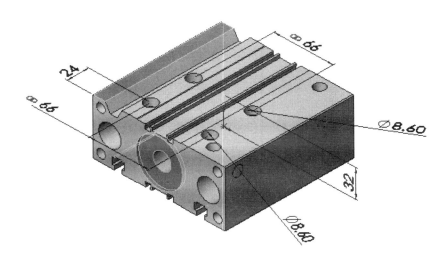

Fit the model to the Graphics window.
10) Press the **f** key.

11) Drag the **dimensions** off the model to display the values.

The distance from the front edge to the first hole is 24mm.

Measure the distance between the front face to the back left Cbore.
12) Click **Tools, Measure** from the Main menu.

13) Click the **front face.** Face<1> is displayed.

14) Click the **back left Cbore cylindrical face** as illustrated. Face<2> is displayed. The Center Distance is 72mm.

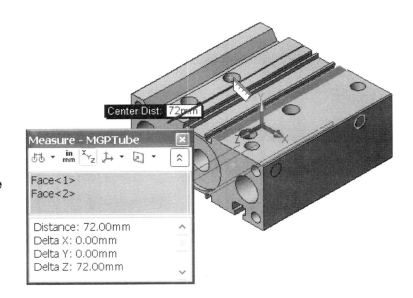

Deselect the faces.

15) Right-click in the **selected box**.

16) Click **Clear Selections**.

Measure the distance between the back left Cbore to the back right Cbore.

17) Click the **back left Cbore cylindrical face**.

18) Click the **back right Cbore cylindrical face**. The Center Distance is 66mm.

Close the open documents.

19) Click **Close** from the Measure box.

20) Click **Window**, **Close All** from the Main menu.

21) Click **No** to Save changes.

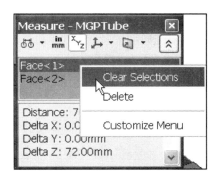

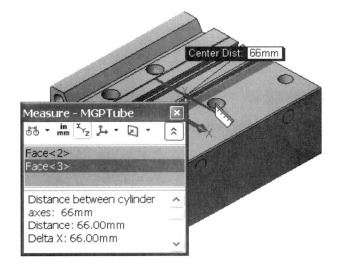

Review the hole placement.   Vertical: 72mm – 24mm = 48mm.

                                               Horizontal: 66mm on center.

Review the hole type: Cbore: $\varnothing$14.

                                                 Thru Hole: $\varnothing$8.6.

                                                 Common Metric fastener required.

The SolidWorks Measure Tool contains the following options:

- Arc/Circle Measurements.

- Units/Precision.

- Show XYZ Measurements.

- XYZ Relative To.

- Projected On.

The XYZ coordinates display different results. Select a vertex to display the XYZ coordinates in the Status bar.

Select the Show XYZ Measurements option to display dX, dY, or dZ.

Un-Select the Show XYZ Measurements option to display the center distance between two selected entities.

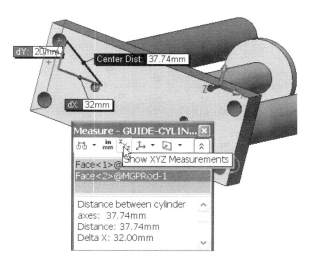

Activity: Geometric and Functional Requirements – PLATE-A and RODLESS-CYLINDER

Open the RODLESS-CYLINDER assembly.
22) Click the **SMC\MY1M50G-500LS** folder from the Design Library.

23) Click and drag the **RODLESS-CYLINDER** icon into the Graphic window.

24) Click **Yes** to rebuild. The RODLESS-CYLINDER assembly is displayed.

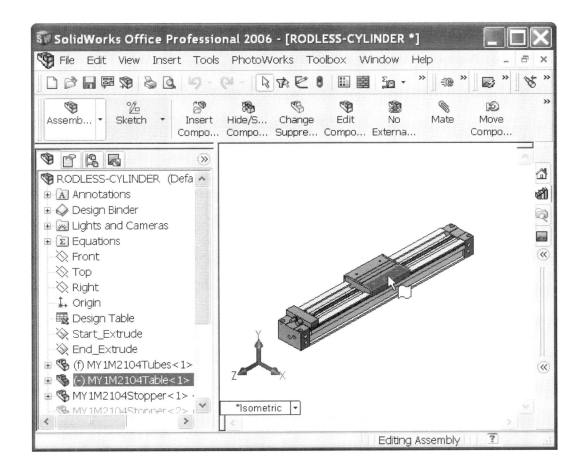

Open the MY1M2104Table.

25) Right-click **MY-1M2104Table<1>** from the FeatureManager.

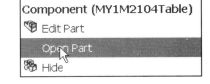

26) Click **Open Part**. The part is displayed in the Graphics window.

Fit the model to the Graphics window.

27) Press the **f** key.

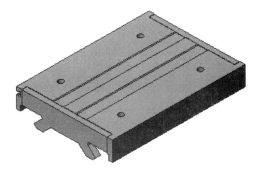

Locate the Table features.
28) Position the **mouse pointer** on the right side of the Table. The feature tool tip Table is displayed. Table is an Extruded Base feature.

29) Position the **mouse pointer** on the top-hole circumference. The feature tool tip Table_Holes is displayed.

Display the feature dimensions.
30) Double-click **Table** from the FeatureManager. View the dimensions.

31) Double-click **Table_Holes** from the FeatureManager. View the dimensions.

Close the MY1M2104Table.
32) Click **File**, **Close** from the Main menu. The RODLESS-CYLINDER remains open.

33) Click **No** to save changes.

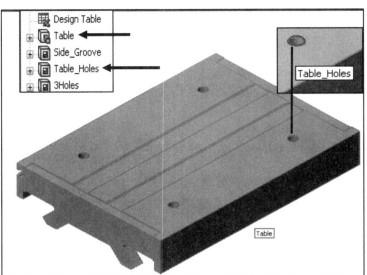

PLATE-A part

The dimensions in the mating parts determine the feature dimensions in PLATE-A. The Table_Holes are not aligned with the GUIDE-CYLINDER Cbore Holes.

PLATE-A requires two patterns of holes.

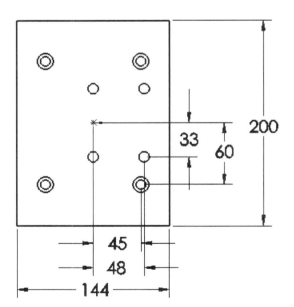

Where should the PLATE-A reference planes be located? Answer: Review the RODLESS-CYLINDER\MY1M2104Table part to locate the planes of symmetry.

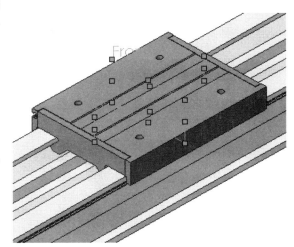

The MY1M2104Table part identifies the overall sketch dimensions and orientation of the PLATE-A part.

The MY1M2104Table part is centered on the Front and Right Plane.

The first feature of the PLATE-A part is an Extruded Base feature. The Top Plane is the Sketch plane. Center the rectangular sketch on the Front and Right Plane.

Utilize 15mm Aluminum plate stock. The PLATE-A part utilizes the custom PART-MM-ANSI-AL6061 Template created in Project 1.

Plan Mate types before creating the Base feature of the part.

Review the Mates between the PLATE-A part and the MY1M2104Table part.

Mate Type:	PLATE-A part:	RODLESS-CYLINDER\ MY1M2104Table part:
Coincident	Bottom face	Top face
Concentric	Lower right hole	Lower right hole
Concentric	Upper left hole	Upper left hole

Align the component in the same orientation as the assembly to avoid unnecessary use of Rotate Component in the assembly. Create the Extruded Base feature vertical and horizontal dimensions in the same orientation as the MY1M2104Table Extruded Base feature.

The PLATE-A part requires two sets of four holes. The first set contains four Cbores.

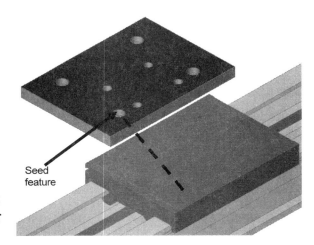

Seed feature

The second set contains four Thru Holes.

Create a 2x2 Linear Pattern for both hole types. Utilize the Hole Wizard.

The seed feature of the Linear Pattern is the first Cbore. The PLATE-A part positions the seed feature in its lower right corner. Utilize the seed feature and Linear Pattern in the assembly.

Display Cbore Holes and the Thru Holes in the ANSI Metric standard. Other standards may be selected when using the Hole Wizard or SolidWorks\Toolbox.

Prepare for future design changes. If the overall size of PLATE-A changes, the hole location remains constant. Select the Front and Right Plane for a Symmetric Reference for the Cbore. Select the Front Plane for a Symmetric Reference for the Thru Holes. Select the Right plane for a Coincident Reference.

Activity: PLATE-A

Display the RODLESS-CYLINDER reference planes.

34) Expand **MY1M2104Table** from the RODLESS-CYLINDER FeatureManager as illustrated.

35) Click **Front** Plane from the FeatureManager.

36) Hold the **Ctrl** key down.

37) Click **Right** Plane from the FeatureManager.

38) Release the **Ctrl** key.

39) Right-click **Show**. The Front and Right Planes are displayed in the Graphics window.

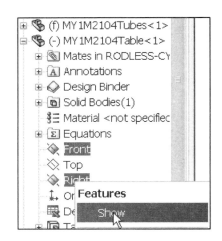

Create a new part.
40) Click **File**, **New** from the Main menu.

41) Click the **MY-TEMPLATES** tab.

42) Double-click the **PART-MM-ANSI-AL6061** Part Template. The Part FeatureManager is displayed.

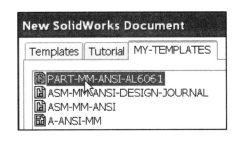

Save the new part.
43) Click **Save** from the Main menu.

44) Select the **DELIVERY-STATION-** folder from the Save in list box.

45) Enter **PLATE-A** for File name.

46) Click **Save**. The PLATE-A FeatureManager is displayed.

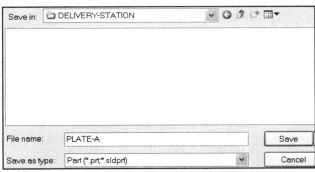

By default, the Bill of Materials utilizes the File name field for the Part Number column and the Description field for the Description column.

Utilize Custom Properties in Project 5 to control the Description and Part number.

Sketch the profile.
47) Click **Top Plane** from the FeatureManager for the Sketch plane.

48) Click **Sketch** Sketch .

49) Click **Rectangle** Rectan... from the Sketch toolbar.

50) Sketch a **rectangle** approximately centered about the Origin.

51) Click **Centerline** Centerl... from the Sketch toolbar.

52) Sketch a centerline between the **two diagonal endpoints** of the rectangle as illustrated.

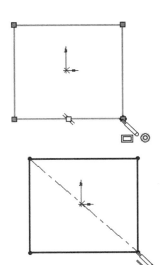

Add a Midpoint relation.

53) Right-click **Select** in the Graphics window.

54) Click the **Origin**.

55) Hold the **Ctrl** key down.

56) Click the **Centerline**. The Properties PropertyManager is displayed.

57) Release the **Ctrl** key.

58) Click **Midpoint** from the Add Relations box. Midpoint0 is displayed in the Existing Relations box.

59) Click **OK** from the Properties PropertyManager.

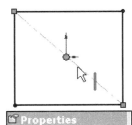

Add a vertical dimension.

60) Click **Smart Dimension** from the Sketch toolbar.

61) Click the right **vertical** line.

62) Click a **position** to the right of the vertical line.

63) Enter **200**. Click ✓.

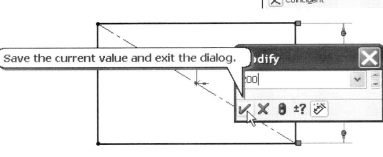

Add a horizontal dimension.

64) Click the bottom **horizontal** line.

65) Click a **position** below the horizontal line.

66) Enter **144**. Click ✓.

67) Click **OK** from the Dimension PropertyManager.

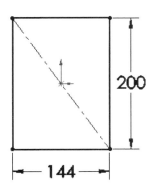

Extrude the sketch.

68) Click **Extruded Boss\Base** from the Features toolbar.

69) Enter **Mid Plane** for End Condition.

70) Enter **15** for Depth.

71) Click **OK** from the Extrude PropertyManager. Extrude1 is displayed in the FeatureManager

Use the Hole Wizard. Create an M8 CBORE Hole.
72) Click the **top face** of PLATE-A in the lower right corner. Extrude1 is highlighted in the FeatureManager.

73) Click **Hole Wizard** Hole Wizard from the Features toolbar. The Hole Specification PropertyManager is displayed.

74) Click **Counterbore** for Hole Specification.

75) Select **Ansi Metric** for Standard.

76) Select **Socket Head Cap Screw** for Type.

77) Select **M8** for Size.

78) Select **Through All** for End Condition.

79) Click the **Positions** tab.

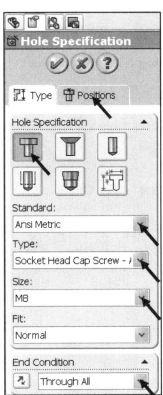

Insert dimensions.

80) Click **Smart Dimensions** 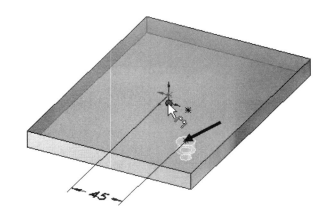 from the Sketch toolbar.

81) Click the **Origin**.

82) Click the **Cbore center point**.

83) Click a **position** below the horizontal profile line.

84) Enter **45**.

85) Click ✔.

86) Click the **Origin**.

87) Click the **Cbore center point**.

88) Click a **position** to the right of the vertical profile line.

89) Enter **60**.

90) Click ✔.

91) Click **OK** 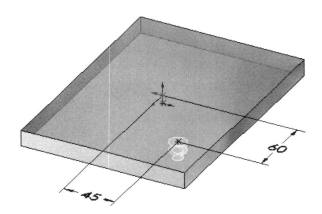 from the Dimension PropertyManager

92) Click **OK** from the Hole Position PropertyManager. CBORE for M8 SHCS1 is displayed in the FeatureManager.

93) Click **Hidden Lines Visible**.

The CBORE for M8 SHCS1 is displayed in the Graphics window. CBORE for M8 SHCS1 is the seed feature for the first Linear Pattern.

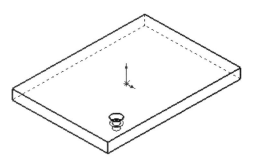

Create a Linear Pattern.

94) Click **Linear Pattern** Linear Pattern from the Features toolbar. The Linear Pattern PropertyManager is displayed.

Display the Top view.
95) Click **Top** view.

96) Click the **bottom edge** of PLATE-A for Direction1.

97) If required, click **Reverse Direction**. The direction arrow points to the left.

98) Enter **90** for Direction1.

99) Enter **2** for Instances.

100) Click the **left vertical line** for Direction2.

101) If required, click **Reverse Direction**. The direction arrow points upward.

102) Enter **120** for Direction2.

103) Enter **2** for Instances.

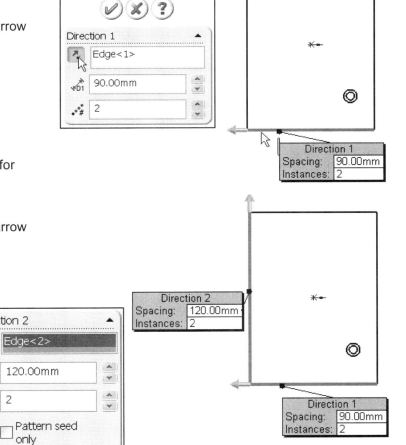

104) Check **Geometry pattern** from the Options box.

105) If required, click inside the **Features to Pattern** box. Expand **PLATE-A** in the Graphics window. Click **CBORE for M8 SHCS1**. CBORE for M8 SHCS1 is displayed in the Features to Pattern box.

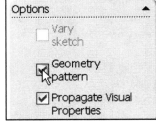

106) Click **OK** 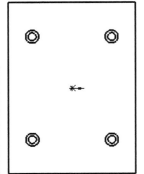 from the Linear Pattern PropertyManager. LPatten1 is created in the FeatureManager.

The checked Geometry pattern option copies only the geometry (faces and edges) of the features. The unchecked Geometry pattern option results in a calculated solution for every instance in the pattern.

The geometry pattern option usually decreases the time required to create and rebuild a pattern.

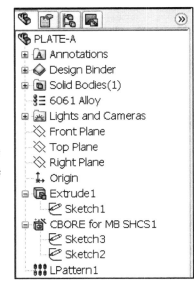

Use the Hole Wizard. Create an M10 Thru Hole.

107) Click the **top face** of PLATE-A in the lower right hand corner. Extrude1 is highlighted in the FeatureManager.

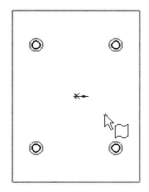

108) Click **Hole Wizard** Hole Wizard from the Features toolbar. The Hole Specification PropertyManager is displayed.

109) Click **Hole** for Hole Specification.

110) Select **Ansi Metric** for Standard.

111) Select **Drill sizes** for Type.

112) Select **10** for Size.

113) Select **Through All** for End Condition.

114) Click the **Positions** tab.

Dimension the hole.

115) Click **Smart Dimensions** Smart Dimens... from the Sketch toolbar.

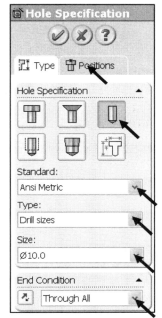

116) Click the **Origin**.

117) Click the **hole center point** as illustrated.

118) Click a **position** below the horizontal profile line.

119) Enter **48**.

120) Click ✔.

121) Click the **Origin**.

122) Click the **hole center point**.

123) Click a **position** to the right of the vertical profile line.

124) Enter **33**.

125) Click ✔. Click **OK** ✔ from the Dimension PropertyManager.

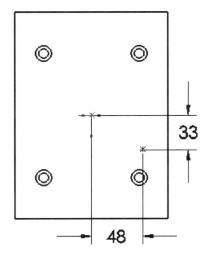

126) Click **OK** ✅ from the Hole Position PropertyManager. The M10 Thru Hole is the seed feature for the second Linear Pattern.

Create the second Linear Pattern.

127) Click **Linear Pattern** Pattern from the Features toolbar. The Linear Pattern PropertyManager is displayed.

128) Click the **bottom edge** for Direction1. Edge<1> is displayed. If required, click **Reverse Direction**. The direction arrow points to the left.

129) Enter **48** for Direction1.

130) Enter **2** for Instances.

131) Click the **left vertical edge** for Direction2. The direction arrow points upward.

132) Enter **33*2** for Direction2.

133) Enter **2** for Instances.

134) If required, click inside the **Features to Pattern** box. Expand **PLATE-A** in the Graphics window. Click **10.0 (10) Diameter Hole1**.

135) Click **OK** ✅ from the Linear Pattern PropertyManager. LPattern2 is displayed in the FeatureManager.

Display an Isometric view.
136) Click **Isometric** view.

Save the PLATE-A part.
137) Click **Save**.

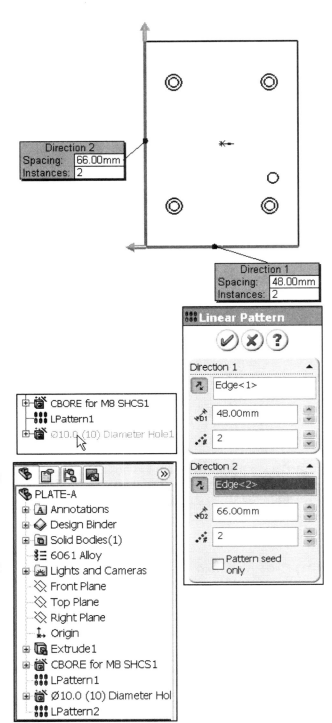

Activity: New Folder in SolidWorks Design Library

Create a new parts folder in the SolidWorks Design Library.

138) Click the **Design Library** 📚 icon.

139) Expand **Design Library**.

140) Click the **Push Pin** 📌 to pin the Design Library open.

141) Right-click on **parts** in the folder area.

142) Click **New Folder**.

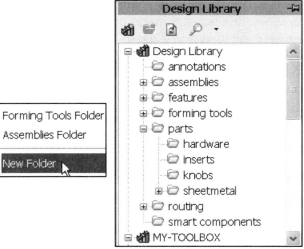

143) Enter **plates** for Folder name.

144) Double-click the **plates** folder. The folder is empty.

Insert PLATE-A into the plates file folder.

145) Drag the **PLATE-A** 📎 PLATE-A part icon from the top of the FeatureManager into the plates folder.

146) Click **Save** to save PLATE-A into the plates folder. PLATE-A is contained in the Parts\plates folder.

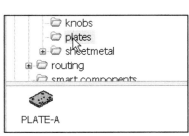

147) Click the **Push Pin** 📌 to un-pin the Design Library.

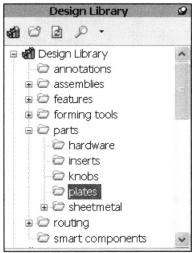

💡 Utilize Tools, Options, File Locations, Design Library to insert additional folders into the Design Library.

Assembly Mating Techniques

The action of assembling components in SolidWorks is defined as Mates. Mates simulate the construction of the assembly in a manufacturing environment. In dynamics, components possess linear motion along the x, y, and z-axes and rotational motion around the x, y, and z-axes. In an assembly, each component contains six degrees of freedom: three translational (linear) and three rotational. All components behave as rigid bodies. Components do not flex or deform.

In a static analysis, there is no motion. How do static and dynamic principles translate to component Mates? Answer: Mates remove degrees of freedom.

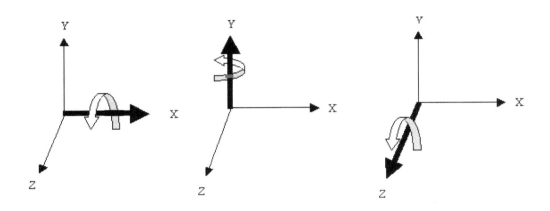

☀ Understand the engineering mechanics of the component before creating Mates.

Example 1:

Static: Fasten the DELIVERY-STATION assembly to the MOUNTING-PLATE part. The MOUNTING PLATE part is fixed to the Origin of the final assembly. The MOUNTING-PLATE part does not translate or rotate.

Example 2:

Dynamic: Assemble the PLATE-A part to the RODLESS-CYLINDER\ MY1M2104Table part. The MY1M2104Table part slides along the MY1M2104Tubes part. The PLATE-A part travels at the same velocity as the MY1M2104Table part. Insert the Mates between the PLATE-A part and the MY1M2104Table part.

Assembly modeling requires practice and time. Below are a few helpful techniques to address component mating. Utilize these techniques throughout the development of the 3AXIS-TRANSFER assembly and sub-assemblies.

Mating Techniques:
Right-click in the assembly Graphics window to avoid mouse pointer "movement" to the assembly toolbar and the assembly FeatureManager.
Use the Zoom and Rotate commands to select the geometry in the mate process. Zoom to select the correct face. Right-click Select Other for hidden geometry.
Use View Orientation, Named Views to display a key area of the model.
Apply various colors to features and components to improve display.
Utilize Reference Planes and axes to assemble complex geometry.
Activate Temporary axes and Show Planes when required for Mates, otherwise Hide All Types from the View menu. Create Shortcut keys to activate View commands.
Select Reference Planes from the FeatureManager for complex components. Expand the FeatureManager to view the correct plane.
Remove display complexity. Hide components when visibility is not required.
Suppress components when Mates are not required. Group fasteners at the bottom of the FeatureManager. Suppress fasteners and their assembly patterns to save rebuild time and file size. Utilize caution with suppressed components. Suppressed Mates may cause related components to translate and rotate. Use View Mates to understand mating dependencies.
Utilize Section views to select internal geometry. Utilize Transparency to see through components required for mating.
Use the Move Component and Rotate Component commands before Mating. Position the component in the correct orientation.
Use a Coincident Mate when the distance value between two entities is zero. Utilize a Distance Mate when the distance value between two entities is not zero.
Cylindrical components require a Concentric and Coincident Mate. They are not fully defined.
Verify the position of the components. Use Top, Front, Right and Section views.
Rename Mates, key features and Reference Geometry with descriptive names.
Avoid unwanted references. Confirm the geometry name you selected in the Mate Property Manager.
Uncheck the Show preview option to prevent components from moving out of the Graphics window during mating.

LINEAR-TRANSFER assembly

The RODLESS-CYLINDER assembly is the Base (first) component in the LINEAR-TRANSFER assembly.

All components of the RODLESS-CYLINDER assembly remain stationary, except for the MY1M2104Table part.

The MY1M2104Table part linearly translates along the MY1M2104Tubes part.

Perform the following tasks to complete the LINEAR-TRANSFER assembly.

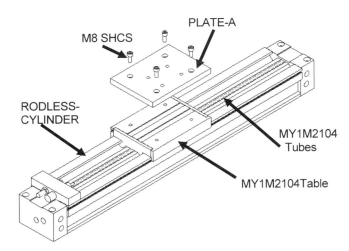

LINEAR-TRANSFER assembly

- Create the LINEAR-TRANSFER assembly.

- Fix the RODLESS-CYLINDER assembly to the Origin of the LINEAR-TRANSFER assembly.

- Assemble the PLATE-A part to the RODLESS-CYLINDER\MY1M2104Table part.

- Determine the diameter and length of the SHCS. Mate the SHCS with the SolidWorks\Toolbox.

The PLATE-A part, LINEAR-TRANSFER assembly and the RODLESS-CYLINDER assembly remain open during this project.

Activity: Insert Component and Shortcut Keys

Deactivate the Large Assembly Mode.
148) Click **Tools, Options** from the Main menu.

149) Click **Assembles**.

150) Uncheck **Use Large Assembly Mode**.

151) Click **OK**.

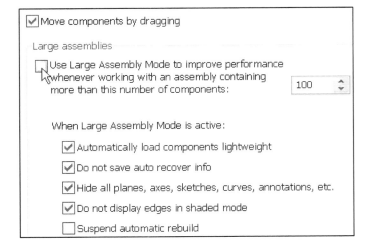

Create the LINEAR-TRANSFER assembly.

152) Click **Make Assembly from Part/Assembly** 🔩 from the Standard toolbar.

153) Click the **MY-TEMPLATES** tab.

154) Double-click **ASM-MM-ANSI**.

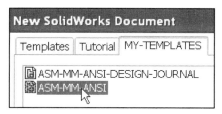

The Insert Component PropertyManager is displayed. In order to select multiple components from the Part/Assembly to Insert, Open documents box, select the Push Pin. The PropertyManager remains open. Utilize the Browse button to select components not displayed in the Open documents box.

Inset the ROD-CYLINDER assembly.

155) Click **View**, **Origins** from the Main menu.

156) Click **Push Pin** 🔘 from the Insert Component PropertyManager.

157) Click **RODLESS-CYLINDER** from the Open documents box.

158) Click the **Origin** ↳ of the assembly. The mouse pointer displays the Insert Component fixed at Origin icon 🔩.

159) Click **PLATE-A** in the Open documents box.

160) Click a **position** above the RODLESS-CYLINDER as illustrated.

161) Click **OK** ✅ from the Insert Component PropertyManager.

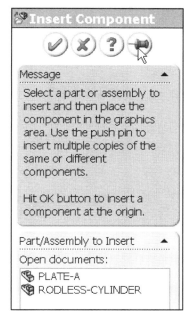

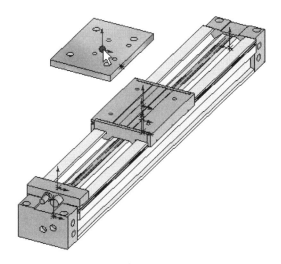

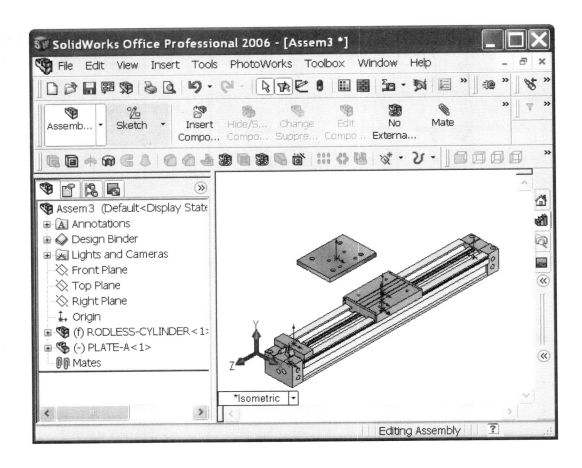

Save the assembly.
162) Click **Save**.

163) Select the **DELIVERY-STATION** for Save in folder.

164) Enter **LINEAR-TRANSFER** for File name.

165) Click **Save**. The LINEAR-TRANSFER assembly FeatureManager is displayed.

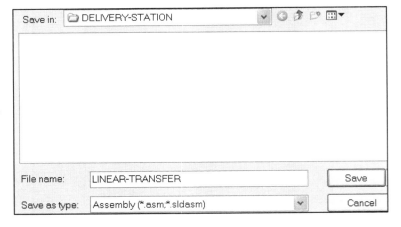

Hide the Origin.
166) Click **View,** uncheck **Origins** from the Main menu

Customize the Keyboard

Customize your keyboard to create Shortcut keys for reference geometry. Create
Shortcut keys to check or uncheck Hide All Types, Planes, Axes, Temporary Axes, and
Origins. Large Assembly Mode hides all Reference geometry by default.

Create a new view in the View Orientation dialog box. An enlarged view saves time in
assembling the MY1M2104Table holes to the PLATE-A holes.

Activity: Customizing the Keyboard

Create four View Shortcut keys.
167) Click **Tools, Customize** from the Main menu.

168) Click the **Keyboard** tab.

169) Click **View** from the Categories box.

Create the Planes Shortcut key.
170) Select **Planes** from the
Commands box.

171) Enter **Shift + P** in the Press new
Shortcut key.

172) Click **Assign**.

Create the Axes Shortcut key.
173) Select **Axes** from the Commands
box.

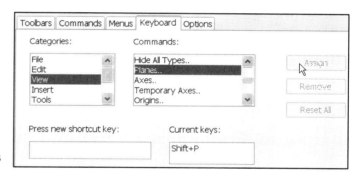

174) Enter **Shift + A** in the Press new
Shortcut key.

175) Click **Assign**. SolidWorks pre-
assigned the A key to the Select
Others command option toggle.

Create the Temporary Axes Shortcut key.
176) Select **Temporary Axes** from the Commands list box.

177) Enter **Shift + T** in the Press new Shortcut key.

178) Click **Assign**.

Create the Origins Shortcut key.
179) Select **Origins** from the Commands list box.

180) Enter **Shift + O** in the Press new Shortcut key.

181) Click **Assign**.

182) Click **OK**.

Review the created Shortcut keys.
183) Press **P** to show Planes.

184) Press **P** to hide Planes.

185) Press **T** to show Temporary Axes.

186) Press **T** to hide Temporary Axes.

187) Press **O** to show Origins.

188) Press **O** to hide Origins.

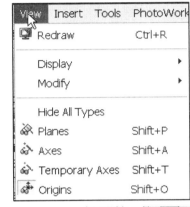

Create a new view.
189) **Zoom to area** on the MY1M2104Table.

190) Rotate the **MY1M2104Table** as illustrated.

191) Press the **Space Bar to** display the View
Orientation dialog box.

192) Click **Pin** 🖈 from the Orientation box.

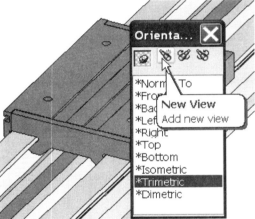

193) Click **New View** 🦯 .

194) Enter **table-view** for view name.

195) Click **OK** from the Named View box.

Display an Isometric view.
196) Click **Isometric** view.

Display the table-view.
197) Click **table-view** from the
Orientation box.

198) Click **Close** from the Orientation
box.

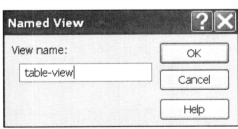

The default programmed Shortcut Keys for the default views are as follows:

- Ctrl+1 – Front.
- Ctrl+2 – Back.
- Ctrl+3 – Right.
- Ctrl+4 – Left.
- Ctrl+5 – Top.
- Ctrl+6 – Bottom.
- Ctrl+7 – Isometric.
- Ctrl+8 – Normal To.
- Ctrl+Shift+Z – Previous view.

Note: Custom Shortcut keys are set on the current keyboard. To save/restore settings to another computer, utilize the Start, All Programs, SolidWorks, SolidWorks Tools, Copy Settings Wizard. For best practice, System Administrators copy settings to network computers and roaming user profiles.

Modifying the Base component; Fix / Float options

By default, the first component in an assembly is fixed with respect to the assembly Origin.

The Insert Component fixed at the Origin icon ensures that the component Origin is coincident with the assembly Origin.

The component receives an (f) in the FeatureManager.

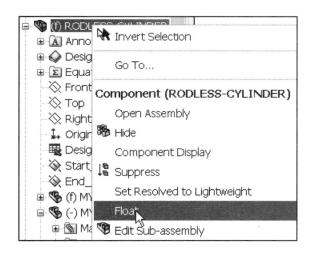

As components increase in complexity, visualizing the icon becomes more challenging. In many design situations, the first component orientation and position with respect to the assembly Origin requires modification.

How do you address these issues? Answer: Modify the Fixed state to a Float state.

The Float state displays a minus (-) in the FeatureManager. Move and rotate the component with respect to the assembly Origin.

Mate the first component to reference assembly geometry.

Explore the Fixed/Float state for the first component in Project 3.

Standard and Advanced Mates, SmartMates, and InPlace Mates

Establishing the correct component relationship in an assembly requires forethought on component interaction. Mates are geometric relationships that align and fit components in an assembly. Mates remove degrees of freedom from a component.

Mates require geometry from two different components. Selected geometry includes Planar Faces, Cylindrical faces, Linear edges, Circular/Arc edges, Vertices, Axes, Temporary axes, Planes, Points, and Origins.

Standard and Advanced Mates:

The Mate Property Manager displays Standard Mate Types and Advanced Mate Types. Components are assembled with various Mate Types. The Standard Mate Types are:

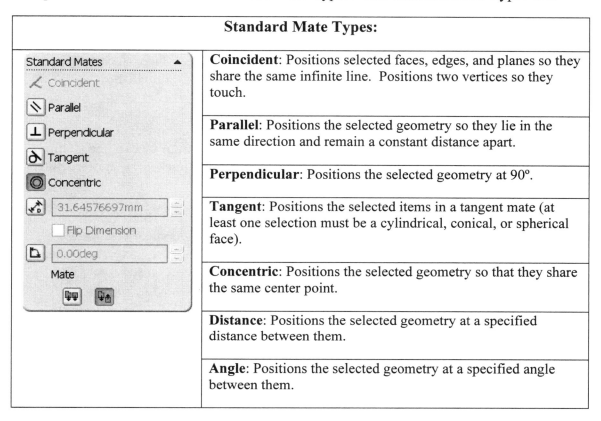

Standard Mate Types:	
	Coincident: Positions selected faces, edges, and planes so they share the same infinite line. Positions two vertices so they touch.
	Parallel: Positions the selected geometry so they lie in the same direction and remain a constant distance apart.
	Perpendicular: Positions the selected geometry at 90°.
	Tangent: Positions the selected items in a tangent mate (at least one selection must be a cylindrical, conical, or spherical face).
	Concentric: Positions the selected geometry so that they share the same center point.
	Distance: Positions the selected geometry at a specified distance between them.
	Angle: Positions the selected geometry at a specified angle between them.

The Mate, Show popup dialog box, displays the Pop-up toolbar during the Mate options. The Standard Mate Types, Aligned/Anti-Aligned, Undo and OK are displayed in the Pop-up toolbar.

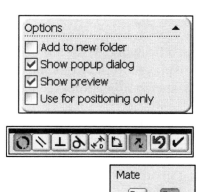

There are two Mate Alignment options. The Aligned option positions the components so that the normal vectors from the selected faces point in the same direction.

The Anti-Aligned option positions the components so that the normal vectors from the selected faces point in opposite directions.

Advanced Mates:

The Advanced Mate Types are:

Advanced Mate Types:	
	**Symmetric**: Positions two selected entities to be symmetric about a plane or planar face. A Symmetric Mate does not create a Mirrored Component.
	Cam: A cam-follower mate is a type of tangent or coincident mate. It positions a cylinder, plane, or point to a series of tangent extruded Cam faces. The Cam profile is comprised of tangent lines, arcs, and/or splines in a closed loop.
	Gear: Positions two components to rotate relative to one another about selected axes. The axis of rotation includes: cylindrical and conical faces, axes, and linear edges. Gear components are not required for a Gear Mate. Example, two rolling cylinders.
	Limit: Defines a range of motion for a Distance Mate or Angle Mate. Specify a starting value, minimum value and maximum value.

SolidWorks Help Topics list the rules governing Mate type valid geometry. The valid geometry selection between components in a Coincident Mate is displayed in the Coincident Mate Combinations Table.

SolidWorks Help Topics also display Standard Mates by Entity. Specific combinations of geometry create valid Mates.

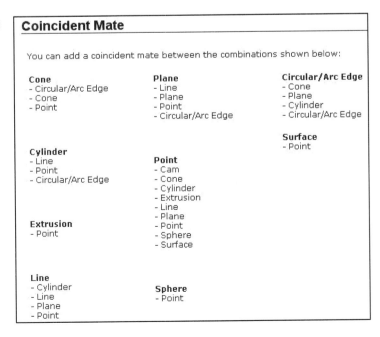

Coincident Mate

You can add a coincident mate between the combinations shown below:

Cone
- Circular/Arc Edge
- Cone
- Point

Cylinder
- Line
- Point
- Circular/Arc Edge

Extrusion
- Point

Line
- Cylinder
- Line
- Plane
- Point

Plane
- Line
- Plane
- Point
- Circular/Arc Edge

Point
- Cam
- Cone
- Cylinder
- Extrusion
- Line
- Plane
- Point
- Sphere
- Surface

Sphere
- Point

Circular/Arc Edge
- Cone
- Plane
- Cylinder
- Circular/Arc Edge

Surface
- Point

Mates reflect the physical behavior of a component in an assembly. In this project, the two most common Mate Types are Concentric and Coincident.

Concentric Mate – 2 Conical faces   Concentric Mate – 2 Conical faces

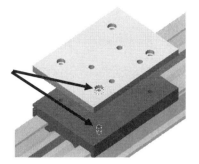
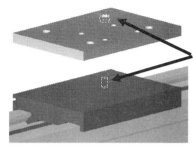

Utilize two Concentric Mates between the two sets of holes from the PLATE-A part and the RODLESS-CYLINDER assembly.

Utilize one Coincident Mate between the two planar faces from the PLATE-A part and the RODLESS-CYLINDER assembly.

Coincident Mate – 2 Planar faces

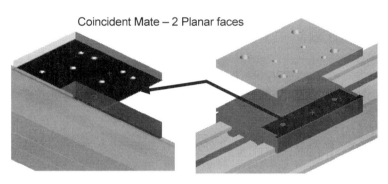

The two Concentric Mates and the one Coincident Mate remove all six degrees of freedom for the PLATE-A part.

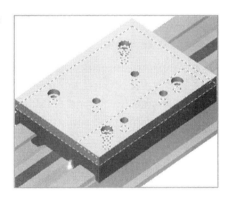

The PLATE-A part is fully defined in the LINEAR-TRANSFER assembly.

The operation of the Mate tool is as follows.

1. Select the entity from the free component to assemble.

2. Select Mate from the Assembly toolbar.

3. Select the entity from the target assembly.

4. Select the Mate type.

5. Select OK from the Mate PropertyManager.

The Mates entry in the FeatureManager displays the Mates Types.

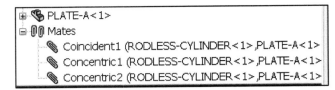

🔆 Organize your Mates in the FeatureManager. A Mates list for a 100 component assembly has 200 – 300 Mate Types. Group Mates from the same component. Utilize folders to organize Mates. Select the free component entity to assemble and then select the target assembly entity.

SmartMates

A SmartMate is a Mate that automatically occurs when a component is placed into an assembly. There are three categories of SmartMates:

- Geometry-based.

- Feature-based.

- Pattern-based.

Geometry-based

The mouse pointer displays a SmartMate feedback symbol when common geometry and relationships exist between the component and the assembly.

SmartMates are Concentric or Coincident.

A Concentric SmartMate assumes that the geometry on the component has the same center as the geometry on an assembled reference.

A Coincident Plane SmartMate assumes that a plane on the component lies along a plane on the assembly.

Mating entities	Type of mate	Pointer
2 linear edges	Coincident	
2 planar faces	Coincident	
2 vertices	Coincident	
2 conical faces, or 2 axes, or 1 conical face and 1 axis	Concentric	
2 circular edges (the edges do not have to be complete circles)	Concentric (conical faces) - and - Coincident (adjacent planar faces)	

As the component is dragged into place, the mouse pointer provides feedback such as:

- Concentric ![icon] .

- Coincident ![icon] .

Feature-based

The Feature-based SmartMate adds automatic Mates between features that have a "peg-in-hole" relationship. One of the features must be a Base or Boss, and the other must be a Hole or a Cut. Only Extruded and Revolved features utilize Feature-based Mates.

Pattern-based

The Pattern-based SmartMate inserts up to three SmartMates at once. Each component contains a circular pattern of cylindrical holes or bosses on a planar face with a circular edge.

Geometry-base SmartMates are utilized in the next activity. Additional examples of Feature-based and Pattern-based SmartMates are available in SolidWorks Help, SmartMates.

Review the following table on methods to invoke SmartMates.

Methods to Invoke Smart Mates:	
Option 1: Within the assembly	Hold the Alt key down. Click the mating entity of the free component. Drag the component to the assembly reference. Release the Alt key.
Option 2: Within the assembly	Click Move Component. Click SmartMates from the Move Component PropertyManager. Option A: Double-click and drag the mating entity of the free component to the target mating entity of the assembly. Release the left mouse button. Option B: Double-click the mating entity of the free component. Single click on the target mating entity of the assembly.
Option 3: From an open document	Tile Horizontally with the free component and the target assembly. Select a face, edge or vertex on the free component. Drag to the target mating entity of the assembly in the second window.

Press the Tab key after the Concentric/Coincident icon is displayed to control the Aligned or Anti-Aligned option.

InPlace Mates

Components added In-Context of the assembly automatically receive an InPlace Mate within the Mates entry in the FeatureManager. The InPlace Mate is a Coincident Mate created between the Front Plane of a new component and the selected planar geometry of the assembly.

Tab key
Aligned/Anti-Aligned

The component is fully defined by the InPlace Mate. No additional Mates are required to position the component. The InPlace1 Mate is added to the FeatureManager.

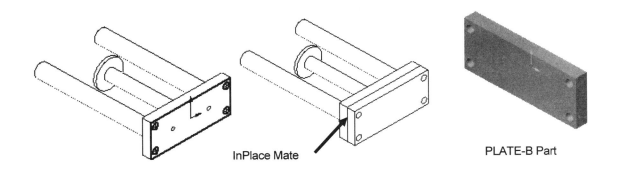

InPlace Mate   PLATE-B Part

The PLATE-B part is created In-Context of the GUIDE-CYLINDER assembly.

The InPlace Mate is created between the PLATE-B Part Front Plane and the GUIDE-CYLINDER assembly right face.

InPlace Mates are explored in Project 3 and Project 4. The next activity utilizes SmartMate Geometry based techniques to assemble the PLATE-A part to the MY1M2104Table part.

Utilize SmartMates with the Alt key to create two Concentric Mates. Utilize SmartMates from within the Move Component PropertyManager to create one Coincident Mate. The SmartMate icon indicates SmartMate mode. Practice the different methods and options.

Activity: Inserting SmartMates

Hide the MYM1M2104Tubes part.
199) Right-click **MY1M2104Tubes** from the FeatureManager.

200) Click **Hide**.

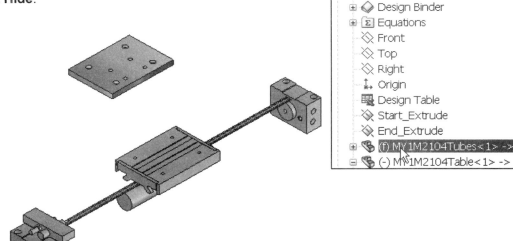

Insert a Concentric SmartMate.
201) Hold the **Alt** key down.

202) Click and drag the PLATE-A **CBORE face** to the front right Table_Hole face, as illustrated. The Concentric

    icon is displayed. Note: Zoom in on the area.

203) Release the **Alt** key. Concentric is selected by default from the Mate Pop-up menu.

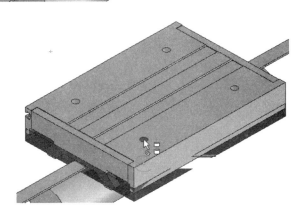

204) Click ✔.

View the created Mate.
205) Expand **Mates** from the FeatureManager. View the inserted Concentric mate.

The Smart Mate 🖰🖋 icon indicates SmartMate mode. The Move option remains active.

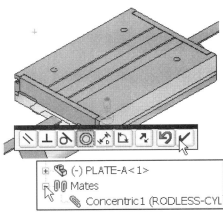

Move the PLATE-A part.

206) Click the **PLATE-A** part in the Graphics window.

207) Drag the **PLATE-A part** upward until you view the upper left CBORE as illustrated.

Fit the model to the Graphics window.
208) Press the lower case **z key** until the MYM2104Table part and the PLATE-A part are displayed in the Graphics window.

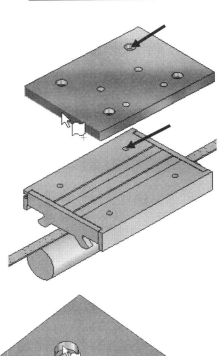

Insert the second Concentric SmartMate.
209) Press the **Down arrow** to view the inside face of the Cbore as illustrated.

210) Hold the **Alt** key down.

211) Click and drag the PLATE-A **CBORE face** to the back left Table_Hole as illustrated. The Concentric

🖰🖾 icon is displayed.

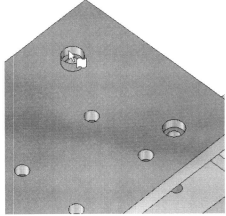

212) Release the **Alt** key. Concentric is selected by default from the Mate Pop-up menu.

213) Click ✔ .

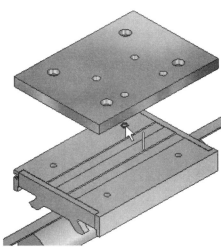

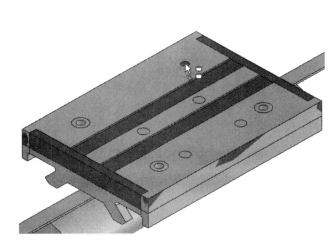

View the created Mate.
214) Expand **Mates** from the FeatureManager. View the second inserted Concentric mate.

- ⊞ 🦴 (-) PLATE-A<1>
- ⊟ 📎 Mates
  - 📎 Concentric1 (RODLESS-CYLINDE
  - 📎 Concentric2 (RODLESS-CYLINDE

Insert a Coincident SmartMate.
215) Fit the model to the Graphics window. Press the **f** key.

Move
216) Click **Move Component** Compo... from the Assembly toolbar. The Move Component PropertyManager is displayed.

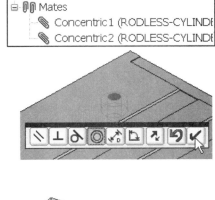

217) Click and drag **PLATE-A** upward and rotate until its bottom face is visible. Click the **SmartMates** 🖱 icon in the Move box.

218) Double-click the **bottom face** of PLATE-A. The SmartMate icon is displayed.

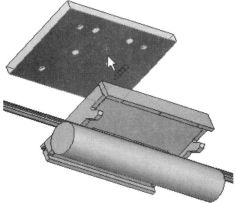

219) Click **table-view**.

220) Click the **top face** of the MYM2104Table. Coincident is selected by default from the Mate Pop-up.

221) Click ✔.

222) Click **OK** ✅ from the SmartMates PropertyManager.

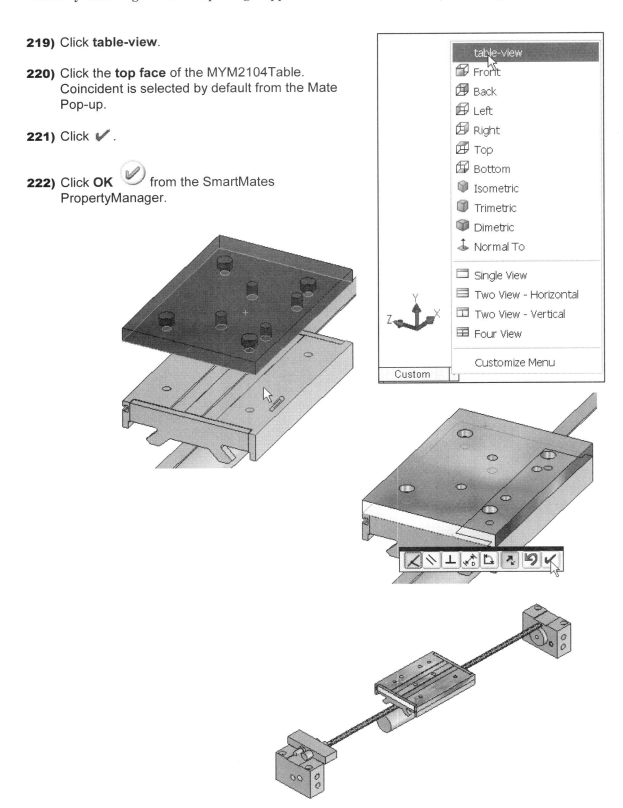

Show the MYM1M2104Tubes part.
223) Right-click **MY1M2104Tubes** from the FeatureManager.

224) Click **Show**.

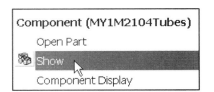

Minimize entries in the FeatureManager.
225) Click the **Minus** icon in the
FeatureManager to minimize the
PLATE-A part.

226) Click the **Minus** icon to minimize the
RODLESS-CYLINDER assembly.

Expand the LINEAR-TRANSFER\Mates
entry.
227) Expand **Mates** from the LINEAR-
TRANSFER FeatureManager.

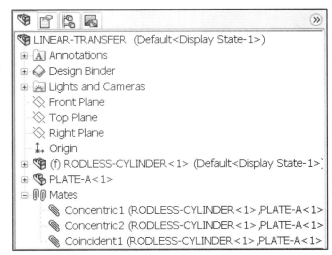

The three SmartMates created two
Concentric Mates and one Coincident
Mate. The PLATE-A part cannot
translate or rotate.

🔆 Design for change. For
easier recognition, Mates that
require future modification
should be renamed to a
descriptive name.

Note: Mate name numbers
increment by one. If you delete
a Mate and insert a new Mate in
the same session of SolidWorks,
the new Mate name is
incremented by one.

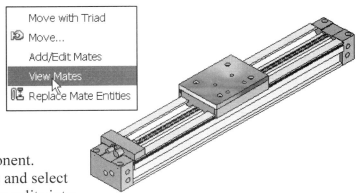

The View Mates option displays
all the Mates for a selected component.
Right-click on a component name and select
View Mates. The FeatureManager splits into
two sections.

How do you enable the PLATE-A part to translate in the
LINEAR-TRANSFER assembly? Answer: Modify the
Component Property Solve as option from Rigid to Flexible.

Rigid and Flexible

There are two states to solve Mates in an assembly:

- Rigid.

- Flexible.

By default, components inserted into an assembly solve Mates as
Rigid. Rigid components do not translate or rotate.

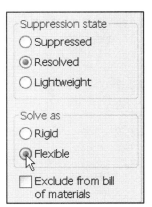

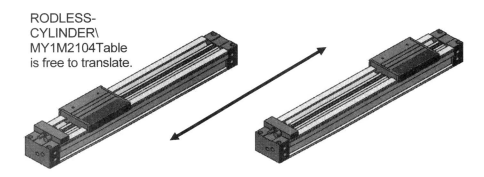

RODLESS-
CYLINDER\
MY1M2104Table
is free to translate.

Flexible components translate or rotate
based on the behavior of their Mates.

In the flexible state, the MY1M2104Table
part and PLATE-A part are free to translate
in the LINEAR-TRANSFER assembly.

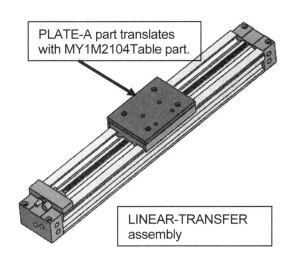

PLATE-A part translates
with MY1M2104Table part.

LINEAR-TRANSFER
assembly

Activity: Rigid and Flexible

Modify the Component Properties.
228) Right-click **RODLESS-CYLINDER** from the FeatureManager.

229) Click **Component Properties**.

230) Click **Flexible** in the Solve as box.

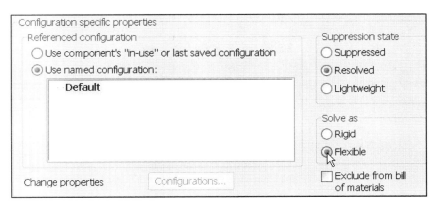

231) Click **OK** from the Component Properties box.

Move PLATE-A.
232) Click and drag the **PLATE-A** part in the LINEAR-TRANSFER assembly from left to right. The flexible state parameter is displayed in the FeatureManager at the component level.

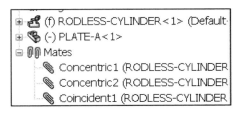

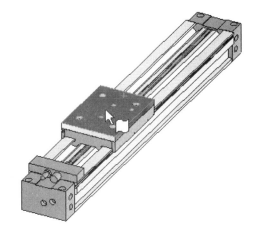
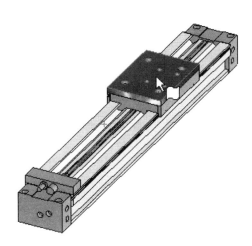

Save the LINEAR-TRANSFER assembly.
233) Click **Isometric** view.

234) Click **Save** from the Main menu.

Selection

Selecting geometry in SolidWorks as it relates to Mates and SmartMates requires practice. Review the following options:

Think big. If you can clearly see an edge or face in the Graphics window, SmartMates picks up the reference. Utilize the Zoom and Rotate functions of the mouse, Pop-up menus, Shortcut keys, tools, and commands:

Mouse

A mouse with a center wheel provides additional functionality in SolidWorks.

- Roll the center wheel downward to enlarge the model in the Graphics window.

- Hold the center wheel down. Drag the mouse in the Graphics window to rotate the model. Hold the Ctrl key down. Drag the mouse to pan the model.

Pop-up menu

Right-click a position in the Graphics window. Click the various view tools.

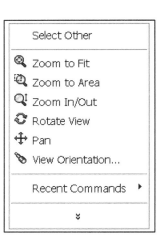

Move with Triad

The Move with Triad Pop-up option provides the ability to move or rotate components in the assembly.

The Triad is divided into three areas: Arm (3 axes), Wing, and Center.

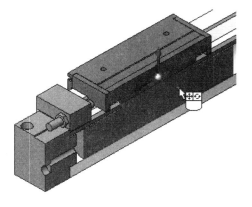

Utilize the left mouse button to translate a component as follows:

- Drag the arm of the triad to move along one of the three axes.

- Drag the wing of the triad to move along the reference plane coincident with the wing.

- Drag the center sphere to a linear or planar entity to align the triad with the entity.

Utilize the right mouse button to rotate a component as follows:

- Drag the arm of the triad to rotate about the axis coincident with the arm.

- Drag the center sphere to a linear or planar entity to align the triad with the entity.

Shortcut keys:

Command:	Shortcut key:
Rotate the model horizontally or vertically:	**Arrow** key
Rotate the model horizontally or vertically 90 degrees.	**Shift** + **Arrow** keys
Rotate the model clockwise or counterclockwise	**Alt** + left or right **Arrow** keys
Pan the model	**Ctrl** + **Arrow** keys
Zoom in	**Shift** + **z** keys
Zoom out	**z** key
Zoom to fit	**f** key
Previous view	**Ctrl** + **Shift** + **z keys**

Display the Previous view quickly. The default, Ctrl+Shift+z is difficult to press with speed. Assign the Shortcut key, b to go back to the previous view.

Zoom to Selection

Select an entry from the FeatureManager.
Click Zoom to Selection.

Window-select in the Graphics window. Click
Zoom to Selection.

Select Other

For hidden geometry or small faces and edges,
right-click in the Graphics window and click
the Select Other option. The current face
disappears.

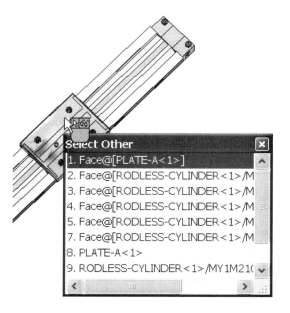

The Select Other option provides a list of
geometry to select based on the geometry
below the mouse pointer position.

While in the Select Other mode, right-click on
visible geometry to remove other faces. To
toggle transparency, hold the Shift key down
and select the face.

Other Assembly Tools

Utilize the Section view tool to visualize internal
components for mating.

Hide components not required for mating.

Right-click on the component in the Graphics window.
Click Hide.

Right-click on the component entry in the FeatureManager.
Click Hide.

Utilize the Ctrl-Select keys to select multiple components in
the Graphics window or FeatureManager.

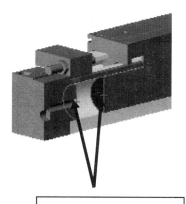

Section view to see
internal components

Utilize Shift-Select to select a sequential listing of entries in the FeatureManager.

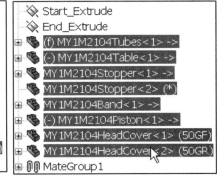

Click an entry in the FeatureManager. Hold the Shift key down. Select the bottom entry. All entries between are selected.

Minimize mouse travel between the Graphics window and the FeatureManager.

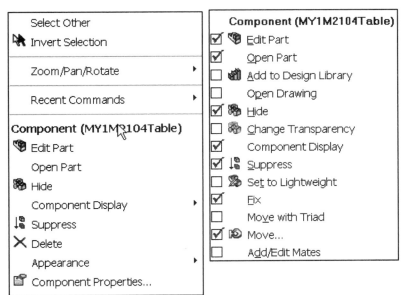

Utilize the Pop-up menu in the Graphics window for Component or Part options.

The Move Component option is always activated in the SolidWorks assembly.

The Component PropertyManager is not displayed when you drag a component in the Graphics window.

Customize the Pop-up menu to include the Move option if your models are dynamic and require any of the following Move options:

- Standard Drag.
- Collision Detection.
- Physical Dynamics.

The Move Component PropertyManager displays when the Move option is selected.

Fasteners

Screws, bolts, and fasteners are used to join parts. Use standard available fasteners whenever possible. This will decrease product cost and reduce component purchase lead times. The American Society for Mechanical Engineers, (ASME) and the International Standardization Organization, (ISO) provides standards on various hardware components.

Below are general selection and design guidelines that are utilized in this text:

- Use standard industry fasteners where applicable.

- Utilize industry fasteners that are supplied by qualified vendors and suppliers.

- Know the customer geographic location of the assembly and the fastener when dealing with both millimeter and inch units.

- Reuse common fastener types where applicable. Dissimilar screws and bolts may require additional tools for assembly, additional part numbers and increase inventory storage and cost.

- Decide on the fastener type before creating holes. Dissimilar fastener types require different geometry.

- Create notes on all fasteners. This will assist in the development of a Parts list and Bill of Materials.

- Caution should be used in positioning holes. Do not position holes too close to an edge. Review manufacturer's specifications for punching and machining to determine minimum hole spacing.

- Design for service support. Insure that the model can be serviced in the field and or on the production floor.

Use standard M8 x 1.25 SHCS in this exercise.

- M8 represents a metric screw: 8mm major outside diameter.

- 1.25 thread pitch (mm per thread).

Determine the proper overall length with the Tools, Measure option from the Main menu.

How do you determine the proper overall length of the M8 SHCS?

Answer: The depth of PLATE-A (15mm) plus the required blind depth of the Table_Hole (15mm) provided by the manufacturer. The SHCS top is recessed, below the top face of the Table.

When using fasteners to connect plates, a rule of thumb is to use at least 75% - 85% of the second plate blind depth to avoid fastener failure.

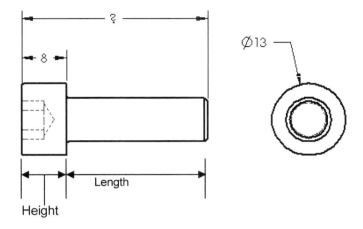

In some processes, it is easier to manufacture a thru thread, rather than a blind one. In this instance, have a least enough thread engagement to equal the diameter of the fastener.

The metric fasteners from your supplier are available in 5mm increments for lengths greater than 20mm.

Determine the length of the fastener.

- PLATE-A thickness = 15mm.

- Table-Hole blind depth = 15mm.

- Height of the 8M x 1.25 Socket Head = 8mm.

- Length = (PLATE-A thickness + Table_Hole blind depth) – Height Socket Head.

- Length = 15mm +15mm – 8mm = 22mm.

What length do you utilize; 20mm or 25mm? Answer: 20mm. The 20mm SHCS is engaged within 75% - 85% of the Table_Hole blind depth. The 25mm is too long since the holes are drilled and tapped at the vendor's facility.

A few screw manufacturers produce a 22mm SHCS, however, your machine shop does not stock this size. Integrating a new part number for hardware costs time and money.

You decide the 20mm SHCS is your choice. SolidWorks Toolbox automatically creates two SmartMates between the SHCS and the CBORE Hole. Copies of the SolidWorks Toolbox SHCS required for this project are located in the MY-TOOLBOX\SHCS folder.

Utilize the SHCS copies in the next activity to explore SmartMates between Graphic windows. Review the optional method of utilizing SolidWorks\Toolbox directly.

Toolbox parts are listed in the FeatureManager in two ways:

- Configuration Name: B18.31M-8x1.25x20Hex SHCS-20NHX.

- User defined name: SHC-91.

The B18.3.1M-8x1.25x20 Hex SHCS – 20NHX configuration name is defined as follows:

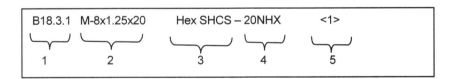

1. B18.3.1M is the ASME B18.3.1M Socket Head Cap Screw Metric Standard.

2. M-8×1.25×20:

   - M is Metric, 8mm is the diameter; 1.25 is the thread pitch, 20 is the length.

3. Hex SHCS is the fastener type.

4. 20NHX is the length of thread.

5. <1> is the first instance of the SHCS.

The User defined name corresponds to the part number utilized by Manufacturing, Purchasing and Inventory personnel.

Open the B18.3.1M-8x1.25x20 Hex SHCS – 20 NHX part. Drag the SHCS part into the LINEAR-TRANSFER assembly. Utilize the

Concentric/Coincident SmartMates  to position the SHCS in the PLATE-A Cbore. The Concentric Mate aligns the SHCS to the cylindrical face of the Cbore. The Coincident Mate aligns the screw head bottom edge to the PLATE-A Cbore bottom edge.

There are three types of Component Patterns in an assembly:

- Linear.

- Circular.

- Feature Driven.

A Linear Pattern creates multiple instances of selected components along one or two linear paths.

A Circular Pattern creates multiple instances of selected components about an axis.

A Feature Driven Pattern (Derived) creates multiple instances of selected components based on an existing pattern.

Utilize a Feature Driven Pattern to copy the SHCSs based on the PLATE-A Linear Pattern of Cbores.

Activity: Fastener – SmartMate

Open the SHCS.

235) Click the **Design Library** 📎 icon.

236) Expand **MY-TOOLBOX**.

237) Click the **SHCS** folder.

238) Right-click on the **B18.3.1M-8x1.25x20 Hex SHCS – 20 NHX** icon.

239) Click **Open**. The Hex SHCS is displayed in the Graphics window.

Display an Isometric view.
240) Click **Isometric** view.

Insert the Hex SHCS.
241) Click **Window**, **Tile Horizontally** from the Main menu.

242) **Zoom in** and **Rotate** the LINEAR-TRANSFER assembly until the inside seed Cbore is displayed.

243) Click and drag the **bottom circular edge** of the SHCS to the inside bottom circular edge of the Cbore. The mouse pointer displays the

Concentric/Coincident SmartMates .

244) Release the **left mouse button** to create the two SmartMates.

245) **Maximize** the LINEAR-TRANSFER assembly.

Fit the Model to the Graphics window.
246) Press the **f** key.

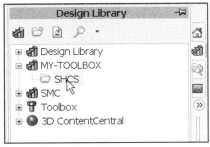

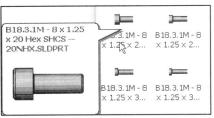

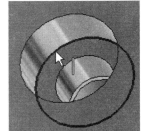

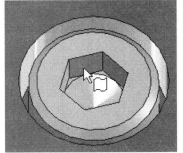

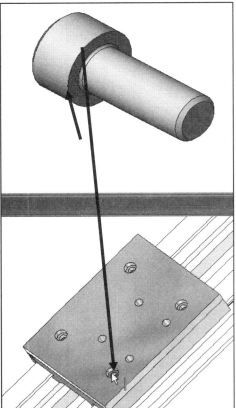

Review the Inserted mates.
247) Expand **Mates** from the FeatureManager.

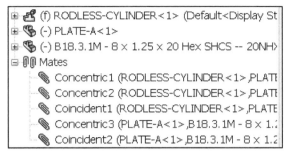

The SHCS is free to rotate about its axis. Multiple Hex-shaped fasteners require a Parallel Mate to orient faces in the same direction. Fully defined fasteners rotate together.

An additional Parallel Mate between the Hex head face and the PLATE-A narrow face prevents rotation.

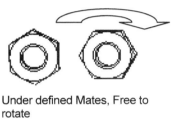

Under defined Mates, Free to rotate

Fully defined

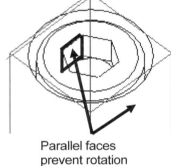

Parallel faces prevent rotation

The SHCS top face is positioned below the PLATE-A top face, there are no interferences. No Parallel Mate is created to fully define the SHCS.

💡 Save mate time and rebuild time. Utilize a Concentric/Coincident Mate for screws, nuts, washers, and bolts. Utilize the Parallel Mate to locate the head direction for hex geometry when required for interference detection or appearance.

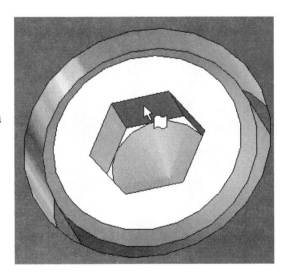

Create a Derived Component Pattern.

248) Click **Insert**, **Component Pattern**, **Feature Driven** from the Main menu. The Feature Driven PropertyManager is displayed.

249) Expand **LINEAR-TRANSFER** from the Graphics window.

250) Click **B18.3.1M-8x1.25x20 Hex SHCS – 20 NHX** from the FeatureManager. Hex SHCS is displayed in the Components to Pattern box.

251) Click a **position** inside the Driving Feature box.

252) Expand **PLATE-A<1>** from the FeatureManager.

253) Click **LPattern1**. LPattern1 is displayed in the Driving Feature box.

254) Click **OK**  from the Feature Driven PropertyManager.

DerivedLPattern1 is listed in the assembly FeatureManager and contains three instances of the SHCS.

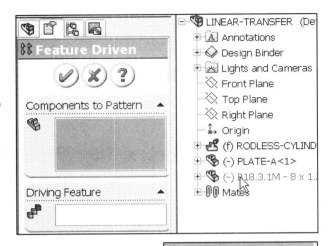

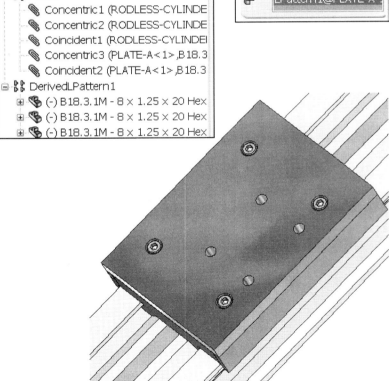

Save the LINEAR-TRANSFER
assembly.
255) Click **Isometric** view.

256) Click **Save**.

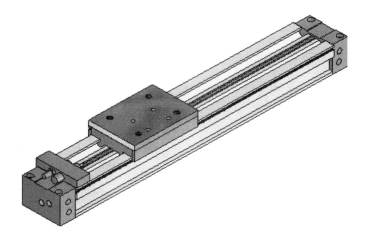

Activity: Toolbox Activity

Activate the Toolbox Browser.
257) Click **Tools, Add-Ins** from the Main menu.

258) Check **SolidWorks Toolbox** and **Toolbox Browser**.

259) Click **OK** from the Add-Ins box.

Set the Toolbox directory.
260) Click **Toolbox** from the Main menu.

261) Click **Browser Configuration**. The
Configure Browser box is displayed.

262) Click **Document Properties**.

263) Check **Always create copy**.

264) Click **Browse**.

265) Select **\ASSEMBLY-SW-FILES-2006\
MY-TOOLBOX**.

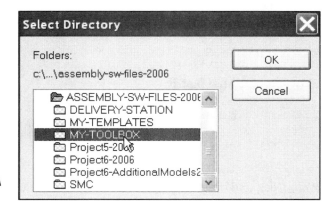

266) Click **OK** from the Select Directory box.

267) Click **OK** from the Configure Browser box

SolidWorks copies the Toolbox parts utilized in this project from their default file
location to the MY-TOOLBOX folder.

Delete the existing SHCS.
268) Click the **B18.3.1M-8x1.25x20 Hex SHCS – 20 NHX** from the FeatureManager.

269) Right-click **Delete**.

270) Click **Yes** to delete dependent entities and mates. The DerivedPattern is also deleted.

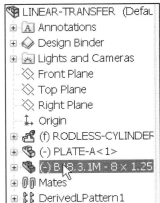

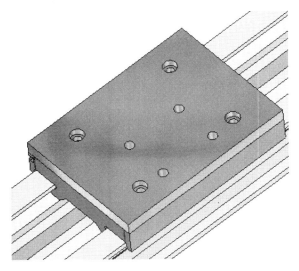

Insert an M8x1.25x20 Hex SHCS into the LINEAR-TRANSFER assembly.
271) Click the **Design Library** icon.

272) Expand **Toolbox**.

273) Expand **Ansi Metric**.

274) Expand **Bolts and Screws**.

275) Click **Socket Head Screws**.

276) Click and drag the **Cap (B18.3.1M)** icon into the assembly Graphics window.

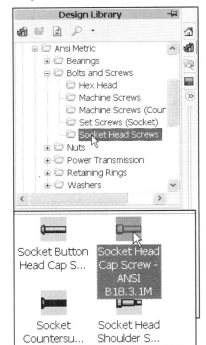

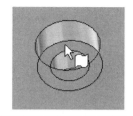

277) Release the **mouse pointer** on the CBORE face of the lower right seed feature. The Socket Head Cap Screw Properties dialog box is displayed.

278) Enter **M8** for Size.

279) Enter **20** for Length.

280) Click **OK** from the Socket Head Cap Screw box.

281) Click **Cancel** 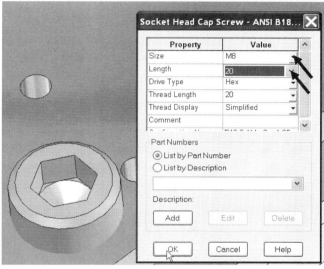 from the Insert Component PropertyManager.

As an exercise, insert a Component Pattern. Follow the instructions in the previous activity.

A Concentric and Coincident Mate is displayed in the FeatureManager.

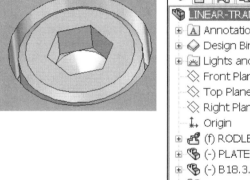

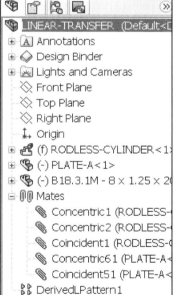

Mate References specify one or more entities of a component to utilize for automatic mating.

Mate References

A Mate Reference specifies one or more geometric component entities to utilize for automatic mating. As you drag a component into the assembly, SolidWorks finds combinations of entities with the same Mate Reference or Mate Type. The SHCS utilizes the bottom head circular edge for the Mate Reference, Primary Reference Entity.

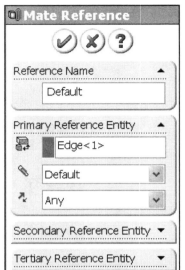

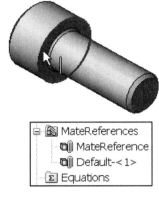

To create a new Mate Reference, click Insert, Reference Geometry, Mate Reference from the Main menu. Select up to three Reference Entities in the Mate Reference PropertyManager.

Mate References are listed in the FeatureManager MateReferences folder. Mate References are commonly used for library parts. Note: Mates, SmartMates, and Mate References provide the tools to assemble components. As geometry complexity increases, utilize the standard Mate tool to assemble components to planes, axes, and other reference geometry.

Configurations

A configuration is a variation of a part or assembly within a single document. Create configurations at multiple assembly levels. Develop new configurations for the RODLESS-CYLINDER assembly and the LINEAR-TRANSFER assembly.

There are three methods to create configurations:

• Method 1: Add Configuration.

• Method 2: Design Table.

• Method 3: Combination of Method 1 and Method 2.

Build configurations for the RODLESS-CYLINDER assembly to illustrate dynamic motion and physical location. Utilize the Configuration Manager, Add Configuration option. Create two RODLESS-CYLINDER configurations:

- Normal.

- Extended.

Default   Normal   Extended

By default, all assemblies contain a configuration named, Default. The Flexible configuration name is used for all assemblies that contain components which translate or rotate.

The Normal and Extended configuration names represent the first and second position for all pneumatic components.

In the Default configuration, the MY12014Table part is free to translate in the RODLESS-CYLINDER assembly.

The Default (Flexible) configuration is a derived configuration from the Default configuration that allows the PLATE-A part to translate. SolidWorks creates this configuration when the Solve as state changes from Rigid to Flexible.

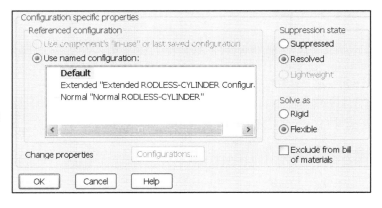

The RODLESS-CYLINDER Default configuration changes from ⊦□ to ⊟⊦✖ when SolidWorks add the Default (Flexible) derived configuration and a Design Table exists.

The Default (Flexible) derived configuration is not displayed in the Design Table. The Default (Flexible) derived configuration name and parameters are determined from the Default configuration.

⚡ Save time. Plan your configurations, names, behavior and properties early in the design process.

Review the RODLESS-CYLINDER assembly.

The MY1M2104Table part slides along the MY1M2104Tubes part.

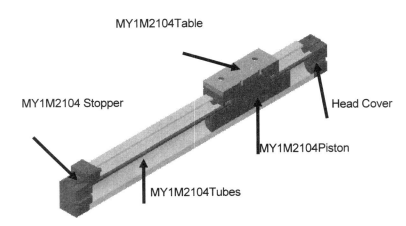

Use the Collision Detection tool to determine the physical location of the MY1M2104 Table part in the Normal and Extended configurations.

Add the Normal and Extended configurations.

Insert a Distance Mate between the MY1M2104Piston Part and the MY1M2104HeadCover Part. The RODLESS-CYLINDER assembly is in the Normal position when the Distance Mate value equals 0.

The RODLESS-CYLINDER assembly is in the Extended position when the Distance Mate value equals 500.

Collisions occur when one component impacts another component. You can detect collisions with other components when moving or rotating a component.

Customize the Pop-up menu to include the Move option.

The Move option provides access to the Move PropertyManager and the Collision Detection option.

Note: The Default configuration name can be renamed. The Default name is utilized in the projects.

Activity: Collision Detection and Distance Mate

Open the RODLESS-CYLINDER assembly.
282) Right-click **RODLESS-CYLINDER** from the
LINEAR-TRANSFER FeatureManager.

283) Click **Open Assembly**.

Customize the Pop-up menu.
284) Click **MY1M2104Table** from the
FeatureManager.

285) Right-click **Customize Menu**.

286) Check **Move**.

Locate the collision between the components.
287) Double-click **Move** in the Customize Menu box. The
Move Component PropertyManager is displayed.

288) Click the **Collision Detection** check box.

289) Check the **Stop at Collision** box.

290) Drag the **MY1M2104Table** part until it meets the
MY1M2104Stopper part.

291) Click **OK**  from the Move Component PropertyManager.
The colliding faces are displayed in green.

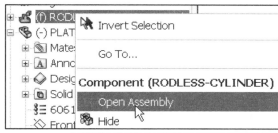

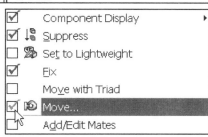

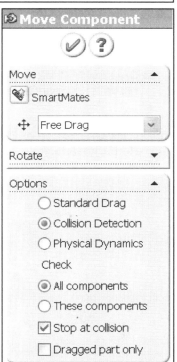

MY1M2104Stopper

Display the Section view.

292) Click **Right** Plane from the FeatureManager. Right Plane is highlighted in the FeatureManager.

293) Click **Section view** 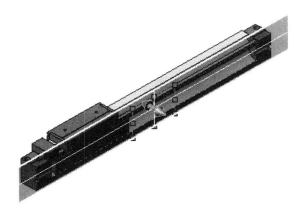 from the View toolbar. The Section View PropertyManager is displayed. View the section view in the Graphics window.

294) Click **OK** from the Section View PropertyManager.

Locate the collision between the components.

295) Right-click **MY1M2104Table** from the FeatureManager.

296) Click **Move**. The Move Component PropertyManager is displayed.

297) Click the **Collision Detection** check box.

298) Check the **Stop at Collision** box.

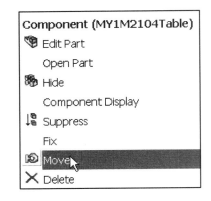

299) Drag the **MY1M2104Table** part until it meets the MY1M2104HeadCover part.

300) Click **OK** from the Move Component PropertyManager.

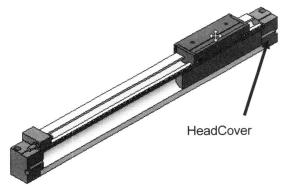

HeadCover

Expand MateGroup1.
301) Double-click the **RODLESS-CYLINDER\
MateGroup1**.

The three broken paperclip icons indicate Suppressed Mates.

The list contains two Mates for the MY1M2104Tubes part and the MY1M2104Table part.

The MY1M2104Table part is free to translate along the MY1M2104Tubes part.

H is a renamed Distance Mate. The MY1M2104Piston part translates along the MY1M2104 Tubes part with a Concentric Mate.

View the internal components with a Section view.

Create a Distance Mate.
302) Click the **MY1M2104Piston front face**.

303) Click **Mate** Mate from the Assembly toolbar.
Face<1>@MY1M2104Piston-1 is displayed in the Mate PropertyManager.

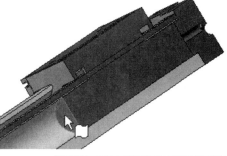

304) Click the **MY1M2104HeadCover left inside face**.
Face<2>MY1M2104HeadCover is displayed in the Mate PropertyManager.

305) Click **Distance**.

306) Enter **0**.

307) Click ✔.

308) Click **OK** ✅ from the Mate PropertyManager.

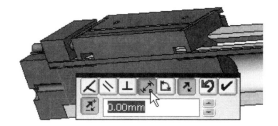

Display an Isometric view
309) Click **Isometric** view.

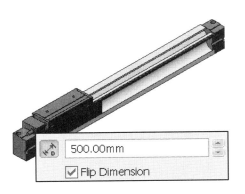

Modify the Distance1 Mate.
310) Right-click the **Distance1** mate from the FeatureManager.

311) Click **Edit Feature**.

312) Enter **500** for new distance.

313) Click **OK**  from the Distance1 PropertyManager.

314) Click **OK** from the Mate PropertyManager.

Rename Distance1 Mate.

315) Double-click **Distance1** in the FeatureManager.

316) Click **inside** the text box.

317) Enter **Stroke**. Spelling must be exact. Do not leave spaces in Mate names. The variable is utilized in the configurations.

Display a full view.
318) Click **Section View** 🗐 from the View toolbar.

Locate and modify the Stroke
value. Utilize the
FeatureManager. Position the
dimension off the profile.

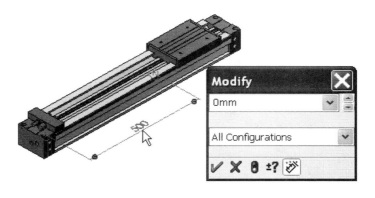

Modify the distance value.
319) Double-click **Stroke** from the
FeatureManager. The value
500 is displayed.

320) Drag the **500** dimension
outward.

321) Double-click **500**.

322) Enter **0**.

323) Click **Rebuild** from the Modify box. The
MY1M2104Table part moves to the left.

324) Click ✔.

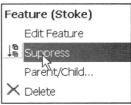

325) Click **OK** ⊘ from the Dimension
PropertyManager

Suppress the Distance Mate.
326) Right-click the **Stroke** Mate.

327) Click **Suppress**. The Stroke entry in the
FeatureManager changes from black to light
gray.

Save the RODLESS-CYLINDER assembly.
328) Click **Save**.

☀ Drag the distance dimension outward to
improve visibility. The "0" value contains no
dimension lines. Utilize a Distance Mate to
modify the value between mating component
entities.

Activity: RODLESS-CYLINDER Configurations

Display the ConfigurationManager.

329) Click the **ConfigurationManager** 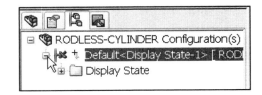 icon. The Default configuration is named Default.

330) Expand ⊟ 📕 **Default [RODLESS-CYLINDER].** The derived flexible configuration is named, ⊢ Default [RODLESS-CYLINDER]. The RODLESS-CYLINDER Default configuration changes from ⊢ to ⊟ 📕 when SolidWorks adds the Default (Flexible) derived configuration and a Design Table exists.

Add the RODLESS-CYLINDER assembly (Normal) configuration.

331) Right-click **RODLESS-CYLINDER Configuration(s)** at the top of the ConfigurationManager.

332) Click **Add Configuration**. The Add Configuration PropertyManager is displayed.

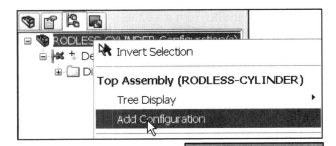

333) Enter **Normal** for Configuration name.

334) Enter **Normal RODLESS-CYLINDER** for Description.

335) Enter **RODLESS-CYLINDER 500MM, STROKE-DISTANCE = 0** for Comment.

336) Select **User Specified Name** in the Bill of Materials Options box.

337) Enter **015801** for Part number displayed when used in a bill of materials.

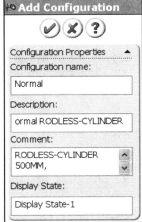

338) Click **OK** ✔ from the Add Configuration PropertyManager. The Normal configuration is displayed in the ConfigurationManager.

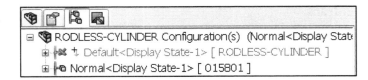

339) Click the **Assembly FeatureManager**  icon. The configuration name (Normal) is displayed to the right of the RODLESS-CYLINDER assembly name.

Set the Stroke value.
340) Double-click **MateGroup1** from the FeatureManager.

341) Right-click **Stroke**.

342) Click **Unsuppress**.

343) Double-click **Stroke**.

344) Double-click **0**.

345) Enter **0** for Distance.

346) Select **This Configuration** from the Modify drop down list.

347) Click **Rebuild** from the Modify box.

348) Click ✔. Click **OK** from the Dimension PropertyManager.

RODLESS-CYLINDER (Normal)

💡 The Add Configuration option is available from the FeatureManager or Pop-up Component menu in the assembly.

💡 Locate Distance Mate values quickly. If you cannot locate the value in the Graphics window, select Edit Definition from the Distance Mate FeatureManager.

Add the RODLESS-CYLINDER (Extended) configuration.
349) Click the **ConfigurationManager** icon.

350) Right-click **RODLESS-CYLINDER Configuration(s)**.

351) Click **Add Configuration**.

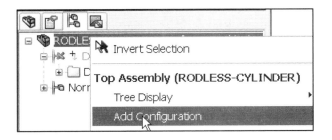

352) Enter **Extended** for Configuration Name.

353) Enter **Extended RODLESS-CYLINDER** for Description.

354) Enter **RODLESS-CYLINDER 500MM, STROKE-DISTANCE = 500** for Comment.

355) Select **User Specified Name** in the Bill of Materials Options box.

356) Enter **015801** for Part number displayed when used in a bill of materials.

357) Click **OK** 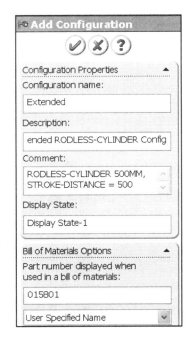 from the Add Configuration PropertyManager. The Extended configuration is displayed in the Configuration Manager.

358) Click the **Assembly FeatureManager** icon. The configuration name (Extended) is displayed to the right of the RODLESS-CYLINDER assembly name.

Set the Stroke value.
359) Double-click **MateGroup1** from the FeatureManager.

360) Double-click **Stroke**.

361) Double-click **0**.

362) Enter **500**.

363) Click **This Configuration**.

364) Click **Rebuild**. The MY1M2104Table moves to the second position.

365) Click ✔.

366) Click **OK** 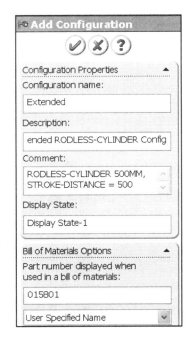 from the Dimension PropertyManager.

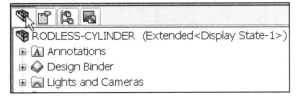

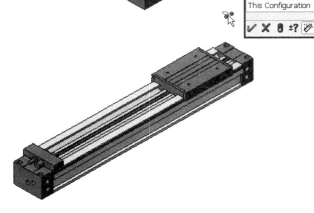

Verify the four Configurations.

367) Click the **ConfigurationManager** icon.

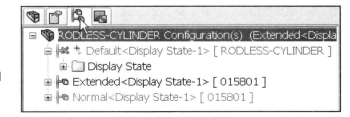

368) Double-click **Default**, **Normal**, and **Extended** from the Configuration Manager. Note: The Default (Flexible) configuration is listed under the Default configuration in the ConfigurationManager.

Return to the Default configuration.

369) Double-click the **Default** configuration.

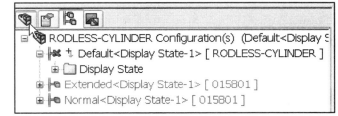

Return to the Assembly FeatureManager.

370) Click the **Assembly FeatureManager** icon.

Save the RODLESS-CYLINDER assembly.

371) Click **Save**.

Default   Normal   Extended

💡 Save parts and assemblies in their Default configuration. Select configuration names in Component Properties.

Parent/Child Relations in an assembly

A parent is an existing feature on which other features are dependent. A child is a dependent feature related to a previously built feature (its parent). During a parent modification, a child is modified automatically. Parent\child relationships in the assembly are available from the FeatureManager or Pop-up Component menu.

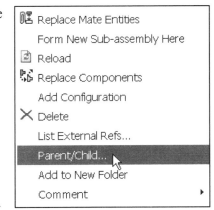

Example: Right-click MY1M2104Table from the FeatureManager. Click Parent/Child.

The first SHCS has three child relations with the three additional components in the DerivedLPattern1. Double-click the Mates icon in the Children column to display the Parent components.

Review the Parent/Child relationships in an assembly before you develop configurations that require Suppress/Unsuppress states. When you suppress a component, the corresponding Mates are suppressed.

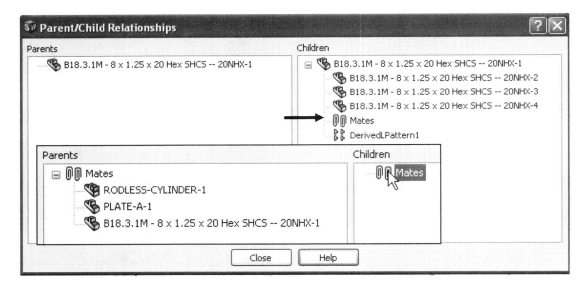

LINEAR-TRANSFER Configurations

Add the configurations to the LINEAR-TRANSFER assembly. Utilize the RODLESS-CYLINDER configurations to create three different configurations in the LINEAR-TRANSFER assembly. The LINEAR-TRANSFER configuration names are:

- Normal.
- Extended.
- Fastener.

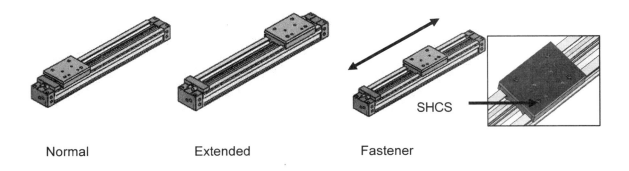

Normal   Extended   Fastener

💡 Physical dynamics analysis and finite element analysis are computer intensive. Utilize configurations to develop simplified parts and assemblies. Develop simplified parts by suppressing fillet and draft features. Develop simplified assemblies by suppressing hardware and insignificant components.

Control three entries in the LINEAR-TRANSFER configurations:

- RODLESS-CYLINDER configuration name.
- Suppress/Unsuppress B18.3.1M-8x1.25x20 Hex SHCS.
- Suppress/Unsuppress DerivedLPattern1.

The LINEAR-TRANSFER (Normal) configuration utilizes the RODLESS-CYLINDER (Normal) configuration and the Suppressed SHCSs.

The LINEAR-TRANSFER (Extended) configuration utilizes the RODLESS-CYLINDER (Extended) configuration and the Suppressed SHCSs.

The LINEAR-TRANSFER (Fastener) configuration utilizes the RODLESS-CYLINDER (Default) configuration and the Unsuppressed SHCSs.

Activity: LINEAR-TRANSFER Configurations

Review the LINEAR-TRANSFER FeatureManager.
372) Open the **LINEAR-TRANSFER** assembly. The LINEAR-TRANSFER assembly is displayed in the Graphics window.

View the Component Properties.
373) Right-click **RODLESS-CYLINDER** from the LINEAR-TRANSFER FeatureManager.

374) Click **Component Properties**. The Configuration name is Default. The Extended and Normal configurations are displayed in the Used named configuration box.

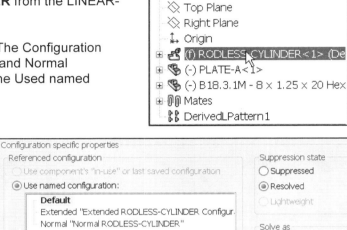

375) Click **OK** from the Component Properties box.

Suppress the Hex SHCS.
376) Click **B18.3.1M-8x1.25x20 Hex SHCS** from the FeatureManager.

377) Hold the **Ctrl** key down.

378) Click **DerivedLPattern1**.

379) Release the **Ctrl** key.

380) Right-click **Suppress**.

Add the LINEAR-TRANSFER (Normal) configuration.

381) Click the **ConfigurationManager**.

382) Right-click the **LINEAR-TRANSFER Configuration(s)**. Click **Add Configuration**.

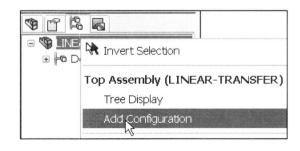

Enter parameters.

383) Enter **Normal** for Configuration name.

384) Enter **Normal (LINEAR-TRANSFER)** for Description.

385) Enter **Use RODLESS-CYLINDER (Normal)**, **Suppress SHCS** for Comment.

386) Click **OK**  from the Add Configuration PropertyManager.

Modify the LINEAR-TRANSFER (Normal) Referenced configuration.

387) Click the **Assembly FeatureManager** icon. The configuration name (Normal) is displayed to the right of the LINEAR-TRANSFER assembly name.

388) Right-click **RODLESS-CYLINDER** from the FeatureManager.

389) Click **Component Properties**.

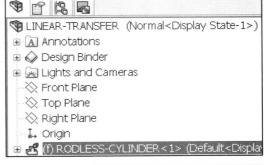

390) Select **Normal** from the Used named configuration box. Flexible is checked in the Solve as box.

391) Click **OK**. The Normal configuration is added to the ConfigurationManager.

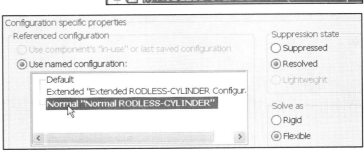

Add the LINEAR-TRANSFER (Extended) Configuration.

392) Click the **ConfigurationManager** .

393) Right-click the **LINEAR-TRANSFER Configuration(s)**.

394) Click **Add Configuration**.

Enter parameters.

395) Enter **Extended** for Configuration name.

396) Enter **Extended (LINEAR-TRANSFER)** for Description.

397) Enter **Use RODLESS-CYLINDER (Extended)**, **Suppress SHCS** for Comment.

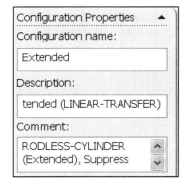

398) Click **OK** ✅ from the Add Configuration PropertyManager. The Extended configuration is added to the ConfigurationManager.

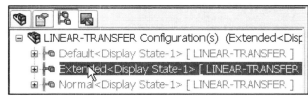

Modify the LINEAR-TRANSFER (Extended) Referenced configuration.

399) Click the **Assembly FeatureManager** 🔷 . The configuration name (Extended) is displayed to the right of the LINEAR-TRANSFER assembly name.

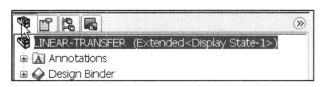

400) Right-click the **RODLESS-CYLINDER** from the FeatureManager.

401) Click **Component Properties**.

402) Select **Extended** from the Used named configuration box. Flexible is checked in the Solve as box.

403) Click **OK**.

Add the LINEAR-TRANSFER (Fastener) Configuration.

404) Click the **ConfigurationManager** 📇 .

405) Right-click the **LINEAR-TRANSFER Configuration(s)**.

406) Click **Add Configuration**.

Enter parameters.
407) Enter **Fastener** for Configuration name.

408) Enter **Fastener (LINEAR-TRANSFER)** for Description.

409) Enter **Use RODLESS-CYLINDER (Default)**, **Unsuppress SHCS** for Comment.

410) Click **OK** from the Add Configuration PropertyManager. The Fastener configuration is added to the ConfigurationManager.

Modify the LINEAR-TRANSFER (Fastener) Referenced configuration.
411) Click the **Assembly FeatureManager** . The configuration name (Fastener) is displayed to the right of the LINEAR-TRANSFER assembly name.

412) Right-click **RODLESS-CYLINDER** from the FeatureManager.

413) Click **Component Properties**.

414) Select **Default** from the Use named configuration box. Flexible is checked in the Solve as box.

415) Click **OK**.

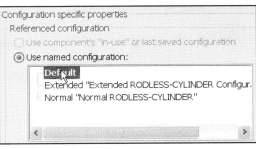

Un-suppress the Hex SHCS.
416) Click **B18.3.1M-8x1.25x20 Hex SHCS** from the FeatureManager.

417) Right-click **Set to Resolved**.

418) Click **DerivedLPattern1**.

419) Right-click **Unsuppress**.

Verify the Configurations.

420) Click the **ConfigurationManager** 🖳 .

421) Double-click **Default**, **Normal**, **Extended,** and **Fastener** from the Configuration Manager.

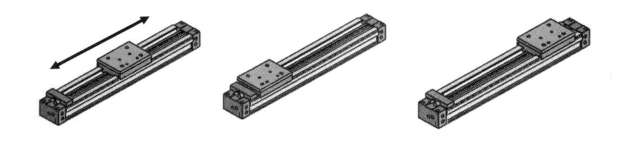

Default   Normal   Extended

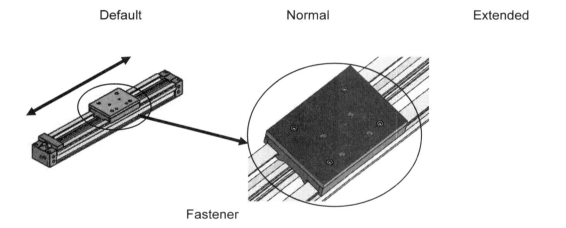

Fastener

Return to the Default configuration.

422) Double-click the **Default** Configuration. Note: In the default state, items are suppressed and need to be resolved.

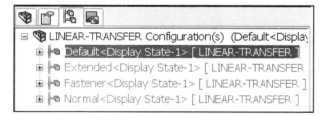

423) Click the **Assembly FeatureManager** .
LINEAR-TRANSFER (Default) is displayed.

Display an Isometric view.
424) Click **Isometric** view.

Save the LINEAR-TRANSFER assembly.
425) Click **Save**.

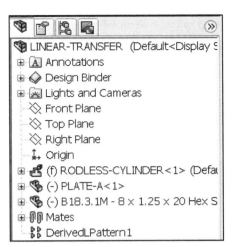

The configurations are complete for the LINEAR-TRANSFER assembly. The LINEAR-TRANSFER assembly is the first component in the 3AXIS-TRANSFER assembly.

Additional components and configurations are created in Project 3.

Preparing for the Next Assembly

Determine the components and features in the LINEAR-TRANSFER assembly that are utilized in the next assembly. What key component and feature is required for the next phase of the project? Answer: The GUIDE-CYLINDER assembly is the next key component. The next key feature is the four Thru Holes.

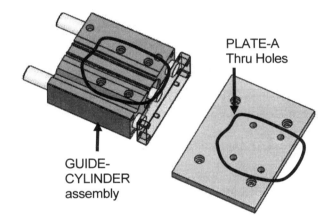

PLATE-A
Thru Holes

GUIDE-
CYLINDER
assembly

Mount the GUIDE-CYLINDER assembly to the four PLATE-A Thru Holes.

Rename the Thru Hole Linear Pattern2 for clarity in the next step.

The Linear Pattern2 is referenced in Project 3.

The GUIDE-CYLINDER is the base (first) component in the 2AXIS-TRANSFER assembly.

The project leader incorporates the GUIDE-CYLINDER into the 2AXIS-TRANSFER assembly versus the LINEAR-TRANSFER assembly for modularity.

The LINEAR-TRANSFER assembly becomes a future sub-assembly in another application.

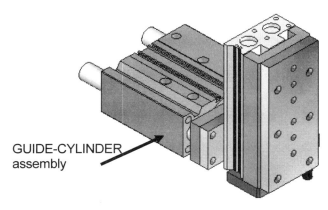

GUIDE-CYLINDER assembly

2AXIS-TRANSFER assembly
Project 3

Activity: Preparing for the Next Assembly

Open the PLATE-A part.
426) Right-click **PLATE-A** from the FeatureManager.

427) Click **Open Part**.

Display an Isometric view.
428) Click **Isometric** view.

Rename Linear Pattern2 in the PLATE-A part.
429) Click **LPattern2** from the FeatureManager.

430) Click **inside** the name text box.

431) Enter **LPattern2-ThruHoleGuideCylinder**.

Save the PLATE-A part.
432) Click **Save**.

Close all parts and assemblies.
433) Click **Windows**, **Close All** from the Main menu.

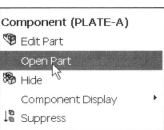

Component (PLATE-A)
- Edit Part
- Open Part
- Hide
- Component Display ▸
- Suppress

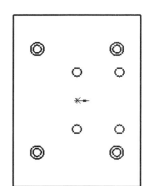

PLATE-A
- Annotations
- Design Binder
- Solid Bodies(1)
- 6061 Alloy
- Lights and Cameras
- Front Plane
- Top Plane
- Right Plane
- Origin
- Extrude1
- CBORE for M8 SHCS1
- LPattern1
- Ø10.0 (10) Diameter Hole1
- LPattern2-THruHoleGuideCylinde

Project Summary

A Bottom-Up Design Assembly modeling approach was utilized to create the LINEAR-TRANSFER assembly. You created the PLATE-A part based on the features of the RODLESS-CYLINDER\MY1M2104Table part and the GUIDE-CYLINDER assembly.

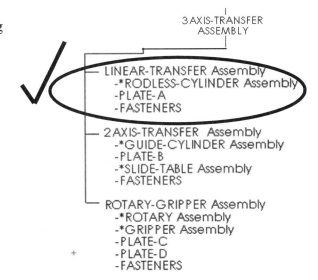

The LINEAR-TRANSFER assembly consisted of the RODLESS-CYLINDER assembly, the PLATE-A part and four M8x1.25x20 SHCS.

The RODLESS-CYLINDER assembly contained three configurations:

- Default.
- Normal.
- Extended.

The LINEAR-TRANSFER assembly contained four configurations:

- Default.
- Fastener.
- Normal.
- Extended.

In Project 3 develop the 2AXIS-TRANSFER assembly. In Project 4 develop the ROTARY-GRIPPER assembly.

Discuss the assemblies with your project team leader. Ask if the customer has provided any additional input that would constitute a design change. For now, there are no design changes. Discuss the PLATE-A part fabrication with a machinist. The machinist recommends modifying the four Thru Holes to four tapped holes.

There will be additional design changes in the future. Planning for change in the assembly and configurations is key to your success. You utilized symmetry, reused geometry and obtained models from other sources to save time. Review the project questions and exercises.

Questions

1. Describe the components and features utilized to determine the geometric and functional requirements of the PLATE-A part.

2. List the sketch tools and feature options that build symmetry into a part.

3. Identify the locations of the PLATE-A Reference planes.

4. True or False. The Hole Wizard does not require dimensions or relationships to define the position of a hole.

5. Assembling components in SolidWorks is defined as _____

6. Each component has _____ degrees of freedom.

7. Identify the view type that displays internal geometry.

8. Describe the difference between a Distance Mate with a 0 value and a Coincident Mate.

9. Describe the SHCS abbreviation. What does it stand for?

10. Identify the two SmartMates that are used to assemble a SHCS to a hole in the PLATE-A part.

11. Identify the command utilized to create a Component Pattern in an assembly that references an existing feature for another component.

12. Describe configurations. Are they useful? Explain your answer.

13. A sub-assembly named Flexible is inserted into an assembly. The Flexible sub-assembly is Rigid. Identify the option that would regain a flexible state?

14. Review the SmartMate .avi files with SW help. Identify other types of Smart Mates. Explain.

Mating entities	Type of mate	Pointer	Click for example
2 linear edges	Coincident		Show Me
2 planar faces	Coincident		Show Me
2 vertices	Coincident		Show Me
2 conical faces, or 2 axes, or 1 conical face and 1 axis	Concentric		Show Me
2 circular edges (the edges do not have to be complete circles)	Concentric (conical faces) - and - Coincident (adjacent planar faces)		Show Me

Exercises

Exercise 2-1a: Customize your keyboard. Create a Shortcut key for a Mate command. Use the M key to create the Shortcut key.

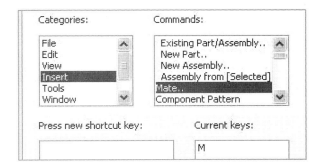

Exercise 2-2: Create three new configurations for the RODLESS-CYLINDER assembly:

- Stroke100.

- Stroke250.

- Stroke400.

The Distance Mates are: 100, 250, & 400.

Create three new configurations for the LINEAR-TRANSFER assembly. All fasteners are suppressed in the three configurations.

Exercise 2-3: Create a new PLATE-A configuration with a thickness of 20mm. Utilize Add Configuration and the Edit Feature option in the PLATE-A FeatureManager. Modify the Thru Holes to Tapped Holes.

Exercise 2-4: Create a SUPPORT-PLATE part. The SUPPORT-PLATE is 10mm thick. The SUPPORT-PLATE Part is symmetric about the Origin of the RODLESS-CYLINDER assembly.

The SUPPORT-PLATE utilizes a Bottom-Up Design Assembly modeling approach. Determine the fasteners required to assemble the RODLESS-CYLINDER assembly to the SUPPORT-PLATE part.

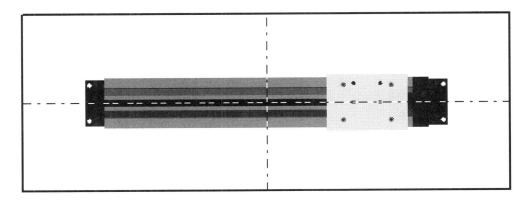

Exercise 2-5: The purchased components utilized in this exercise are available in the ASSEMBLY-SW-FILES\EXERCISES\EXERCISE-PROJECT2 folder.

A) BEARING-SHAFT assembly.

Create a 1″, (25.4mm) SHAFT for the PILLOW-BLOCK-BEARING. The length of the SHAFT is 8″, (203.2mm).

Create the BEARING-SHAFT assembly. The PILLOW-BLOCK-BEARING is a fixed component. The SHAFT rotates inside the BEARING. The SHAFT is centered in the BEARING.

The PILLOW-BLOCK-BEARING utilizes imported geometry. Axes and Planes have been added to assist you during the assembly process. Assemble the Temporary Axis of the SHAFT to the Axis of the BEARING.

Assemble two Flange Bolts from the Design Library.

Create a BEARING-SHAFT configuration named Fastener. The Fastener configuration contains the Flange Bolts. The Flange Bolts are suppressed in the Default configuration.

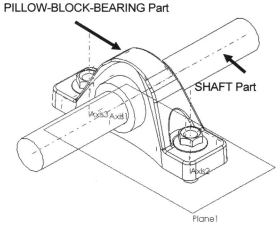

PILLOW-BLOCK-BEARING Part

SHAFT Part

BEARING-SHAFT Assembly

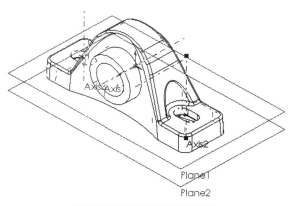

PILLOW-BLOCK-BEARING
Model Courtesy of Boston Gear

B) GEAR-40-BEARING-SHAFT assembly.

The 1″, (25.4mm) SHAFT supports a CHANGE-GEAR40 with 14-1\2° Pressure Angle, 12 Diametral Pitch, 3.333″ Pitch Diameter and 40 teeth.

CHANGE-GEAR40

GEAR40-BEARING-SHAFT Assembly
Model Courtesy of Boston Gear
(GEAR tooth profile has been simplified)

Modify the SHAFT. Create an Extruded Cut feature named keyway. The keyway size corresponds to the CHANGE-GEAR40 keyway.

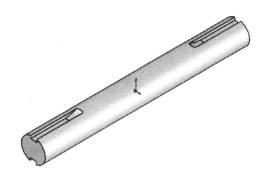

The CHANGE-GEAR40 is an imported part. An axis has been created to assist in the assembly process. A Concentric Mate cannot be created with the imported surface. Assemble the CHANGE-GEAR40 axis to the SHAFT temporary axis. Utilize SmartMates to assemble keyway edges and vertices between the SHAFT and the CHANGE-GEAR.

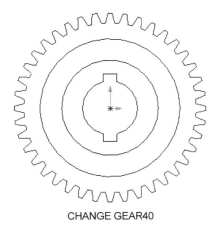

CHANGE GEAR40

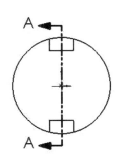

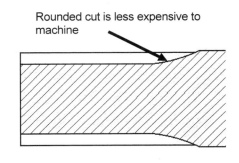

Rounded cut is less expensive to machine

SHAFT with KEYWAY Extruded Cut

The CHANGE-GEAR40 is fixed to the end of the SHAFT. The CHANGE-GEAR40 rotates when the SHAFT rotates.

The current keyway requires a square end cut that is costly to manufacture. Modify the SHAFT keyway feature to slope outward. Utilize a Fillet feature to round the sharp edges.

Utilize the same Fillet radius that is produced by your milling process.

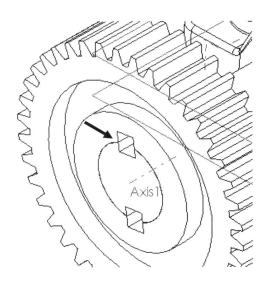

C) GEAR-RACK-BEARING assembly.

Create the GEAR-RACK - BEARING Assembly. As the SHAFT rotates, the GEAR-RACK translates through a groove in the BASE-PLATE-RG.

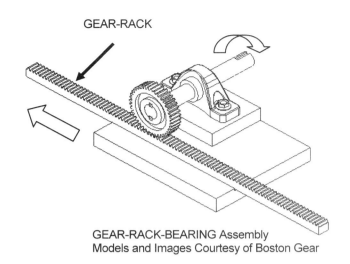

GEAR-RACK-BEARING Assembly
Models and Images Courtesy of Boston Gear

The Boston Gear web site contains information about the GEAR-RACK (Part No. L515-4) and the CHANGE-GEAR40 (Part No GD40B). The GEAR-RACK Part and CHANGE-GEAR40 Part contain the same 14-1\2° Pressure Angle and 12 Diametral Pitch.

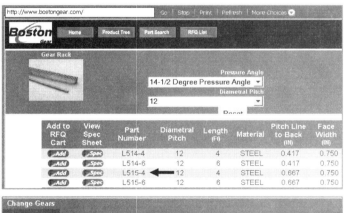

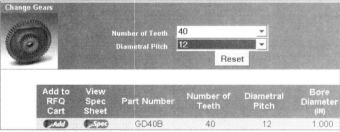

Create the BASE-PLATE-RG part.

Utilize the dimensions from the GEAR-RACK and the GEAR-40-BEARING-SHAFT Assembly. Note: Answers will vary.

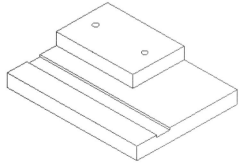

BASE-PLATE-RG Part

Exercise 2-6: GEAR Mate and Simulation.

The SolidWorks\Toolbox components utilized in this exercise are available in the ASSEMBLY-SW-FILES\EXERCISES\EXERCISE-PROJECT2 file folder.

Open the 2-GEARS assembly. Review the Coincident and Concentric Mates.

Position the mating teeth. Insert a Gear Mate. Select the two cylindrical hole faces. As you rotate the right gear clockwise, the left gear turns counter-clockwise.

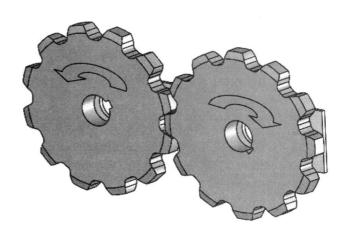

Physical Simulation

Physical Simulation simulates the effects of motors, springs, and gravity on assemblies. Physical Simulation combines these options with SolidWorks Mate tools and Physical Dynamics to move components and rotate components.

Insert a Rotary Motor on the front face of the right gear. Calculate the simulation. Play the Simulation.

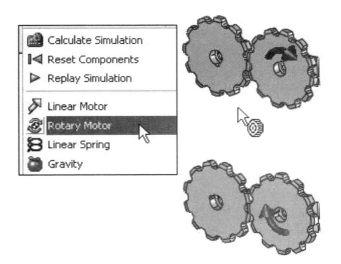

Additional notes about gears:

- Gear teeth are memory intensive.
  Utilize configurations to represent simplified versions in an assembly.

- Utilize Coincident and Concentric Mates first to position gears based on pitch diameter. Then insert a Gear Mate to simulate rotation.

- Imported gear geometry may not support a Gear Mate.

- Gear teeth can contain only one point of contact between teeth for simulation to run.

Exercise 2-7: Industry Collaborative Exercise.

You now work with a team of engineers on a new industrial application. The senior engineer specifies a ½HP AC Motor. The Parts department stocks the motor. Create the SPEED REDUCER Assembly. Reduce the input speed of the motor at a ratio of 30:1. An enclosed gear drive, called a Speed Reducer, reduces the speed of the motor. The enclosed gear drive is a purchased part. The Motor is fastened to the Speed Reducer.

Determine the parts to design. PLATE-SR contains a 150mm x 60mm notched section with 4 equally spaced holes. The Speed Reducer is mounted to the PLATE-SR with 4 fasteners. All holes on PLATE-SR use the same fastener.

Obtain vendor information from the Purchasing Department. The ½ HP Motor is manufactured by Boston Gear, Quincy, MA. The Motor part number is FUTF. No drawings of the Motor exist in the Engineering Department.

Utilize 3DContentCentral.com. Visit the Boston Gear website: www.bostongear.com. Click the BostSpec2 button. Click the BostSpec2 button again. The Boston Gear Product Tree is displayed to the left. Click the Part Search Button. Enter FUTF for the part number.

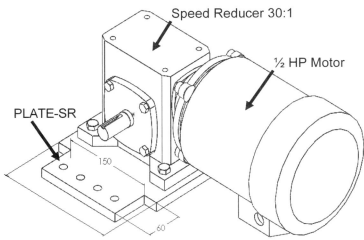

SPEED REDUCER Assembly

Speed Reducer 30:1

½ HP Motor

PLATE-SR

150

60

All Models and Images
Courtesy of Boston Gear

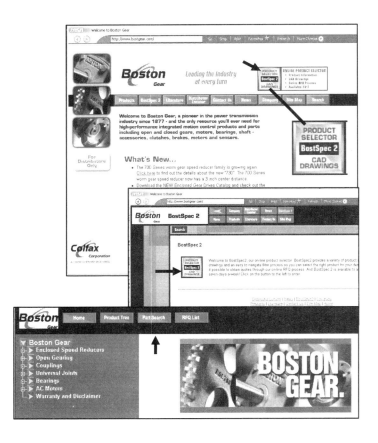

Click the View Spec Sheet button to display the motor specification. Click the 3D CAD button to view the part.

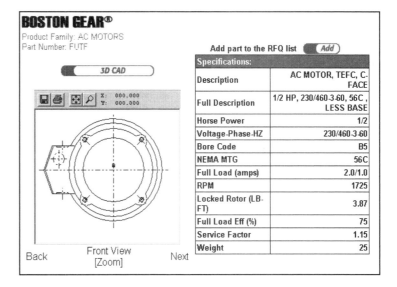

Click the 3D Formats button. Select the SolidWorks Assembly to download.

Find the Enclosed Speed Reducer. Click the Product Tree button. Click the Worm Gear Speed Reducers, Single Reduction option. Click the Type B – G icon in the second row.

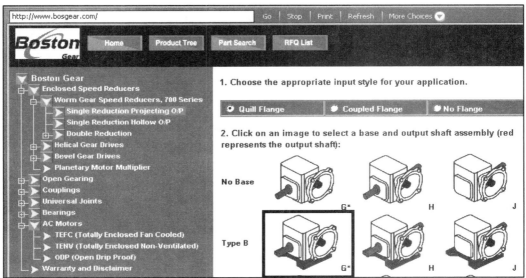

There are over 100 Speed Reducers listed. Select ½ in the Motor HP (Class I) list box. The number of entries reduces to 10. Select 30 in the Ratio list box. A single part number remains. View the Speed Reducer specification and download the SolidWorks Assembly.

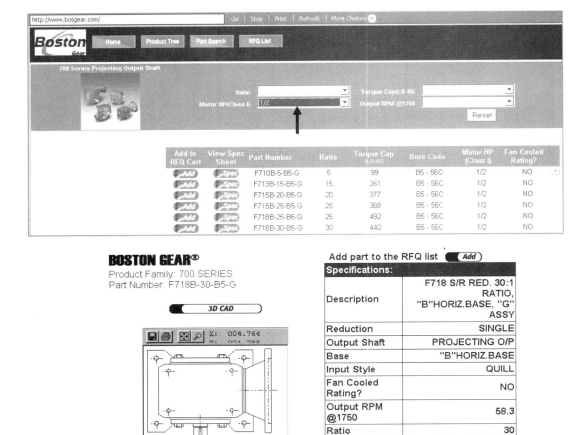

The Speed Reducer ships with HHCS (4) 3\8-16 x 1 inch, (Heavy Hex Cap Screw 3\8 inch diameter, 16 threads per inch, 1 inch length). Create a sub assembly between the Motor and Speed Reducer. Mate the four HHCS between the Motor and the Speed Reducer.

Measure the size and location of the Speed Reducer mounting holes. Create the part, PLATE-SR. Create the SPEED REDUCER Assembly. Mate the sub assembly to the PLATE-SR. Utilize fasteners from the SolidWorks\Toolbox or use the Flange Bolt from the Design Library.

Project 3
Top Down Design – In-Context

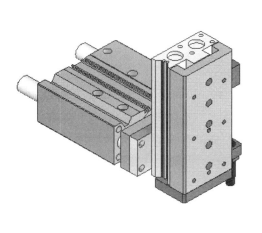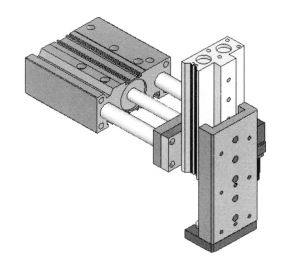

Below are the desired outcomes and usage competencies based on the completion of this Project.

Project Desired Outcomes:	Usage Competencies:
• 2AXIS-TRANSFER assembly.	• Ability to create assemblies with multiple configurations.
• PLATE-B part.	• An understanding of In-Context methods in a Top-Down assembly modeling approach.
	• Ability to create, lock and redefine External references.
• Configurations for the GUIDE-CYLINDER, SLIDE-TABLE, and 2AXIS-TRANSFER assemblies.	• Knowledge to develop and incorporate assembly configurations at various levels with the ConfigurationManager and Design Table.
	• Ability to create and modify Mates related to configurations.

Notes:

Project 3 – Top-Down Design – In-Context

Project Objective

Create the 2AXIS-TRANSFER assembly. Design the PLATE-B part In-Context of the GUIDE-CYLINDER and SLIDE-TABLE assemblies. The new part develops In-Context features.

Utilize the ConfigurationManager to create configurations for the GUIDE-CYLINDER and SLIDE-TABLE.

Utilize a Design Table to create configurations for the new 2AXIS-TRANSFER assembly. The 2AXIS-TRANSFER assembly is the second component in the 3AXIS-TRANSFER assembly.

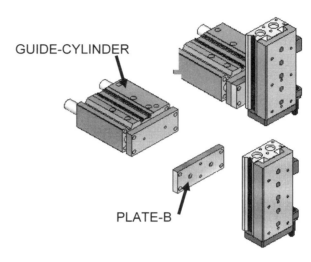

2AXIS-TRANSFER assembly

On the completion of this project, you will be able to:

- Apply a Top-Down Design assembly modeling approach to develop components In-Context of the assembly.

- Review External reference and InPlace Mate syntax to create the PLATE-B part.

- Apply a Bottom-Up Design assembly modeling approach to assemble additional components.

- Select the appropriate hole types and fasteners required in the assembly.

- Obtain the required dimensions, measure, and insert features.

- Calculate the interference between components and edit Mates and redefine External references.

- Add configurations to assembly components with the ConfigurationManager.

- Develop a Design Table and utilize parameters to control configurations and state.

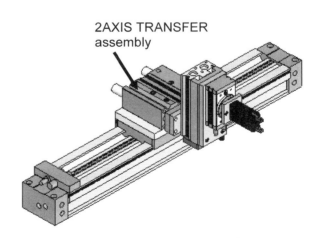

3AXIS-TRANSFER assembly

SolidWorks Tools and Commands

In Project 3, utilize the following SolidWorks tools and commands.

SolidWorks Tools and Commands:		
$Configuration	Edit Part, Edit Sub-assembly	Rename
$STATE	Extrude Boss/Base	Replace Components
Add Configuration	Feature Palette	Replace Mate Entities
Autodimension	Fixed/Float	Rotate Component
Coincident Mate	Hide	Section view
Component Pattern	Hole Wizard	Selection Filters toolbar
Component Properties	InPlace Mate	Select Other
Concentric Mate	Interference Detection	Shortcut keys
Configurations	Insert Component, New Part	Show
Customize keyboard	List External References	Show Update Holders
Design Library	Lock All	Sketch relations: On Entity, Midpoint, Coincident, Horizontal, Vertical
Design Table	Mate Types	Sketch tools: Centerline, Dimension
Dimensions/Relations toolbar	Measure	SmartMate
Display/Delete Relations	Move Component	Suppress/Set to Resolved
Distance Mate	Move with Triad	Suppress/Unsuppress
Do not create External References	New view	Suspend Automatic Rebuild
Edit Component	Open part, Open assembly	View Planes, Origins, Temporary Axis

Build modeling skill and speed. Project 3 primarily utilizes Pop-up menus and Shortcut keys to execute the tools in the Assembly toolbar.

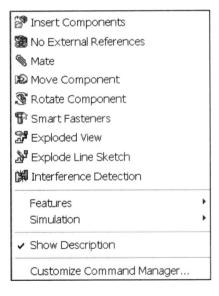

Project Overview

The 2AXIS-TRANSFER assembly is the second sub-assembly for the 3AXIS-TRANSFER assembly.

The 2AXIS-TRANSFER assembly combines the GUIDE-CYLINDER assembly and the SLIDE-TABLE assembly.

The SLIDE-TABLE assembly vertically lifts the GRIPPER 100mm. The GUIDE-CYLINDER assembly moves 100mm horizontally.

The SLIDE-TABLE assembly cannot be fastened directly to the GUIDE-CYLINDER assembly.

Design the PLATE-B part as an interim part to address this issue. Create PLATE-B In-Context of the GUIDE-CYLINDER assembly.

The 2AXIS-TRANSFER assembly consists of the following models:

- GUIDE-CYLINDER assembly.

- PLATE-B part.

- SLIDE-TABLE assembly.

- SHCS.

Add the configurations for the GUIDE-CYLINDER, SLIDE-TABLE, and 2AXIS-TRANSFER assemblies to represent physical positions.

Utilize the ConfigurationManager to create the GUIDE-CYLINDER configurations named; Default, Normal, and Extended.

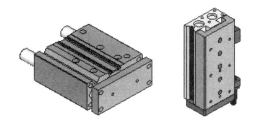

GUIDE-CYLINDER assembly   SLIDE-TABLE assembly

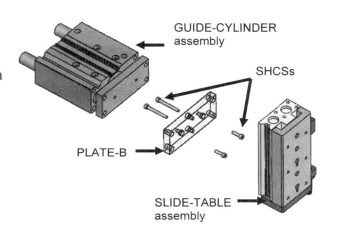

GUIDE-CYLINDER assembly

SHCSs

PLATE-B

SLIDE-TABLE assembly

2AXIS-TRANSFER assembly

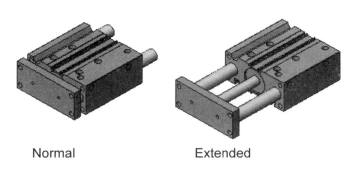

Normal   Extended

GUIDE-CYLINDER Configuration

Utilize the ConfigurationManager to create the SLIDE-TABLE configurations named; Default, Normal, and Extended.

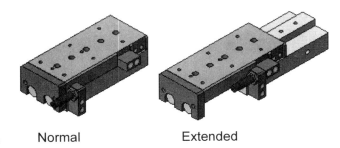

Normal　　　　　　　Extended

SLIDE-TABLE Configurations

Combine the GUIDE-CYLINDER Normal configuration and Extended configuration with the SLIDE-TABLE Normal configuration and Extended configuration to create the following four 2AXIS-TRANSFER configurations:

1. Normal-Normal.

2. Normal-Extended.

3. Extended-Normal.

4. Extended-Extended.

The GUIDE-CYLINDER configuration is listed first, followed by the SLIDE-TABLE configuration.

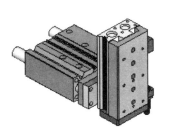

Normal-Normal

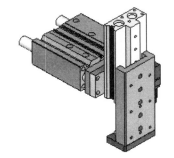

Normal-Extended

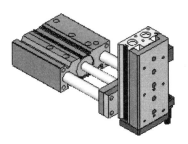

Extended-Normal

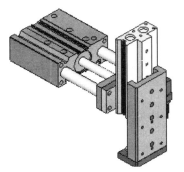

Extended-Extended

Create the fifth 2AXIS-TRANSFER configuration named Fastener.

Un-suppress the SHCSs in the Fastener configuration.

Suppress the SHCSs in the other four configurations.

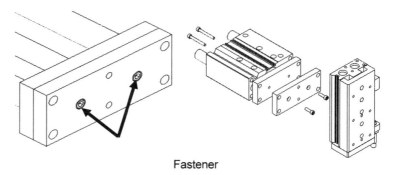

Fastener

2AXIS-TRANSFER Configurations

Top Down Design Assembly Modeling Approach

In the Top Down design assembly modeling approach, the major design requirements are translated into assemblies, sub-assemblies, and components. You do not need all of the required component design details. The model requires individual relationships between components. There are two methods to begin a Top Down design assembly approach:

- Method 1: Start with a Layout Sketch in the assembly.
- Method 2: Start with a component in the assembly.

In Method 1, all major components are positioned based on a 2D sketch. Relationships between sub-assemblies must be maintained for proper fit. Utilize Method 1 in Project 6.

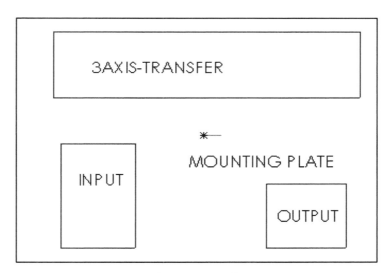

Delivery Station Layout Sketch

In Method 2, relationships are derived from an existing component in the assembly. Utilize Method 2 for the PLATE-B part.

Develop the PLATE-B part In-Context of the existing GUIDE-CYLINDER assembly. The PLATE-B part contains In-Context relations.

An In-Context relation is a reference between a sketch entity in a part and an entity in another component. Relations that are defined In-Context are listed as External references. In-Context relations and External references are powerful tools in the design phase. Begin with an empty part and utilize existing components in the assembly.

Determine the geometric and functional requirements of the part.

Mastering assembly modeling techniques with In-Context relations requires practice and time. Planning and selecting the correct reference and understanding how to incorporate changes are important.

Explore various techniques using InPlace Mates and External references developed in the context of an assembly.

Assembly Modeling Techniques with InPlace Mates:
1. Plan the Top-Down design method. Start from a Layout sketch or with a component in the assembly.
2. Prepare the references. Utilize descriptive feature names for referenced features and sketches.
3. Utilize InPlace Mates sparingly. Load all related components into memory to propagate changes. Do not use InPlace Mates for purchased parts or hardware.
4. Group references. Select references from one component at a time.
5. Ask questions! Will the part be used again in a different assembly? If the answer is yes, do not use InPlace Mates. If the answer is no, use InPlace Mates.
6. Will the part be used in physical dynamics or multiple configurations? If the answer is yes, do not use InPlace Mates.
7. Examine how to redefine External references. Use List References and Lock References to locate and protect geometry. Existing references do not update in a locked state. Locate the locked references. Create new references for the sketch and the feature.
8. Reduce the size of the FeatureManager. Hide Update Holders for In-Context features.
9. Work in the Edit Part mode to obtain the required external references in the assembly. Create all non-referenced features in the Part, not in the assembly.
10. Obtain knowledge of your company's policy on InPlace Mates or develop one as part of an engineering standard. .
11. Use the Break All command from keeping External references from updating.

Note: The Break All command is not utilized in this project. The authors prefer other techniques based on experience.

2AXIS-TRANSFER assembly

Create an assembly called 2AXIS-TRANSFER assembly.

Determine the specific features required to create the PLATE-B part using the Top Down design assembly approach.

Utilize Insert, Component, New Part from the Main menu to create PLATE-B In-Context of the GUIDE-CYLINDER assembly.

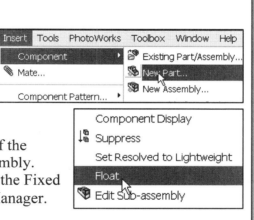

Redefine the orientation of the GUIDE-CYLINDER assembly. The Float option removes the Fixed constraint in the FeatureManager.

Utilize the 2AXIS-TRANSFER default reference planes: Front Plane, Top Plane, and Right Plane. The reference planes provide an accurate method to locate the first component in an assembly at the required orientation.

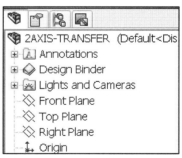

Note: To rotate a component by an exact value, select Rotate Component. Select the By Delta XYZ option. Enter an angular value.

Deactivate the Large Assembly Mode.

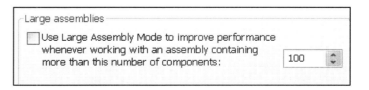

Activity: 2AXIS-TRANSFER assembly

Close all documents.
1)   Click **Window**, **Close** All from the Main menu.

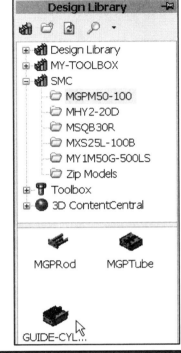

Deactivate the Large Assembly Mode.
2)   Click **Tools, Options** from the Main menu.

3)   Click **Assemblies**. Uncheck **Use Large Assembly Mode**.

4)   Click **OK**.

Open the GUIDE-CYLINDER assembly from the Design Library.
5)   Double-click **MGPM50-100** from the SMC folder.

6)   Click and drag **GUIDE-CYLINDER** into the Graphics window. The GUIDE-CYLINDER assembly is displayed in the Graphic window.

Create a new assembly.
7)   Click **Make Assembly from Part/Assembly** 🎯 from the Standard toolbar.

8)   Select the **MY-TEMPLATES** tab.

9)   Double-click **ASM-MM-ANSI**. The Insert Component PropertyManager is displayed.

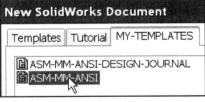

10)   Click **View**, check **Origins** from the Main menu.

11)   Click a **position** to the left of the new assembly Origin. Do not click the assembly Origin.

12)   If required, click **View**. Uncheck **Planes** to hide all planes.

Display an Isometric view.
13)   Click **Isometric** view.

Save the assembly.
14)   Click **Save** 💾 .

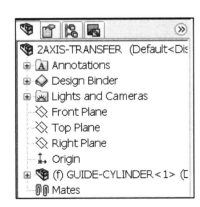

15)   Select **DELIVERY-STATION** for Save in: file folder.

16)   Enter **2AXIS-TRANSFER** for File name.

17)   Click **Save**. The 2AXIS-TRANSFER FeatureManager is displayed. Click **View**, un-check **Origins** from the Main menu.

Float the GUIDE-CYLINDER.

18) Right-click **GUIDE-CYLINDER** from the FeatureManager.

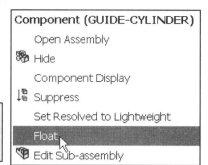

19) Click **Float**. The GUIDE-CYLINDER entry changes from fixed, (f) to under-defined, (-).

Rotate the GUIDE-CYLINDER.

20) Right-click **GUIDE-CYLINDER** from the FeatureManager.

21) Click **Move with Triad**.

22) Hold the **right mouse button** down on the green vertical arrow.

23) Drag the **mouse pointer** to the left to rotate the component as illustrated.

24) Release the **right mouse button**.

Mate the GUIDE-CYLINDER. Create a Coincident mate.

25) Expand **GUIDE-CYLINDER** from the FeatureManager.

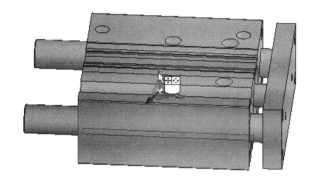

26) Click **GUIDE-CYLINDER\Plane3**.

27) Click **Mate** Mate . The Mate PropertyManager is displayed.

28) Click **2AXIS-TRANSFER\Front Plane**. Coincident is selected by default.

29) Click ✔.

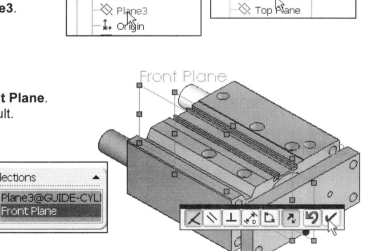

Create the second Coincident mate.
30) Click **GUIDE-CYLINDER\Plane2**.

31) Click **2AXIS-TRANSFER\Top Plane**.
Coincident is selected by default.

32) Click ✔.

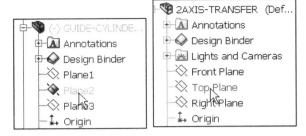

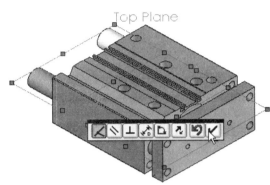

Create the third Coincident mate.
33) Click **GUIDE-CYLINDER\Plane1**.

34) Click **2AXIS-TRANSFER\Right Plane**.
Coincident is selected by default.

35) Click ✔.

36) Click **OK** ✅ from the
Mate PropertyManager.

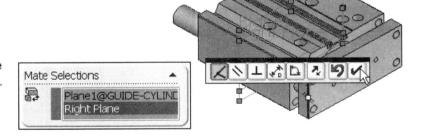

Expand the Mates.
37) Expand **Mates** from the
FeatureManager. View
the 3 Mates. The
GUIDE-CYLINDER is
fully defined in the
2AXIS-TRANSFER
assembly.

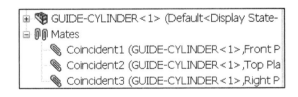

🔆 The Fix option provides a fast technique in assembly modeling. As models become more complex, it is difficult to determine where the component Origin is in space. Mating the first component to three planes takes more time but provides orientation flexibility and greater accuracy.

Hide the MGPTube component.
38) Right-click **MGPTube<1>** from the FeatureManager.

39) Click **Hide**.

Expand the MGPRod part.
40) Expand **MPGRod<1>** from the 2AXIS-TRANSFER FeatureManager. If required, Set to Resolve.

41) Click **MountHoles2** from the FeatureManager. The four holes are selected in the Graphics window and displayed in green.

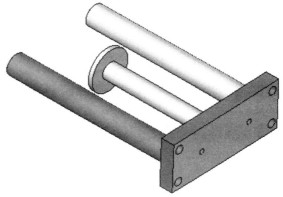

The PLATE-B part references the MountHoles2 feature.

In-Context, External References, and InPlace Mates

An In-Context relationship is a geometric relationship between a sketch entity in one part, and a feature on a component in the assembly.

An External reference is a relationship that exists between a sketch entity and geometry outside the sketch. Example: The GUIDE-CYLINDER utilizes reference planes to develop the Base Extrude feature for the MGPTube.

An External reference develops an In-Context relationship when geometry is referenced outside the part. Example: Create the new PLATE-B part in the context of the 2AXIS-TRANSFER assembly that references the MGPRod component.

Components added in the context of an existing assembly automatically receive an InPlace Mate. The InPlace Mate is a Coincident Mate created between the Front Plane of a new component and the selected planar geometry of the assembly. The component is fully defined; no additional Mates are required to position the component. By default, SolidWorks uses the default templates for new parts and assemblies developed In-Context of an existing assembly.

To select a custom Template, define the System Options, Document Templates option before you insert a new component into the assembly.

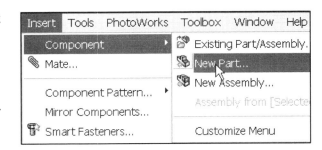

Create the PLATE-B part In-Context of the 2AXIS-TRANSFER assembly, select Insert, Component, New Part 🖆 New Part....

Select the custom Part Template from the MY-TEMPLATES folder.

Enter PLATE-A for the new part.

Select the MGPRod right face to create an InPlace Mate reference with the PLATE-B Front Plane. SolidWorks automatically selects the Edit Component 🖆 Compo... icon when inserting a new component. The PLATE-B blue text appears in the FeatureManager. The default blue color indicates that the part is actively being edited.

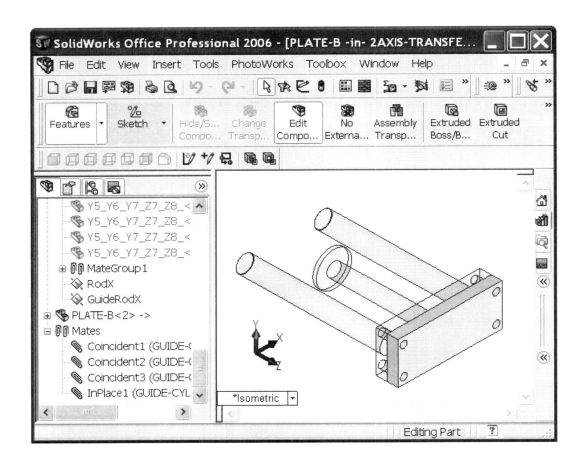

The right face of the MGPRod part is the current
Sketch plane. The current sketch name is Sketch1. The
current Graphics window title displays the sketch and
name.

Example:

"Sketch1 of PLATE-B -in- 2AXIS-
TRANSFER."

PLATE-B is the name of the component
created in the context of the 2AXIS-
TRANSFER assembly. SolidWorks
automatically selects Sketch 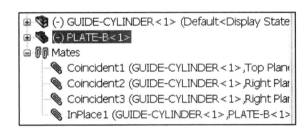Sketch .

The Mate, InPlace1 (GUIDE-
CYLINDER<1>, PLATE-B<1>) fully
defines PLATE-B in the 2AXIS-
TRANSFER assembly.

The Assembly toolbar, FeatureManager and
Pop-up Assembly menu display different
options.

Review Edit Component, Edit Part, and Edit
Sub-assembly tools.

- For parts and assemblies, utilize the Edit
  Component Compo... from the Assembly
  toolbar.

- For parts only, utilize Edit Part and
  Open Part.

- For assemblies only, utilize Edit Sub-
  assembly and Open Assembly.

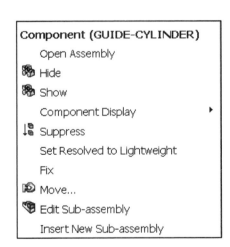

SolidWorks creates External references from the PLATE-B part to the GUIDE-CYLINDER assembly.

Example: The Extrude1 feature develops an External reference from the sketch plane. Sketch1 develops External references from the Convert Entities Sketch tool.

The No External References Externa... option develops no InPlace Mate or External references. Select this option before you select Insert, Component, New Part from the Main menu. Customize the Assembly toolbar in the next activity to include this important option.

The procedure to create a component in the context of an assembly with no External references is the same as creating a new part with External references. Select a Sketch plane and create the sketch.

If you utilize Convert Entities and Offset Entities Sketch tools, no External references develop. The new part requires dimensions and relations to fully define the geometry and Mates to constrain its position in the assembly. The Do not create External references option toggles on and off. Insert this option into the Assembly toolbar.

Activity: In-Context, External References, and InPlace Mates

Set the Default Template option.
42) Click **Tools**, **Options**, **System Options** tab from the Main menu.

43) Click **Default Templates**.

44) Check **Prompt user to select document template**.

45) Click **OK** from the System Options box.

Parts
C:\Program Files\SolidWorks\data\templates\Part.prtdot

Assemblies
C:\Program Files\SolidWorks\data\templates\Assembly.asmdot

Drawings
C:\Program Files\SolidWorks\data\templates\Drawing.drwdot

○ Always use these default document templates
⦿ Prompt user to select document template

Insert the new PLATE-B part.
46) Click **Insert**, **Component**, **New Part** from the Main menu.

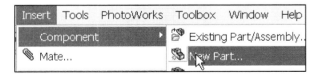

47) Double-click **PART-MM-ANSI-AL6061**.

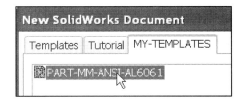

48) Select **DELIVERY-STATION** for Save in: file folder.

49) Enter **PLATE-B** for file name.

50) Click **Save**.

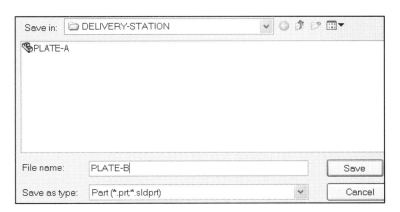

Locate the new part with an InPlace Mate.

51) The Component Pointer icon is displayed on the mouse pointer. The PLATE-B component is empty and requires a sketch plane. Click the **right** face of the MGPRod part as illustrated. SolidWorks creates the InPlace1 Mate.

52) Click **Hidden Lines Visible**.

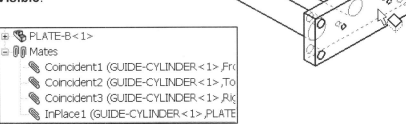

Convert existing edges.
53) Click the **right face**.

54) Click **Convert Entities** Convert from the Sketch toolbar.

55) Click the **top left MountHoles2 circle**.

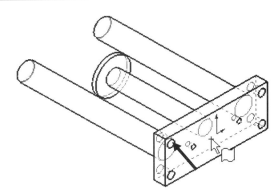

56) Hold the **Ctrl** key down.

57) Select the **three MountHoles2 circles**.

58) Release the **Ctrl** key.

59) Click **Convert Entities** Convert .

Extrude Sketch1.

60) Click **Extruded Boss/Base** Boss/B... from the
Features toolbar.

61) Enter **15** for Depth.

62) Click **OK** from the Extrude PropertyManager.
The name of PLATE-B is displayed in blue. The
PLATE-B part is edited In-Context of the 2AXIS-
TRANSFER assembly.

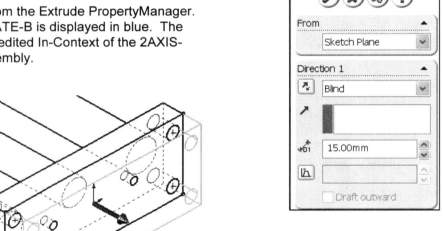

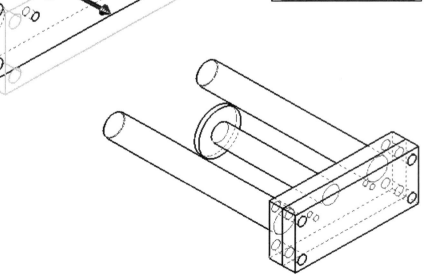

Return to the 2AXIS-TRANSFER assembly.
63) Right-click a **position** in the Graphics window.

64) Click **Edit Assembly: 2AXIS-TRANSFER**.

65) Right-click **PLATE-B** from the FeatureManager.

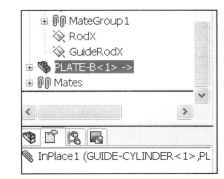

66) Click **View Mates**. The InPlace1 Mate lists the component references; GUIDE-CYLINDER<1>, PLATE-B<1>.

Display the MGPTube part.
67) Expand **GUIDE-CYLINDER<1>** from the FeatureManager.

68) Right-click **MGPTube** from the FeatureManager.

69) Click **Show**.

70) Click **Shaded With Edges**.

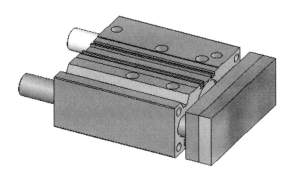

Save the 2AXIS-TRANSFER assembly.
71) Click **Isometric** view.

72) Click **Save** from the Main menu.

Open PLATE-B.
73) Right-click **PLATE-B** from the FeatureManager.

74) Click **Open Part**. PLATE-B is displayed in the Graphics window.

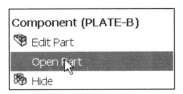

Review External references in PLATE-B.

75) The "->" symbol indicates that there are External references for the PLATE-B part. Right-click **PLATE-B**.

76) Click **List External Refs**. The External Reference list contains the Feature, Data, Status, Reference Entity, and Feature Component. All External references are defined.

77) Click **OK**.

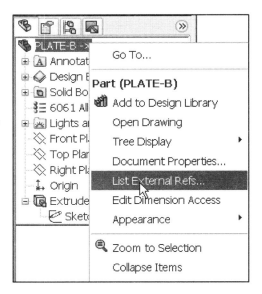

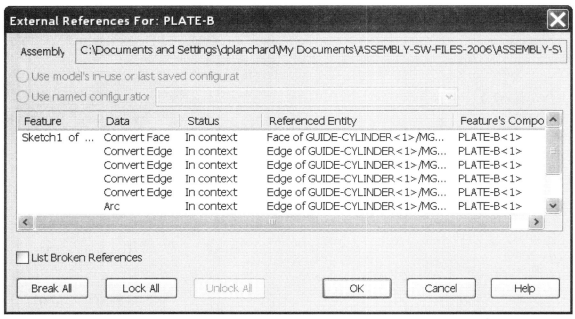

External References For: PLATE-B

Assembly | C:\Documents and Settings\dplanchard\My Documents\ASSEMBLY-SW-FILES-2006\ASSEMBLY-S\

○ Use model's in-use or last saved configurat

○ Use named configuration

Feature	Data	Status	Referenced Entity	Feature's Compo
Sketch1 of ...	Convert Face	In context	Face of GUIDE-CYLINDER<1>/MG...	PLATE-B<1>
	Convert Edge	In context	Edge of GUIDE-CYLINDER<1>/MG...	PLATE-B<1>
	Convert Edge	In context	Edge of GUIDE-CYLINDER<1>/MG...	PLATE-B<1>
	Convert Edge	In context	Edge of GUIDE-CYLINDER<1>/MG...	PLATE-B<1>
	Convert Edge	In context	Edge of GUIDE-CYLINDER<1>/MG...	PLATE-B<1>
	Arc	In context	Edge of GUIDE-CYLINDER<1>/MG...	PLATE-B<1>

☐ List Broken References

| Break All | Lock All | Unlock All | | OK | Cancel | Help |

Customize the Assembly toolbar.

78) Click **Tools**, **Customize** from the Main menu. The Customize box is displayed.

79) Click the **Commands** tab.

80) Select **Assembly** from the Categories list.

81) Click the **No External References** 🗑 icon.

82) Drag the **icon** into the Assembly toolbar.

83) Click **OK**.

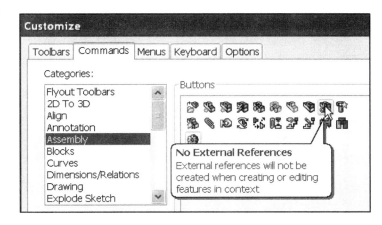

Base-Extrude Sketch1 contains three types of External references.

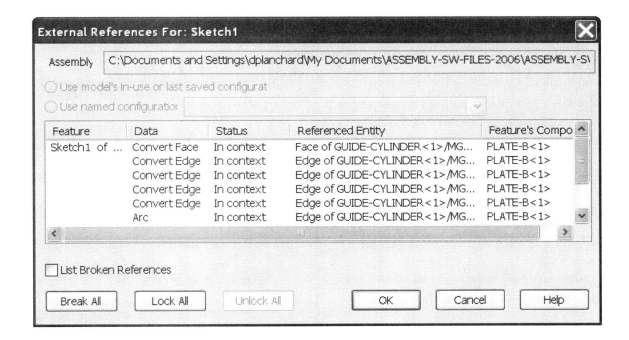

Convert Face entry occurs when you select the sketch plane. Convert Edge and Arc entries occur when you select Convert Entities in Sketch1. The Data column lists External references.

- Convert Face.

- Convert Edge.

- Arc.

The Convert Entities of the MGPRod's right face results in four Convert Edge references. The four Convert Edge references are:

- Bottom Horizontal Line.

- Right Vertical Line.

- Top Horizontal Line.

- Left Vertical Line.

There are four Arc references. The Convert Entities of the four MountHoles2 circles created the Arc references.

From the 2AXIS-TRANSFER assembly, utilize two additional methods to access External references.

Method 1: Right-click on a component in the FeatureManager or in the Graphics window. Click List External Refs.

Method 2: Right-click on the top level assembly icon. Click Show Update Holders.

SolidWorks creates an Update Holder for each External sketch reference. The Update Holders are displayed at the bottom of the FeatureManager.

The Update Holder entry contains the option to List
External Refs. Reduce the size of the FeatureManager.
Select the default Hide Update Holders.

Hole Selection

Hole selection becomes an important decision in machine
design. You decide on the hole type, placement, and feature
selection. Four ∅10mm SHCSs fasten the PLATE-B part to
the GUIDE-CYLINDER assembly. Should the holes utilize
a counterbore? Answer: No. The holes are too close to the
edge of the PLATE-B part. Do you enlarge PLATE-B to
accommodate the counterbore? Answer: No. Increasing the
part size adds additional weight and cost.

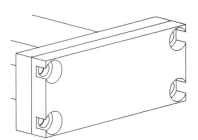

You must decide whether to create the PLATE-B holes in a
Top Down design approach with External
references, or a Bottom-Up Design approach with
no External references.

Examine the SLIDE-TABLE assembly to
determine the fastener type. Are additional holes
required to mount the SLIDE-TABLE assembly to
PLATE-B? Answer: Yes. Add two additional
holes.

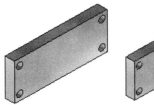

PLATE-B

There are two major components in the SLIDE-
TABLE assembly:

1.) MXSL-Body.

2.) MXSL-Table.

The MXSL-Body back face mates to the PLATE-B
front face. Simplify the mate process. Hide the
MXSL-Table.

MXSL-Table

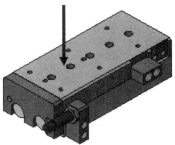

SLIDE-TABLE assembly

Utilize BodyThruHole4 and BodyThruHole5, closest to the bottom face. Create two M6 Cbores in the PLATE-B part that correspond to the ThruHoles in the MXSLTable. No External references are created in this Bottom Up approach.

🔆 Minimize the use of External references from multiple parts. Multiple part references lead to problems in higher levels of the assembly. External references require additional modification when dissolving components and forming sub-assemblies used in other projects.

🔆 Avoid unnecessary references. Do not work continuously in Edit Component mode for the individual part. Open the part. Insert additional features at the part level. The individual part is less complex than an assembly. Rebuild time is quicker.

Activity: Hole Selection

Hide the GUIDE-CYLINDER assembly.
84) Return to the 2AXIS-TRANSFER assembly. Click **Window, 2AXIS-TRANSFER** from the Main menu.

85) Right-click **GUIDE-CYLINDER** from the FeatureManager.

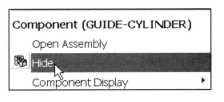

86) Click **Hide**. PLATE-B is displayed in the Graphics window.

Display the Origin.
87) Click **View, Origins** from the Main menu.

Note: Do not suppress the GUIDE-CYLINDER assembly. The Mates will be suppressed and the 2AXIS-TRANSFER assembly will no longer be constrained.

Note: The 2AXIS-TRANSFER assembly determines the location of the PLATE-B Origin.

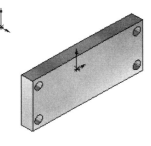

Open the SLIDE-TABLE assembly.
88) Double-click the **SMC\MXS25L-100B** folder from the Design Library.

89) Right-click **SLIDE-TABLE**.

90) Click **Open**. The SLIDE-TABLE is displayed in the Graphics window.

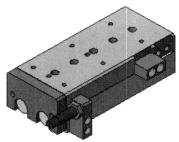
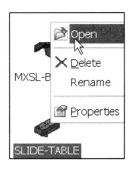

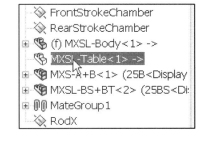

Determine the SLIDE-TABLE/MXSLBody Thru Hole locations.

91) Right-click **MXSL-Table<1>** from the FeatureManager.

92) Click **Hide**.

93) Right-click **MXSL-Body<1>** from the FeatureManager.

94) Double-click **MXSL-Body<1>** from the FeatureManager to view the ThruHole sketch.

95) Double-click **ThruHoles** from the FeatureManager. The ∅6.6mm holes are spaced 35mm apart and 32mm from the MXSLBody Top face.

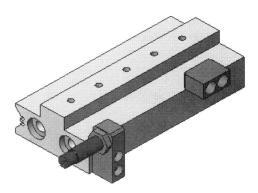

96) Click **BodyThruHole4** and **BodyThruHole5** to display the Thru Hole feature.

Display the SLIDE-TABLE/MXSL-Table part.

97) Right-click **SLIDE-TABLE/ MXSL-Table** from the FeatureManager.

98) Right-click **Show**.

Display an Isometric view.

99) Click **Isometric** view.

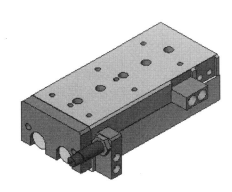

Open the PLATE-B part.
100) Click **Window**, **PLATE-B** from the Main menu. PLATE-B is displayed.

101) Click **Hidden Lines Visible**.

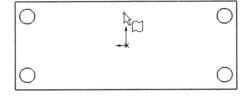

Add two Cbore Holes to the back face of the PLATE-B part. Use the Hole Wizard.
102) Click **Back** view.

103) Click the **back face** above the Origin.

Hole
104) Click **Hole Wizard** Wizard from the FeatureManager.

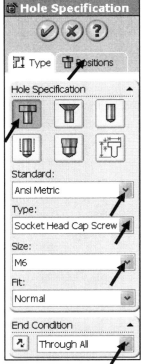

Create Cbore Hole1.
105) Click **Counterbore** for Hole Specification.

106) Select **Ansi Metric** for Standard.

107) Select **Socket Head Cap Screw** for Type.

108) Select **M6** for Size.

109) Select **Through All** for End Condition.

110) Click the **Positions** tab.

Create a Cbore Hole2.
111) Click a **position** below the Top plane, aligned with the Origin. The center point of Cbore Hole2 is displayed in blue. Note: Blue indicates that dimensions and relations are required.

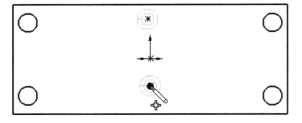

Add a Vertical relation.
112) Right-click **Select** in the Graphics window.

113) Click the **Origin**.

114) Hold the **Ctrl** key down.

115) Click the **Hole1 center point** and **Hole2 center point**.

116) Release the **Ctrl** key.

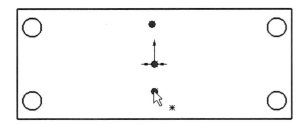

117) Click **Vertical** from the Add Relations box.

118) Click **OK** from the Properties PropertyManager.

Add a Symmetric relation.

119) Click **Centerline** Centerl... from the Sketch toolbar.

120) Sketch a **horizontal centerline** from the Origin to the midpoint of the right vertical edge as illustrated.

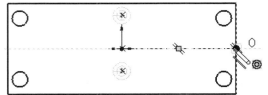

121) Right-click **Select**.

122) Click the **centerline**.

123) Hold the **Ctrl** key down.

124) Click the **Hole1 center point** and the **Hole2 center point**.

125) Release the **Ctrl** key.

126) Click **Symmetric** from the Add Relations box.

127) Click **OK** from the Properties PropertyManager.

Add a vertical dimension.

128) Click **Smart Dimension** Dimens... from the Sketch toolbar.

129) Click the **Hole1 center point** and the **Hole2 center point**.

130) Enter **35**. Click ✔. The hole center points are fully defined.

131) Click **OK** from the Dimension PropertyManager.

132) Click **OK** from the Hole Position PropertyManager.

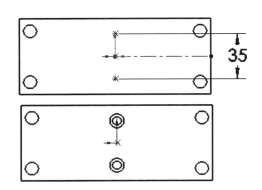

Display an Isometric view.
133) Click **Isometric** view.

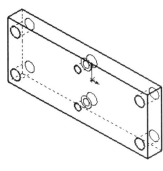

Save the PLATE-B part.
134) Click **Save** from the Main menu.

Return to the 2AXIS-TRANSFER assembly.
135) Click **Window, 2AXIS-TRANSFER** from the Main menu. Click **Yes** to the Rebuild now message.

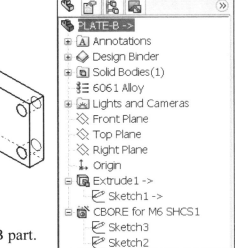

PLATE-B changed by adding two Cbore Holes. The 2AXIS-TRANSFER assembly contains the PLATE-B part. Utilize a Section view to display the new Cbores.

Update the 2AXIS-TRANSFER assembly.
136) Right-click **GUIDE-CYLINDER** from the FeatureManager.

137) Click **Show**.

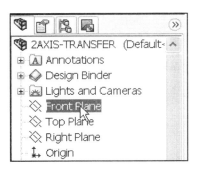

View the Cbore Hole in the 2AXIS-TRANSFER assembly.
138) Click **Front Plane** from the 2AXIS-TRANSFER FeatureManager.

139) Click **Section View** from the View toolbar. The Cbores are on the back face of the PLATE-B part.

140) Click **Cancel** from the Section View PropertyManager to display the Full view.

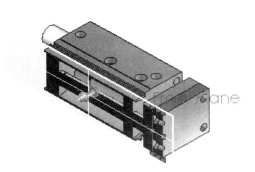

Conserve design time. There are numerous Front Plane, Top Plane, and Right Plane entries in an assembly FeatureManager. Each component contains these reference planes. How do you select the correct Plane? Answer: Locate the component in the FeatureManager. Expand the component entry. Select the reference plane directly below the component name.

Mating the SLIDE-TABLE assembly

The SLIDE-TABLE assembly fastens to the PLATE-B Cbores. Open the SLIDE-TABLE and 2AXIS-TRANSFER assemblies if required. Utilize Tile Horizontally and drag the SLIDE-TABLE assembly icon into the 2AXIS-TRANSFER assembly. Position the SLIDE-TABLE in its approximate orientation before creating a Mate.

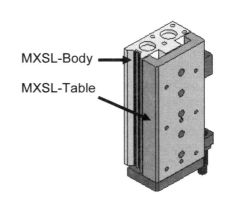

MXSL-Body

MXSL-Table

Hide components when not required. Do not suppress the GUIDE-CYLINDER assembly. Suppressing components suppresses Mates, resulting in parts being free to move and rotate.

There are many holes on the MXSL-Body part. What holes do you assemble to PLATE-B? Answer: The two bottom holes on the MXSL-Body part.

Investigate the physical behavior of the SLIDE-TABLE assembly. What part moves? What part remains static? Answer: The MXSL-Table part linearly translates and the MXSL-Body part is fixed.

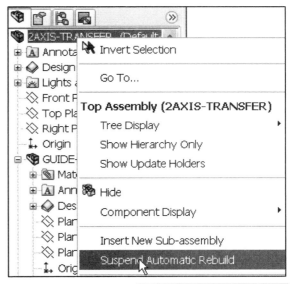

The Suspend Automatic Rebuild defers the updating of Mates in the top level 2AXIS-TRANSFER assembly.

Utilize this option to create and change multiple Mates. The Rebuild command from the Standard toolbar controls the update of the deferred Mates.

Utilize a Section view to see the PLATE-B Cbores and the BodyThruHole4 and BodyThruHole5.

Utilize the Use for positioning only option to move and rotate components based on the Mate type. The Mate is not created or added to the FeatureManager.

Activity: Mating the SLIDE-TABLE assembly.

Insert the SLIDE-TABLE assembly.
141) Click **Window, Tile Horizontally** from the Main menu.

142) Click and drag the **SLIDE-TABLE assembly icon** into the 2AXIS-TRANSFER assembly.

143) Click a **position** in front of the PLATE-B part as illustrated.

144) Maximize the 2AXIS-TRANSFER assembly.

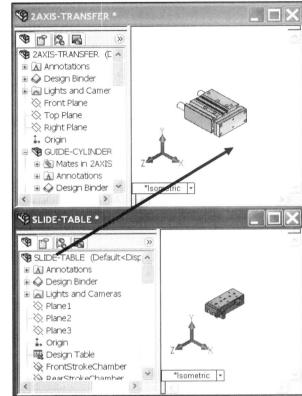

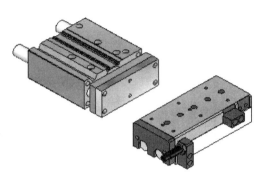

Move and Rotate the SLIDE-TABLE assembly.
145) Right-click **SLIDE-TABLE** from the FeatureManager.

146) Click **Move**.

147) Right-click in the **Graphics window**.

148) Click **Rotate Component**.

149) Click and drag the **SLIDE-TABLE** assembly in front of the PLATE-B part as illustrated.

150) Click **OK** from the Rotate Component PropertyManager.

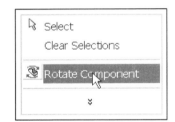

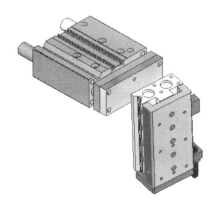

Hide all Components that are not required.
151) Expand **SLIDE-TABLE** from the FeatureManager.

152) Click **MXSL-Table<1>**.

153) Hold the **Shift** key down.

154) Click the **MXSL-BS+BT<2>**.

155) Release the **Shift** key. The MXS-A+B is selected automatically with Shift-Select.

156) Hold the **Ctrl** key down.

157) Click the **GUIDE-CYLINDER** assembly from the FeatureManager.

158) Release the **Ctrl** key.

159) Right-click **Hide**.

Display an Isometric view.
160) Click **Isometric** view.

Create a Coincident mate.
161) Click **Front Plane** from the 2AXIS-TRANSFER FeatureManager.

162) Click **Mate** ^Mate from the Assembly toolbar. The PropertyManager is displayed.

163) Click SLIDE-TABLE/**Plane3**.

164) Click the **Use for positioning only** option. Coincident is selected by Default.

165) Click ✔. Do not move or rotate the MXSL-Body.

166) Click **OK** ✅ from the Mate PropertyManager.

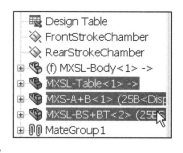
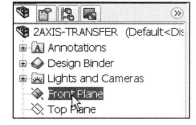
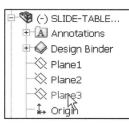
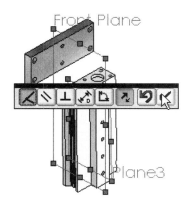

Defer the Mates.
167) Right-click **2AXIS-TRANSFER** from the FeatureManager.

168) Click **Suspend Automatic Rebuild**.

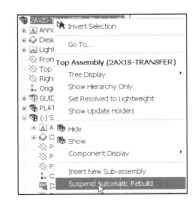

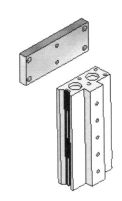

Display the Section view.
169) Click **Front Plane** from the 2AXIS-TRANSFER FeatureManager.

170) Click **Section view** 📦.

171) Click **OK** ✅ from the Section View PropertyManager.

Insert a Concentric Mate.
172) Click the **BodyThruHole4 cylindrical face** as illustrated.

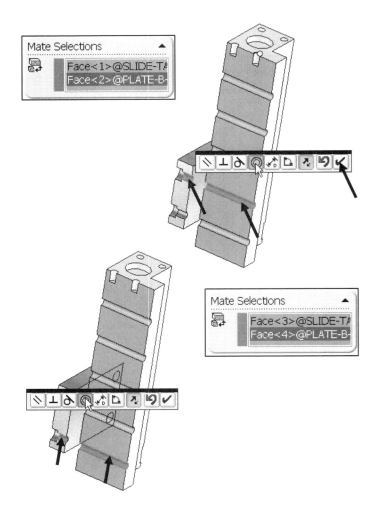

173) Click **Mate** Mate from the Assembly toolbar.

174) Click the top **PLATE-B Cbore cylindrical face**.

175) Click **Concentric**.

176) Click ✔.

Insert the second Concentric Mate.
177) Click the **BodyThruHole5 cylindrical face**.

178) Click the bottom **PLATE-B Cbore cylindrical face**.

179) Click **Concentric**.

180) Click ✔.

Insert a Coincident Mate.
181) Click the **PLATE-B front face**.

182) Click the **MXSL-Body back face**.

183) Click **Coincident**.

184) Click ✔.

185) Click **OK** ✅ from the Mate PropertyManager. The SLIDE-TABLE is fully defined.

Display an Isometric view.
186) Click **Isometric view**.

187) Click **Section view** 🔲.

Save the 2AXIS-TRANSFER assembly.
188) Click **Save**.

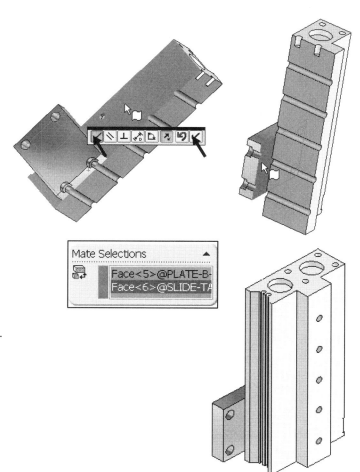

Mate Selections
Face<5>@PLATE-B-
Face<6>@SLIDE-TA

Fasteners

The 2AXIS-TRANSFER assembly requires two different length fasteners.

- Insert two M6x1.0 SHCSs between the PLATE-B part and the SLIDE-TABLE assembly.

- Insert two M6x1.0 SHCSs between the PLATE-B part and the GUIDE-CYLINDER assembly.

- Create an assembly-sketched pattern for the fasteners.

Inserting fastener components simulates the assembly process in manufacturing. Assemble the PLATE-B part to the SLIDE-TABLE assembly. The individual SHCSs were created from SolidWorks Toolbox and stored in the MY-TEMPLATE\SHCS folder.

The Mate References in the SHCS create the Concentric\Coincident SmartMate when dragged to the PLATE-B hole. Utilize the components located in the SHCS folder instead of SolidWorks\Toolbox to practice Replace and Redefine options.

Activity: Fasteners

Measure the thread length distance.
189) Click **Top** view.

190) Click **Hidden Lines Visible**.

191) Click **Tools, Measure** from the Main menu.

192) Click the **inside edge** of the PLATE-B Cbore Hole.

193) Click the **bottom edge** of the hole. The Delta X distance is 57mm. Utilize a 50mm thread length for the SHCS.

194) Click **Close**.

195) Click **Shaded With Edges**.

Position the model.
196) Rotate PLATE-B as illustrated.

197) Zoom in on the **bottom Cbore**.

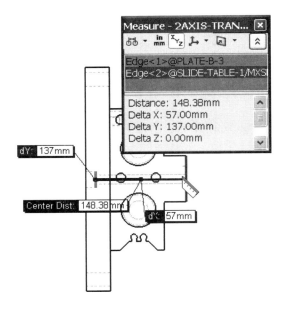

Insert two M6 Hex SHCS from the Design Library.
198) Click the **MY-TOOLBOX\SHCS** folder.

Insert the first Hex SHCS.
199) Click and drag the **B18.3.1M-6x1.0x50 Hex SHCS** to the bottom Cbore. The Coincident\Concentric icon is displayed.

200) Release the mouse pointer on the **inside circular edge** as illustrated.

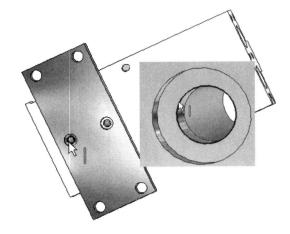

Insert the second M6Hex SHCS from the Design Library.
201) Drag the **B18.3.1M-6x1.0x50 Hex SHCS** to
the top Cbore.

202) Click on the **inside circular edge** as
illustrated.

203) Click **Cancel** 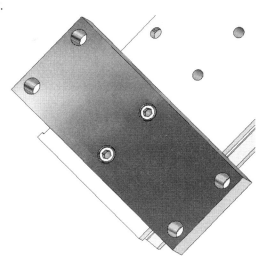 from the Insert Component
PropertyManager.

Fit the Model to the Graphics window.
204) Press the **f** key.

View the created Mates.
205) Expand **Mates** from the
FeatureManager.

Two instances of the M – 6 x 1.0 x 50
SHCS have been added to the
FeatureManager. The B18.3.1M -6 x 1.0
x 50 Hex SHCS<1> is the first instance.
The B18.3.1M – 6 x 1.0 x 50 Hex
SHCS<2> is the second instance. Each
time you insert a SHCS, in the same
session of SolidWorks, the instance number is
incremented. Your instance numbers <1>, <2>,
may be different if a SHCS was deleted.

⊞ 🔩 (-) B18.3.1M - 6 x 1.0 x 50 Hex SHCS -- 50NHX<1>	
⊞ 🔩 (-) B18.3.1M - 6 x 1.0 x 50 Hex SHCS -- 50NHX<2>	

Dragging the
SHCS into the
assembly and
referencing the
Cbore circular
edge created four
SmartMates. Your
numbers may be
different if a Mate
was deleted.

⊟ 🔗 Mates
  🔗 Coincident1 (GUIDE-CYLINDER<1>,Front Plane)
  🔗 Coincident2 (GUIDE-CYLINDER<1>,Top Plane)
  🔗 Coincident3 (GUIDE-CYLINDER<1>,Right Plane)
  🔗 InPlace1 (GUIDE-CYLINDER<1>,PLATE-B<1>)
  🔗 Concentric1 (PLATE-B<1>,SLIDE-TABLE<1>)
  🔗 Concentric2 (PLATE-B<1>,SLIDE-TABLE<1>)
  🔗 Coincident8 (PLATE-B<1>,SLIDE-TABLE<1>)
  🔗 Concentric31 (PLATE-B<1>,B18.3.1M - 6 x 1.0 x 50 Hex SHCS -- 50NHX<1>)
  🔗 Coincident91 (PLATE-B<1>,B18.3.1M - 6 x 1.0 x 50 Hex SHCS -- 50NHX<1>)
  🔗 Concentric41 (PLATE-B<1>,B18.3.1M - 6 x 1.0 x 50 Hex SHCS -- 50NHX<2>)
  🔗 Coincident101 (PLATE-B<1>,B18.3.1M - 6 x 1.0 x 50 Hex SHCS -- 50NHX<2>)

Hide and Show components.
206) Click **SLIDE-TABLE** from the FeatureManager.

207) Hold the **Ctrl** key down.

208) Click **B18.3.1M-6x1.0x50Hex SHCS <1>** from the FeatureManager.

209) Click **B18.3.1M-6x1.0x50Hex SHCS<2>** from the FeatureManager.

210) Release the **Ctrl** key.

211) Right-click **Hide**. Click **Hidden Lines Visible**.

212) Right-click **GUIDE-CYLINDER** from the FeatureManager.

213) Click **Show**.

214) Right-click **MGPTube** from the FeatureManager.

215) Click **Hide**. PLATE-B and the MGPRod parts are displayed.

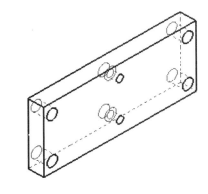

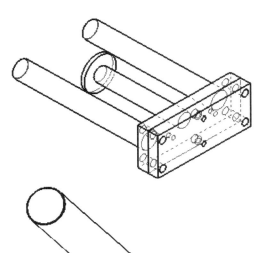

Add an M10x1.5 SHCS to PLATE-B from the Design Library.
216) Click the **MY-TOOLBOX\SHCS** folder. Zoom in on the back top hole as illustrated.

217) Click and drag the **B18.3.1M-10x1.5x25 Hex SHCS** to the back top hole as illustrated.

218) Release the mouse pointer on the **outside circular edge**.

219) Click **Cancel** ✖ from the Insert Component PropertyManager.

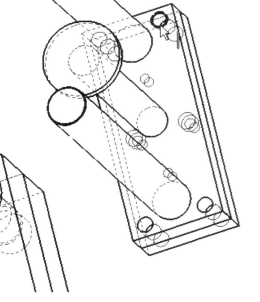

Editing Mates and Redefining Components

Assemblies require the ability to modify Mates and redefined components.

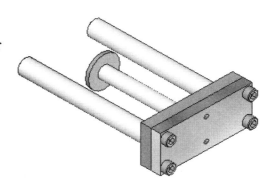

The 2AXIS-TRANSFER assembly requires four M10 SHCSs to fasten the PLATE-B part to the GUIDE-CYLINDER assembly. Errors occur in the modify process. The goal is to learn how to recognize and correct errors.

A Concentric Mate and Coincident Mate define the SHCS placement. Suppress the Coincident Mate in order to flip the alignment.

Modify the Concentric Mate selections from the GUIDE-CYLINDER top back hole to the PLATE-B bottom front hole with the Replace Mate Entities option. Unsuppress the Coincident Mate. Utilize the Replace Mate Entities option to redefine the Coincident Mate selections.

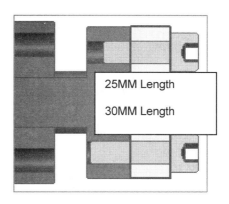

25MM Length

30MM Length

What is the required thread length? Answer: 25mm or 30mm. Try a 25mm SHCS. The 25mm SHCS thread does not provide the minimum engagement of 75% for the MGPRod Plate hole.

Utilize the Replace Component option to modify the 25mm SHCS to a 30mm.

The SHCS fastens PLATE-B to the GUIDE-CYLINDER assembly.

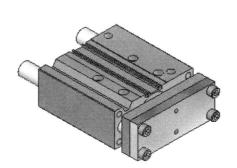

Create a Local Assembly Pattern that corresponds to the MountHoles2 position. Record the dimensions between the holes.

The Local Assembly Pattern of the M10 SHCS requires the 130mm and 40mm dimensions.

Identify the location of the pattern. Locate the pattern at the top level of the 2AXIS-TRANSFER assembly.

There is a visual interference between the lower right fastener and the
SLIDE-TABLE assembly. What is the solution? Answer: Utilize the
second set of MGPRod M6 holes, named MountHoles.

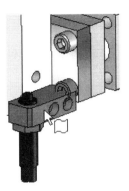

Activity: Editing Mates and Redefining Components

Suppress the last Coincident Mate.
220) Right-click **Coincident** from the
FeatureManager as illustrated.

221) Click **Suppress**.

Redefine the Concentric Mate as illustrated.
222) Right-click **Concentric** from the
FeatureManager.

223) Click **Replace Mate Entities**. The Mated
Entities PropertyManager is displayed.

224) Click the **Face of GUIDE-CYLINDER** from
the Mate Entities box.

225) Click the **PLATE-B front bottom hole
face** as illustrated. The SHCS head points
towards PLATE-B. Click the **Flip Mate Alignment** button if
required.

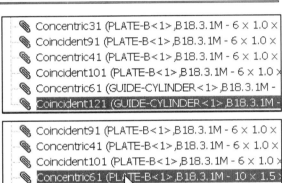

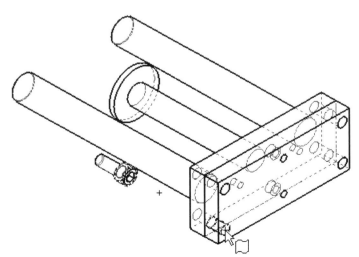

226) Click **OK** 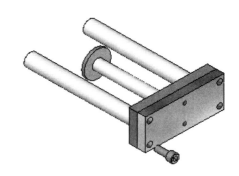 from the Mated Entities PropertyManager.

Move the SHCS into position.
227) Click and drag the **SHCS** in front of PLATE-B as illustrated.

228) Click **Shaded With Edges**.

Modify the last Coincident Mate.
229) Right-click **Coincident** as illustrated.

230) Click **Unsuppress**.

231) Click **Rebuild** from the Main menu.

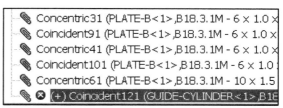

The What's Wrong box displays two errors. The first error is a general error statement about the 2AXIS-TRANSFER Mate group. The 2AXIS-TRANSFER entry displays an error flag in red 2AXIS-TRANSFER. The Mates entry displays an error flag Mates in red.

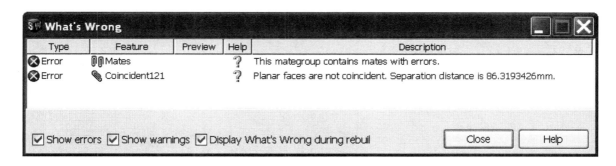

The second error lists the Feature, Coincident and provides a description about the error condition. The separation distance value is based on the SHCS position in the Graphics window. To maintain coincident faces, utilize Replace Mate Entities and select the front PLATE-B face.

232) Click **Close** from the What's Wrong box.

Redefine the Concentric Mate as illustrated.
233) Right-click **Concentric** from the FeatureManager.

234) Click **Replace Mate Entities**. The Mated Entities PropertyManager is displayed. Red error flags are displayed on the Mate Entities.

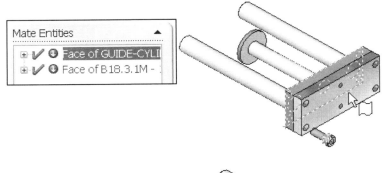

235) Click **Face of GUIDE-CYLINDER** from the Mate Entities box.

236) Click the **GUIDE-CYLINDER front face** as illustrated. Green check marks are displayed on the Mate Entities.

237) Click **OK** from the Mated Entities PropertyManager.

Display an Isometric view.
238) Click **Isometric** view.

Create a Section view.
239) Click the **Front** face of PLATE-B.

240) Click **Section View** .

241) Enter **-8** for Offset Distance.

242) Click **OK** from the Section View PropertyManager.

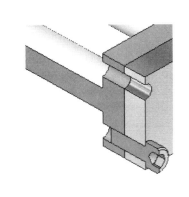

Replace the SHCS.

243) Right-click **B18.3.1M-10x1.5x25 Hex SHCS** from the FeatureManager.

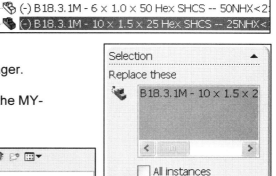

244) Click **Replace Components**. The Replace PropertyManager is displayed.

245) Click **Browse** from the Replace PropertyManager.

246) Select **B18.3.1M-10x1.5x30 Hex SHCS** from the MY-TOOLBOX\SHCS folder.

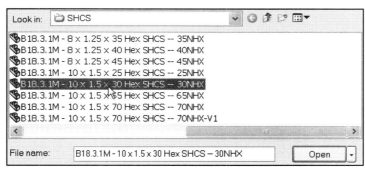

247) Click **Open**.

248) Click **OK** from the Replace PropertyManager.

249) Click **OK** from the Mated Entities PropertyManager

Display the full view.

250) Click **Section View** .

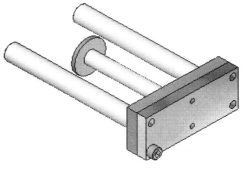

Show the MGPTube.

251) Right-click **MGPTube** from the FeatureManager.

252) Click **Show**.

The Mated Entities PropertyManager displays the Concentric and Coincident references for the Mates.

The SHCS updates in the Graphics window. The FeatureManager displays the new entries with the part icon and Mates entries.

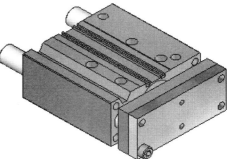

The Mate Entities PropertyManager provides the ability to change Mate selection. Explore additional Mate errors and their recovery in Project 4.

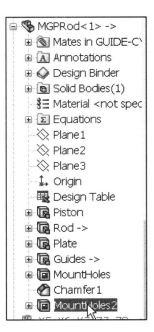

View the dimensions required for a Local Pattern.
253) Expand **GUIDE-CYLINDER** from the FeatureManager.

254) Expand **MGPRod**.

255) Double-click **MountHoles2**. View the dimensions.

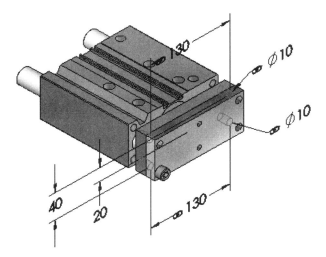

Create a Local Assembly Pattern.
256) Click **B18.3.1M-10x1.5x30Hex SHCS** from the 2AXIS-TRANSFER FeatureManager for the seed component.

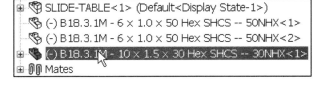

257) Click **Insert**, **Component Pattern**, **Linear Pattern** from the Main menu. The Linear Pattern PropertyManager is displayed.

258) Click the **bottom horizontal edge** for Direction 1. The arrow points to the right

259) Enter **130** for Spacing.

260) Enter **2** for Instances.

261) Click the **left vertical edge** for Direction 2. The arrow points upward.

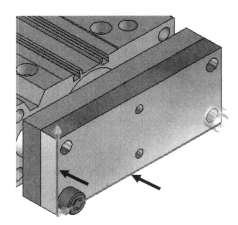

262) Enter **40** for Spacing.

263) Enter **2** for Instances.

264) Click **OK** 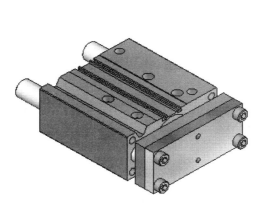 from the Linear Pattern PropertyManager. LocalPattern1 is displayed in the FeatureManager.

Show the SLIDE-TABLE components.

265) Right-click **SLIDE-TABLE** from the FeatureManager.

266) Click **Show**.

267) Expand **SLIDE-TABLE** from the FeatureManager.

268) Click **MXS-A+B<1>**.

269) Hold the **Ctrl** key down.

270) Select **MXSL-BS+BT<2>**.

271) Release the **Ctrl** key.

272) Right-click **Show**.

Rotate the 2AXIS-TRANSFER assembly.

273) Rotate the 2AXIS-TRANSFER assembly to view the **MXSL-BS+BT** as illustrated.

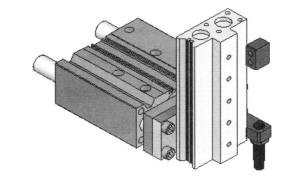

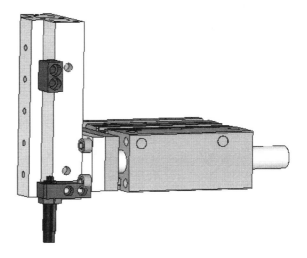

Perform an Interference Detection on the assembly.

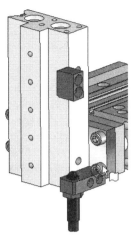

274) Click **Interference Detection** from the Assembly toolbar.

275) Right-click a **position** in the Selected components box.

276) Click **Clear Selections**.

277) Click **B18.3.1M-10x1.5x30 Hex SHCS** from the Graphics window.

278) Click **MXSL-BS+BT** from the Graphics window, as illustrated.

279) Click **Calculate**. The results display the Interference1 volume.

280) Click **OK** from the Interference Detection PropertyManager.

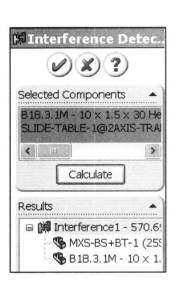

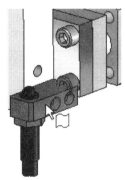

The Interference results in a design decision. Review the four options:

- Modify the positions of the PLATE-B four holes.

- Mount the SLIDE-TABLE to PLATE-B utilizing BodyHole3 and BodyHole4.

- Increase the overall size of PLATE-B and modify the four through holes to countersink or counterbore.

- Locate additional holes on the MGPRod component.

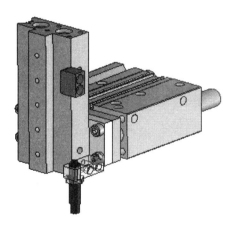

The first option results in modification of a purchased part. The second and third options cause interference with other components. Proceed with the fourth option.

Locate two MountHoles on the MGPRod. Insert two M6 Cbores in PLATE-B with the Holes Wizard.

Delete the M10 SHCS and Local Pattern.

281) Click **B18.3.1M-10x1.5x30 Hex SHCS** from the 2AXIS-TRANSFER FeatureManager.

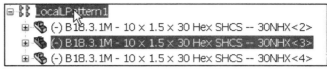

282) Hold the **Ctrl** key down.

283) Click **LocalPattern1** from the FeatureManager.

284) Release the **Ctrl** key.

285) Press the **Delete key**.

286) Click **Yes to All** to delete the dependent Mates.

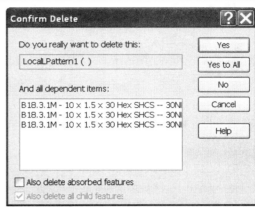

Hide the SLIDE-TABLE and the GUIDE-CYLINDER/MGPTube.

287) Click **SLIDE-TABLE** from the FeatureManager.

288) Hold the **Ctrl** key down.

289) Click **GUIDE-CYLINDER/MGPTube** from the FeatureManager.

290) Release the **Ctrl** key.

291) Right-click **Hide**.

292) Hide the remaining **B18.3.1M-10x1.5x30 Hex SHCS** as illustrated.

293) Click **Hidden Lines Visible**.

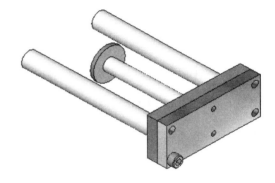

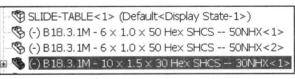

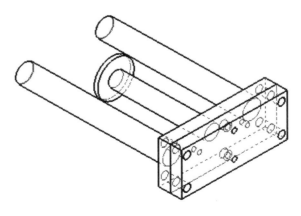

Edit PLATE-B In-Context of the 2AXIS-TRANSFER assembly.

294) Right-click **PLATE-B** from the FeatureManager.

295) Click **Edit Part**. The PLATE-B part name is displayed in blue.

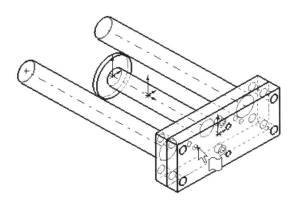

Display Temporary Axes.
296) Click **View**, **Temporary Axes** from the Main menu.

Display the Origins.
297) Click **View**, **Origins** from the Main menu.

Insert an M6 Cbore. Use the Hole Wizard.
298) Click the **PLATE-B face** to the left of the Origin.

Hole
299) Click **Hole Wizard** Wizard from the FeatureManager.

300) Click **Countbore** for Hole Specification.

301) Select **Ansi Metric** for Standard.

302) Select **Socket Head Cap Screw** for Type.

303) Select **M6** for Size.

304) Select **Through All** for End Condition.

305) Click the **Positions** tab.

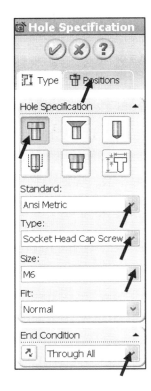

Position the second M6 hole center point.
306) Click **Right** view.

307) Click a **position** to the right of the Origin.

308) Right-click **Select**.

There are two methods to reference the center point of a Hole Wizard hole or Circle Sketch tool. The first method is to "wake up" the center point of an existing hole by dragging the mouse pointer over circular geometry.

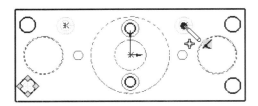

A Coincident relationship is inferred. This method requires that the referenced circular geometry and the new center point are on the same plane or face.

The second method utilizes the Temporary axis of an existing hole and the new center point. Work in an Isometric view to display the Temporary axis and the center point. Utilize this method in the next step.

Select the Axis filter.
309) Click **Filter Axes**.

Add a Coincident relation to the left Cbore.

310) Click the **left MGPRod/MountHole Temporary Axis**.

311) Click **Clear All Filters**.

312) Hold the **Ctrl** key down.

313) Select the **left Cbore center point**.

314) Release the **Ctrl** key.

315) Click **Coincident** from the Add Relations box. The hole is fully defined.

316) Click **OK** ✅ from the Properties PropertyManager.

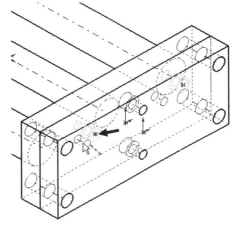

Add a Coincident relation to the right Cbore.

317) Click **Filter Axes**.

318) Click the **right MGPRod/MountHole Temporary Axis.**

319) Click **Clear All Filters**. Hold the **Ctrl** key down.

320) Click the **right Cbore center point**.

321) Release the **Ctrl** key.

322) Click **Coincident** from the Add Relations box. The hole is fully defined.

323) Click **OK** ✅ from the Properties PropertyManager.

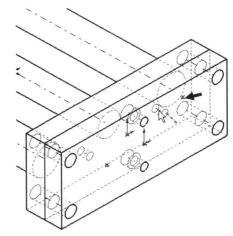

Return to the 2AXIS-TRANSFER assembly.

324) Click **OK** 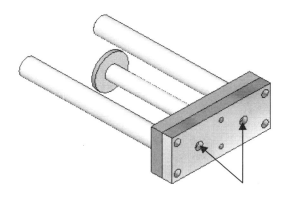 from the Hole Position
PropertyManager.

325) Click **Shaded With Edges**.

326) Right-click **2AXIS-TRANSFER** from the
FeatureManager.

327) Click **Edit Assembly**.

328) Deactivite the **Origins** and **Temporary Axis**.

Save the 2AXIS-TRANSFER assembly.
329) Click **Save**.

Size and insert two M6 SHCSs. This action is
an exercise at the end of the project. Utilize
the four outside mounting holes in a different
assembly.

If required, suppress the SHCSs.
330) Click **B18.3.1M – 6 x 1.0 x 50 Hex SHCS
<1>** from the FeatureManager.

331) Hold the **Ctrl** key down.

332) Click **B18.3.1M – 6 x 1.0 x 50 Hex
SHCS <2>** from the FeatureManager.

333) Release the **Ctrl** key.

334) Right-click **Suppress**.

Display the Hidden components.
335) Display the **hidden components** as
illustrated.

336) Display an **Isometric** view.

Save the model.
337) Click **Save**.

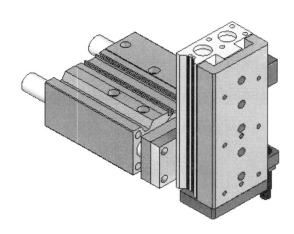

Redefine External References

External references defined in the context of an assembly become out of context when the referenced geometry is either deleted or not loaded into memory.

The company has instituted a policy. Utilize InPlace Mates and External references when required in the initial design phase of an assembly. Redefine all InPlace Mates and External part references before the assemblies, parts, and drawings are released to manufacturing.

PLATE-B requires that the GUIDE-CYLINDER be loaded into memory. How can a component developed In-Context of an assembly be modified for the independent Bottom-Up design assembly modeling approach? Answer: Redefine all External references. Delete all InPlace Mates. Add dimensions and relations to fully define the PLATE-B sketches. Insert Mates to constrain PLATE-B in the 2-AXIS TRANSFER assembly.

The Lock All command protects the part. New references are created when the part is locked. Existing references are not updated.

PLATE-B FeatureManager lists the locked references with an "*" symbol, after the part name, feature, and or sketch.

Redefine External references with a systematic approach. Review both the feature and the sketch. Start with Sketch1 of the Extrude1 feature. Review geometric relations with Display/Delete Relations. Delete external references. Redefine design intent such as symmetry, dimensions, and geometric relations. Work through the FeatureManager until all external references developed In-Context of an assembly are redefined.

Sketch relation symbols indicate the geometric relations added to a sketch. Check the View, Sketch Entities option to display sketch relations symbols in the sketch. The On Entity ⊞ icon is displayed for External references in the Sketch.

Relations	Icons
Horizontal	
Perpendicular	
Parallel	
Horizontal and tangent	
Horizontal and coincident	
Vertical, horizontal, intersection, and tangent	
Horizontal, vertical, and equal	
Concentric	
Horizontal	

In the next activity you will define relations and dimensions. There are two additional Sketch tools that assist you in redefining a sketch.

- Fix.

- Autodimension.

A Fix relation results in the size and location of the selected entities without having to add dimensions or other relations.

These entities cannot be moved or changed. As easy and tempting as this action may sound, the Fix relation can lead to headaches later on when you want to make a change to a dimension. There are no dimensions to double-click and modify. Therefore, use the Fix relation tool appropriately and sparingly.

The Autodimension tool in the Dimensions/Relations toolbar automatically dimensions sketches and drawings.

Select the dimensioning Scheme option: Chain, Baseline, or Ordinate. Select a reference for the Horizontal Dimensions and Vertical Dimensions.

The Autodimension tool takes into account the defined geometric relations.

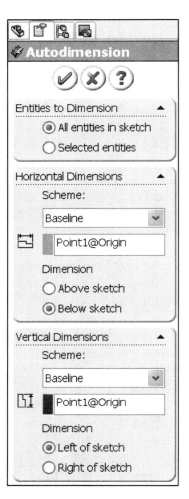

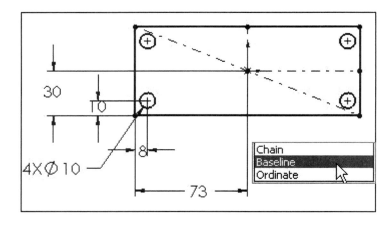

Activity: Redefine External References

Redefine the PLATE-B references.

338) Right-click **PLATE-B** from the 2AXIS-TRANSFER FeatureManager.

339) Click **List External Refs**. The features and sketches referenced from the 2AXIS-TRANSFER/PLATE-B are displayed.

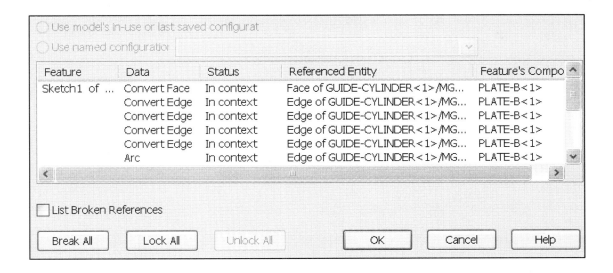

340) Lock all GUIDE-CYLINDER assembly references. Click the **Lock All** button.

341) Click **OK**. The warning message is displayed, "All external references for the model, PLATE-B will be locked. You will not be able to add any new external references until you unlock the existing references."

342) Click **OK**. The "->∗" symbol is displayed next to the part name, PLATE-B in the FeatureManager. PLATE-B contains External references that are locked.

Open the PLATE-B part.

343) Right-click **PLATE-B** from the 2AXIS-TRANSFER FeatureManager.

344) Click **Open Part**. PLATE-B is displayed in the Graphics window.

345) Click **Rebuild**.

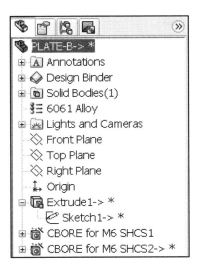

Delete the Sketch1 External references.
346) Double-click **Extrude1** from the FeatureManager.

347) Right-click **Sketch1**.

348) Click **Edit Sketch**.

Delete the Locked references.
349) Right-click **Display/Delete Relations**. Delete the 8 On Edge references. The "*" symbol indicates the Lock All command was activated.

350) Click **Delete All** from the Relations box.

351) Click **OK** 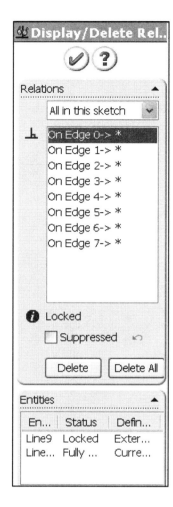 from the Display/Delete Relations PropertyManager.

The On Entity ▦ symbol indicates the Sketch entities with External references.

Redefine the Geometry relations and dimensions.
352) Click **Centerline** Centerl... from the Sketch toolbar.

353) Sketch a **diagonal centerline** between the upper left corner and the lower right corner.

354) Click **View**, **Sketch Relations** from the Main menu.

Add a Midpoint relation.
355) Right-click **Select**.

356) Click the **Centerline**.

357) Hold the **Ctrl** key down.

358) Click the **Origin**.

359) Release the **Ctrl** key.

360) Click **Midpoint** from the Add Relations box.

361) Click **OK** from the Properties PropertyManager.

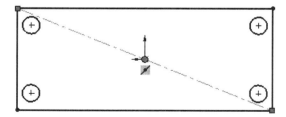

Add a Horizontal relation.
362) Click the **top horizontal** line. Hold the **Ctrl** key down.

363) Click the **bottom horizontal line**. Release the **Ctrl** key.

364) Click **Horizontal**.

365) Click **OK** 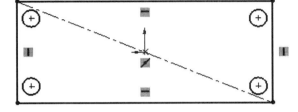 from the Properties PropertyManager.

Add a Vertical relation.
366) Click the **right vertical** line. Hold the **Ctrl** key down.

367) Click the **left vertical** line. Release the **Ctrl** key.

368) Click **Vertical**. Click **OK** from the Properties PropertyManager.

Add dimensions.

369) Click **Smart Dimension** Smart Dimens... from the Sketch toolbar.

370) Click the **right vertical** line.

371) Drag the vertical dimension **60** to the right of the profile. Click ✔.

372) Click the **bottom horizontal** line.

373) Drag the horizontal dimension **146** below the profile.

374) Click ✔.

375) Click **OK** 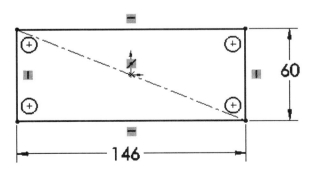 from the Dimension PropertyManager. The rectangular sketch is fully defined and is displayed in black. The four circles are undefined and are displayed in blue.

376) Click **View**. Uncheck **Sketch Relations** from the Main menu.

Sketch the Construction geometry.

377) Click **Centerline** Centerl... from the Sketch toolbar.

378) Sketch a **horizontal centerline** from the Origin to the midpoint of the right vertical line.

379) Sketch a **vertical centerline** from the Origin to the midpoint of the top horizontal line.

Add an Equal relation to the four circles.
380) Right-click **Select**.

381) Click the **circumference** of the upper right circle.

382) Hold the **Ctrl** key down. Click the **circumference** of the remaining three circles.

383) Release the **Ctrl** key.

384) Click **Equal**.

385) Click **OK** ✅ from the Properties PropertyManager.

Add a Symmetric relationship to the top right and bottom right circles.
386) Click the **horizontal centerline**.

387) Hold the **Ctrl** key down. Click the **top right circle**.

388) Click the **bottom right circle**. Release the **Ctrl** key.

389) Click **Symmetric**. Click **OK** ✅ from the Properties PropertyManager.

Add a Symmetric relationship between the top right circle and the top left circle.
390) Click the **vertical centerline**.

391) Hold the **Ctrl** key down. Click the **top right circle**.

392) Click the **top left circle**. Release the **Ctrl** key.

393) Click **Symmetric**. Click **OK** ✅ from the Properties PropertyManager.

Add a Symmetric relationship between the top left circle and the bottom left circle.

394) Click the **horizontal centerline**. Hold the **Ctrl** key down.

395) Click the **top left circle**. Click the **bottom left circle**.

396) Release the **Ctrl** key. Click **Symmetric**.

397) Click **OK** ✅ Properties PropertyManager.

Add dimensions.

398) Click **Smart Dimensions** Smart Dimens….

399) Click the **center points** of the two top circles.

400) Drag the dimension **130** above the profile. Click ✔.

401) Click the **center points** of the two right circles. Drag the dimension **40** to the right of the profile. Click ✔.

402) Click the **circumference** of the top right circle. Drag the diameter **10** off the profile.

403) Click ✔. Click **OK** ✅ from the Dimension PropertyManager. The sketch is fully defined and is displayed in black. Click **Exit Sketch**. Click **Rebuild**.

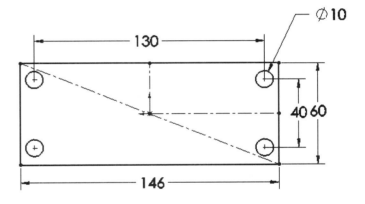

💡 Color indicates that a sketch is under defined (blue), fully defined (black) or over defined (red). The status of a sketch is displayed in the lower right corner of the Graphics window.

The External references are deleted from Extrude1 and Sketch1. Sketch1 is fully defined in the FeatureManager. The In-Context locked "->*" symbol is removed.

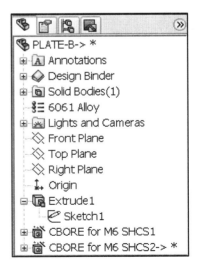

Redefine the CBORE for M6 SHCS2.

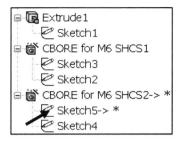

404) Expand **CBORE for M6 SHCS2** from the FeatureManager.

405) Right-click **Sketch5->***.

406) Click **Edit Sketch**.

407) Right-click **Display/Delete Relations**.

408) Delete the locked **Coincident0->*** and **Coincident1->*** relations.

409) Click **Delete All**.

410) Click **OK** ✅ from the PropertyManager.

Sketch a vertical centerline.
411) Sketch a **vertical centerline** from the Origin to the midpoint of the top horizontal line as illustrated.

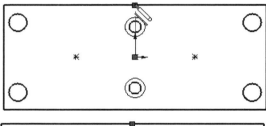

Add a Symmetric relation.
412) Right-click **Select**. Click the **left center point**. Hold the **Ctrl** key down.

413) Click the **right center point**. Click the **centerline**. Release the **Ctrl** key.

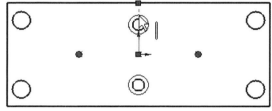

414) Click **Symmetric**. Click **OK** ✅ from the Properties PropertyManager.

Add a Horizontal relation.
415) Click the **Origin**. Hold the **Ctrl** key down.

416) Click the **two center points**. Release the **Ctrl** key.

417) Click **Horizontal**. Click **OK** ✅ from the Properties PropertyManager.

Add dimension.

418) Click **Smart Dimension** Smart Dimens….

419) Click the **two center points**.

420) Drag the dimension **66** above the top horizontal line.

421) Click .

422) Click **OK** 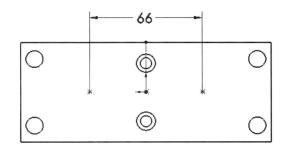. The center points are fully
defined. The External references for PLATE-
B are redefined.

Close the Sketch.

423) Click **Exit Sketch** Exit Sketch .

Save PLATE-B.
424) Click **Save**.

Insert PLATE-B into the plates folder.
425) Click and drag the **PLATE-B** part
icon into the plates folder. If
required, Pin the Design Library.

426) Click **Save**.

Note: Utilize PLATE-B in other
assemblies. PLATE-B contains no
External references or InPlace
Mates.

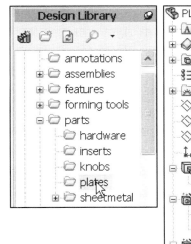

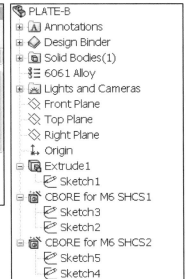

Return to the 2AXIS-TRANSFER assembly.
427) Click **Window**, **2AXIS-TRANSFER** from the
Main menu.

428) Click **Yes** to update the models.

Find the InPlace Mate with the Go To command.
429) Right-click **2AXIS-TRANSFER** from the
FeatureManager.

430) Click **Go To**. Enter **InPlace1**.

431) Click **Find Next**. The Mate, InPlace1 is
found in the FeatureManager.

432) Click **Close**.

433) Right-click **InPlace1** from the
FeatureManager as illustrated.

434) Click **Delete**.

435) Click **Yes** to confirm delete.

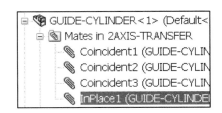

436) Right-click **2AXIS-TRANSFER icon** from the FeatureManager.

437) Click **Go To**.

438) Click **Find Next**. No other InPlace Mates are found. Click **Close**.

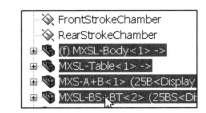

Hide components.
439) Hide the **following components** as illustrated.

PLATE-B is free to translate and rotate. Create three new Smart Mates to fully define PLATE-B in the 2AXIS-TRANSFER assembly.

Move PLATE-B.
440) Click and drag **PLATE-B** in the Graphics window to create a gap between the GUIDE-CYLINDER assembly and the PLATE-B part as illustrated.

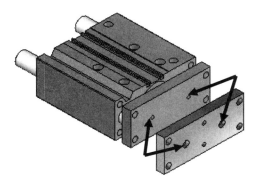

Create the first Concentric SmartMate.
441) Hold the **Alt** key down.

442) Drag the **PLATE-B left hole face** to the GUIDE-CYLINDER left Cbore face. The Coincident\Concentric icon is displayed.

443) Release the **Alt** key. Concentric is selected by default.

444) Click ✔.

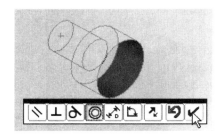

Create the second Concentric SmartMate.
445) Hold the **Alt** key down.

446) Drag the **PLATE-B right hole face** to the GUIDE-CYLINDER right Cbore face. The Coincident\Concentric icon is displayed.

447) Release the **Alt** key. Concentric is selected by default.

448) Click ✔.

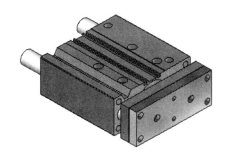

Create the first Coincident SmartMate.
449) Hold the **Alt** key down.

450) Drag the **PLATE-B back face** to the GUIDE-CYLINDER face. The Coincident icon is displayed.

451) Release the **Alt** key. Coincident is selected by default.

452) Click ✔.

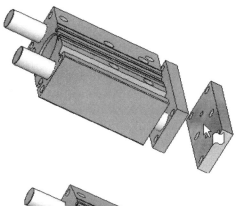

View dependent InPlace Mates and External references.
453) Right-click **2AXIS-TRANSFER** from the FeatureManager.

454) Click **Tree Display**.

455) Check **View Mates and Dependencies**. The PLATE-B part contains no InPlace Mates or External references. Search for other InPlace Mates. No other InPlace Mates exist. Note: The Go To option also identifies InPlace Mates.

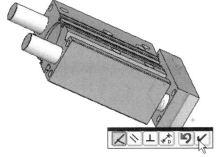

Display the SLIDE-TABLE assembly.
456) Show **MXSL-BODY**, **MXSL-Table**, **MXS-A+B**, and **MXSL-BS+BT**.

457) Click **Show**.

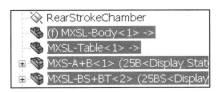

Check for Interference.
458) Click **PLATE-B** from the Graphics window.

Interfer...
459) Click **Interference Detection** Detection from the Assembly toolbar.

460) Click **SLIDE-TABLE/MXS-BS-BT** from the Graphics window.

461) Click **Calculate**. There are No Interferences.

462) Click OK  from the Interference Detection PropertyManager.

Display an Isometric view.
463) Click **Isometric** view.

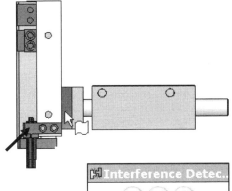

Save the 2AXIS-TRANSFER assembly.
464) Click **Save**.

The 2AXIS-TRANSFER assembly is complete. The Default configuration displays the
GUIDE-CYLINDER assembly, the PLATE-B part, and the SLIDE-TABLE assembly.
All fasteners are suppressed.

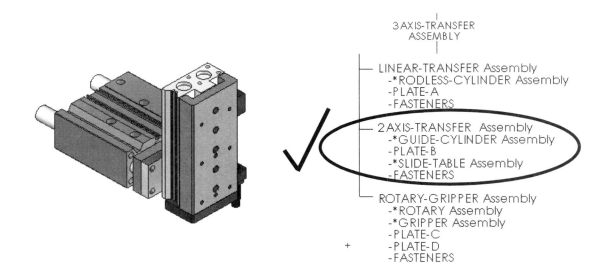

Develop the 2AXIS-TRANSFER configurations. Utilize assembly configurations to
control visualization of components, Suppress/Resolve states, Color, Mate characteristics,
sub-assembly configurations, and part configurations.

Explore the Fastener configuration in the project exercises. The Fastener Configuration
contains Resolved and Visible SHCSs.

☼ Organize hardware components. Create folders for fasteners in an assembly. Utilize
assembly configuration to control the Suppress state and Display state of fasteners,
washers, nuts, and other hardware.

___

Configurations and Design Tables

Configurations create multiple variations of a part or assembly. A Design Table is an
Excel spreadsheet utilized to create multiple configurations of a part or assembly.

Utilize the ConfigurationManager to create two configurations for the GUIDE-
CYLINDER and SLIDE-TABLE.

Utilize a Design Table to combine the GUIDE-CYLINDER configurations and the
SLIDE-TABLE configurations to create the 2AXIS-TRANSFER configurations.

The GUIDE-CYLINDER configurations require a Distance Mate between the GUIDE-CYLINDER/MGPTube part and the GUIDE-CYLINDER/MGPRod part. Review the existing Mates. Modify the existing Coincident Mate to a Distance Mate.

The GUIDE-CYLINDER assembly is in the Default configuration. The current configuration of the GUIDE-CYLINDER assembly is named Default. The Distance Mate value equals 0.

Create two GUIDE-CYLINDER configurations:

- Normal.

- Extended.

The GUIDE-CYLINDER assembly is in the Normal configuration when the Distance Mate value equals 0. The GUIDE-CYLINDER is in the Extended configuration when the Distance Mate value equals 100.

Default   Normal   Extended

GUIDE-CYLINDER Configurations

The SLIDE-TABLE requires a Distance Mate between the SLIDE-TABLE/MXSL-Body part and SLIDE-TABLE/MXSL-Table part. Modify the existing Coincident Mate to a Distance Mate.

The SLIDE-TABLE assembly is in the Default configuration. The current configuration of the SLIDE-TABLE assembly is named Default. The Distance Mate is 0.

Create two SLIDE-TABLE configurations:

- Normal.

- Extended.

The SLIDE-TABLE assembly is in the Normal configuration when the Distance Mate is 0.

The SLIDE-TABLE assembly is in the Extended configuration when the Distance Mate is 100.

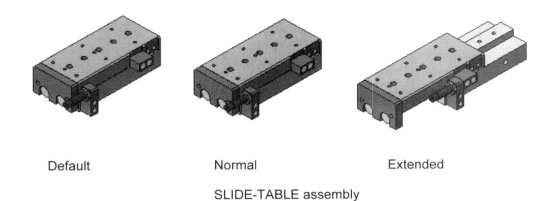

Default   Normal   Extended

SLIDE-TABLE assembly

Utilize a Design Table to combine the GUIDE-CYLINDER Normal configuration and the GUIDE-CYLINDER Extended configuration with the SLIDE-TABLE Normal configuration and the SLIDE-TABLE Extended configuration.

Create four 2AXIS-TRANSFER configurations: Normal-Normal, Normal-Extended, Extended-Normal, and Extended-Extended.

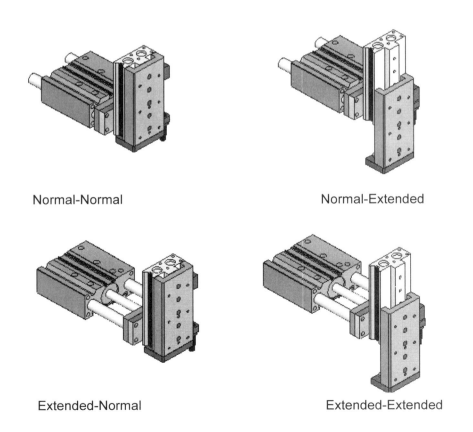

Normal-Normal   Normal-Extended

Extended-Normal   Extended-Extended

In the 2AXIS-TRANSFER configurations, the configuration name of the GUIDE-CYLINDER assembly is listed first followed by the configuration name of the SLIDE-TABLE assembly. SHCS are suppressed in the Normal-Normal, Normal-Extended, Extended-Normal, and Extended-Extended configurations.

Develop the Fastener configuration in the project exercises. SHCSs are resolved in the Fastener configuration.

Before creating new configurations with models obtained from other sources, review Design Table properties. The manufacture's Design Table lists the defined properties in Row 2. Example: The Custom Property $PRP@Stroke.

Avoid problems with configurations. Utilize unique names in your configurations that do not conflict with names selected by the manufacturer.

The 2AXIS-TRANSFER assembly requires the Stroke distance to be controlled through 2 positions. Rename the Distance Mate to Distance-Stroke.

The new MGPM12-10 GUIDE-CYLINDER-12MM, downloaded in Project 1, contains only the individual configuration information.

The FeatureManager contains no Design Table. Utilize the ConfigurationManager, Custom Properties, Configuration Specific option to list properties defined in an assembly.

Activity: GUIDE-CYLINDER Configurations and Design Tables

Open the GUIDE-CYLINDER.

465) Right-click **GUIDE-CYLINDER** from the 2AXIS-TRANSFER FeatureManager.

466) Click **Open Assembly**. The GUIDE-CYLINDER is displayed in the Graphics window.

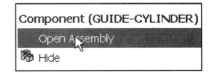

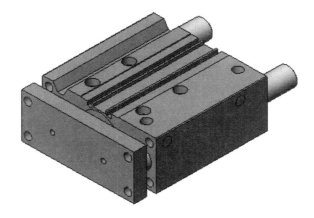

Locate and Redefine the GUIDE-CYLINDER
Coincident Mate.

467) Expand **MateGroup1**.

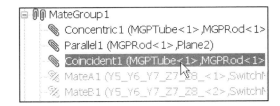

468) Click **Coincident1** as illustrated. The
Coincident1 Mate is between the face of the
MGPTube part and the face of the MGPRod
part.

469) Right-click **Edit Feature**.

470) Click **Distance** from the Standard Mates box.
The Distance value is 0.

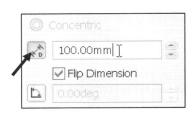

471) Enter **100**.

472) Click **OK** ✅ from the Distance1
PropertyManager.

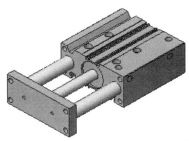

473) Click OK ✅ from the Mate PropertyManager.

Rename the Distance Mate.

474) Rename the Distance1 Mate to **Distance-
Stroke**.

475) Double-click **Distance-Stroke**.

476) Drag the **100** dimension text off the profile.

Modify the Distance.

477) Double-click the **100** dimension text.

478) Enter **0**.

479) Click **Rebuild**.

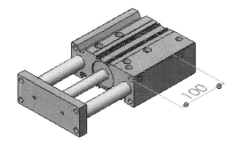

480) Click ✔.

481) Click **OK** ✅ from the Distance
PropertyManager. The Default
configuration value is 0 for the
Distance Mate named Stroke.

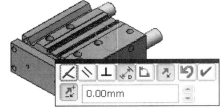

Create the GUIDE-CYLINDER Normal and
Extended Configurations.

482) Drag the **Split bar** downward to
divide the FeatureManager and the
Configuration Manager.

483) Click the **ConfigurationManager**
icon.

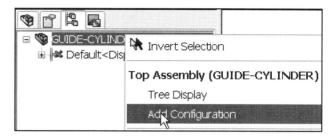

484) Right-click **GUIDE-CYLINDER
Configuration(s)**.

485) Click **Add Configuration**. The Add
Configuration PropertyManager is
displayed.

486) Enter **Normal** for Configuration name.

487) Enter **GUIDE-CYLINDER Normal
configuration** for Description.

488) Enter **Distance-Stroke Value
= 0** for Comment.

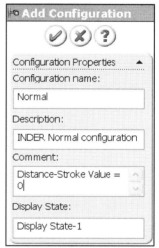

489) Click **OK** 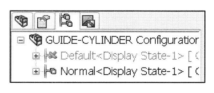 from the Add
Configuration
PropertyManager. The
Normal configuration is
currently the same as the
Default configuration.

490) Right-click **GUIDE-
CYLINDER
Configuration(s).**

491) Click **Add Configuration**.

492) Enter **Extended** for
Configuration Name. Enter
**GUIDE-CYLINDER
Extended configuration** for
Description.

493) Enter **Distance-Stroke Value = 100**
for Comment.

494) Click **OK** from the Add
Configuration PropertyManager.

Extended [GUIDE-CYLINDER] is the current configuration.

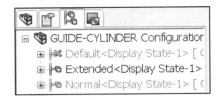

495) Click the **FeatureManager** icon. The configuration name, (Extended) is displayed after the GUIDE-CYLINDER assembly name.

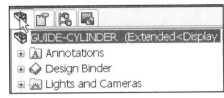

Enter informative comments for future use that explain Mates, parameters, and design intent. Team members on the next project require helpful comments on the GUIDE-ROD assembly.

Modify the Stroke value.
496) Double-click **Distance-Stroke** from MateGroup1.

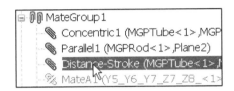

497) Double-click **0**.

498) Enter **100**.

499) Click **This Configuration** from the drop down list.

500) Click **Rebuild**.

501) Click ✔.

502) Click **OK** ✅ from the Dimension PropertyManager.

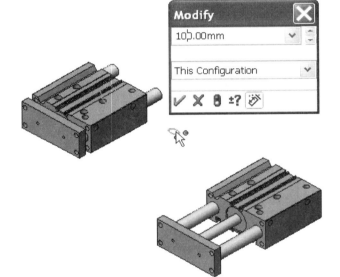

Test the configurations.
503) Click the **ConfigurationManager** icon.

504) Double-click **Normal configuration** and **Extended configuration**. View the configuration.

505) Double click the **Default** configuration. The Default configuration displays the Excel icon, displayed in green.

Return to the assembly FeatureManager.
506) Click the **FeatureManager** icon.

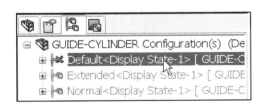

Save the GUIDE-CYLINDER assembly.
507) Click **Save**.

Return to the 2AXIS-TRANSFER assembly.
508) Open the **2AXIS-TRANSFER** assembly.

Locate and Redefine the SLIDE-TABLE Mate.
509) Right-click **SLIDE-TABLE** from the 2AXIS-TRANSFER
     assembly FeatureManager.

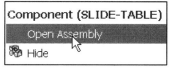

510) Click **Open Assembly**.

511) Expand **MateGroup1**.

512) Click **Coincident6** Mate as illustrated.

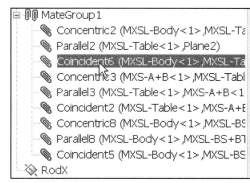

513) Right-click **Edit Feature**.

514) Click **Distance**.

515) Enter **100** for Distance value.

516) Click **OK** ![OK] from the Distance1
     PropertyManager. Click **OK** ![OK] from the Mate
     PropertyManager.

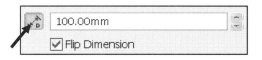

Rename the Distance Mate.
517) Rename **Distance1** to **Distance-Stroke**.

518) Double-click **Distance-Stroke**.

519) Drag the **100** dimension text off
     the profile.

520) Double-click **100**.

521) Enter **0**. Click **Rebuild**.

522) Click ✔.

523) Click **OK** ![OK] from the Distance
     PropertyManager.

The Distance-Stroke value equals 0
for the Default configuration.

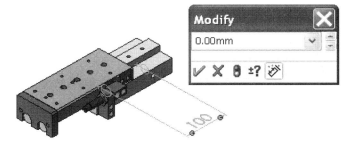

Create the SLIDE-TABLE Normal and Extended Configurations.

524) Drag the **Split bar** downward to divide the FeatureManager and ConfigurationManager.

525) Click the **ConfigurationManager** icon.

526) Right-click **SLIDE-TABLE Configuration(s)**.

527) Click **Add Configuration**. The Add Configuration PropertyManager is displayed.

528) Enter **Normal** for Configuration name.

529) Enter **SLIDE-TABLE Normal** for Description.

530) Enter **Distance-Stroke = 0** for Comment.

531) Click **OK**  from the Add Configuration PropertyManager. Currently, the Normal Configuration is the same as the Default Configuration.

532) Right-click **SLIDE-TABLE Configuration(s)**.

533) Click **Add Configuration**.

534) Enter **Extended** for Configuration Name.

535) Enter **SLIDE-TABLE Extended** for Description.

536) Enter **Distance-Stroke = 100** for Comment.

537) Click **OK**  from the Add Configuration PropertyManager. Extended [SLIDE-TABLE] is the current configuration.

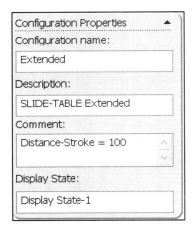

Return to the assembly FeatureManager.
538) Click the **FeatureManager** icon.

The configuration name (Extended) is displayed after the SLIDE-TABLE name.

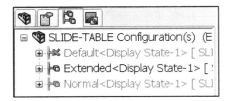

Modify the Distance-Stroke value.
539) Expand **MateGroup1**.

540) Double-click **Distance-Stroke**.

541) Double-click **0**.

542) Enter **100**.

543) Click **This Configuration** from the drop down list.

544) Click **Rebuild**.

545) Click ✓.

546) Click **OK** 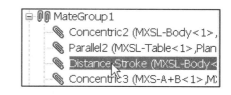 from the Dimension PropertyManager.

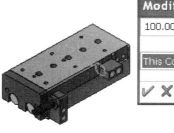

Test the Configurations.
547) Double-click **Normal** configuration and **Extended** configuration. View the configurations.

548) Double-click **Default** configuration.

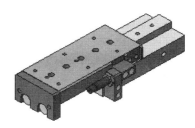

Return to the assembly FeatureManager.
549) Click the **FeatureManager** icon.

Save the SLIDE-TABLE assembly in the Default configuration.
550) Click **Save**.

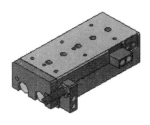

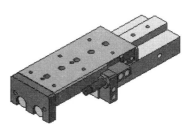

Default   Normal   Extended

SLIDE-TABLE assembly

Return to the 2AXIS-TRANSFER assembly.

551) Click **Window**, **2AXIS-TRANSFER** from the Main menu. The GUIDE-CYLINDER(Default) and SLIDE-TABLE (Default) are the current configurations in the 2AXIS-TRANSFER assembly FeatureManager. The SHCSs are displayed in light gray.

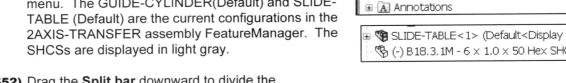

552) Drag the **Split bar** downward to divide the FeatureManager and Configuration Manager.

Design Table and 2AXIS-TRANSFER Configurations

A Design Table is an Excel spreadsheet utilized to create configurations and control parameters in a part or assembly. Insert a Design Table to control the Normal and Extended configurations for the GUIDE-CYLINDER and SLIDE-TABLE assemblies.

The 2AXIS-TRANSFER Design Table controls the parameters $Configuration and $STATE for each component in the assembly. The $Configuration parameter is the configuration name. The $STATE parameter is the Suppressed/Resolved state of a component in the assembly. Design Tables utilizing additional parameters at the part and assembly level will be utilized in Project 4.

The model name associated with the Design Table is located in Cell A1. Define the 2AXIS-TRANSFER configuration names in the first column of an Excel spreadsheet. Define the parameters in the second row. Enter values in the Cells that correspond to the configuration name and the parameter name. Leave Cell A2 blank.

Entering individual configurations with the ConfigurationManager is a cumbersome task. Avoid spelling issues. Utilize the Auto-create option to insert SHCS $STATE parameters into the Design Table.

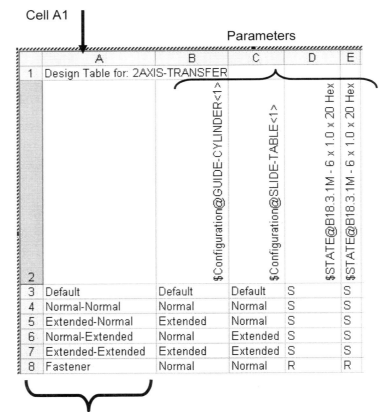

2AXIS-TRANSFER configuration names

Additional part and assembly parameters control Dimensions, Color, and Comments. All parameters begin with a $, except Dimension.

Enter parameters carefully. The "$", "@" and "<>" symbol format needs to match exactly for the result to be correct in the BOM.

The Summary of Design Table Parameters is as follows:

Summary of Design Table Parameters:		
Parameter Syntax (Header Cell)	**Legal Values (Body Cell)**	**Default if Value is Left Blank**
Parts only:		
$configuration@part_name	configuration name	not evaluated
$configuration@<feature_name>	configuration name	not evaluated
Parts and Assemblies:		
$comment	any text string	empty
$part number	any text string	configuration name
$state@feature_name	Suppressed, S Unsuppressed, U	Unsuppressed
dimension@feature	any legal decimal value for the dimension	not evaluated
$parent	parent configuration name	property is undefined
$prp@ property	any text string	property is undefined
$state@equation_number@equations	Suppressed, S Unsuppressed, U	Unsuppressed
$state@lighting_name	Suppressed, S Unsuppressed, U	Unsuppressed
$state@sketch relation@sketch name	Suppressed, S Unsuppressed, U	Unsuppressed
$user_notes	any text string	not evaluated
$color	32-bit integer specifying RGB (red, green, blue) color. See Online Help, color for more info.	zero (black)
Assemblies only:		
$show@component<instance>	Yes, Y No, N	No
$state@component<instance>	Resolved, R, Suppressed, S	Resolved
$configuration@component<instance>	configuration name	Component's "in-use" or last saved configuration. NOTE: If the component uses a derived configuration, and the value is left blank, the configuration used is linked to its parent.

Insert a new Design Table into the 2AXIS-TRANSFER assembly. Insert the configuration names and parameters. The SHCSs are suppressed.

The Design Table PropertyManager is divided into three sections:

- Source.

- Edit Control.

- Options.

Source:

The Blank option inserts an empty Design Table. The designer fills in the parameters.

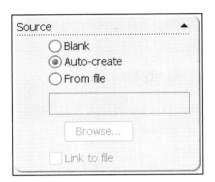

The Auto-create option automatically creates a new Design Table and loads all different configured parameters and values entered in the ConfigurationManager. In an assembly, the Auto-create option loads the $STATE of components into a Design Table.

🔆 Utilize Auto-create with maximum results. The Auto-create option inserts only parameters that are *different*. Example: Create two configurations. The first configuration is the Default. Insert as many parameters into the second configuration. Auto-create will then insert the parameters from the second configuration into the Design Table. The PLATE-D Design Table activity provides an example with multiple parameters.

The From file option utilizes a pre-existing Excel spreadsheet. Browse to locate the spreadsheet. Checking the Link to file check box option means that any changes made in the spreadsheet outside SolidWorks are updated in the model during the next SolidWorks session. If the Allow model edits to update the design table option is checked, the spreadsheet reflects the model changes.

Edit Control:

The Allow model edits to update the design table option results in the Design Table to update when the model changes. Utilize this option in the beginning of the design process to permit changes.

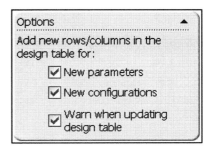

The Block model edits that would update the design table option prohibits any changes that update the Design Table. The GUIDE-CYLINDER Design Table and SLIDE-TABLE Design Table provided by SMC both utilize these options.

Options:

The New parameters option inserts new rows and columns into the Design Table when you add a new parameter to the part/assembly.

The New configurations option inserts new rows and columns into the Design Table when you add a new configuration to the part/assembly.

The Warn when updating design table option produces a warning message that the Design Table will change based on the parameters updated in the part/assembly.

Activity: Design Table and 2AXIS-TRANSFER Configurations

Insert a Design Table.
553) Click **Insert**, **Design Table** from the Main menu.

Select the parameters.
554) Check **Auto-create**.

555) Click **OK**  from the Design Table PropertyManager.

Cell A1 contains the 2AXIS-TRANSFER assembly name. Cell A3 contains the 2AXIS-TRANSFER Default configuration name.

Insert the $Configuration parameters.
556) Click **Cell B2**.

557) Enter **$Configuration@GUIDE-CYLINDER<1>**.

558) Click **Cell C2**.

559) Enter **$Configuration@SLIDE-TABLE<1>**.

Note: If your GUIDE-CYLINDER or SLIDE-TABLE entry in the FeatureManager lists a different instance number in brackets <1>, utilize that number. The component spelling and instance number must match exactly.

560) Copy **Cell A3** to **Cell B3** and **Cell C3**.

Note: Click a position outside the Design Table and you exit EXCEL and return to SolidWorks. To return to the Design Table, right-click Design Table from the FeatureManager. Click Edit Table.

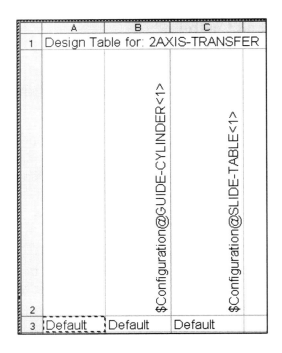

Insert the configuration names.
561) Click **Cell A4**.

562) Enter **Normal-Normal**.

563) Click **Cell A5**.

564) Enter **Extended-Normal**.

565) Click **Cell A6**.

566) Enter **Normal-Extended**.

567) Click **Cell A7**.

568) Enter **Extended-Extended**.

3	Default	Default	Default
4	Normal-Normal		
5	Extended-Normal		
6	Normal-Extended		
7	Extended-Extended		

Resize Column A
569) Position the **mouse pointer** between the A and B Column header. The mouse pointer displays the Resize ⟷ icon.

570) Drag the **mouse pointer** to the right until Cell A7 is completely visible.

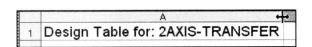

Enter the values for the GUIDE-CYLINDER configurations.
571) Click **Cell B4**. Enter **Normal**.

572) Click **Cell B5**. Enter **Extended**.

573) Click **Cell B6**. Enter **Normal**.

574) Click **Cell B7**. Enter **Extended**.

Enter the values for the SLIDE-TABLE configurations.
575) Click **Cell C4**. Enter **Normal**.

576) Click **Cell C5**. Enter **Normal**.

577) Click **Cell B6**. Enter **Extended**.

578) Click **Cell C7**. Enter **Extended**.

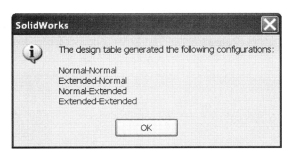

Default	Default	Default
Normal-Normal	Normal	Normal
Extended-Normal	Extended	Normal
Normal-Extended	Normal	Extended
Extended-Extended	Extended	Extended

Build the configurations.
579) Click a **position** inside the SolidWorks Graphics window.

580) Click **OK** to the message: "The design table generated the following configurations:"

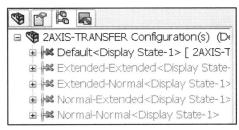

View the configurations.
581) Click the **ConfigurationManager** icon.

582) Double-click **Normal-Normal**, **Normal-Extended**, **Extended-Normal** and **Extended-Extended** to verify the position.

Return to the Default Configuration.
583) Double-click **Default**.

Return to the FeatureManager.
584) Click the **FeatureManager** icon.

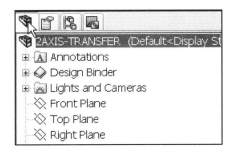

Edit the Design Table.
585) Right-click **Design Table** from FeatureManager.

586) Click **Edit Table**. The Add Rows and Columns dialog box is displayed.

587) Click **Cancel**.

Insert the SHCSs $STATE parameters.
588) Hold the **Ctrl** key down.

589) Select the two **$STATE** entries in the parameters box. Note: If the part is suppressed, then the $STATE parameter is displayed.

590) Click **OK**.

591) Release the **Ctrl** key. The $STATE entries are displayed in Cell D2 and E2. The S value in Cells D3 through E7 indicates the Suppressed State.

Insert the Fastener configuration.
592) Enter **Fastener** in Cell A8.

593) Enter **Normal** in Cell B8 and Cell C8.

594) Enter **R** in Cell D8 and E8. The R value indicates the Resolved State in an assembly.

Update the configurations.
595) Click a **position** inside the Graphics window.

596) Click **OK**.

View the configurations.
597) Click the **ConfigurationManager**.

598) Double-click **Fastener** to verify the unsuppressed SHCSs.

Return to the Default Configuration.
599) Double-click **Default**. Click the **FeatureManager**.

Save the 2AXIS-TRANSFER assembly.
600) Click **Save**.

Close all parts and assemblies.
601) Click **Windows**, **Close All** from the Main menu.

Project Summary

In this project you utilized a Top Down design assembly modeling approach with InPlace Mates and features developed in the context of the 2AXIS-TRANSFER assembly. The 2AXIS-TRANSFER assembly consists of following:

- GUIDE-CYLINDER assembly.

- PLATE-B part.

- SLIDE-TABLE assembly.

- SHCSs parts.

You created the PLATE-B part In-Context of the GUIDE-CYLINDER assembly and SLIDE-TABLE assembly. Interference problems were detected and resolved before any parts were manufactured.

You built configurations for the GUIDE-CYLINDER assembly and the SLIDE-TABLE assembly utilizing the ConfigurationManager. The GUIDE-CYLINDER configurations and SLIDE-TABLE configurations were combined in a Design Table to form the 2AXIS-TRANSFER configurations: Normal-Normal, Normal-Extended, Extended-Normal, and Extended-Extended.

Review the assemblies with your project team leader. Ask if the customer has provided any additional input that would constitute a design change. For now, there are no changes. There will be changes in the future. Planning your assembly and configurations determines your success.

How do you control positions of the ROTARY-GRIPPER assembly? Answer: Utilize configurations in Project 4. Review the questions and exercises before moving on to Project 4.

Questions

1. Describe the two design methods utilized in a Top Down design assembly modeling approach.

2. Define an In-context relation.

3. Describe the procedure to rename a feature, sketch or Mate name.

4. Define an InPlace Mate.

5. True or False. An InPlace Mate cannot be deleted from an assembly.

6. Describe the procedure to create a rectangular sketch centered about the part Origin. The rectangular sketch contains only one vertical and one horizontal dimension.

7. True or False. A Concentric SmartMate is created between two cylindrical faces from the same part.

8. True or False. External references cannot be redefined.

9. Identify the two components that determine the geometric and functional requirements for PLATE-B.

10. How do you redefine a component in an assembly?

11. True or False: External references defined In-context become out of context when the corresponding components are not loaded into memory.

12. Describe the procedure to block updates to a Design Table in the 2AXIS-TRANSFER assembly.

13. The GUIDE-CYLINDER has two configurations. The SLIDE-TABLE has two configurations. Describe the process of combining the GUIDE-CYLINDER configurations and the SLIDE-TABLE configurations to create the 2AXIS-TRANSFER configurations.

14. Identify the following icons in the Assembly toolbar.

a	b	c	d	e	f	g	h	i	j	k	l	m

Exercises

Exercise 3-1: Size and assemble the two SHCSs between PLATE-B and the GUIDE-CYLINDER in the 2AXIS-TRANSFER assembly.

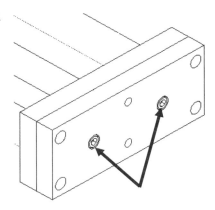

Exercise 3-2: Size and assemble the SHCSs to fasten the PLATE-B part to the SLIDE-TABLE assembly.

Note: You must complete Exercise 3-1 and 3-2 before performing Exercise 3-3.

Exercise 3-3: Modify the Fastener configuration in the 2AXIS-TRANSFER Design Table to include the two SHCSs utilized to assemble PLATE-B to the SLIDE-TABLE assembly.

Create an Exploded view for the 2AXIS-TRANSFER assembly. Hint: Right-click the Fastener Configuration, New Exploded View. Click on a component to Explode. Drag the Triad red axis to position components approximately 1in (25mm) in the Graphics window. Modify the distances between the Explode steps to display the individual components.

Right-click ExplView1 from the ConfigurationManager. Click Animate collapse to display the animation. Select Stop from the Animation Controller.

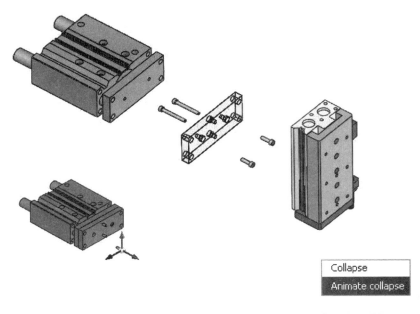

Exercise 3-4: Create two new 2AXIS-TRANSFER Configurations. The first configuration is named MIDDLE. The second configuration is named UPPER.

Redefine the two Concentric Mates between the PLATE-B part and the SLIDE-TABLE assembly. The MIDDLE configuration utilizes BodyThruHole2 and BodyThruHole3. The UPPER configuration utilizes BodyThruHole1 and BodyThruHole2.

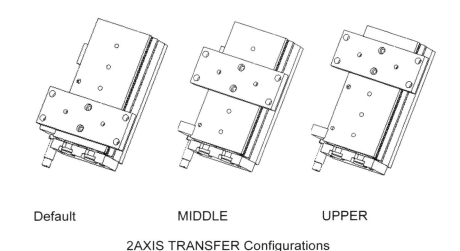

Default   MIDDLE   UPPER

2AXIS TRANSFER Configurations

Exercise 3-4A:

Note: Exercise 3-4A and Exercise 3-4B require your own dimensions. Manually sketch your ideas on paper. Add dimensions. Label each part and each assembly.

The SMALL-BLOCK part translates freely along the SLOTTED-BLOCK part in the SLIDER assembly. The SMALL-BLOCK and SLOTTED-BLOCK are symmetric about the Front Plane. The SLOTTED-BLOCK is fixed to the SLIDER assembly Origin. The SMALL-BLOCK contains a Thru Hole.

Determine the two positions where the SMALL-BLOCK collides with the SLOTTED-BLOCK.

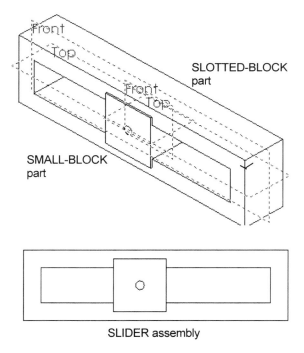

SLOTTED-BLOCK part

SMALL-BLOCK part

SLIDER assembly

Exercise 3-4B:

Create the MECHANISM assembly. The SLIDER assembly is the first component in the MECHANISM assembly.

LINK part

Create the first LINK part. Assemble the LINK part to the SMALL-BLOCK part. The LINK part is free to rotate in the MECHANISM assembly.

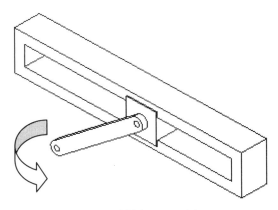

MECHANISM assembly

Create the second LINK as a configuration. Assemble the second LINK configuration to the first LINK part.

Create a PIN part. Assemble a PIN at each LINK Thru Hole.

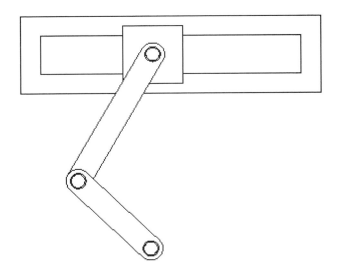

Exercise 3-5: Industry Collaborative exercise.

In Exercise 2-5 you developed the BEARING-SHAFT assembly utilizing a Bottom Up assembly modeling approach. The SHAFT now requires additional BEARINGs for support.

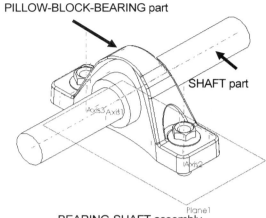

PILLOW-BLOCK-BEARING part

SHAFT part

BEARING-SHAFT assembly

Utilize a Top Down assembly modeling approach to develop the PLATE-BG in context of the BEARING-SHAFT assembly.

With some imported geometry, Top Down design requires a few additional steps. You cannot select faces for a Sketch Plane. Utilize Plane2 for the PLATE-BG Sketch Plane. Sketch a rectangle centered on the Right plane. The overall size supports three BEARINGS.

Utilize the BEARING Slot Cut edges and Convert Entities. Select the Slot Cut lines and check For Construction.

Converted lines from Slot Cut

Open the PLATE-BG part. Utilize the Slot Cut construction lines to complete the profile. Extrude the sketch.

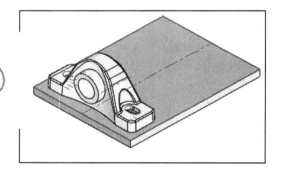

Create a Linear Pattern of Slot Cuts in PLATE-BG. Utilize a derived Component Pattern to complete the assembly.

Note: You can also create the Slot Cut and the Rectangle in the same profile. Utilize the Faces to Pattern option in the PLATE-BG Linear Pattern to create additional Slot Cuts. Select the four inside faces.

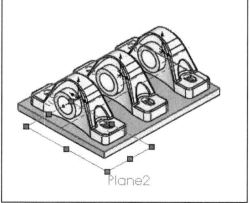

Exercise 3-6: Industry Collaborative exercise.

Read the entire project before you begin.

In Exercise 2-6 you sized and downloaded components from Boston Gear based on the Senior engineer's specifications. You created the SPEED-REDUCER assembly. The SPEED-REDUCER assembly consisted of a 1/2HP MOTOR part, SPEED REDUCER 40:1 assembly and the PLATE-SR part.

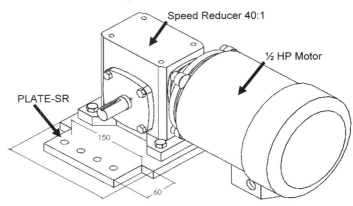

SPEED REDUCER assembly
Models and Images
Courtesy of Boston Gear

The Senior engineer provides a drawing for a new project. You are responsible to create the final MOTOR-GEAR-BOX assembly. The MOTOR-GEAR-BOX assembly consists of purchased components from Boston Gear. The Boston Gear components are available in the ASSEMBLY-SW-FILES-2006/EXERICISE/PROJECT3 file folder. CHANGE GEAR 40 and CHANGE GEAR 60 tooth profiles are simplified.

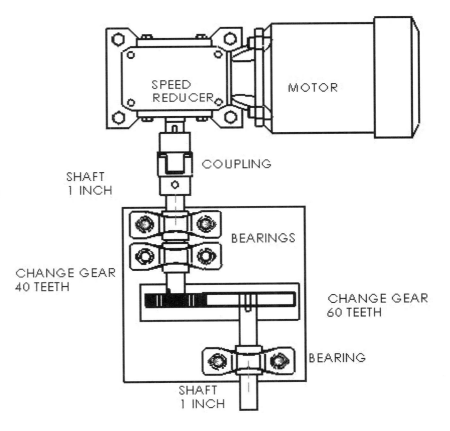

MOTOR-GEAR-BOX assembly
Models and Images Courtesy of Boston Gear

The purchased components are:

QTY:	DESCRIPTION:	FILE NAME:	Boston Gear Part No.:
1	½ HP MOTOR	futf-default-11950.sldprt	FUTF
1	SPEED-REDUCER 40:1	f721-40b5-g-2.sldasm	F721B-40-B5-G
1	COUPLING	fc20_1-default-37402.sldprt	FC20-1
1	CHANGE GEAR 40 Teeth	gd40b-simpletooth.sldprt	GD40B
1	CHANGE GEAR 60 Teeth	gd60b-simpletooth.sldprt	GD60b
2	PILLOW BLOCK BEARING	bg-1in-pillow-block.sldprt	SRP16

You are required to create the following parts:

- SHAFT part (Qty2).
- PLATE-SR40 part.
- PLATE-BEARING part.

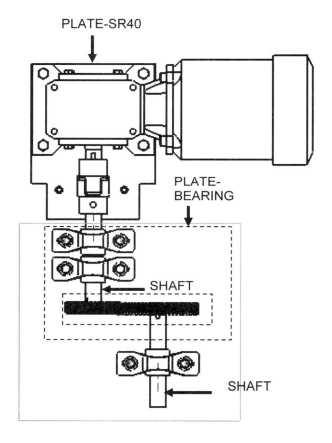

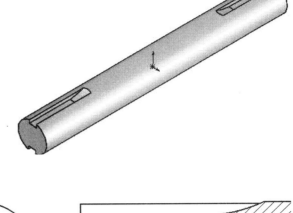

Create the SHAFT part. The SHAFT dimensions are 1″, (25.4mm) diameter by 8″, (203.2mm) length. The SHAFT contains grooves, called keyseats. Approximate the size of the keyseats that correspond to the CHANGE GEAR and COUPLING keyways.

Note: Exact dimensions and tolerance for standard keys, keyways and keyseats for gears and shafts are available in ASME B17.1, ASME B17.2 and the Machinery's Handbook.

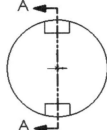

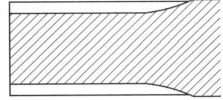

Create the PLATE-SR40 part. Utilize an In-context feature to determine the hole locations from the SPEED-REDUCER.

Create the BEARING-PLATE part. The BEARING-PLATE part contains the Thru Hole locations to fasten the PILLOW BLOCK BEARINGs. Create an Extruded Cut feature in the BEARING-PLATE. Note: Design for CHANGE GEAR clearance.

Simplify the MOTOR-GEAR-BOX assembly. Create three sub-assemblies:

- SPEED-REDUCER40 assembly.

- GEAR40-BEARING assembly.

- GEAR60-BEARING assembly.

GEAR40-BEARING assembly　　　　　　GEAR60-BEARING assembly

View the Axis and Temporary Axis. The
SHAFT part is free to rotate. The GEAR part is
fixed to the SHAFT part. Utilize edges and or
vertices to align the GEAR keyway to the
SHAFT keyway.

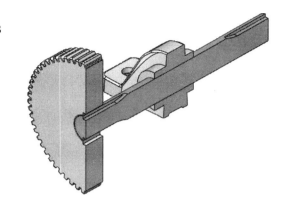

The PILLOW
BLOCK
BEARING part
was imported as an
IGES file.
Reference Planes,
Axes and Sketches
were added.
Utilize the
sketched point and
axis in the middle
of the Slot Cut to
locate the fasteners.

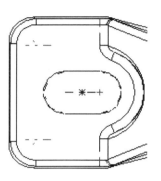

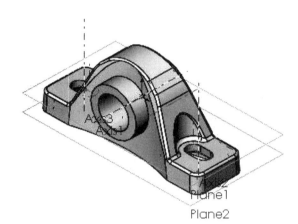

The Pitch Diameter of the
CHANGE-GEAR determines the
horizontal distance between the
SHAFTs. The CHANGE-
GEAR40 Pitch Diameter is 3.333
inch. The CHANGE-GEAR60
Pitch Diameter is 5.000 inch.
The horizontal distance between
the two SHAFTs is
(3.333+5.000)/2 = 4.167 inch
[105.84mm].

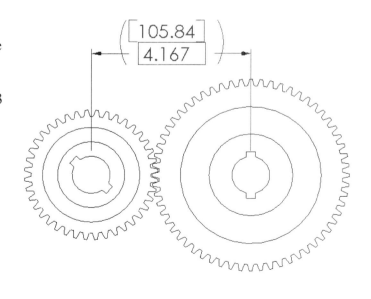

The CHANGE GEAR Tooth profile has been simplified to save file size and rebuild time. The actual tooth profile consists of a series of curves and fillets.

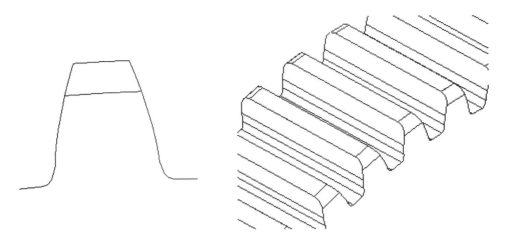

Return to the Boston Gear web site www.bostongear.com. See Exercise 2.6. Utilize the Boston Gear Part No. from the table in Exercise 2.6. Determine the material, pressure angle and maximum Torque Rating for each CHANGE GEAR.

Determine the inside Bore Diameter for the COUPLING. Determine the dimensions of the output key on the SPEED-REDUCER from the F72B1B-B5 Outline drawing.

Note: There is more than one answer.

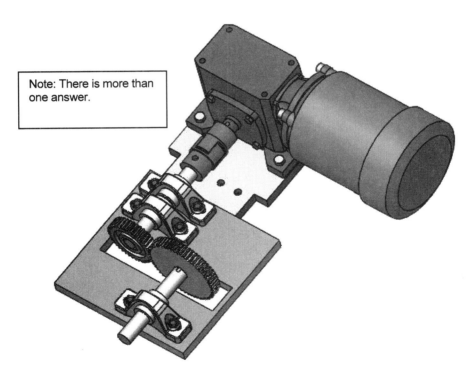

MOTOR-GEAR-BOX Assembly
Models and Images Courtesy of Boston Gear
www.bostongear.com

Notes:

Project 4

Configurations, Custom Properties, Design Tables, & References

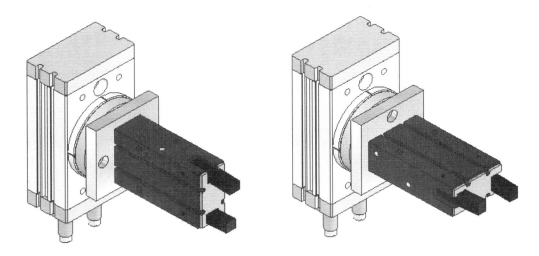

Below are the desired outcomes and usage competencies based on the completion of this project.

Project Desired Outcomes:	Usage Competencies:
• ROTARY-GRIPPER assembly.	• Ability to create parts defined in the context of an assembly.
• PLATE-D part.	• Ability to recognize and modify External references.
• PLATE-C part.	• Ability to develop an empty part and Copy/Paste sketches from different components.
• ROTARY and ROTARY-GRIPPER configurations. • PLATE-D and ROTARY-GRIPPER Design Table.	• Knowledge to develop and incorporate configurations at various assembly levels. • An understanding of Design Tables for parts and assemblies.
• PLATE-D Custom Properties. • PLATE-D drawing.	• Ability to utilize configurations in a multi-sheet drawing with Notes linked to Custom Properties.

Notes:

Project 4 – Configurations, Custom Properties, Design Tables, & References

Project Objective

Create the ROTARY-GRIPPER assembly. The ROTARY-GRIPPER assembly is the third component in the 3AXIS-TRANSFER assembly.

Design the PLATE-D part In-Context of the ROTARY assembly and GRIPPER assembly.

Create the PLATE-C part. Insert the PLATE-C part into the 2AXIS-TRANSFER assembly.

Utilize the ConfigurationManager and Design Tables to create configurations in the ROTARY assembly, ROTARY-GRIPPER assembly, and the PLATE-D part. Develop Custom Properties for the PLATE-D part.

Create the PLATE-D drawing. Insert multiple views and configurations into the PLATE-D drawing.

On the completion of this project, you will be able to:

- Apply Top-Down and Bottom-Up design assembly modeling techniques.

- Develop levels of configurations in an assembly with parts and sub-assemblies.

- Recognize and redefine External references.

- Define an empty part in an assembly with reference planes.

- Copy/Paste sketches from one component to another.

- Create Configuration Specific Custom Properties and utilize SolidWorks Properties.

- Manipulate views and configurations in a drawing.

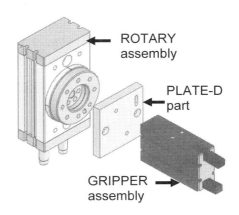

ROTARY-GRIPPER assembly

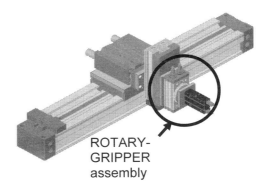

3AXIS-TRANSFER assembly

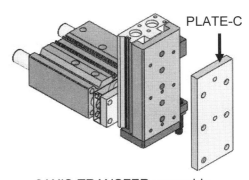

2AXIS-TRANSFER assembly

SolidWorks Tools and Commands

In Project 4, utilize the following SolidWorks tools and commands.

SolidWorks Tools and Commands:		
$color	Edit Part, Edit Sub-assembly	Move Component, Move with Triad
$configuration	Extruded Boss/Base, Cut	New drawing
$PARTNUMBER	Feature Properties	Note
$prp@property	Fixed/Float	Open part, Open assembly, Open drawing
$state	Hide	Properties
$user_notes	Hole Wizard	Projected view
Add Configuration	InPlace Mate	Rename
Add Sheet	Interference Detection	Rotate Component
Annotations	Insert Component, New Part	Selection Filters toolbar
Component Properties	Insert Model View	Shortcut keys
Configurations	Linear Pattern	Show
Configuration Specific	Linked Note	Show Update Holders
Copy/Paste views	Link to Property	Sketch relations: On Entity, Midpoint, Coincident, , Tangent
Custom Properties	List External References	Sketch tools: Centerline, Dimension
Dimension@feature	Lock All	SmartMate
Design Table	Mass Properties	Suppress/Set to Resolved
Display/Delete Relations	Mate Types: Coincident, Concentric, Distance	Suppress/Unsuppress
Do not create External References	Materials Editor	Suspend Automatic Rebuild
Drawing View Properties	Make Assembly from Part/Assembly	View Planes, Origins, Temporary Axis
Edit Component	Make Drawing from Part/Assembly	View Properties

Build modeling skill and speed. Project 4 utilizes Pop-up menus to execute the tools in the Assembly and Drawing toolbar.

Project Overview

Project 4 develops additional skill sets in recognizing and editing External references.

The ROTARY-GRIPPER assembly incorporates configurations at the part and sub-assembly level.

Utilize the ConfigurationManager and Design Tables to manipulate parameters and their values.

SolidWorks Properties and Custom Properties link model information to the drawing.

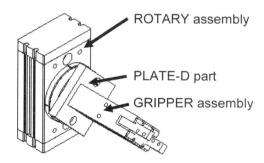

ROTARY-GRIPPER assembly

The ROTARY-GRIPPER assembly consists of the following:

- ROTARY assembly.
- GRIPPER assembly.
- PLATE-D part.

The ROTARY assembly and GRIPPER assembly are SMC components. Develop the PLATE-D part In-Context of the ROTARY assembly and GRIPPER assembly.

In the initial design phase, the PLATE-C part was listed in the Assembly Layout Diagram as a component of the ROTARY-GRIPPER assembly. You encounter a situation to rethink the location of the PLATE-C part.

Develop the PLATE-C part as a component in the 2AXIS-TRANSFER assembly. Utilize three reference planes to mate PLATE-C to the 2AXIS-TRANSFER reference planes. Obtain geometry for PLATE-C features from the SLIDE-TABLE assembly and ROTARY assembly.

The ROTARY assembly rotates 360°. The GRIPPER assembly requires a vertical and horizontal position. The rotation of the GRIPPER assembly depends on the rotation of the ROTARY assembly. At a 0° ROTARY position, the GRIPPER moves to a vertical position. At a 90° ROTARY position, the GRIPPER moves to a horizontal position.

Begin complex configurations at the lowest assembly level. Develop the ROTARY assembly configurations.

Incorporate the ROTARY configuration into the ROTARY-GRIPPER configurations.

Create three configurations for the ROTARY assembly:

- Flexible.
- Rotation0.
- Rotation90.

A small dowel pin slot indicates the ROTARY position.

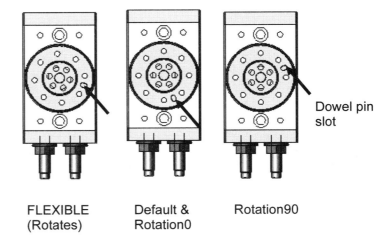

FLEXIBLE   Default &   Rotation90
(Rotates)   Rotation0

Dowel pin
slot

ROTATRY Configurations

Create three configurations for the ROTARY-GRIPPER assembly:

- Flexible.
- Rotation0.
- Rotation90.

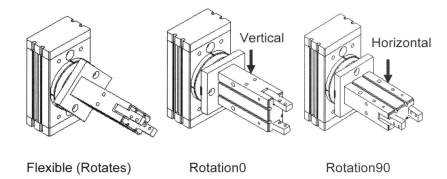

Flexible (Rotates)   Rotation0   Rotation90

ROTARY-GRIPPER configurations

Create the PLATE-D Design Table. The Design Table configurations control the depths of the Extruded-Base feature:

- 10mm.
- 15mm.
- 20mm.

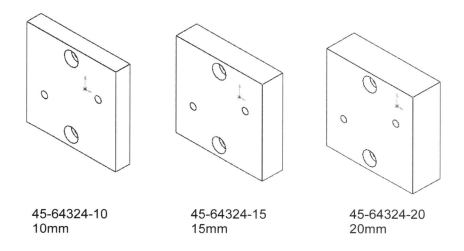

45-64324-10   45-64324-15   45-64324-20
10mm   15mm   20mm

PLATE-D configurations

Properties are parameters defined in a single document that can be accessed and utilized by multiple documents. The PLATE-D part requires three Properties:

- MASS.
- MATERIAL.
- DESCRIPTION.

Combine the PLATE-D configurations and modify the ROTARY-GRIPPER configurations:

- Horizontal-10.
- Horizontal-15.
- Horizontal-20.

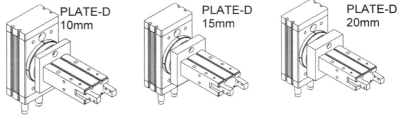

Horizontal-10   Horizontal-15   Horizontal-20

- Vertical-10.
- Vertical-15.
- Vertical-20.

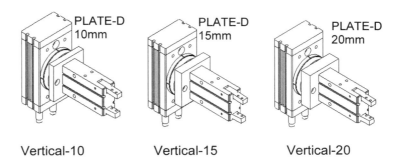

Vertical-10   Vertical-15   Vertical-20

ROTARY-GRIPPER configurations

Create the PLATE-D drawing with multiple sheets, configurations, and Custom Properties.

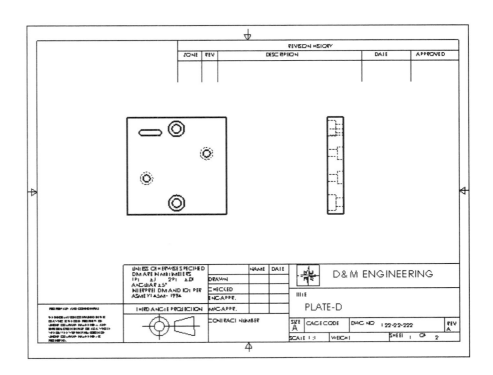

ROTARY-GRIPPER assembly

Create the ROTARY-GRIPPER assembly. Insert the
ROTARY assembly as the first component. Modify the
default orientation. Utilize Rotate Component or Move
with Triad to rotate the component in the assembly.

Insert the GRIPPER assembly. Determine the specific
features required to create the PLATE-D part using the
Top Down design approach.

Create PLATE-D as a new part, In-Context of the
ROTARY assembly and the GRIPPER assembly.

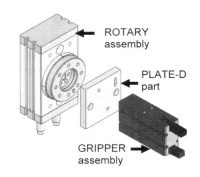

ROTARY-GRIPPER assembly

Activity: ROTARY-GRIPPER assembly

Close all documents.
1) Click **Window**, **Close All** from the Main menu.

Deactivate the Large Assembly Mode.
2) Click **Tools, Options** from the Main menu.

3) Click **Assemblies** from the System Options tab.

4) Uncheck **Use Large Assembly Mode**.

5) Click **OK**.

Expand the SMC folder from the Design Library.
6) Expand the **SMC** folder.

Open the ROTARY assembly.
7) Click the **MSQB30R** folder.

8) Click and drag the **ROTARY** icon into the Graphic
window. The ROTARY assembly is displayed in the
Graphics window.

Create a new assembly.

9) Click **Make Assembly from Part/Assembly** 🎯 from the
Standard toolbar. Select the **MY-TEMPLATES** tab.

10) Double-click **ASM-MM-ANSI**. The Insert Component
PropertyManager is displayed.

11) Click **View**, **Origins** from the Main menu.

12) Click a **position** to the left of the new assembly Origin.
Do not select the Assembly Origin.

ROTARY

Save the assembly.
13) Click **Save** from the Main menu.

14) Select **DELIVERY-STATION** for Save in: folder.

15) Enter **ROTARY-GRIPPER** for File name.

16) Click **Save**. The ROTARY-GRIPPER
FeatureManager is displayed.

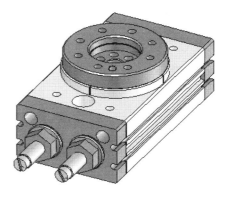

Hide the Origins.
17) Click **View**, un-check **Origins** from the Main menu.

Float the ROTARY component.
18) Right-click **ROTARY** from the FeatureManager.

19) Click **Float**. The ROTARY entry changes from fixed,
(f) to under-defined, (-).

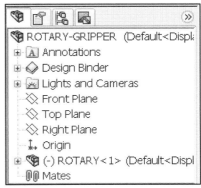

Rotate the ROTARY component.
20) Click **ROTARY** from the FeatureManager.

Rotate
21) Click **Rotate Component** Compo... from the Assembly
toolbar.

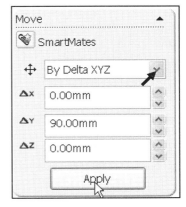

Create the first rotation.
22) Select **By Delta XYZ** from the Rotate drop down list.

23) Enter **0** for ΔX.

24) Enter **90°** for ΔY.

25) Enter **0** for ΔZ.

26) Click **Apply**.

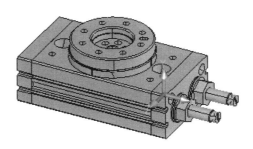

Create the second rotation.

27) Enter **0** for ΔX.

28) Enter **0** for ΔY.

29) Enter **-90°** for ΔZ.

30) Click **Apply**.

31) Click **OK** 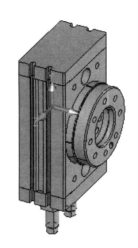 from the Rotate Component PropertyManager.

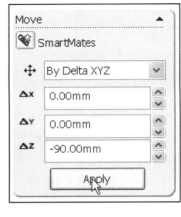

Mate the ROTARY component to the assembly planes.

32) Click **ROTARY/Plane3** from the FeatureManager.

33) Click **Mate** Mate . The Mate PropertyManager is displayed.

34) Click **ROTARY-GRIPPER/ Front Plane**. Coincident is selected by default.

35) Click ✔ .

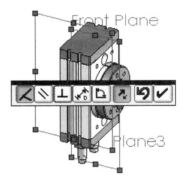

36) Click **ROTARY/Plane1** from the FeatureManager.

37) Click **ROTARY-GRIPPER/ Top Plane** from the FeatureManager. Coincident is selected by default.

38) Click ✔ .

39) Click **ROTARY/Plane2** from the FeatureManager.

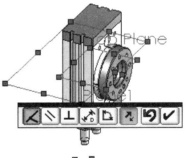

40) Click **ROTARY-GRIPPER/ Right Plane** from the FeatureManager. Coincident is selected by default. Click ✔ .

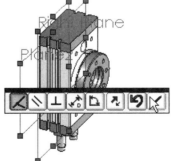

41) Click **OK** 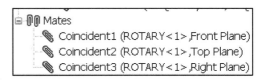 from the Mate PropertyManager.

Expand the Mates.
42) Expand **Mates** to display the three Coincident Mates. The ROTARY component is fully defined in the ROTARY-GRIPPER assembly.

Insert the GRIPPER component using the Design Library.
43) Click the **SMC/MHY2-20D** folder.

44) Click and drag the **GRIPPER** icon into the ROTARY-GRIPPER Graphics window. Position the GRIPPER to the left of the ROTARY component as illustrated.

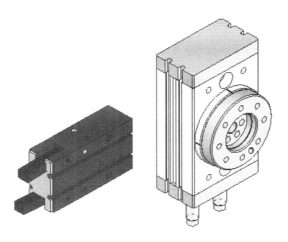

45) Click **Cancel** 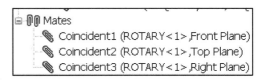 from the Insert Components PropertyManager.

Move and Rotate the GRIPPER.
46) Right-click **GRIPPER** from the FeatureManager.

47) Click **Move with Triad**. Click and drag the left mouse button along the **horizontal red axis** to move the GRIPPER in front of the ROTARY component.

48) Drag the right mouse button along the **green vertical axis** to rotate the GRIPPER as illustrated. The two middle small holes of the GRIPPER are in the top view.

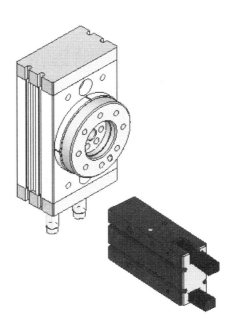

Save the ROTARY-GRIPPER assembly.
49)   Click **Save** from the Main menu.

Dynamic Behavior of Components

In static modeling, components do not move. In dynamic modeling, components translate and rotate. Mates reflect the dynamic behavior of the physical components.

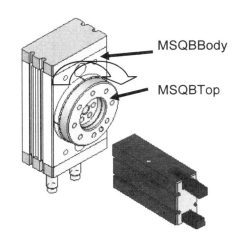

MSQBBody

MSQBTop

Investigate the dynamic behavior of the components before you assemble them. Determine the design intent of the ROTARY and GRIPPER assemblies as individual components and as a sub-assembly.

The ROTARY assembly contains the MSQBTop part. The ROTARY/MSQBTop part rotates about the X-axis.

The GRIPPER assembly position depends on the MSQBTop part position. The GRIPPER assembly requires two positions:

- Position One at 0°.

- Position Two at 90°.

Control the GRIPPER assembly rotation through the configurations of the ROTARY assembly.

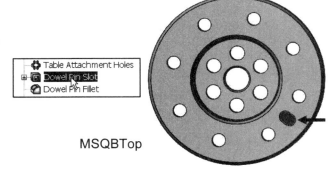

MSQBTop

The ROTARY/MSQBTop part contains an Extruded Cut feature named Dowel Pin Slot. The Dowel Pin Slot indicates the 0° home position.

Control rotation of the ROTARY/MSQBTop part. Create Coincident and Perpendicular Mates between the ROTARY/MSQBBody/Front and the ROTARY/MSQBTop/Side.

Activity: Dynamic Behavior of Components

Open the ROTARY assembly.

50) Click **ROTARY** from the ROTARY-GRIPPER FeatureManager.

51) Right-click **Open Assembly**. The ROTARY assembly is displayed in the Graphics window.

52) Click **Top** view.

53) Click **ROTARY/MSQBTop** from the FeatureManager.

Rotate

54) Click **Rotate Component** Compo... . The Rotate Component PropertyManager is displayed.

55) Position the **Dowel Pin Slot** approximately in the lower right corner as illustrated.

56) Click **OK** from the Rotate Component PropertyManager.

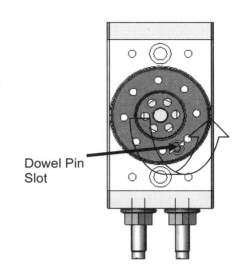
Dowel Pin Slot

Insert a Coincident Mate between the MSQBTop and the MSQBBody.

57) Expand **MSQBBody** from the FeatureManager.

58) Click **MSQBBody/Front**.

59) Click **Mate** Mate . The Mate PropertyManager is displayed.

60) Expand **MSQBTop** from the FeatureManager.

61) Click **MSQBTop/Side**. Coincident is selected by default.

62) Click .

63) Click **OK** from the Mate PropertyManager.

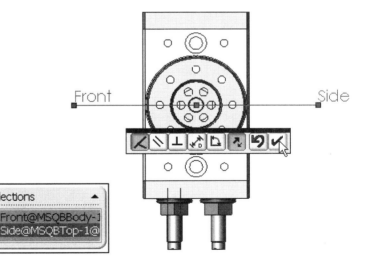
Front   Side

Mate Selections

Front@MSQBBody-1
Side@MSQBTop-1@

The MSQBBody/Front and MSQBTop/Side planes are horizontal. This is the Default and Rotation0 configuration position of the ROTARY assembly.

Control the Suppress/UnSuppress state of Mates through configurations.

Rename and Suppress the Coincident Mate.
64) Expand **ROTARY/MateGroup1**.

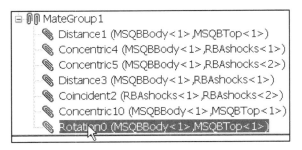

65) Click the **Coincident** Mate at the bottom of MateGroup1.

66) Rename to **Rotation0**.

Suppress the Mate.
67) Right-click **Rotation0**.

68) Click **Suppress**. A Suppressed Mate Paperclip icon is displayed in light gray. Note: Light gray indicates a Suppressed Mate.

Insert a Perpendicular Mate.
69) Expand **ROTARY** assembly.

70) Click **MSQBBody/Front**.

71) Click **Mate** Mate.

72) Click **MSQBTop/Side**.

73) Click **Perpendicular**. The Dowel Pin Slot rotates to the upper right corner. Click the **Flip** check box if required.

74) Click ✔.

75) Click **OK** from the Mate PropertyManager.

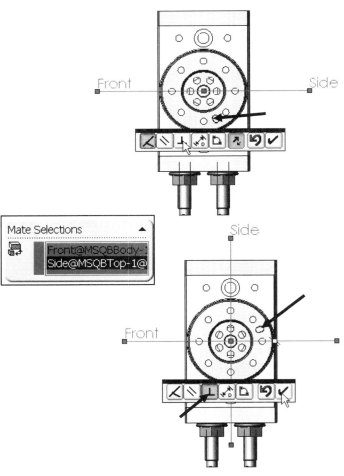

76) Expand **ROTARY/MateGroup1**.

77) Click the **Perpendicular1** Mate.

78) Rename to **Rotation90**.

Suppress the Mate.
79) Right-click **Rotation90**.

80) Click **Suppress**.

Save the ROTARY assembly.
81) Click **Save** from the Main menu.

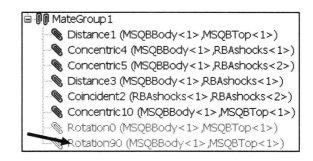

In the next activity, work with the Rotation0 and Rotation90 Mates. Reposition Mates in MateGroup1 to locate quickly in the FeatureManager. Note: Rotation0 and Rotation90 contain no dependency on any other Mate.

Reposition the Mates.
82) Drag the **Rotation0** Mate from the bottom of MateGroup1 to the top of MateGroup1. The Move feature in tree ⏎ icon is displayed above the Distance1 Mate.

83) Repeat the above procedure for the **Rotation90** Mate.

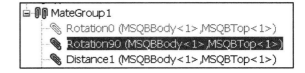

Utilize an Angle Mate when configurations require multiple angle values. Modify the Angle value in the configuration.

In some mating situations at 180°, the Mate Alignment flips and the Mate becomes invalid. Utilize an Angle Mate to resolve this issue.

In the project exercises, modify the mate scheme. Replace the Rotation0 Mate and Rotation90 Mate; utilize one Angle Mate and modify the values in the configuration.

Suppress the Angle Mate in the Flexible configuration.

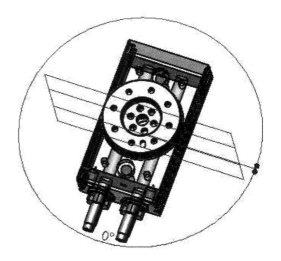

ROTARY configurations

Create the three ROTARY configurations:

- Rotation0.

- Rotation90.

- Flexible.

Utilize the ConfigurationManager, Add Configuration option. Suppress/UnSuppress the Rotation0 Mate and the Rotation90 Mate to create three configurations.

Utilize a separate Flexible configuration and fixed Default configuration for additional control. Suppress the Rotation0 Mate and the Rotation90 Mate to create the Flexible configuration. Unsuppress the Rotation0 Mate to create a fixed Default configuration.

Avoid rotation when defining In-Context features. Utilize the Default configuration to create PLATE-D defined in the context of the assembly. Utilize the three ROTARY configurations with the PLATE-D configurations.

Activity: ROTARY configurations

Modify the ROTARY (Default) configuration.
84)   Right-click **Rotation0**.

85)   Click **Unsuppress**.

Insert the ROTARY (Rotation0) configuration.
86)   Click the **ROTARY ConfigurationManager**.

87)   Right-click **ROTARY Configuration(s)**.

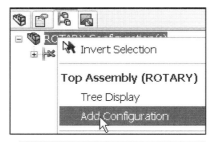

88)   Click **Add Configuration**. The Add Configuration PropertyManager is displayed.

89)   Enter **Rotation0** for Configuration name.

90)   Enter **ROTARY Rotation0** for Description.

91)   Enter **UnSuppress Mate Rotation0** and **Suppress Mate Rotation90** for Comment.

92) Click **OK**  from the Add Configuration PropertyManager. The Rotation0 configuration name is added to the ConfigurationManager.

Insert the ROTARY (Rotation90) configuration.
93) Right-click **ROTARY Configuration(s)**.

94) Click **Add Configuration**.

95) Enter **Rotation90** for Configuration name.

96) Enter **ROTARY Rotation90** for Description.

97) Enter **Suppress Mate Rotation0** and **UnSuppress Mate Rotation90** for Comment.

98) Click **OK**  from the Add Configuration PropertyManager. The Rotation90 configuration name is added to the ConfigurationManager.

Define the Rotation90 configuration Mate state.
99) Click the **FeatureManager**.

100) Right-click **Rotation0**.

101) Click **Suppress**.

102) Right-click **Rotation90**.

103) Click **UnSuppress**. The Dowel Pin Slot rotates to Position90.

Return to the ConfigurationManager.
104) Click the **ConfigurationManager**.

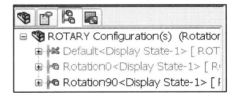

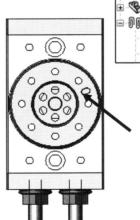

Insert the ROTARY (Flexible) configuration.
105) Right-click **ROTARY Configuration(s).**

106) Click **Add Configuration**.

107) Enter **FLEXIBLE** for Configuration name.

108) Enter **ROTARY Flexible** for Description.

109) Enter **Suppress Mate Rotation0** and **Suppress Mate Rotation90** for Comment.

110) Click **OK** 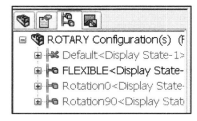 from the Add Configuration PropertyManager. The FLEXIBLE configuration name is added to the ConfigurationManager.

Define the Flexible configuration Mate state.
111) Return to the **FeatureManager**.

112) Right-click **Rotation90**.

113) Click **Suppress**. The Dowel Pin Slot rotates freely.

Work with multiple Mates to control configurations. Suppress related Mates. UnSuppress the Mates required to achieve dynamic behavior through the configurations.

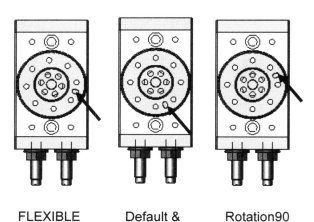

FLEXIBLE   Default &   Rotation90
(Rotates)   Rotation0

ROTATRY Configurations

Example: Suppress the Rotation0 Mate and Suppress the Rotation90 Mate. UnSuppress either the Rotation0 Mate or the Rotation90 Mate. The Mates would be over defined if both the Rotation0 and the Rotation90 Mates were UnSuppressed.

Verify the ROTARY configurations.
114) Double-click **Default**, **FLEXIBLE**, **Rotation0,** and **Rotation90**. The FLEXIBLE configuration rotates.

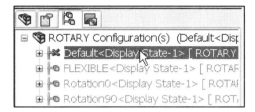

Display the Default configuration.
115) Double-click **Default** from the ConfigurationManager. The Dowel Pin Slot is located in the lower right corner.

Return to the FeatureManager.
116) Click the **FeatureManager**.

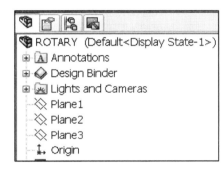

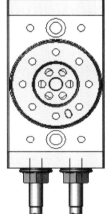

Save the ROTARY assembly.
117) Click **Save** from the Main menu.

Configurations are an integral part of the design process. Define the ROTARY positions before mating the GRIPPER assembly.

Why maintain a Default configuration and a Rotation0 configuration when both positions are the same? Answer: The Default configuration remains a "safety fall back" configuration.

The Default configuration is recognized by the members of the design team. The Rotation0 configuration affects four levels of assemblies: ROTARY, ROTARY-GRIPPER, 3AXIS-TRANSFER, and DELIVERY-STATION.

Each assembly and their components contain configurations. Issues can and will occur in the development process. The Default configuration provides assistance in solving issues.

The Default configuration remains a static configuration. All multiple configuration components utilize the Default configuration.

Assemble the GRIPPER assembly to the ROTARY assembly

Utilize two Coincident Mates and one Distance Mate to assemble the GRIPPER assembly to the ROTARY assembly. The ROTARY-GRIPPER assembly currently contains nine components. As components and geometry increase in complexity, utilize the FeatureManager to select planes in the mating process. Expand the sub-assembly entries to select the planes to constrain the model.

Example: The ROTARY/MSQBBody part is fixed. Mate selections to this component result in a non-rotating GRIPPER assembly. The ROTARY/MSQBTop part rotates. Mate selection to this component result in a rotating GRIPPER assembly.

The Distance Mate mates the back face of the GRIPPER/Body part to the front face of the ROTARY/MSQBTop part. You wait for team members to provide critical dimensions for the location of the GRIPPER fingers with respect to other DELIVERY-STATION components. Allow for future design changes. Create a 10mm gap between the ROTARY assembly and the GRIPPER assembly. Note: Later you will create 15mm and 20mm gaps and adjust the gaps based on the position of the INPUT and OUTPUT components.

View the GRIPPER assembly position with the three ROTARY configurations:

- Default.
- Rotation0.
- Rotation90.

The MSQBTop part rotates in the ROTARY (FLEXIBLE) configuration. When the ROTARY (FLEXIBLE) configuration is inserted into the ROTARY-GRIPPER assembly, SolidWorks solves the Mates as rigid.

The MSQBTop is fixed. Modify the Solve As option from Rigid to Flexible in the ROTARY Component Properties.

Activity: Assemble the GRIPPER assembly to the ROTARY assembly

Hide the ROTARY/MSQBBody part.
118) Click **ROTARY/MSQBBody** from the FeatureManager.

119) Right-click **Hide**.

120) Click **RBAshocks<1>** from the FeatureManager.

121) Hold the **Ctrl** key down.

122) Click **RBAshocks<2>** from the FeatureManager.

123) Release the **Ctrl** key.

124) Right-click **Hide**.

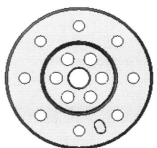

Return to the ROTTERY-GRIPPER assembly.
125) Click **Windows**, **ROTARY-GRIPPER** from the
Main menu.

Display an Isometric view.
126) Click **Isometric** view.

Select the GRIPPER assembly.
127) Click the **right face** of the GRIPPER assembly
between the two FINGERS.

128) Click **Section view** 🔲.

129) Enter **–80** for Offset Distance.

130) Click **OK** ✅ from the Section
View PropertyManager.

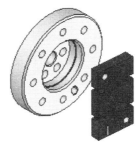

Assemble the GRIPPER
assembly to the ROTARY
assembly.

Insert the first Coincident Mate.
131) Click
ROTARY/MSQBTop/Front
from the FeatureManager.

132) Click **Mate** Mate .

133) Click **GRIPPER/Right** from
the FeatureManager.
Coincident is selected by
default. Click ✔ .

Mate Selections
Front@ROTARY-1@
Right@GRIPPER-1@

💡 Locate the correct Mate
selections quickly. Select Planes from the
FeatureManager. Split the FeatureManager in half if
numerous Reference planes exist in the Graphics
window. Display the first component in the top half, the
Mate PropertyManager in the lower half.

Expand the assembly entry in the Graphics window.
Position the model to the right of the text.

Insert the second Coincident
Mate.
134) Click
ROTARY/MSQBTop/Side
from the FeatureManager.

135) Click **GRIPPER/Front** from
the FeatureManager.
Coincident is selected by
default.

136) Click ✔ .

Mate Selections
Side@ROTARY-1@R
Front@GRIPPER-1@

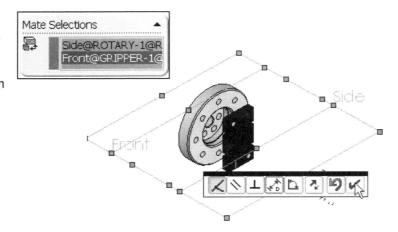

Insert a Distance Mate.

137) Click the **back face** of the GRIPPER assembly.

138) Click the **front face** of the ROTARY assembly.

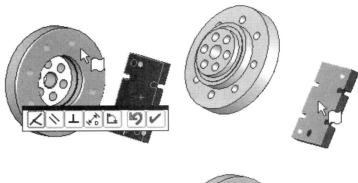

139) Click **Distance**.

140) Enter **10**.

141) Click  .

142) Click **OK** ✅ from the Mate PropertyManager.

143) Click **Isometric** view.

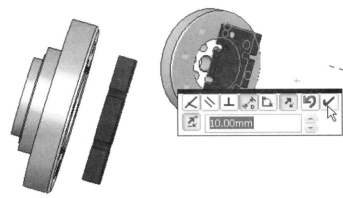

Display the Full view.

144) Click **Section view** 🔳. The GRIPPER assembly is fully defined in the ROTARY-GRIPPER assembly.

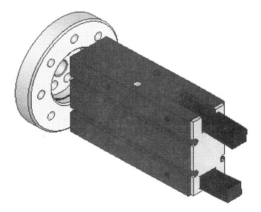

Select the ROTARY(FLEXIBLE) configuration.

145) Right-click **ROTARY** from the ROTARY-GRIPPER FeatureManager.

146) Click **Component Properties**.

147) Select **Flexible** for the Solve as option. Select **FLEXIBLE** for the Referenced configuration.

148) Click **OK**.

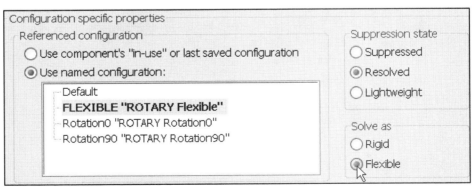

149) Drag the **GRIPPER** assembly in the ROTARY-
GRIPPER Graphics window. The GRIPPER assembly
is free to rotate.

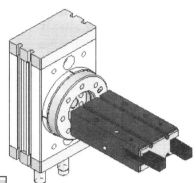

Select the ROTARY (Rotation0) configuration.
150) Right-click **ROTARY** from FeatureManager.

151) Click **Component Properties**.

152) Select **Rotation0**
"ROTARY
Rotation0" for the
Reference
configuration.

Default
FLEXIBLE "ROTARY Flexible"
Rotation0 "ROTARY Rotation0"
Rotation90 "ROTARY Rotation90"

153) Click **OK**.

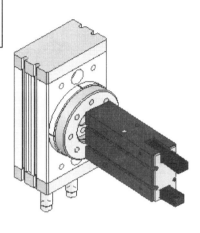

Select the ROTARY (Rotation90) configuration.
154) Right-click **ROTARY** from the ROTARY-GRIPPER
FeatureManager.

155) Click **Component Properties**.

156) Select **Rotation90** for the Reference configuration.

157) Click **OK**.

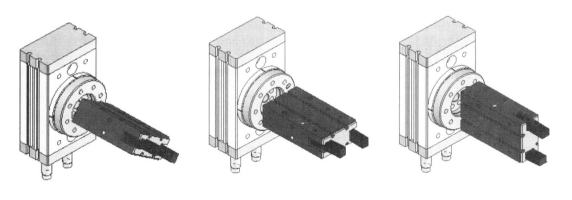

Flexible   Rotation90   Rotation0

ROTARY-GRIPPER configurations

Return to the ROTARY(Default) configuration.

158) Right-click **ROTARY** from the ROTARY-GRIPPER FeatureManager.

159) Click **Component Properties**.

160) Select **Default**.

161) Click **OK**.

162) Click **Right** view. The Default configuration of the ROTARY/MSQBTop/DowelPinSlot is located in the lower right corner in the Graphics window.

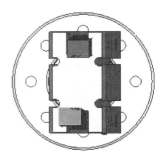

Default Configuration

PLATE-D part with In-Context features

The ROTARY/MSQBTop part contains eight, 5mm holes. The GRIPPER assembly contains two, 4mm holes. The GRIPPER assembly mounting holes do not align to the ROTARY/MSQBTop part mounting holes. Create the PLATE-D part as an interim part between the ROTARY/MSQBTop part and the GRIPPER assembly.

Develop the PLATE-D part in the context of the ROTARY-GRIPPER assembly. In the first activity, create the Extruded-Base feature sketched on the front face of the ROTARY assembly. The first sketch references the circular edges of the ROTARY/MSQBTop part. In the second activity, create the holes as in-context features.

Utilize Insert, Component, New Part from the Main menu. Select the ASM-MM-ANSI Template. SolidWorks automatically selects the Sketch tool. The PLATE-D Extruded Base feature sketch is parallel to the MSQBTop Plane1. The PLATE-D entry in the FeatureManager is displayed in blue.

SolidWorks inserts the InPlace Mate as a Coincident Mate between the PLATE-D Front Plane and the MSQBTop circular face. The InPlace Mate fully defines the PLATE-D part in the ROTARY-GRIPPER assembly.

Create the PLATE-D sketch. Sketch a horizontal centerline through the MSQBTop Origin. Sketch a rectangle. The four lines of the rectangle are tangent to the MSQBTop circular edge. Extrude the sketch to the back vertex of the GRIPPER assembly. The depth of the PLATE-D part references the vertex of the GRIPPER assembly.

The Extruded-Base feature of the PLATE-D part is a square shape versus a circular shape. A square flat plate shape costs less to machine than a circular flat plate shape.

You are in the ROTARY-GRIPPER assembly level.

Activity: PLATE-D part with in-context features

Hide the GRIPPER assembly.
163) Right-click **GRIPPER** from the FeatureManager.

164) Click **Hide**.

Insert the new PLATE-D part.
165) Click **Insert**, **Component**, **New Part** from the Main menu.

166) Double-click **PART-MM-ANSI-AL6061**.

167) Select **DELIVERY-STATION** for the Save in folder.

168) Enter **PLATE-D** for File name.

169) Click **Save**.

170) Click the **circular face** of MSQBTop. The InPlace Mate is added to MateGroup1. Edit Component mode is selected.

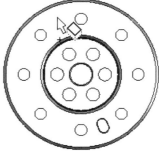

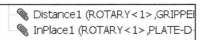

Sketch the profile.
171) Click **Right** view.

172) Click **Rectangle** Rectan... from the Sketch toolbar.

173) Sketch a **rectangle** larger than the MSQBTop circle.

174) Click **Centerline** Centerl... from the Sketch toolbar.

175) Sketch a **diagonal centerline** as illustrated.

Insert a Midpoint relation.
176) Right-click **Select**.

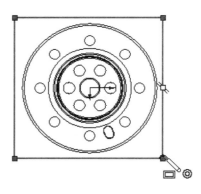

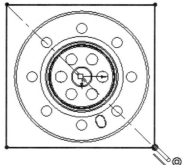

177) Click the MSQBTop **Origin** from the FeatureManager.

178) Hold the **Ctrl** key down.

179) Click the **Centerline**.

180) Release the **Ctrl** key

181) Click **Midpoint** from the Add Relations box.

182) Click **OK** 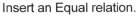 from the Properties PropertyManager.

Select and verify reference geometry with the FeatureManager. Utilize the FeatureManager to select the MSQBTop Origin. Review the entity name in the Selected Entities box, Point1@Origin@ROTARY-1@ROTARY-GRIPPER/MSQBTop-1. Utilize Display/Delete Relations in the part sketch to verify the entity. The syntax is slightly different, Point1@Origin of ROTARY<1>/MSQBTop<1>.

Insert an Equal relation.
183) Click the **top horizontal line** of the rectangle.

184) Hold the **Ctrl** key down.

185) Click the **right vertical line** of the rectangle.

186) Release the **Ctrl** key.

187) Click **Equal** from the Add Relations box.

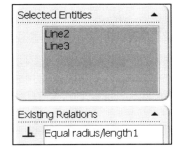

188) Click **OK** from the Properties PropertyManager.

Insert a Tangent relation.
189) Click the **top horizontal line** of the rectangle.

190) Hold the **Ctrl** key down.

191) Click the inside **top circular edge**.

192) Release the **Ctrl** key.

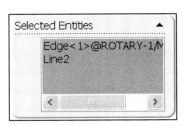

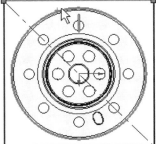

193) Click **Tangent** from the Add Relations box. The black sketch is fully defined.

194) Click **OK** 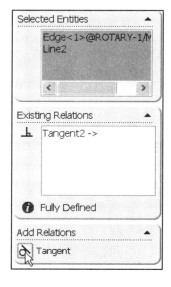 from the Properties PropertyManager.

Display the GRIPPER assembly.
195) Right-click **GRIPPER** from the FeatureManager.

196) Click **Show**.

Display an Isometric view.
197) Click **Isometric** view.

Extrude Sketch1.
198) Click **Extruded Boss/Base** Boss/B... from the Features toolbar.

199) Click **Up To Vertex**.

200) Click the back **Vertex** of the Gripper as illustrated.

201) Click **OK** from the Extrude PropertyManager.

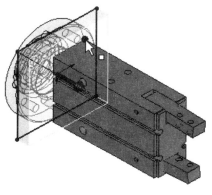

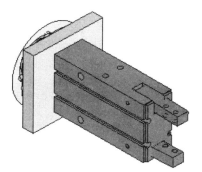

Display the PLATE-D entries.
202) Expand the **PLATE-D/Extrude1** entry in the
     FeatureManager.

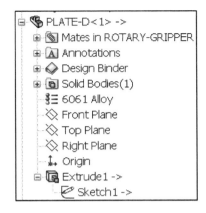

The External References "->" symbol indicates that the
Extrude1 feature and Sketch1 contain solved external
references. PLATE-D is in the Edit Component mode.
The FeatureManager displays the PLATE-D name and
features in blue.

List the PLATE-D External references.
203) Right-click **Extrude1**.

204) Click **List External Refs**. The Status column displays In-Context for the Sketch Arc,
     Sketch Point and Extrude feature. The Referenced Entity column lists the referenced
     geometry from ROTARY<1>/MSQBTop<1> and GRIPPER<1>/MHY2BODY<1>.

205) Click **OK**.

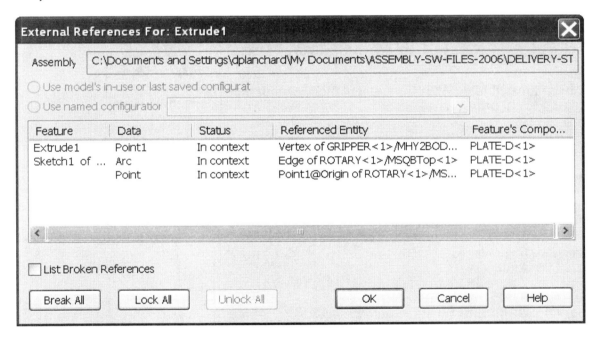

PLATE-D Holes

PLATE-D fastens to the ROTARY/MSQBTop part and to the back face of the GRIPPER assembly. Determine the size and location of the mounting holes.

PLATE-D fastens to the GRIPPER with two 4mm SHCSs. Create the Cbores on the PLATE-D back face, in the context of the GRIPPER/BackHole1 and GRIPPER/BackHole2 features.

PLATE-D fastens to the MSQBTop part with two 5mm SHCSs. Create the Cbores on the PLATE-D front face, In-Context of the MSQBTop/Mounting Holes feature.

Identify your location in the ROTARY-GRIPPER assembly.

The assembly window displays "PLATE-D-in-ROTARY-GRIPPER." The PLATE-D entry in the FeatureManager is displayed in blue.

You are located in the Edit Component mode within the ROTARY-GRIPPER assembly.

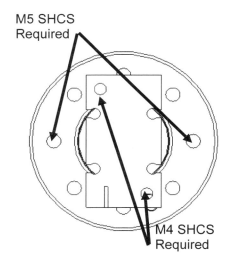

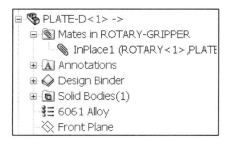

Activity: PLATE-D Holes

Create two 5mm Cbores on the PLATE-D part In-Context.
206) Click **Hidden Lines Visible**.

Display the Right view.
207) Click **Right** view.

Hide the GRIPPER assembly.
208) Click **GRIPPER** from the FeatureManager.

209) Right-click **Hide**. PLATE-D remains in the Edit Component mode.

Select the Sketch Plane for the two 5mm Cbores.
210) Click the **front face of PLATE-D** on the left side as illustrated.

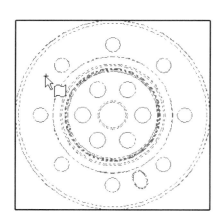

Use the Hole Wizard to create the Cbore.

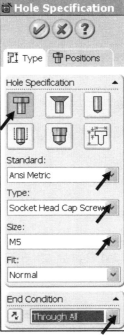

211) Click **Hole Wizard** Hole from the Features toolbar.

212) Click **Counterbore** for Hole Specification.

213) Select **Ansi Metric** for Standard.

214) Select **Socket Head Cap Screw** for Type.

215) Select **M5** for Size.

216) Select **Through All** for End Condition.

217) Click the **Positions** tab.

218) Activate the center point. Drag the **mouse pointer** over the right Mounting Hole of the MSQBTop part.

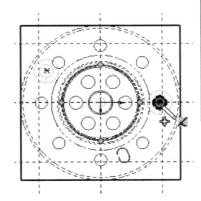

219) Click a **position** on the center point for the right Mounting Hole.

Activate Filters.

220) Click **Edges** and **Sketch Points** from the Selection Filter toolbar.

Add a Concentric relation.
221) Right-click **Select**.

222) Click the **Blue center point**, as illustrated.

223) Hold the **Ctrl** key down.

224) Click the **left Mounting Hole circle**.

225) Release the **Ctrl** key.

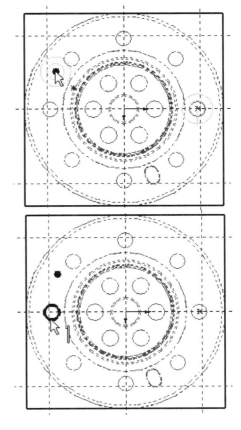

226) Click **Concentric.**

227) Click **OK** 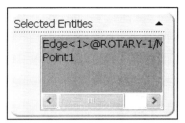 from the Properties PropertyManager.

228) Click **OK** from the Hole Position PropertyManager.

Display the GRIPPER assembly.
229) Right-click **GRIPPER** from the FeatureManager.

230) Click **Show**.

Hide the ROTARY assembly.
231) Right-click **ROTARY** from the FeatureManager.

232) Click **Hide**.

Display the GRIPPER.
233) Right-click **GRIPPER** from the FeatureManager.

234) Click **Show**.

Deactivate Filters.
235) Deactivate **all filters**.

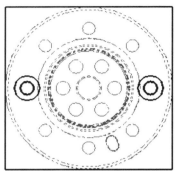

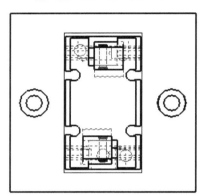

The PLATE-D part remains in the Edit Component mode, (blue).

Note: The action of dragging the mouse pointer over a sketched circle is called "wake up the center point". When sketch entities do not belong to the current sketch, there are three options:

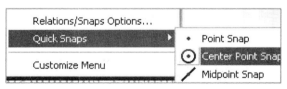

- Add a Concentric relation between the point and the circular edge.

- Add a Coincident relation between the point and the Temporary axis.

- Utilize the Quick Snaps, Center Point Snap option.

Quick Snaps are similar to the AutoCAD O-Snaps (Object Snaps). The mouse pointer snaps to specified geometry. Right-click Quick Snaps on a sketch entity to view the snap options.

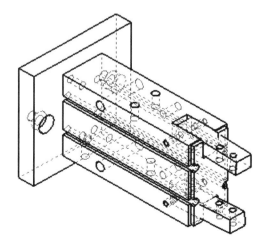

Create two 4mm Cbores on PLATE-D In-Context using Hole Wizard.

236) Click **left** view.

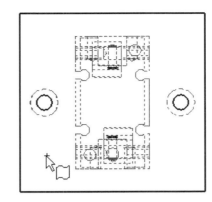

237) Click the **back face of PLATE-D** in the lower left corner as illustrated.

238) Click **Hole Wizard** 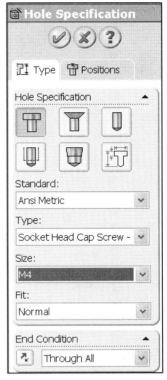 from the Features toolbar.

239) Click **Counterbore** for Hole Specification.

240) Select **Ansi Metric** for Standard.

241) Select **Socket Head Cap Screw** for Type.

242) Select **M4** for Size.

243) Select **Through all** for End Condition.

244) Click the **Position** tab.

245) Click the center point of the GRIPPER/MHY2BODY/**M5 x 0.8BackHole1 circle** as illustrated.

246) Click the center point of the GRIPPER/MHY2BODY/**M5 x 0.8BackHole2 circle** as illustrated.

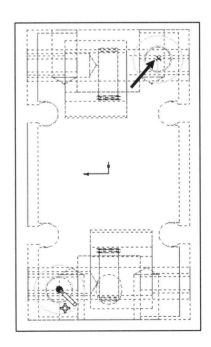

247) Right-click **Select**.

248) Click the **first point** as illustrated.

249) Right-click **Delete**.

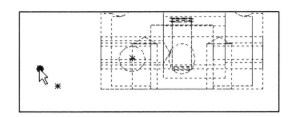

250) Click **OK** ✔ from the Hole Position PropertyManager.

Return to the ROTARY-GRIPPER assembly.
251) Right-click **ROTARY-GRIPPER** from the Graphics window.

252) Click **Edit Assembly: ROTARY-GRIPPER.**

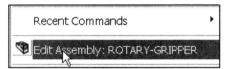

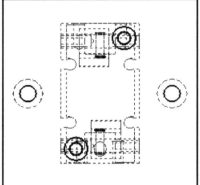

Display the Update Holders.
253) Right-click the **ROTARY-GRIPPER** assembly icon.

254) Click **Show Update Holders**. The FeatureManager lists six entities.

255) Right-click **ROTARY-GRIPPER** from the FeatureManager.

256) Click **Show Update Holders**. View the update Holders.

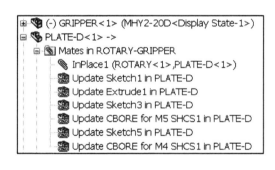

257) Hide the **Update Holders**.

Display the ROTARY assembly and GRIPPER assembly.
258) Show the **features** as illustrated.

The distance between the ROTARY assembly and the GRIPPER assembly controls the depth of the PLATE-D part.

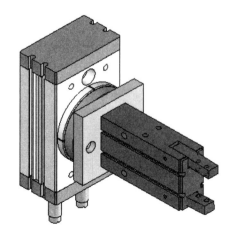

Modify the PLATE-D Distance1 Mate.
259) Expand **ROTARY-GRIPPER/Mates**.

260) Right-click **Distance1**.

261) Click **Edit Feature**.

262) Enter **30**.

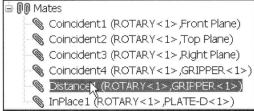

263) Click **OK**  from the Distance1 PropertyManager.

264) Click **OK** from the Mate PropertyManager.

Rename Distance1 Mate.
265) Click **Distance1** in the ROTARY-GRIPPER
FeatureManager.

266) Enter **Distance-PLATE-D-Depth**.

Modify PLATE-D.
267) Double-click **Distance-PLATE-D-Depth**
from the FeatureManager.

268) Double-click **30**.

269) Enter **10**. Click **Rebuild**.

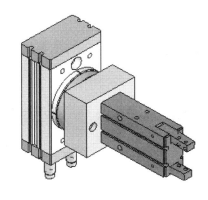

270) Click ✔. Click **OK** .

Save the ROTARY-GRIPPER assembly.
271) Click **Save**.

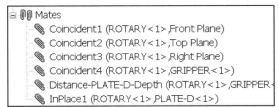

Redefining External References and InPlace Mates

Review InPlace Mates and External references. The PLATE-D part references two assemblies.

- GRIPPER assembly.

- ROTARY assembly.

Utilize the PLATE-D part in a future project without the GRIPPER assembly and the ROTARY assembly. Remove the PLATE-D External references. Redefine features and sketch geometry in the PLATE-D part.

Delete the Inplace1 Mate. The PLATE-D part is free to translate and rotate in the ROTARY-GRIPPER assembly without the Inplace1 Mate. Utilize three SmartMates to assemble the PLATE-D part to the ROTARY assembly. The PLATE-D part contains no External references.

The "->" symbol indicates that the features were developed in-context of another component. The ROTARY assembly and the GRIPPER assembly reside in memory in order for PLATE-D to locate the in-context features. Otherwise, the features are out of context and the "->?" symbol is displayed after each feature.

Example: Close all documents. Open PLATE-D. The FeatureManager displays the out of context "->?" symbol next to the PLATE-D part icon and the three In-Context features.

Open the ROTARY-GRIPPER assembly. Rebuild PLATE-D. The FeatureManager displays the restored In-Context features with the "->" symbol.

The default view orientation of the PLATE-D part differs from its view orientation in the ROTARY-GRIPPER assembly.

The PLATE-D Origin is relative to the ROTARY-GRIPPER assembly.

Activity: Redefining External References and InPlace Mates

Review the External references.
272) Right-click **PLATE-D** in the Graphics window.

273) Click **Open Part**. PLATE-D is displayed in the Graphics window.

274) Click **Hidden Lines Visible**.

Display the PLATE-D part and the ROTARY-GRIPPER assembly.
275) Click **Windows**, **Tile Horizontal** from the Main menu.

List the External references.
276) Right-click **PLATE-D** from the FeatureManager.

277) Click **List External Ref**. Click **Lock All**.

278) Click **OK**. The warning message is displayed, "All external references for the model, PLATE-D will be locked. You will not be able to add any new External references until you unlock the existing references."

279) Click **OK**. The "->∗" symbol is displayed next to the part name, PLATE-D in the FeatureManager. The PLATE-D part contains External references that are locked.

280) Maximize the **PLATE-D** part.

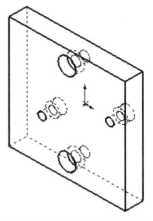

Redefine Sketch1.
281) Right-click **Extrude1**.

282) Click **Edit Sketch**.

283) Right-click **Display/Delete Relations**.

Replace the Midpoint relation. Delete the Tangent relation.

Replace the Midpoint relation.
284) Click the **Midpoint0** relation.

285) Click **Point5** in the Entities box. The External Point5 is the ROTARY Origin.

286) Expand **PLATE-D** from the FeatureManager.

287) Click the **PLATE-D Origin**. The Point1@Origin of PLATE-D is displayed in the entity Replace box.

288) Click the **Replace** button.

The Entities box lists Point1@Origin Defined In the Same Model. The Relations box lists Midpoint0 with no In-Context "->" symbol.

If you delete and redefine relations, the number increments by one. Example: Midpoint1.

Delete the Tangent relation.
289) Click the **Tangent** -> relation.

290) Click the **Delete** button. The sketch is underdefined and is displayed in blue.

Add a Horizontal dimension.

291) Click **Smart Dimension** Dimens…. from the Sketch toolbar.

292) Click the **top horizontal line**.

293) Click a **position** for the 63 dimension above the profile. The black sketch is fully defined.

294) Click **OK** from the Dimension PropertyManager.

Exit the Sketch.

295) Click **Exit Sketch** Sketch .

Sketch1 contains no External references. The Extrude1 feature indicates an External reference. The Depth option, Up to Vertex, references a point on the GRIPPER assembly.

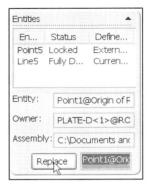

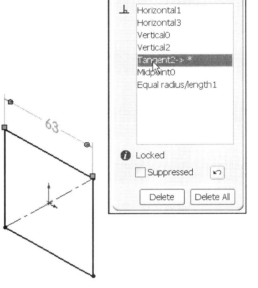

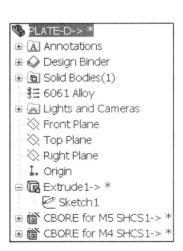

Redefine the depth of the Extrude1 feature.
296) Right-click **PLATE-D/Extrude1** from the FeatureManager.

297) Click **Edit Feature**.

298) Select **Blind** from the Depth list box.

299) Enter **10** for Depth.

300) Click **OK**  from the Extrude1 PropertyManager. The Extrude1 feature is fully defined with no External references.

Redefine the M5 Cbores.
301) Expand **CBORE for M5 SHCS1**. Sketch3 contains an External reference.

302) Click **Sketch3**. Right-click **Edit Sketch**.

303) Right-click **Display/Delete Relations**.

304) Select **Concentric0** and **Concentric1** External references.

305) Click **Delete All**. Click **OK**  from the Display/Delete Relations.

306) Click **Rebuild**.

Sketch a Centerline.
307) Click **Front Plane** from the FeatureManager.

308) Click **Front** view. Click **Centerline** Centerl... from the Sketch toolbar.

309) Sketch a **horizontal centerline** from the Origin to the right vertical midpoint.

Add a Vertical relation.
310) Right-click **Select**.

311) Click the **Origin**. Hold the **Ctrl** key down.

312) Click the **first point** and **second point** as illustrated.

313) Release the **Ctrl** key.

314) Click **Vertical**. Click **OK**  from the Properties PropertyManager.

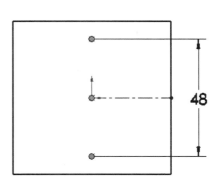

Add a Symmetric relation.
315) Click the **horizontal centerline**.

316) Hold the **Ctrl** key down. Click the **first point** and **second point**.

317) Release the **Ctrl** key. Click **Symmetric**.

318) Click **OK** from the Properties PropertyManager.

Insert a vertical dimension.

319) Click **Smart Dimension** from the Sketch toolbar.

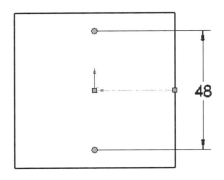

320) Add a **vertical dimension** between the first point and the second point.

321) Enter **48**. The black sketch is fully defined.

322) Click **Exit Sketch**.

Redefine the M4 Cbores.
323) Expand **CBORE for M4 SHCS**. Sketch5 contains the External reference.

324) Click **Sketch5**. Right-click **Edit Sketch**.

325) Right-click **Display/Delete Relations**.

326) Select **Coincident0->*** and **Coincident1->*** locked External references.

327) Click **Delete All**.

328) Click **OK** from the Display/Delete Relations.

329) Click **Rebuild**.

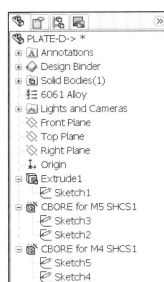

Insert dimensions.

330) Define holes from the Origin to maintain common design intent from the GRIPPER assembly. Click **Smart Dimension**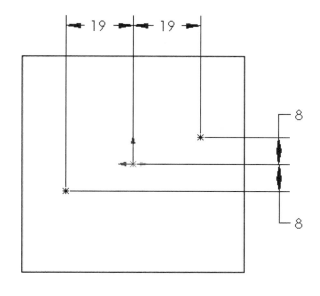

331) Create a **vertical dimension** from the Origin to the first point.

332) Accept **8**.

333) Create a **vertical dimension** from the Origin to the second point. Accept **8**.

334) Create a **horizontal dimension** from the Origin to the first point.

335) Accept **19**. Create a **horizontal dimension** from the Origin to the second point.

336) Accept **19**. The black sketch is fully defined. Click **Exit Sketch**.

Save PLATE-D.

337) Click **Isometric** view.

338) Click **Shaded With Edges**.

339) Click **Save** from the Main menu.

Delete the InPlace1 Mate.

340) Open the **ROTARY-GRIPPER** assembly.

341) Expand **MateGroup1**.

342) Click **Inplace1** from the FeatureManager.

343) Press the **Delete** key. Click **Yes** to confirm delete.

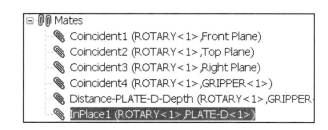

PLATE-D is free to translate and rotate. Create three Mates to define the PLATE-D part in the ROTARY-GRIPPER assembly.

Recall that there are two methods to utilize SmartMates:

- Alt key + Drag.

- SmartMate tool + double-click (component to mate) + click (assembly).

In project 3, you utilized the Alt key. As models become more complex, selecting the correct face while dragging the mouse becomes challenging. Utilize the SmartMate tool located in the Move Component PropertyManager. Double-click the required cylindrical component faces. Click the required assembly face.

Move the PLATE-D part.
344) Click and drag the **PLATE-D** part in the Graphics window to create an approximate 50mm gap between the ROTARY assembly and the PLATE-D part.

Assemble the PLATE-D part.
345) Right-click **Move**. The Move Component PropertyManager is displayed.

346) Click **SmartMate** from the Move Component Property Manager.

Insert the first SmartMate.
347) Double-click the **left inside hole face** on the PLATE-D part.

348) Click the **left hole face** of the ROTARY assembly.

349) Click .

Delete the InPlace Mate. PLATE-D is free to move and rotate.

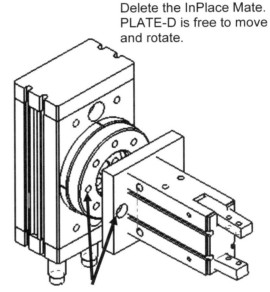

Concentric SmartMate between left holes

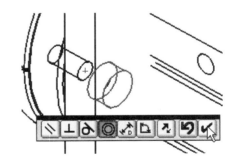

Insert the second SmartMate.
350) Double-click the **right inside hole** face on the PLATE-D part.

351) Click the **right inside hole** face on the ROTARY assembly.

352) Click ✔.

Insert the third SmartMate.
353) Double-click the **back face** on the PLATE-D part.

354) Click the **front face** of the ROTARY assembly.

355) Click ✔.

356) Click **OK**  from the SmartMates PropertyManager.

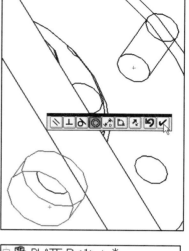

PLATE-D contains no InPlace Mates or External references.

The Lock Reference * symbol remains visible until you close and reopen the ROTARY-GRIPPER assembly.

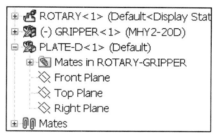

The GRIPPER assembly back face references the ROTARY assembly front face. These Mate Selections are no longer valid in the new design scheme. Redefine the Distance Mate with the PLATE-D front face.

Redefine the Distance-PLATE-D-Depth Mate.
357) Click **Distance-PLATE-D-Depth** Mate.

358) Right-click **Edit Feature**.

359) Click the **ROTARY face** reference.

360) Right-click **Delete**.

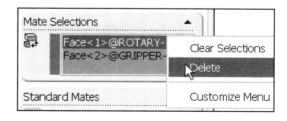

361) Click the **front face** of the PLATE-D part for the Mate Selection.

362) Click **Coincident** from the Pop-up toolbar.

363) Click ✔.

364) Click **OK**  from the Mate PropertyManager.

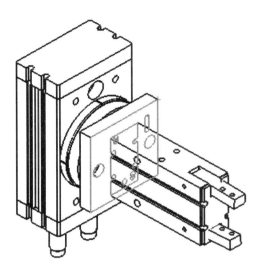

Verify the PLATE-D part.
365) Double-click **PLATE-D** from the Graphics window. The dimensions for the Extrude1 feature are displayed.

366) Double-click **10**.

367) Enter **15**.

368) Click **Rebuild**.

369) Enter **30**.

370) Click **Rebuild**.

Return to the original dimension, 10.
371) Enter **10**. Click **Rebuild**.

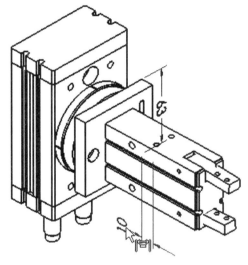

372) Click **OK** from the Dimension PropertyManager.

Save the ROTARY-GRIPPER assembly.
373) Click **Save** from the Main menu.

Close all SolidWorks documents.
374) Click **Windows**, **Close All** from the Main menu.

PLATE-C part

Create PLATE-C. The PLATE-C part is listed in the Assembly Layout Diagram under the ROTARY-GRIPPER assembly.

The ROTARY-GRIPPER assembly cannot be directly fastened to the 2AXIS-TRANSFER assembly. Use the PLATE-C part to assemble the ROTARY-GRIPPER assembly to the 2AXIS-TRANSFER assembly.

Review the PLATE-C design options:

1. Utilize an InPlace Mate in the ROTARY-GRIPPER assembly.

2. Utilize an InPlace Mate in the 2AXIS-TRANSFER assembly.

3. Utilize an InPlace Mate in the 3AXIS TRANSFER assembly.

4. Create an Empty Part with no InPlace Mates.

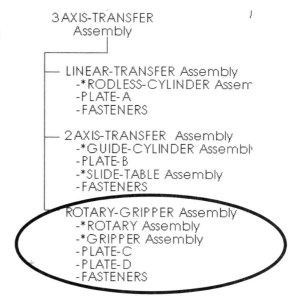

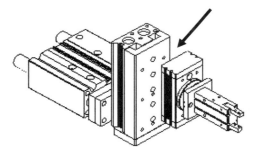

PLATE-C required between two assemblies

Select option 4. An Empty Part is a new part that only contains reference planes. Option 4 creates no InPlace Mates. The three default reference planes orient to the assembly as specified.

Perform the following steps to create the PLATE-C part.

1. Create a new part, PLATE-C.

2. Utilize three Mates to assemble the PLATE-C part reference planes to the 2-AXIS-TRANSFER/SLIDE-TABLE assembly.

3. Select a PLATE-C reference plane for the base feature sketch.

Determine the size and shape of the PLATE-C part.

The 2AXIS-TRANSFER/SLIDE-TABLE assembly and ROTARY assembly determines the geometric and functional requirement for the PLATE-C part.

PLATE-C references the SLIDE-TABLE assembly geometry In-Context of the 2AXIS-TRANSFER assembly.

Create two Thru Holes on the PLATE-C part from the copied ROTARY/ MountingHoles sketch geometry.

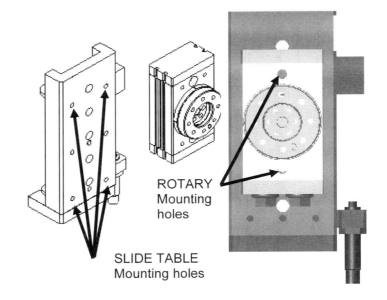

ROTARY
Mounting
holes

SLIDE TABLE
Mounting holes

Design for future changes. Create three different sets of Thru Holes on the PLATE-C part.

Additional mounting holes provide design flexibility for manufacturing, field service and the customer.

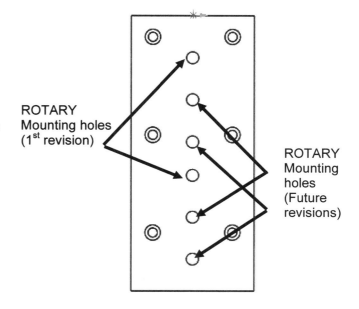

ROTARY
Mounting holes
(1st revision)

ROTARY
Mounting
holes
(Future
revisions)

PLATE-C

Activity: PLATE-C part

Hide the components.
375) Open the **2AXIS-TRANSFER** assembly.

376) Hold the **Ctrl** key down.

377) Select the **GUIDE-CYLINDER**, **PLATE-B**, and the **SLIDE-TABLE/MXSLBody**.

378) Release the **Ctrl** key.

379) Right-click **Hide**.

Create the PLATE-C part
380) Click **File**, **New** from the Main menu.

381) Double-click **PART-MM-ANSI-AL6061**.

382) Click **Save** from the Main menu.

383) Select **DELIVERY-STATION** for Save in: folder.

384) Enter **PLATE-C** for File name.

385) Click **Save**. The PLATE-C FeatureManager is displayed.

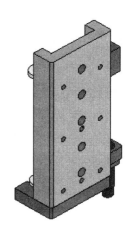

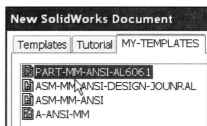

New SolidWorks Document

Templates | Tutorial | MY-TEMPLATES

PART-MM-ANSI-AL6061
ASM-MM-ANSI-DESIGN-JOUNRAL
ASM-MM-ANSI
A-ANSI-MM

Display the Reference Planes.
386) Click **Front Plane** from the PLATE-C FeatureManager.

387) Hold the **Ctrl** key down.

388) Click **Top Plane** and **Right Plane** from the FeatureManager.

389) Release the **Ctrl** key.

390) Right-click **Show**.

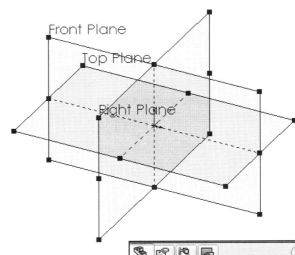

Display an Isometric view.
391) Click **Isometric** view.

Rename the Default Reference Planes.
392) Rename **Front** to **Front-Plate-C**.

393) Rename **Top** to **Top-Plate-C**.

394) Rename **Right** to **Right-Plate-C**.

Save the PLATE-C part.
395) Click **Save**.

Return to the 2AXIS-TRANSFER assembly.
396) Click **Window**, **2AXIS-TRANSFER** from the Main menu.

Insert the PLATE-C part into the 2AXIS-TRANSFER assembly.
397) Click **Insert Component**

   Insert Compo... from the Assembly toolbar,

398) Click **PLATE-C**.

399) Click a **position** to the right of the SLIDE-TABLE assembly. The PLATE-C part is added to the 2AXIS-TRANSFER FeatureManager. The PLATE-C Reference planes are not displayed. All planes are hidden.

400) Click **View**, **Planes** from the Main menu.

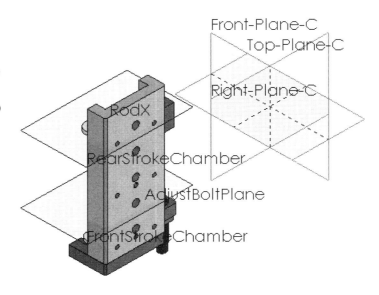

Assemble PLATE-C to the SLIDE-TABLE/MXSL-TABLE.

401) Click the **right face** of the SLIDE-TABLE/ MXSL-TABLE part as illustrated.

402) Click **Mate** Mate . The Mate PropertyManager is displayed.

403) Click **Front-Plate-C** from the FeatureManager.

404) Click **Aligned** . The PLATE-C Plane rotate. The Front-Plate-C Plane is coincident with the front face of the MXSL-TABLE part. The positive side of the Front-Plate-C plane points to the right. Coincident is selected by Default.

405) Click **OK** from the Coincident PropertyManager.

Create the second Mate.

406) Click the **top face** of the MXSL-TABLE part.

407) Click **Top-Plate-C** from the FeatureManager. Coincident is selected by default.

408) Click ✔.

Planes display two colors in an Isometric view. By default, the positive side of a plane is orange. The negative side of a plane is brown.

Create the third Mate.

409) Click the **MXSL-TABLE/Plane3**.

410) Click **Right-Plate-C** from the PLATE-C. Coincident is selected by default.

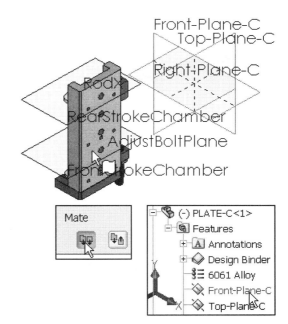

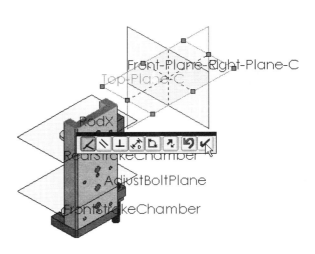

411) Click ✔ .

412) Click **OK** from the Mate PropertyManager.

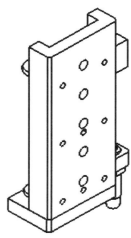

View the three Coincident Mates.
413) Expand the **2AXIS-TRANSFER/Mates**. Note: InPlace Mates are not created.

Select the External References setting.

414) Click **No External References** Externa... from the Assembly toolbar.

415) Click **Hidden Lines Removed**.

416) Hide the **Planes**.

Edit the PLATE-C part In-Context of the 2AXIS-TRANSFER assembly.
417) Right-click **PLATE-C** from the FeatureManager.

418) Click **Edit Part**.

Insert a Sketch.
419) Right-click **Front-Plate-C Plane** from the FeatureManager.

420) Click **Insert Sketch**.

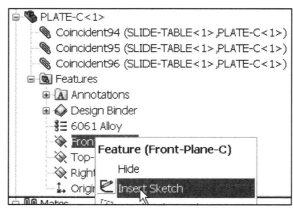

421) Click the **right face** of the SLIDE-TABLE part as illustrated.

422) Click **Convert Entities** Convert from the Sketch toolbar.

Extrude the Sketch.

423) Click **Extrude Boss/Base** Extruded Boss/B... from the FeatureManager toolbar.

424) Enter **15** for Depth. The direction arrow points to the right.

425) Click **OK** from the Extrude PropertyManager.

Note: The Front-PLATE-C Plane is the Extrude1 Sketch plane. The FeatureManager lists no InPlace Mates and no External references. Sketch1 is under-defined.

Edit Component remains selected in the Assembly toolbar. The PLATE-C entry in the FeatureManager is displayed in blue.

The location of the SLIDE-TABLE hole requires the Convert Entity Sketch tool. Obtain the required geometry. Exit Edit Part and return to the 2AXIS-TRANSFER assembly.

Open the PLATE-C part. Create the Cbore and Linear Pattern in the PLATE-C part.

Insert a new Sketch.
426) Click **Hidden Lines Visible**.

427) Click the **right face** of the PLATE-C part.

428) Right-click **Insert Sketch**.

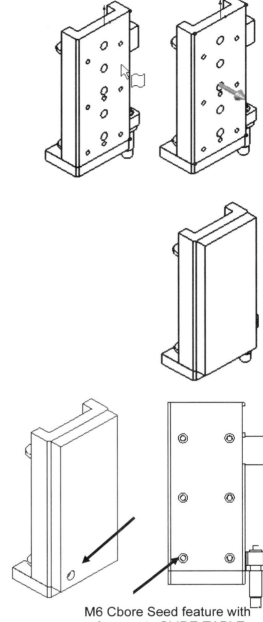

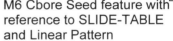

M6 Cbore Seed feature with reference to SLIDE-TABLE and Linear Pattern

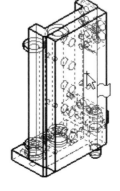

Select the Edge filter.

429) Select the **Edge Filter** .

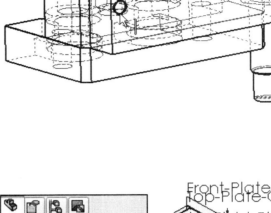

430) Click the **lower left circular edge**. The HolePairs12 of MXSL-Table is displayed.

431) Click **Convert Entities** Convert .

432) Click **Exit Sketch** Exit Sketch .

Return to the assembly.
433) Click **2AXIS-TRANSFER** from the FeatureManager.

434) Right-click **Edit Assembly**.

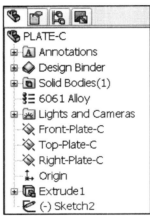

Open the PLATE-C part.
435) Right-click **PLATE-C** from the FeatureManager.

436) Click **Open Part**.

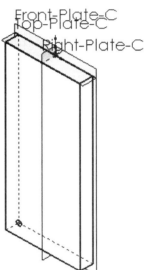

Add a Vertical relation.
437) Right-click **Extrude1**.

438) Click **Edit Sketch**.

Create a Vertical relation.
439) Hold the **Ctrl** key down.

440) Click the **left** and **right** vertical lines of the rectangle.

441) Release the **Ctrl** key.

442) Click **Vertical** from the Add Relations box.

443) Click **OK** 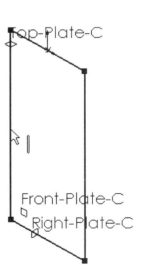 from the Properties PropertyManager.

Create a Horizontal relation.
444) Hold the **Ctrl** key down.

445) Click the **top** and **bottom** horizontal lines of the rectangle.

446) Release the **Ctrl** key.

447) Click **Horizontal** from the Add Relations box.

448) Click **OK** from the Properties PropertyManager.

Display the Front view.
449) Click **Front** view.

Hide the Planes.
450) Click **View**, uncheck **Planes** from the Main menu.

Create a Midpoint relation.
451) Hold the **Ctrl** key down.

452) Click the **top horizontal** line and the **Origin**.

453) Release the **Ctrl** key.

454) Click **Midpoint** from the Add Relations box.

455) Click **OK** from the Properties PropertyManager.

Add dimensions.

456) Click **Smart Dimension** Smart Dimens... from the Sketch toolbar.

457) Add a 197 **vertical dimension** and a 86.41 **horizontal dimension**. The values, 197 and 86.41 are automatically calculated.

458) Double-click **86.41**.

459) Enter **86**. The black sketch is fully defined.

460) Click **Exit Sketch** Exit Sketch .

Save the model.
461) Click **Save**.

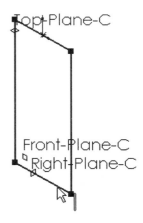

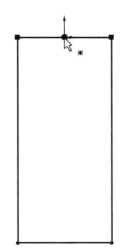

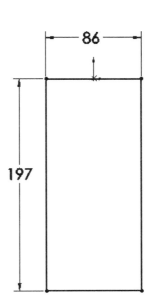

Why was the 86.41 value modified to 86? Answer: To save machining cost. A simple plate in this example does not require 2-place precision.

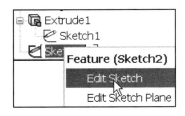

Talk to the machine shop. Identify machined components that can save money and time. Apply precision and tolerance to dimensions in the part. The values propagate to the drawing when inserted from the part.

Edit Sketch2
462) Right-click **Sketch2**.

463) Click **Edit Sketch**.

Add dimensions.

464) Click **Smart Dimension** .

465) Insert a **vertical** and **horizontal dimension**. The dimensions reference the Origin.

466) Insert a **diameter dimension** to fully define the sketch.

467) Click **OK** ✓ from the Dimension PropertyManager.

Modify geometry.
468) Click the **circular edge** as illustrated.

469) Check **For construction**.

470) Click **OK** ✓ from the Circle PropertyManager

471) Click **Exit Sketch** .

Insert the Cbore seed feature. Use the Hole Wizard.
472) Click the **front face**. Extrude1 is displayed in blue.

473) Click **Hole Wizard**  from the Feature toolbar.

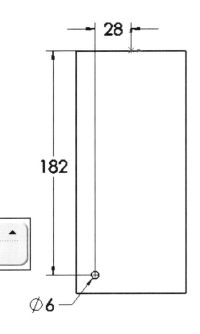

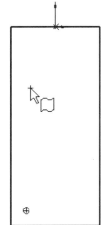

474) Click **Counterbore** for Hole Specification.

475) Click **Ansi Metric** for Standard.

476) Click **Socket Head Cap Screw** for Type.

477) Select **M6** for Size.

478) Select **Through All** for End Condition.

479) Click the **Positions** tab.

480) Right-click **Select**.

Add a Concentric relation.
481) Click the **M6 point.**

482) Hold the **Ctrl** key down.

483) Click the **construction circle**.

484) Release the **Ctrl** key.

485) Click **Concentric**. Click **OK** from the Properties PropertyManager.

486) Click OK from the Hole Position PropertyManager.

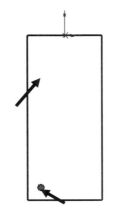

Review the SLIDE-TABLE hole locations.
Double-click SLIDE-TABLE/MXSLTable/
TableHoleLayout sketch. The holes are spaced
56mm x 70mm apart.

Insert a Linear Pattern.

487) Click **Linear Pattern** Linear Pattern from the Features toolbar.

488) Click the **bottom horizontal line** for Direction1. The arrow points to the right.

489) Enter **56** for Direction1.

490) Enter **2** for Number of Instances.

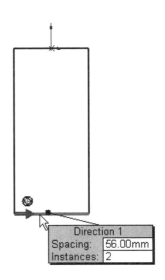

491) Click the **left vertical line** for Direction2. The arrow point up.

492) Enter **70** for Direction2.

493) Enter **3** for Number of Instances.

494) Click **Geometric Pattern**.

495) Click **CBORE for M6** for Features to Pattern.

496) Click **OK**  from the Linear Pattern PropertyManager.

PLATE-C requires two 8.6mm holes. Copy the sketch, ROTARY/MSQBBody/ MountingHoles/Sketch11 to the PLATE-C part.

The dimensions, 21.55mm and 127.10mm determine the location of the first hole and the overall length of the ROTARY body. Modify the dimension values to 22mm and 127mm. The first hole is located 22mm from the PLATE-C edge. The second hole is vertically located 84mm from the first hole.

Open the ROTARY assembly.
497) Click **File**, **Open** from the Main menu.

498) Double-click **ASSEMBLY-SW-FILES-2006/ SMC/MSQB30R/ROTARY.sldasm**.

Review the ROTARY requirements.
499) Open **MSQBBody** from the ROTARY FeatureMaanger.

500) Double-click **MSQBBody/Mounting Holes/Sketch11** from the FeatureManager. View the dimensions.

Copy the MountingHoles Sketch11.
501) Click **Sketch11** from the FeatureManager.

502) Press the **Ctrl+C** Shortcut keys to copy.

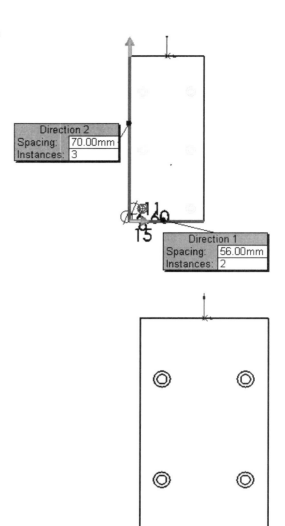

Paste the MountingHoles sketch. Return to PLATE-C.
503) Return to **PLATE-C**.

504) Click **Back** view.

505) Click the **back face** of PLATE-C as illustrated.

506) Press **Ctrl+V** to paste.

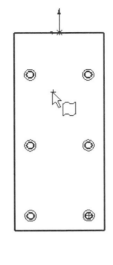
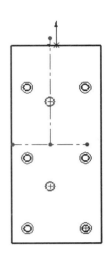

Rename the sketch.
507) Rename **Sketch11** to **Rotary Hole Position**.

Edit the Sketch.
508) Right-click **Rotary Hole Position** from the FeatureManager.

509) Click **Edit Sketch**.

Add a Vertical relation.
510) Click the PLATE-C **Origin**.

511) Hold the **Ctrl** key down.

512) Click the **top center point** and **bottom center point**.

513) Release the **Ctrl** key.

514) Click **Vertical**.

515) Click **OK** from the Properties PropertyManager.

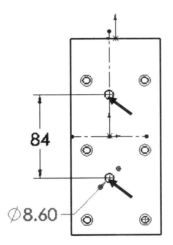
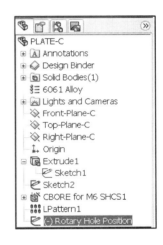

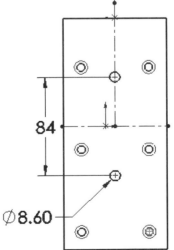

Add a vertical dimension.

516) Click **Smart Dimension** Dimens... from the Sketch toolbar.

517) Create a **vertical dimension** from the Origin to the top center point.

518) Enter **22**. The black sketch is fully defined.

519) Click **OK** from the PropertyManager.

520) Click **Exit Sketch** Sketch .

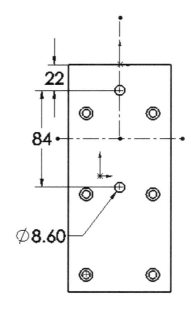

Use the Rotary Hole Position sketch to locate the PLATE-C M8.6 Thru Holes. Create the Thru Holes with the Hole Wizard. Prepare for future design changes. Create three sets of two Thru Holes with a Linear Pattern.

Create two holes. Use the Hole Wizard.
521) Click the **back face** in between the two sketched circles as illustrated.

522) Click **Hole Wizard** Wizard from the Feature toolbar.

523) Click **Hole** for Hole Specification.

524) Click **Ansi Metric** for Standard.

525) Click **Drill size** for Type.

526) Select **8.6** for Size.

527) Select **Through All** for End Condition.

528) Click the **Positions** tab.

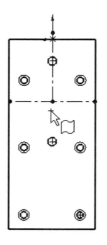

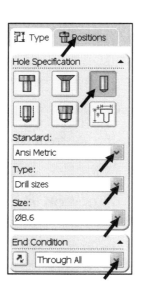

529) Click the **center point** of the first sketched circle.

530) Click the **center point** of the second sketched circle.

531) Right-click **Select**.

532) Click the **first point**.

533) Right-click **Delete**.

534) Click **OK** from the Hole Position PropertyManager.

Hide the Rotary Hole Position sketch.
535) Right-click **Rotary Hole Position** from the FeatureManager.

536) Click **Hide**.

Create a Linear Pattern.
537) Click **8.6(8.6) Diameter Hole1** from the FeatureManager.

538) Click **Linear Pattern** Linear Pattern from the Feature toolbar.

539) Click the **left vertical edge**. The arrow points downward.

540) Enter **25** for Distance.

541) Enter **3** for Number of Instances.

542) Click **OK** from the Linear Pattern PropertyManager.

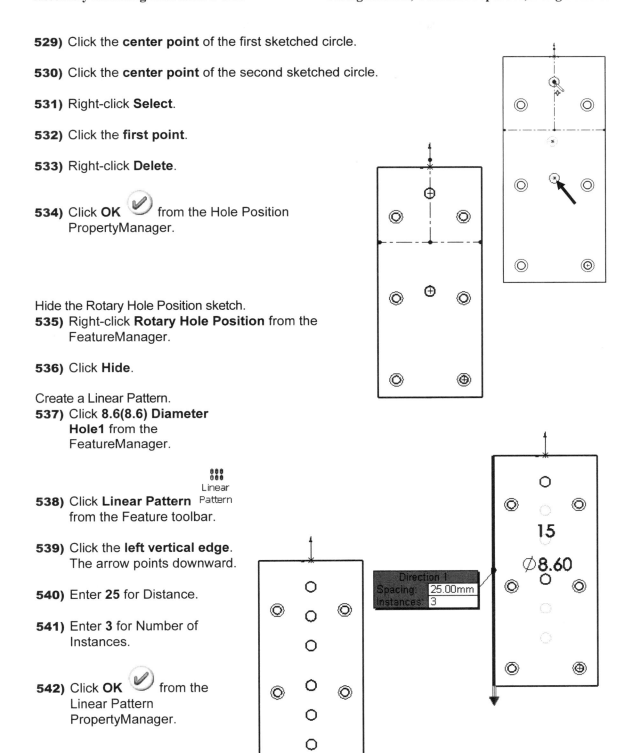

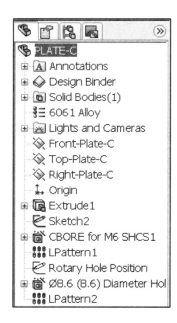

Confirm dimensions and precision when copying geometry between parts. Check the precision of the copied part.

Example 1: In inch units, the value .375 is rounded to .38. Two decimal places are selected for linear units.

Example 2: In millimeter units, the value 27.5 is rounded to 28. Zero decimal places are selected for linear units.

Save the PLATE-C part.
543) Click **Save** from the Main menu.

Open the 2AXIS-TRANSFER assembly.
544) Open the **2AXIS-TRANSFER** assembly.

545) Click **Yes** to Update the assembly.

Display Hidden Components.
546) Click the **GUIDE-CYLINDER**.

547) Hold the **Ctrl** key down.

548) Click **PLATE-B, GUIDE-CYLINDER,** and **SLIDE-TABLE/MXSL-Body** from the FeatureManager.

549) Release the **Ctrl** key.

550) Right-click **Show**.

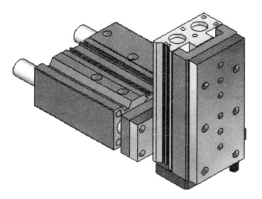

Save the 2AXIS-TRANSFER assembly.
551) Click **Save**.

Close all components.
552) Click **Windows, Close All** from the Main menu.

Identify the fasteners for the PLATE-C part and the PLATE-D part.

Required fasteners for the PLATE-C part:

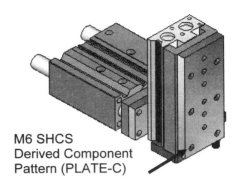

M6 SHCS
Derived Component
Pattern (PLATE-C)

- Six M6 SHCSs to fasten the PLATE-C part to the SLIDE-TABLE assembly.

- Two M8 SHCSs to fasten the PLATE-C part to the ROTARY assembly.

Required fasteners for the PLATE-D part:

- Two M5 SHCSs to fasten the PLATE-D part to the ROTARY assembly.

- Two M4 SHCSs to fasten to the PLATE-D part to the GRIPPER assembly.

Develop the fasteners for the PLATE-D part and the PLATE-C part in the project exercises.

ROTARY-GRIPPER Design Table

Create the ROTARY-GRIPPER Design Table with three configurations: Flexible, Rotation0 and Rotation90. The configuration names refer to the position of the GRIPPER assembly. The Default is the current configuration.

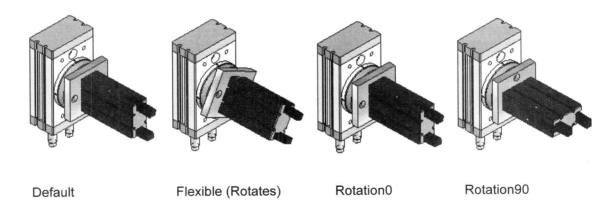

Default   Flexible (Rotates)   Rotation0   Rotation90

ROTARY-GRIPPER configuration

Activity: ROTARY-GRIPPER Design Table

Insert a Design Table.
553) Open the **ROTARY-GRIPPER** assembly.

554) Click **Insert**, **Design Table** from the Main menu.

555) Accept the defaults. Click **OK** .

Enter the ROTARY-GRIPPER configuration names.
556) Enter **Flexible** in Cell A4.

557) Enter **Rotation0** in Cell A5.

558) Enter **Rotation90** in Cell A6.

Enter the ROTARY configuration parameters.
559) Enter **$Configuration@ROTARY<1>** in Cell B2.

560) Copy **Cell A3** through **Cell A6** to Cell B3 through B6.

561) Click a **position** in the Graphics window.

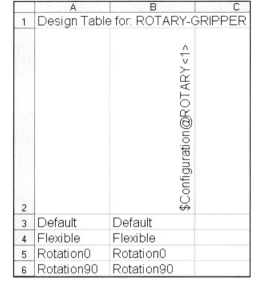

	A	B	C
1	Design Table for: ROTARY-GRIPPER		
2		$Configuration@ROTARY<1>	
3	Default	Default	
4	Flexible	Flexible	
5	Rotation0	Rotation0	
6	Rotation90	Rotation90	

Note: The $Configuration@ROTARY<1> utilizes the name and instance number from the FeatureManager. The values must be identical. Parameters and values are not case-sensitive.

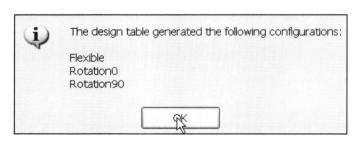

The design table generated the following configurations:

Flexible
Rotation0
Rotation90

OK

Modify the Flexible configuration.
562) Double-click **Flexible** from the ConfigurationManager.

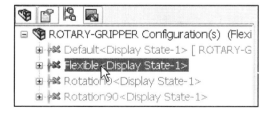

ROTARY-GRIPPER Configuration(s) (Flexi
- Default<Display State-1> [ROTARY-G
- Flexible<Display State-1>
- Rotation0<Display State-1>
- Rotation90<Display State-1>

563) Right-click **ROTARY** from the FeatureManager.

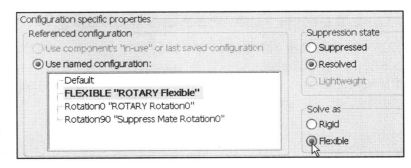

564) Click **Component Properties**.

565) Click **Flexible** for Solve as.

566) Click **OK**. The GRIPPER assembly and the PLATE-D part are free to rotate.

567) Click the **ConfigurationManager**.

Test the configurations.
568) Double-click **Default**, **Flexible**, **Rotation0** and **Rotation90**.

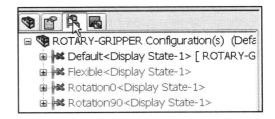

Note: A Rebuild may be required to update the ROTARY-GRIPPER assembly.

Return to the Default configuration.
569) Double-click **Default** configuration.

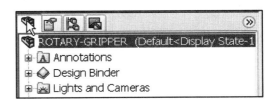

Save the ROTARY-GRIPPER assembly.
570) Click the **FeatureManager**.

571) Click **Isometric** view.

572) Click **Save**.

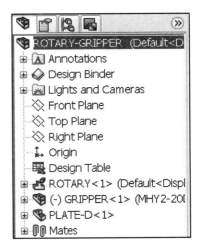

PLATE-D requires three different material thicknesses for testing. How do you control the depth of the Extrude1 feature in the ROTARY-GRIPPER assembly?

Answer: Create three configurations in the PLATE-D part. Incorporate the PLATE-D configuration into the ROTARY-GRIPPER Design Table.

PLATE-D Design Table and Properties

Utilize the Design Table to create three configurations of the PLATE-D part. The configuration name contains a unique part number. Each configuration represents a different extruded depth. Rename the depth dimension parameter and insert the dimension parameter into the Design Table.

Properties are parameters defined in a single document that can be accessed and utilized by multiple documents. Parts and assemblies contain System Properties and User defined Properties.

System Properties

System Properties extract Summary Information values from the current document. System Properties are determined from the SolidWorks documents. Insert System Properties as linked Notes.

System Properties begin with the prefix SW. There are two categories of Properties: System Properties and Drawing Specific System Properties (Project 5). Set System Properties in the File, Properties, Summary Information dialog box as follows:

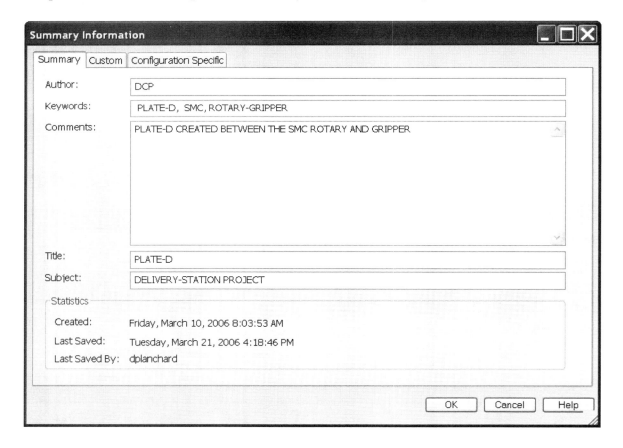

User defined Properties

There are two types of User defined Properties: Custom Properties and Configuration Specific Properties.

Custom Properties apply to all of the configurations of a part or an assembly. Configuration Specific Properties apply to only a single configuration of a part or an assembly.

Assign User defined Property values to named variables in the SolidWorks document.

The default variables are listed in the text file: SolidWorks/ Lang/English/Properties.txt. Create your own User defined Property named variables.

Conserve design time. Utilize System Properties and define Custom Properties and Configuration Specific Properties in the ConfigurationManager and the Design Table.

```
Description
PartNo
Number
Revision
Material
Weight
Finish
StockSize
UnitOfMeasure
Cost
MakeOrBuy
LeadTime
CheckedBy
CheckedDate
DrawnBy
DrawnDate
EngineeringApproval
EngAppDate
ManufacturingApproval
MfgAppDate
QAApproval
QAAppDate
Vendor
VendorNo
Client
Project
Status
DateCompleted
CompanyName
Department
Division
Group
Author
Owner
Source
```

User Defined Properties

PLATE-D Properties

PLATE-D requires four Configuration Specific Properties. Utilize the following PLATE-D Properties in the part drawing and assembly drawing:

- Material.

- Mass.

- Description.

- $PARTNUMBER.

The Materials Editor provides a list of predefined and user defined materials and their physical properties. Link the Material Property to the value, "SW-Material@@Default@ PLATE-D.SLDPRT". This value corresponds to the Material assigned with the Materials Editor. Link the Mass Property to the value "SW-Mass@@Default@PLATE-D.SLDPRT". The value corresponds to the mass calculated through the Mass Properties tool. Create a new Property named, Mass.

A parameter is in the form:

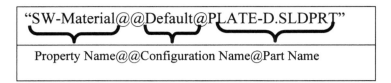

"SW-Material@@Default@PLATE-D.SLDPRT"

Property Name@@Configuration Name@Part Name

Cell entries in the Bill of Materials (BOM) are linked to Properties created in the part and assembly. Create Properties in the part with two techniques:

• Configuration Properties.

• Design Table.

There are three Bill of Materials Options for the part number:

• Document Name (file name).

• Configuration Name.

• User Specified Name.

The $PARTNUMBER Property contains three values in a Design Table:

• $D Document Name (filename).

• $C Configuration Name.

• User Specified Name (not shown).

Do you notice the similarity? Answer: Values entered in the ConfigurationManager correspond to values in the Design Table and vice versa.

In the next activity, define Properties and their values by working between the Design Table and the ConfigurationManager.

Activity: PLATE-D Design Table and Custom Properties

Display the PLATE-D part dimensions.
573) Open the **PLATE-D** part.

574) Click **Isometric** view.

575) Drag the **Rollback bar** below the Extrude1 feature.

576) Right-click the **Annotations** folder.

577) Click **Show Feature Dimensions**.

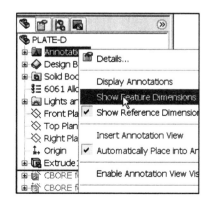

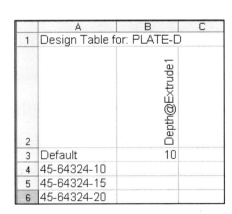

Provide additional control to clearly display feature dimensions for the Design Table. The Show Feature Dimensions option in the Annotations folder displays all feature dimensions. Only entries before the Rollback bar display feature dimensions. Position the Rollback bar to reduce the number of dimensions.

To hide unwanted individual feature dimensions, right-click on the feature entry. Click Hide All Dimensions.

To display hidden feature dimensions, right-click on the feature entry. Click Show All Dimensions.

Rename the Depth dimension.
578) Click the **10** depth dimension of the Extrude1 feature.

579) Right-click **Properties**.

580) Enter **Depth** for Name.

581) Click **OK**.

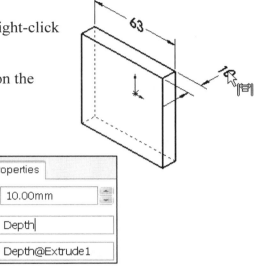

582) Click **OK** ✓ from the Dimension PropertyManager.

Insert a Design Table.
583) Click **Insert**, **Design Table** from the Main menu. Accept the defaults.

584) Click **OK** ✓ from the Design Table PropertyManager.

585) Click **Depth@Extrude1** from the Dimensions box.

586) Click **OK**. The Design Table displays the Depth@Extrude1 parameter in Cell B2. The dimension value 10 is displayed in Cell B3.

Enter the configuration names.
587) Enter **45-64324-10** in Cell A4.

588) Enter **45-64324-15** in Cell A5.

589) Enter **45-64324-20** in Cell A6.

	A	B	C
1	Design Table for: PLATE-D		
2		Depth@Extrude1	
3	Default	10	
4	45-64324-10		
5	45-64324-15		
6	45-64324-20		

Enter the Depth@Extrude1 dimension values.
590) Enter **10** in Cell B4.

591) Enter **15** in Cell B5.

592) Enter **20** in Cell B6.

Create the PLATE-D configurations.
593) Click a **position** outside the Design Table.

594) Click **OK** to generate the three tables.

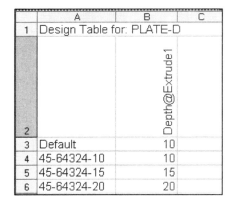

Restore all features.
595) Drag the **Rollback** bar to the bottom of the FeatureManager.

Hide the feature dimensions.
596) Right-click **Annotations**.

597) Uncheck **Show Feature Dimensions**.

Verify the PLATE-D configurations.
598) Drag the **Split bar** to divide the FeatureManager in half.

599) Click the **ConfigurationManager** 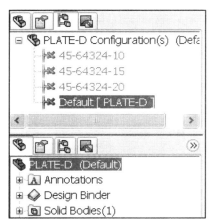.

600) Double-click each configuration: **45-64324-10**, **45-64324-15** & **45-64324-20**.

Return to the Default configuration.
601) Double-click **Default**.

602) Click the **FeatureManager** icon.

Save the PLATE-D part.
603) Click **Save**.

Display the Mass Properties.
604) Click **Tools**, **Mass Properties** from the Main menu.

605) Click **Options**.

606) Click **Use custom settings**.

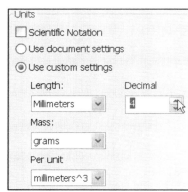

607) Enter **4** for Decimal Places.

608) Click **OK**. The Mass 102.7999 g is displayed. The assigned Material determines the Density 0.0027 g/mm^3.

609) Click **Close**.

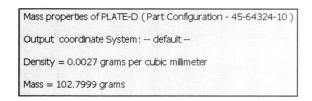

Define Mass and Material in the PLATE-D ConfigurationManager. Enter and modify parameters in the ConfigurationManager and Design Table.

Always check units. Example: The volume of the PLATE-D part is measured in mm^3. Density of Aluminum is $2.700g/cm^3 = 0.0027g/mm^3$. Mass is calculated in grams. Mass = Density x Volume. Mass is multiplied by the gravitational constant of $9.8\ m/s^2$ to obtain the force; weight. In the SI system, force is measured in newtons.

SolidWorks calculates the volume to be $40,634.0433mm^3$. A rough volume calculation based on overall dimensions is 65mm x 65mm x 10mm = $42,250mm^3$. Mass equals $(0.0027g/mm^3)(42250mm^3) = 114.08g$. So why do the calculated values differ from the SolidWorks values. Answer: The rough calculations did not account for the holes.

Add Custom Properties to the PLATE-D part.
610) Click the **ConfigurationManager** .

611) Right-click **Default**.

612) Click **Properties**. The Part number displayed when used in a bill of materials option displays PLATE-D.

613) Click **Custom properties**. The Configuration Specific properties are displayed in a table.

Insert the Configuration Specific Properties.
614) Click the **Configuration Specific** tab.

615) Select **Material** for the Property Name in Row 1. Text is the default Type value.

616) Select **Material** for Value/Text Expression. SolidWorks displays the Evaluated Value, 6061 Alloy.

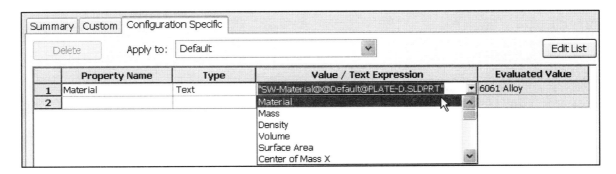

	Property Name	Type	Value / Text Expression	Evaluated Value
1	Material	Text	"SW-Material@@Default@PLATE-D.SLDPRT"	6061 Alloy
2			Material	
			Mass	
			Density	
			Volume	
			Surface Area	
			Center of Mass X	

617) Select **Description** for the Property Name in Row 2.

618) Enter **PLATE**-D for the Value/Text Expression.

619) Enter **Mass** for the Property Name.

620) Select **Mass** for the Value/Text Expression.

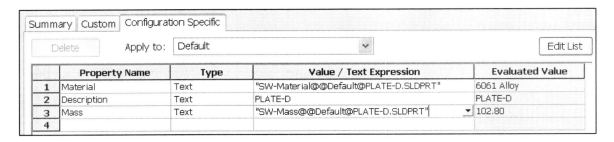

	Property Name	Type	Value / Text Expression	Evaluated Value
1	Material	Text	"SW-Material@@Default@PLATE-D.SLDPRT"	6061 Alloy
2	Description	Text	PLATE-D	PLATE-D
3	Mass	Text	"SW-Mass@@Default@PLATE-D.SLDPRT"	102.80
4				

621) Click **OK** from the Summary Information dialog box.

622) Click **OK** ✅.

Update the Design Table.
623) Right-click **Design Table** from the FeatureManager.

624) Click **Edit Table**. Check **Show unselected items again**.

625) Click **$PRP@Description**.

626) Hold the **Ctrl** key down. Click **$PRP@Mass** and **$PRP@Material**. Release the **Ctrl** key.

627) Click **OK** to insert the parameters and values into the Design Table.

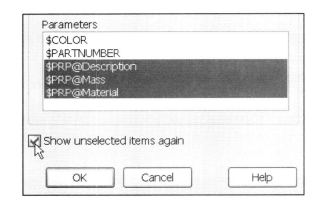

Copy/Paste the default values.
628) Select **Cell C3** through **Cell E3**. A White Cross ✛ icon is displayed.

629) Position the **mouse pointer** at the lower right corner of Cell E3. A small black cross ✚ is displayed.

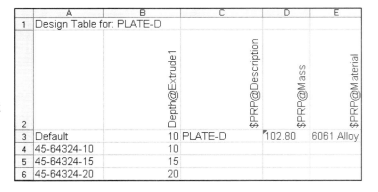

	A	B	C	D	E
1	Design Table for: PLATE-D				
2		Depth@Extrude1	$PRP@Description	$PRP@Mass	$PRP@Material
3	Default	10	PLATE-D	102.80	6061 Alloy
4	45-64324-10	10			
5	45-64324-15	15			
6	45-64324-20	20			

630) Drag the **mouse pointer downward** to fill Cells C4 through E4. The values for the 45-64324-10 configuration are defined.

Return to SolidWorks.
631) Click a **position** outside the Design Table.

	A	B	C	D	E
1	Design Table for: PLATE-D				
2		Depth@Extrude1	$PRP@Description	$PRP@Mass	$PRP@Material
3	Default	10	PLATE-D	102.80	6061 Alloy
4	45-64324-10	10	PLATE-D	102.80	6061 Alloy
5	45-64324-15	15	PLATE-D	102.80	6061 Alloy
6	45-64324-20	20	PLATE-D	102.80	6061 Alloy

Review the 45-64324-10 configuration.
632) Right-click **45-64324-10** from the ConfigurationManager.

633) Click **Properties**.

634) Click **Custom properties**.

635) Click the **Configuration Specific** tab. The Description, Mass, and Material values are displayed.

636) Click **OK**.

Return to the Design Table.
637) Right-click **Design Table** from the FeatureManager.

638) Click **Edit Table**.

639) Select **$PARTNUMBER** from the Add Rows and Columns.

640) Click **OK**.

SolidWorks updates the Description, Mass, and Material values and enters $PARTNUMBER in Cell F2. If $PARTNUMBER is not displayed, select Cell F2. Enter $PARTNUMBER.

Enter $PARTNUMBER used in the Bill of Materials.
641) Cell F3 contains $D for the Document Name. If required, enter **$C** in Cell F4 through Cell F6 for Configuration name.

E	F
$PRP@Material	$PARTNUMBER
6061 Alloy	$D
6061 Alloy	$C
6061 Alloy	$C
6061 Alloy	$C

The $user_notes parameter accepts all text values. Utilize the $user_notes parameter to enter comments that describe the Extrude1 depth in millimeters. Column B contains the values for each configuration. Enter the text, "mm Depth" in Cell I3. The EXCEL Concatenate function combines text strings into a single cell. An absolute reference to an EXCEL cell location contains the "$" symbol before the row and column entry, Example: I3.

Utilize an empty column in the Design Table to separate values not calculated by SolidWorks. If you insert additional rows and columns into the Design Table, verify that you maintained proper absolute cell references.

Enter $user_notes parameter.
642) Click **Cell G2**.

643) Enter **$user_notes**.

644) Click **Cell I3**.

645) Enter **mm Depth**.

646) Click **Cell G3**.

647) Click a **position** inside the formula bar.

648) Enter **=CONCATENATE(B3,I3)**. The value, 10mm Depth is displayed in Cell G3.

649) Copy **Cell G3** to Cell G4 through Cell G6.

🔆 Select Cell entries directly as function arguments. Select the Function *fx* icon. Enter CONCATENATE. Click Cell B3 for the Text1 box. Click Cell I3 for Text2. The values display to the right of the box. Modify Text2 to I3.

🔆 Utilize the "=" Shortcut key to begin a new formula. Utilize the "&" Shortcut key for the CONCATENATE function. Example: =B3&I3

fx =CONCATENATE(B3,I3)

EXCEL Formula Bar

F	G	H	I
$PARTNUMBER	$user_notes		
$D	10mm Depth		mm Depth
$C	10mm Depth		
$C	15mm Depth		
$C	20mm Depth		

Exit the Design Table and Return to SolidWorks.
650) Click a **position** outside the Design Table.

Insert a Custom Property.
651) Right-click **Default** from the ConfigurationManager.

652) Click **Properties**.

653) Click **Custom Properties**.

654) Click the **Custom** tab. Click **Yes** to update.

655) Select **LeadTime** from the Property Name list.

656) Enter **1-2 weeks** for Value.

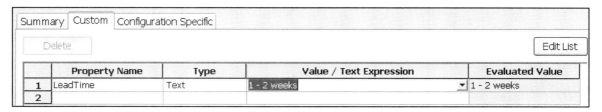

657) Click **OK**.

658) Click **OK** 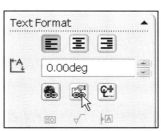.

Insert a Linked Note.
659) Click **Insert**, **Annotations**, **Note** from the Main menu. The Note PropertyManager is displayed.

660) Click a **position** in the lower left corner of the Graphics window.

661) Enter **Lead Time for PLATE-D**.

662) Click **Link to Property** from the Text Format box.

663) Select **LeadTime** from the Link to Property list.

664) Select **OK**. Press **Enter** to start a new line. Enter **Mass equals**.

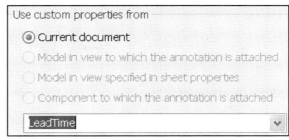

665) Click **Link to Property** from the Text Format box. Select **Mass** from the Link to Property list.

666) Click **OK**. Enter **grams** to complete the note.

667) Click **OK** from the Note PropertyManager.

Hide Annotations.
668) Right-click **Annotations** from the
FeatureManager. Un-check **Display Annotations**.

Save the PLATE-D part.
669) Click **Save**

The LeadTime Custom Property contains the same value across all configurations. The Mass Configuration Specific Property contains different values for each configuration.

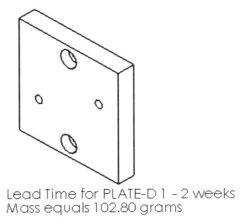

Lead Time for PLATE-D 1 - 2 weeks
Mass equals 102.80 grams

The ROTARY-GRIPPER assembly contains the default configuration for the PLATE-D part. How do you modify the assembly to support multiple configurations of the PLATE-D in a drawing? Answer: Utilize a Design Table.

Edit the ROTARY-GRIPPER Design Table

The ROTARY-GRIPPER incorporates PLATE-D configurations and ROTARY configurations. Edit the ROTARY-GRIPPER Design Table. Delete Rotation0 and Rotation90 configurations. Insert six ROTARY-GRIPPER configurations to define the horizontal and vertical position. Utilize the three PLATE-D configurations: 45-64324-10, 45-64324-15, and 45-64324-20.

Activity: Edit the ROTARY-GRIPPER Design Table

Open the ROTARY-GRIPPER assembly.
670) Click **Window**, **ROTARY-GRIPPER** from the Main menu. The ROTARY assembly and PLATE-D part are set to the Default configurations.

Edit the Design Table.
671) Right-click **Design Table**.

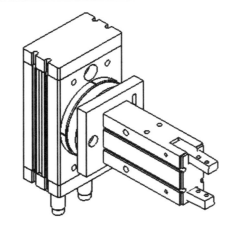

672) Click **Edit Table**.

673) Click **OK**.

674) Select **Row 5** and **Row 6**.

675) Right-click **Delete**.

Insert six configuration names.
676) Enter **Horizontal-10** in Cell A5.

677) Enter **Horizontal-15** in Cell A6.

678) Enter **Horizontal-20** in Cell A7.

679) Enter **Vertical-10** in Cell A8.

680) Enter **Vertical-15** in Cell A9.

681) Enter **Vertical-20** in Cell A10.

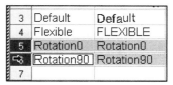

	3	Default	Default
	4	Flexible	FLEXIBLE
	5	Rotation0	Rotation0
	6	Rotation90	Rotation90
	7		

	A	B	C
1	Design Table for: ROTARY-GRIPPER		
2		$Configuration@ROTARY<1>	
3	Default	Default	
4	Flexible	FLEXIBLE	
5	Horizontal-10	Rotation90	
6	Horizontal-15	Rotation90	
7	Horizontal-20	Rotation90	
8	Vertical-10	Rotation0	
9	Vertical-15	Rotation0	
10	Vertical-20	Rotation0	

Insert parameters and values.
682) Enter **ROTATION90** in Cell B5.

683) Copy **Cell B5** to Cell B6-B7.

684) Enter **ROTATION0** in Cell B8.

685) Copy **Cell B8** to Cell B9-B10.

686) Enter **$Configuration@PLATE-D<1>** in Cell C2.

687) Enter **45-64324-10** in Cell C5.

688) Enter **45-64324-15** in Cell C6.

689) Enter **45-64324-20** in Cell C7.

690) Copy **Cell C5-C7** to Cell C8-C10.

691) Click a **position** in the Graphics window to exit the Design Table.

	A	B	C
1	Design Table for: ROTARY-GRIPPER		
2		$Configuration@ROTARY<1>	$Configuration@PLATE-D<1>
3	Default	Default	
4	Flexible	FLEXIBLE	
5	Horizontal-10	Rotation90	45-64324-10
6	Horizontal-15	Rotation90	45-64324-15
7	Horizontal-20	Rotation90	45-64324-20
8	Vertical-10	Rotation0	45-64324-10
9	Vertical-15	Rotation0	45-64324-15
10	Vertical-20	Rotation0	45-64324-20

692) Click **OK** to generate configurations.

693) Click **Yes** to delete the Rotation0 and Rotation90 configurations from the ConfigurationManager.

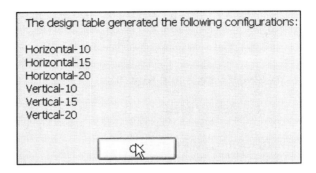

View the six ROTARY-GRIPPER configurations.
694) Double-click **Horizontal-10**, **Horizontal-15**, **Horizontal-20**, **Vertical-10**, **Vertical-15,** and **Vertical-20**.

Return to the Default configuration.
695) Double-click **Default**.

696) Click the **FeatureManager** icon.

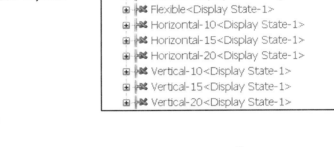

Save the ROTARY-GRIPPER assembly.
697) Click **Save**.

Close the ROTARY-GRIPPER assembly.
698) Click **File**, **Close** from the Main menu.

Horizontal-10   Horizontal-15   Horizontal-20

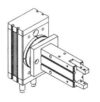

Vertical-10   Vertical-15   Vertical-20

PLATE-D configuration incorporated into
ROTARY-GRIPPER configurations

Display PLATE-D in an Isometric view.
699) Click **Isometric** view. PLATE-D is in the
     Default configuration.

Manufacturing requires a drawing of the three
PLATE-D configurations. Do you create three
separate drawings? Answer: No. Utilize the
configurations in a multi-sheet drawing.

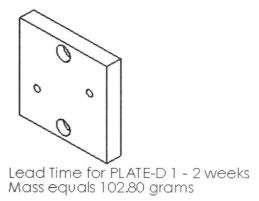

Lead Time for PLATE-D 1 - 2 weeks
Mass equals 102.80 grams

PLATE-D drawing

The PLATE-D drawing contains multiple configurations of the PLATE-D part. Utilize
linked Notes to insert the Custom Properties from the PLATE-D part into the PLATE-D
drawing.

Create the PLATE-D drawing. Control Custom Properties through the View Properties
for Sheet1 and Sheet2. Sheet1 contains Drawing View1 (Front) and Drawing View2
(Right) for the Default configuration. Sheet2 contains Drawing View3 (Front) and
Drawing View4 (Right) for the 45-64324-20 configuration.

Note: View numbers increment if you delete and recreate a view. Views can be renamed.

Activity: PLATE-D drawing

Insert a new drawing for the Default configuration.

700) Click **Make Drawing from Part/Assembly** 🖼 in the
     Standard toolbar.

701) Click the **MY-TEMPLATES** tab.

702) Double-click **A-ANSI-MM** for the Drawing Template.

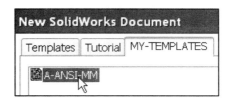

Insert the Front view and Right view.

703) The Model View PropertyManager is displayed. Click **Multiple views** from the Number of Views box.

704) Click ***Right view** from the Orientation box. Note: Front view is activated by default.

705) Click **Hidden Lines Visible** from the Display Style box.

706) Click **OK** 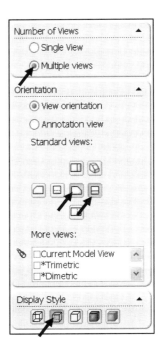 from the Model View PropertyManager.

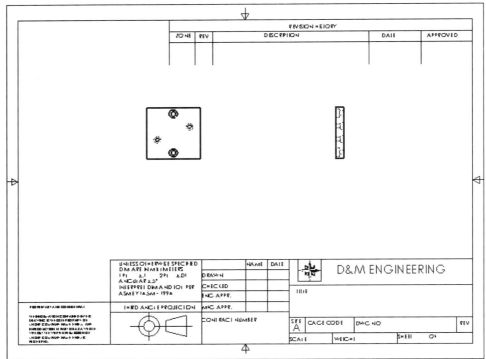

Save the drawing.
707) Click **Save**.

708) Select **DELIVERY-STATION** for Save in: folder.

709) Enter **PLATE-D** for File name. Drawing is the Save as type.

710) Click **Save**.

Insert a linked note.

711) Click **Note** ^A Note from the Annotations toolbar.

712) Click a position below the **Right** view.

713) Enter **MATERIAL**.

714) Click **Link to Property** 🖫.

715) Check the **Model in view to which the annotation is attached** option.

716) Select **Material** from the drop down list.

717) Click **OK**. The parameter $PRPVIEW: "{Material}" displays in the text box.

718) Click **OK** ✅ from the Note PropertyManager. The value 6061 Alloy is displayed in the text box.

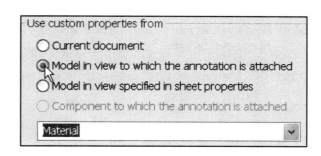

MATERIAL$PRPVIEW:{Material}

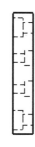

MATERIAL 6061 Alloy

Modify the linked note.
719) Double-click the **note**.

720) Press the **Enter** key to insert a second line.

721) Enter **MASS**.

722) Click **Link to Property** 🖫.

723) Check the **Model in view to which the annotation is attached** option.

724) Select **Mass** from the drop down list.

725) Click **OK**.

726) Enter **grams**.

727) Click **OK**  from the Note PropertyManager.

MATERIAL 6061 Alloy
MASS 102.80 grams

Copy the views from Sheet1 to Sheet2.
728) Click **Drawing View1** from the FeatureManager.

729) Hold the **Ctrl** key down. Click **Drawing View2** from the FeatureManager.

730) Click the **linked note**. Release the **Ctrl** key.

731) Press **Ctrl+C** to copy the views.

732) Right-click the **Sheet1** tab.

733) Click **Add Sheet**. Click **Browse**.

734) Double-click **a-format** from the MY-TEMPLATES folder. Click **OK**.

735) Click a **position** in the center of Sheet2.

736) Press **Ctrl+V** to paste the views and text.

Modify the Drawing View Properties in Sheet2.
737) Click in the **Front view boundary**.

738) Hold the **Ctrl** key down.

739) Click the projected **Right view boundary**.

740) Right-click **Properties**. The Drawing View Properties box is displayed.

741) Release the **Ctrl** key.

742) Click **45-64324-20** in the Used named configuration list box.

743) Click **OK**. The 45-64324-20 reflects changes to the Mass linked note and the View Properties.

744) Click the **Sheet1** tab.

Fit the drawing to the Graphics window.
745) Press the **f** key.

Save the PLATE-D Drawing.
746) Click **Save**.

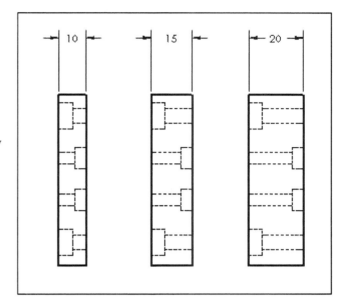

💡 Control the positions of notes in the drawing. Notes attached to a view move with the view.

💡 Save detailing time. Insert Model Items (dimensions) before copying a view and changing the configuration name. The copied dimensions update to reflect the new configuration.

Editing the PLATE-D part and Design Table

The PLATE-D part requires an Extruded Cut feature. The $STATE configuration parameter controls the Suppress/UnSuppress state of the Extrude Cut. Modify the PLATE-D Design Table.

Utilize a slot-shaped profile. This sketch utilizes 3 equal centerlines to control the width of the slot relative to the edges of the profile.

Activity: Editing the PLATE-D part and Design Table

Open the PLATE-D part from the drawing.
747) Right-click inside the **view boundary**.

748) Click **Open plate-d**. The Default configuration is displayed.

749) Click the **front face** of PLATE-D.

Sketch a Rectangle.
750) Click **Front** view.

751) Click **Sketch** .

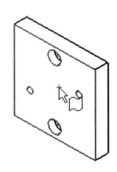

752) Click **Rectangle** Rectan... from the Sketch toolbar.

753) Sketch a **rectangle** in the upper left corner as illustrated.

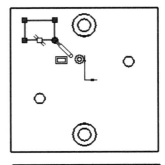

754) Click **Trim** Trim from the Sketch toolbar.

755) Select the **two vertical lines** to be removed.

756) Click **OK** from the Trim PropertyManager.

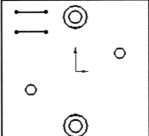

757) Click **Tangent Arc** Tangent Arc from the Sketch toolbar.

758) Sketch **two arcs** on each end of the two horizontal lines.

759) Click **Centerline** Centerl....

760) Sketch three **centerlines** as illustrated

Add an Equal relation.
761) Right-click **Select**. Select the **vertical centerline**. Hold the **Ctrl** key down.

762) Click the **two horizontal centerlines**. Release the **Ctrl** key. Click **Equal**. Click **OK** from the Properties PropertyManager.

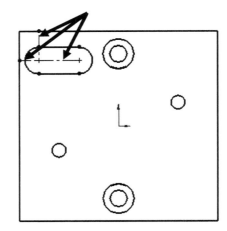

Dimension the Sketch.

763) Click **Smart Dimension** Smart Dimens....

764) Insert a **horizontal dimension**. Enter **10**. The All Configurations option is selected by default. Insert a **radial dimension**.

765) Enter **2**. The All Configurations option is selected by default. Click **OK** from the Dimension PropertyManager.

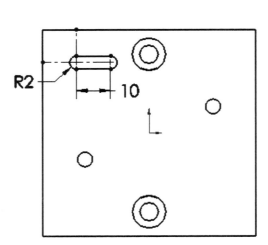

Extrude the Sketch.

766) Click **Extruded Cut** from the Feature toolbar.

767) Select **Thru All** for Depth.

768) Click **OK** from the Cut-Extrude PropertyManager.

Rename the feature.
769) Rename **Cut-Extrude1** to **Cut-Extrude1-Slot**.

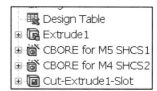

Control the Suppressed/Unsuppressed state of the Cut-Extrude1-Slot feature through Feature Properties and the $State parameter in the Design Table.

Suppress the Cut-Extrude1-Slot feature through Feature Properties.
770) Right-click **Cut-Extrude1-Slot**.

771) Click **Feature Properties**.

772) Click **All Configurations** from the drop down list.

773) Click the **Suppressed** check box.

774) Click **OK**.

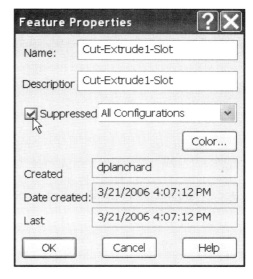

Edit the PLATE-D Design Table.
775) Right-click **Design Table** from the FeatureManager.

776) Click **Edit Table**.

777) Select **$COLOR** from the Parameters box.

778) Hold the **Ctrl** key down.

779) Select **$STATE@Cut-Extrude1-Slot**.

780) Release the **Ctrl** key.

781) Click **OK**.

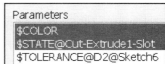

SolidWorks inserts the $COLOR parameter into Cell H2. The value 14933469 indicates the default light gray part color. The $COLOR parameter controls part color. The value in each cell represents the 32-bit integer specifying RGB (red, green & blue).

The $STATE@Cut-Extrude1-Slot parameter controls the Suppressed/Unsuppressed feature state. The S indicates the feature is suppressed.

The U indicates the feature is unsuppressed. Column J, the blank column, determines the end of the evaluated Design Table.

Modify the $COLOR values.
782) Enter **0** in Cell H4 (black).

783) Enter **255** in Cell H5 (red).

784) Enter **65280** in Cell H6 (green).

Modify the STATE values.
785) Enter **U** in Cell I3.

G	H	$STATE@Cut-Extrude1-Slot	J	K
$user_notes	$COLOR			
10mm Depth	14933469	U		mm Depth
10mm Depth	0	S		
15mm Depth	255	S		
20mm Depth	65280	S		

The Cut-Extrude1-Slot is UnSuppressed in the Default Configuration. The Cut-Extrude1 Slot is Suppressed in the other configurations.

☀ Additional integer color values are located in the SW help, Colors, Parameter in design tables.

Update the three PLATE-D configurations.
786) Click a **position** outside the Design Table.

Verify the three configurations.
787) Double-click **45-63424-10**, **45-63424-15** & **45-63424-20**. A different color is displayed.

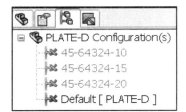

Return to the Default Configuration.
788) Click **Default**. Click the **FeatureManager**.

Save the PLATE-D part.
789) Click **Isometric** view. Click **Save**.

Return to the PLATE-D drawing.
790) Press **Ctrl-Tab**. The Cut-Extrude1-Slot feature is added to the Sheet1.

The Cut-Extrude1-Slot is suppressed in Sheet2. Project 4 is complete. Save and close all open documents.

Project Summary

In this project, you utilized a Top Down design assembly modeling approach with In-Context features. You developed the ROTARY-GRIPPER assembly. The PLATE-D part was developed In-Context of the ROTARY assembly and GRIPPER assembly.

You utilized a Bottom Up design assembly modeling approach to model the PLATE-C part. PLATE-C was created as an empty part and assembled to the 2AXIS-TRANSFER assembly. The InPlace Mates and External references were redefined in the PLATE-D part.

You developed three configurations for the ROTARY assembly:

- Flexible.
- Rotation0.
- Rotation90.

You developed six configurations for the ROTARY-GRIPPER assembly:

- Horizontal-10.
- Horizontal-15.
- Horizontal-20.
- Vertical-10.
- Vertical-15.
- Vertical-20.

You developed three configurations for the PLATE-D part.

- 45-63424-10.
- 45-63424-15.
- 45-63424-20.

Material, Mass and Description were developed as Configuration Specific Properties in the ConfigurationManager. The $PARTNUMBER, $COLOR and $STATE parameters were inserted into the PLATE-D Design Table.

The PLATE-D drawing contained notes linked to Custom Properties in the part. The PLATE-D drawing contained two sheets with multiple configurations.

Utilize the configurations and parameters defined in this project in the 3AXIS-TRANSFER Bill of Materials. Combine the LINEAR-TRANSFER assembly, 2AXIS-TRANSFER assembly and the ROTARY-GRIPPER assembly to complete the 3AXIS-TRANSFER assembly. Review the questions and exercises before moving on to Project 5.

Questions

1. Identify the two components that determine the geometric and functional requirements for the PLATE-D part.

2. True or False. The small dowel pin slot on the ROTARY assembly moves linearly along the Right plane of the assembly.

3. Utilize a _____ to create 100 PLATE-D configurations.

4. True or False. A drawing contains only one configuration of a part or assembly.

5. Describe the two modeling methods that are utilized to create the ROTARY-GRIPPER assembly.

6. True or False. Suppressed Mates are not loaded into memory.

7. Describe the process to split the FeatureManager and to display the reference planes from two different components.

8. True or False. Mates in SolidWorks guarantee that a component can be physically assembled in your factory.

9. What does the "->"symbol and "->?" symbol indicate after a feature entry in the FeatureManager?

10. True or False. Configuration names entered in a Design Table are displayed in the ConfigurationManager.

11. Describe the components that determine the geometric and functional requirements for the PLATE-C part.

12. Mass, Density and Volume are calculated utilizing _____.

13. Describe the difference between a Custom Property and a Configuration Specific Property.

14. True or False. Properties are utilized between a part and a drawing.

15. In a drawing, configurations are selected from the _____ Properties dialog box.

16. Identify the location in the FeatureManager to assign Material to a part.

17. Describe the differences between System Properties and User defined Properties.

18. $COLOR and $STATE are two parameters defined in a Design Table. Where do you locate other SolidWorks parameters and their syntax?

Exercises

Exercise 4-1: Identify the fastener types and lengths required for the ROTARY-GRIPPER assembly. Insert the fasteners into the ROTARY-GRIPPER assembly.

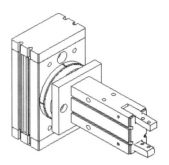

Exercise 4-2: Insert the Fastener configuration to the ROTARY-GRIPPER assembly. The Fastener configuration contains the M5 and M4 SHCSs. Suppress the fasteners in all other configurations.

Exercise 4-3: Create the ROTARY-GRIPPER drawing with two Front views. The first view displays the GRIPPER in a horizontal position. PLATE-D is 10mm. The second view displays the GRIPPER in a vertical position. PLATE-D is 20mm.

Exercise 4-4: Create PLATE-D Sheet3. Add a 15mm configuration. Insert three linked notes to display the Mass, Description and Material Configuration Specific Properties.

Exercise 4-5: Utilize a Design Table to create the PLATE-C part with 20mm and 25mm configurations. Add the Configuration Specific Properties: Mass, Description and Material. Create a PLATE-C drawing. Place each configuration on a separate Sheet. Insert the Properties into Sheet1 and Sheet2.

Exercise 4-6: Model a bolt circle with a Circular Pattern feature for the PLATE-D part that corresponds to the ROTARY/ MSQBTop part. Insert the required fasteners.

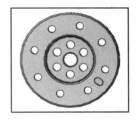

Utilize Tools, Interference Detection and Move, Collision Detection to determine if the fasteners interfere with the GRIPPER assembly.

Identify the holes to utilize in your written manufacturing procedure.

SHCS with Coincident and   SHCS with Coincident Mate suppressed.
Concentric Mates   Drag SHCS outward to display interference.

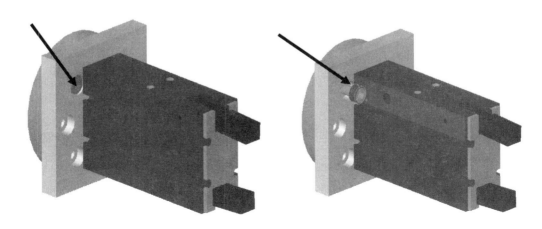

Exercise 4-7: Modify the ROTARY assembly. Delete the Rotation90 Mate. Modify the Rotation0 Mate to an Angle Mate. Control the Angle value in the ROTARY configuration. Modify the ROTARY configurations to utilize the Angle values 0° and 90°.

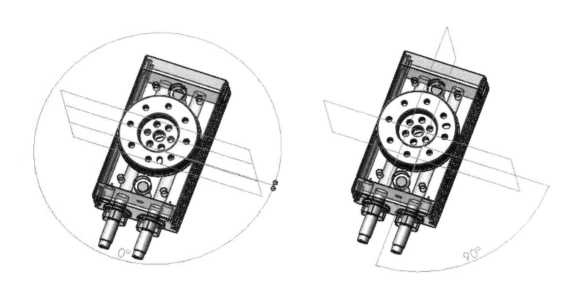

Exercise 4-8: A four bar mechanism is currently analyzed based on three design options. Create a part named LINK. Create a part named JOINT. Create a Design Table to represent the lengths of the required LINKs. Create the 4BAR-LINK assembly. Create three configurations to represent the three design options for the 4-BAR-LINK assembly.

LINK

The first JOINT is fixed to the 4-BAR-LINK Origin. The bottom face of each JOINT is fixed to the Top Plane. The four bar mechanism is free to rotate. Dimensions are given in inches.

Option 1:

- a = 2
- b = 4.5
- c = 7
- d = 9

Option 2:

- a = 2
- b = 3.5
- c = 7
- d = 9

Option 3:

- a = 2
- b = 4
- c = 6
- d = 8

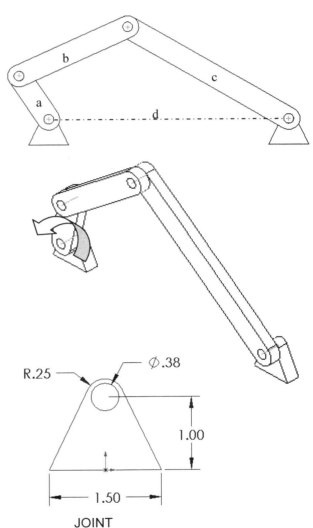

JOINT

Reference: Design of Machinery,
Robert Norton, McGraw Hill 2nd Edition 2003, used with permission.

Notes:

Project 5

Assembly Drawing

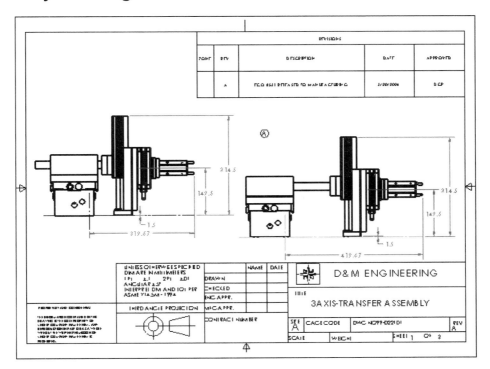

Below are the desired outcomes and usage competencies based on the completion of this Project. An assembly drawing refers to a SolidWorks drawing that contains a SolidWorks assembly.

Project Desired Outcomes:	Usage Competencies:
• 3AXIS-TRANSFER assembly.	• Ability to apply parameters in a Design Table in order to develop assemblies with multiple configurations.
• 3AXIS-TRANSFER drawing. • Sheet1 • Sheet2 • Sheet3	
	• An understanding of Custom Properties in a part/assembly and linked notes in a drawing.
	• Ability to create an assembly drawing using multiple configurations and multiple sheets.
	• Knowledge to incorporate Exploded Views and Bill of Materials into a drawing.

Notes:

Project 5 – Assembly Drawing

Project Objective

Create the 3AXIS-TRANSFER assembly. Utilize a Design Table to create eight configurations for the 3AXIS-TRANSFER assembly.

Create the 3AXIS-TRANSFER drawing. Add Custom Properties to the components in the 3AXIS-TRANSFER assembly.

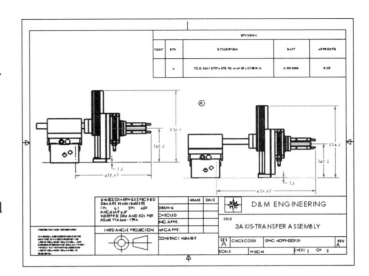

Develop an Exploded View, Linked Notes, Revision Table, and Bill of Materials in the 3AXIS-TRANSFER drawing.

On the completion of this project, you will be able to:

- Apply a Design Table to manipulate multiple configurations of sub-assemblies.

- Define Custom Properties utilized in a Bill of Materials.

- Create and insert Exploded Views.

- Recognize and redefine different configurations in drawing views.

- Develop a multi-sheet assembly drawing and incorporate working dimensions to utilize in the design process.

- Insert a Revision Table in the drawing. Insert a Revision Property from the part as a Linked Note in the drawing.

- Understand a method to control ECO part revisions with SolidWorks Explorer.

SolidWorks Tools and Commands

In Project 5, utilize the following SolidWorks tools and commands.

SolidWorks Tools and Commands:		
$show	Edit Sheet/Edit Sheet Format	Note
$state	Exploded View	Open part, Open assembly, Open drawing
Add Sheet	Fixed/Float	Properties
Annotations	Hide	Rename
Assembly Feature Extruded Cut	Insert Model View	Rotate Component
Auto Balloon	Linked Note	Sheet Properties
Balloon	Link to Property	Shortcut keys
Bill of Material	Mass Properties	Show
Configuration Properties	Mate Types: Coincident, Concentric, Distance	Sketch tools: Centerline, Smart Dimension, Text
Configuration Specific	Materials Editor	SmartMate
Copy/Paste views	Make Assembly from Part/Assembly	Suppress/Set to Resolved
Custom Properties	Make Drawing from Part/Assembly	Suppress/Unsuppress
Design Table	Move Component, Move with Triad	View Planes, Origins, Temporary Axis
Drawing View Properties	New drawing	View Properties

Develop modeling skill and speed. Project 5 primarily utilizes Pop-up menus and Shortcut keys to execute the tools in the Assembly toolbar, Features toolbar, and Drawing toolbar.

Project Overview

Create the 3AXIS-TRANSFER assembly. The assembly contains three sub-assemblies:

- LINEAR-TRANSFER assembly.

- 2AXIS-TRANSFER assembly.

- ROTARY-GRIPPER assembly.

The 3AXIS-TRANSFER assembly includes a Design Table. The Design Table contains eight configurations that represent the various positions during operation.

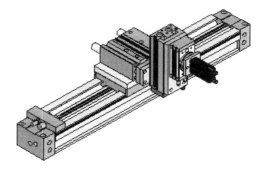

3AXIS-TRANSFER assembly

Create the 3AXIS-TRANSFER drawing. The 3AXIS-TRANSFER drawing includes three sheets:

- Sheet1.
- Sheet2.
- Sheet3.

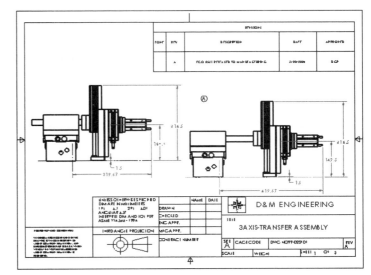

Sheet1 contains two configurations. Insert dimensions for the 3AXIS-TRANSFER assembly.

Sheet2 contains an Exploded View of the 3AXIS-TRANSFER assembly and Fastener configurations. Insert a Bill of Materials and utilize Custom Properties.

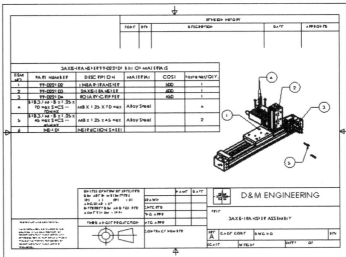

Sheet3 contains a Section view of the 3AXIS-TRANSFER assembly.

Modify the Section view properties to display the 3AXIS-TRANSFER assembly components.

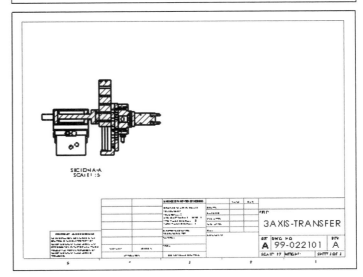

Project 5 incorporates parts, assemblies, drawings, Custom Properties, Design Tables and Bill of Materials. The design environment with Engineering Change Orders, numerous projects and customers that change their minds require you to work with multiple SolidWorks documents.

While you were on vacation, your company revised its drawing standards and instituted a new policy on filenames. The new filename policy states: part and drawing document names are the same as the physical part number.

Example: PLATE-A part is named: 45-63421.sldprt.

PLATE-A drawing is named: 45-63421.slddrw.

The assembly and assembly drawing document names are the same as the part number.

Example: LINEAR-TRANSFER assembly is named: 99-022102.sldasm.

LINEAR-TRANSFER drawing is named: 99-022102.slddrw.

To save time in this project, all the assemblies and models you developed in Project 1 through Project 4 have been renamed and stored in a new folder on the CD in the book.

Obtain the Project5-2006 folder from the provided CD in the book. Copy the folder to your hard drive. The Project5-2006 file folder contains two sub-folders:

- DeliveryStation-Project5.
- Project5-SMC.

Utilize the following part number prefixes to categorize parts in the Delivery Station assembly project:

Category:	Prefix:
Vendor Parts	0
Machined Parts	45-
Assemblies	99-
Socket Head Cap Screws	SHC-

The following table lists a summary of the Project5-SMC vendor components.

Summary of Project5-SMC Vendor Components:			
Assembly Shaded Images: **Note: Not to Scale.**	**New Assembly Name:**	**File Folder Location: (SMC Part Number)**	**Old Assembly Name:**
	015082	MGPM50-100	GUIDE-CYLINDER
	015085	MHY2-20D	GRIPPER
	015084	MSQB30R	ROTARY
	015083	MXS25L-100B	SLIDE-TABLE
	015081	MY1M50G-500LS	RODLESS-CYLINDER

The DeliveryStation-Project5 file folder contains the renamed machined parts: PLATE-A, PLATE-B, PLATE-C, and PLATE-D. The following table lists a summary of the DeliveryStation-Project5 machined parts.

Summary of DelveryStation-Project5 Machined Parts:		
Part: **Note: Not to Scale.**	**New Part Name contained in Project5 file folder:**	**Old Part Name:**
	45-63421	PLATE-A
	45-63422	PLATE-B
	45-63423	PLATE-C
	45-63424	PLATE-D

The DeliveryStation-Project5 file folder contains the renamed assemblies: LINEAR-TRANSFER, 2AXIS-TRANSFER, and ROTARY-GRIPPER.

The following table lists a summary of the DeliveryStation-Project5 assemblies.

Summary of DeliveryStation-Project5 assemblies:		
Assembly:	**New Assembly Name:**	**Old Assembly Name:**
	99-022102	LINEAR-TRANSFER
	99-022103	2AXIS-TRANSFER
	99-022104	ROTARY-GRIPPER

Note: These components contain additional configurations not developed in Project 1 through Project 4.

3AXIS TRANSFER assembly

The 99-022101, 3AXIS-TRANSFER assembly consists of three sub-assemblies. The three sub-assemblies are:

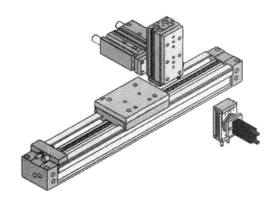

1. 99-022102, LINEAR-TRANSFER assembly.

2. 99-022103, 2AXIS-TRANSFER assembly.

3. 99-022104, ROTARY-GRIPPER assembly.

Each sub-assembly contains multiple configurations. Set each sub-assembly to its Default configuration.

Insert and assemble the 99-022102, LINEAR-TRANSFER assembly to the 99-022101, 3AXIS-TRANSFER assembly. Mate the Front, Top and Right Planes to orient the 99-022102, LINEAR-TRANSFER assembly.

Insert and assemble the 99-022103, 2AXIS-TRANSFER assembly. Insert and assemble the 99-022104, ROTARY-GRIPPER assembly.

The assemblies utilized in this project contain numerous sub-assemblies. To avoid problems with memory and referenced document locations, close any existing SolidWorks session you have open and start a new one.

An assembly contains absolute references to its components. An absolute reference is the complete path name. Example: E:\ASSEMBLY-SW-FILES-2006\PROJECT5-2006\ DELIVERYSTATION-PROJECT5\PLATE-A.sldprt. The individual component does not have references back to the assembly. When an assembly document opens, the referenced documents of the assembly load into memory. SolidWorks searches for referenced documents in the following order:

- SolidWorks documents loaded into Random Access Memory (RAM).

- Paths specified in the System Options, File Locations, Folders list.

- Last accessed path you specified to open the document.

- Last accessed path SolidWorks utilized to open the document.

- The path referenced by the parent document.

- SolidWorks prompts you to browse and locate the document.

Review additional information on search order in On-line help\Search\File Reference Locations.

Activity: 3AXIS-TRANSFER assembly

Copy the Project5 folder.
1)　Copy the **Project5-2006 folder** from the CD in the book to the ASSEMBLY-SW-FILES-2006 folder.

Open the LINEAR-TRANSFER assembly.
2)　Double-click **ASSEMBLY-SW-FILES-2006\ Project5-2006\ DeliveryStation-Project5\99-022102** assembly.

Review the configurations.
3)　Drag the **Split-bar** half way downward to divide the FeatureManager.

4)　Click the **ConfigurationManager** in the lower half of the FeatureManager.

5)　Double-click each **configuration**.

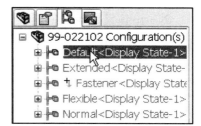

The 99-022102, LINEAR-TRANSFER assembly has five configurations:

- Default.
- Extended.
- Fastener.
- Flexible.
- Normal.

Select the Default configuration.
6)　Click **Default**.

Open the 2AXIS-TRANSFER assembly.
7)　Double-click **ASSEMBLY-SW-FILES-2006\Project5-2006\ DeliveryStation-Project5\99-022103** assembly.

Review the configurations.

8)   Drag the **Split-bar** half way downward to divide the FeatureManager.

9)   Click the **ConfigurationManager** in the lower half of the FeatureManager.

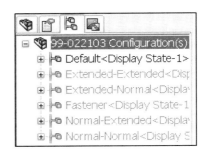

10) Double-click each **configuration**. View the configuration.

The 2AXIS-TRANSFER assembly has six configurations:

- Default.

- Extended-Extended.

- Extended-Normal.

- Fastener.

- Normal-Extended.

- Normal-Normal.

Select the Default configuration.
11) Click **Default**.

Open the ROTARY-GRIPPER.
12) Double-click **ASSEMBLY-SW-FILES-2006\Project5-2006\DeliveryStation-Project5\99-022104** assembly.

Review the configurations.
13) Drag the **Split-bar** half way downward to divide the FeatureManager. Click the **ConfigurationManager** in the lower half of the FeatureManager. Double-click each **configuration**.

The ROTARY-GRIPPER assembly has five configurations:

- Default.

- Fastener.

- Flexible.

- Horizontal.

- Vertical.

Select the Default configuration.
14) Click **Default**.

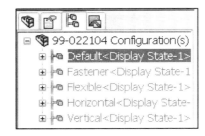

Create a new assembly from the 99-022102, LINEAR-TRANSFER assembly.

15) Click **Window**, **Tile Horizontally** to display the active models.

16) Click inside the **99-022102** Graphics window.

17) Click **Make Assembly From Part/Assembly** 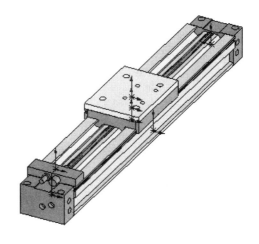 from the Main menu·

18) Click the **MY-TEMPLATES** tab.

19) Double-click **ASM-MM-ANSI**. The Insert Component PropertyManager is displayed.

20) Click **View**, **Origins** from the Main menu.

21) Click a **position** to the left of the Assem1 Origin. The 3AXIS-TRANSFER assembly is displayed in the Graphics window.

Save the 3AXIS-TRANSFER assembly.

22) Click **Save** from the Main menu.

23) Select **DeliveryStation-Project5** for Save in folder.

24) Enter **99-022101** for File name.

25) Click **Save**.

Float the 99-022102 component.

26) Right-click **99-022102** from the FeatureManager.

27) Click **Float**.

Hide the Origins.

28) Click **View**, uncheck **Origins** from the Main menu.

Mate the 99-022102 component.
29)   Click the 99-022101 **Front Plane**.

30)   Click **Mate** ^{Mate} from the Assembly toolbar.

31)   Click the **99-022102 Front** Plane. Coincident is selected by default.

32)   Click ✔ .

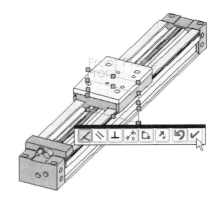

33)   Click the 99-022101 **Right Plane**.

34)   Click the **99-022102 Right** Plane. Coincident is selected by default.

35)   Click **OK** ✔ .

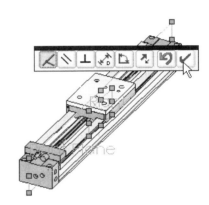

36)   Click the 99-022101 **Top Plane**.

37)   Click the **99-022102 bottom left face**. Coincident is selected by default.

38)   Click ✔ .

39)   Click **OK** ⊘ from the Mate PropertyManager.

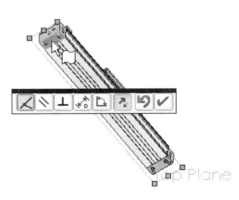

Display the open documents.
40)   Click **Windows**, **Tile Horizontally** from the Main menu.

Insert the 2AXIS-TRANSFER component.
41)   Click and drag the **99-022103** ⬚ 99-022103 icon from the top of the FeatureManager to the right of the LINEAR-TRANSFER component. Do not select the 99-022101 Origin.

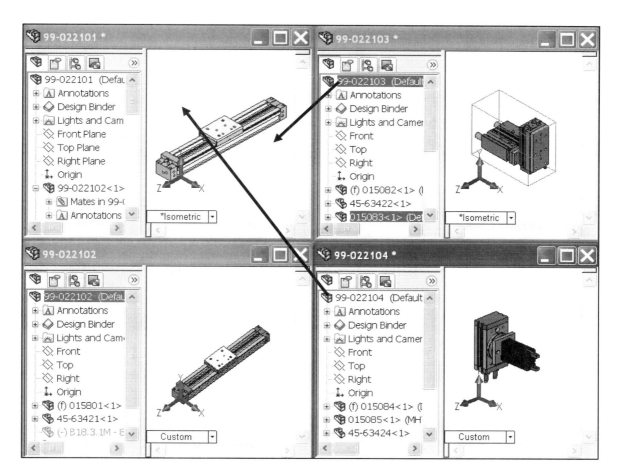

Insert the ROTARY-GRIPPER
component.

42)   Click and drag the **99-022104** icon
          from the top of the
          FeatureManager to the left of the
          LINEAR-TRANSFER component.
          Do not select the 99-022101
          Origin.

Maximize the assembly.

43)   **Maximize** the 99-022101, 3AXIS-
          TRANSFER Graphics window.

Fit all components in the Graphics
window.

44)   Press the **f** key.

Save the 99-022101, 3AXIS-TRANSFER
assembly.

45)   Click **Save**.

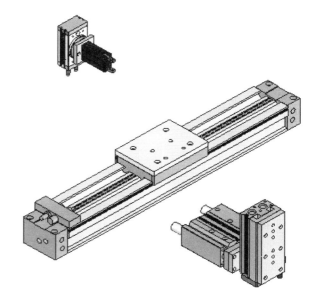

Hide the ROTARY-GRIPPER component.
46)   Right-click the **99-022104** component from the 99-022101 FeatureManager.

47)   Click **Hide**.

☀ Window-select a component in the Graphics window to save mouse travel time to the FeatureManager. To Window-select a component, click the upper left corner, drag the mouse pointer and click the lower right corner. Right-click a position in the Graphics window. Select the Component options such as Move or Hide. Utilize the Ctrl key to select multiple separate areas in the Graphics window.

Move the 2AXIS-TRANSFER component.
48)   Click and drag the **99-022103**, 2AXIS-TRANSFER component above the LINEAR-TRANSFER component as illustrated.

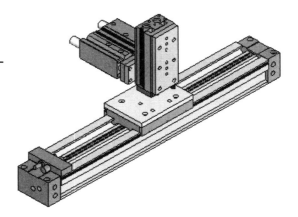

☀ Prepare for SmartMates. Zoom in and rotate the model before selecting the SmartMate geometry. For Concentric SmartMates, orient the model to view the inside cylindrical face.

Insert three SmartMates.

49) Right-click **Move Component** from the Graphics window.

50) Click **SmartMate** ✎ from the Move Component PropertyManager.

Insert a Concentric SmartMate.

51) Double-click the **bottom left Cbore cylindrical face** of the GUIDE-CYLINDER.

52) Click the **bottom left M8 Thru hole cylindrical face** of PLATE-A. Do not select the Cbore face of the PLATE-A part.

53) Click **OK** ✔.

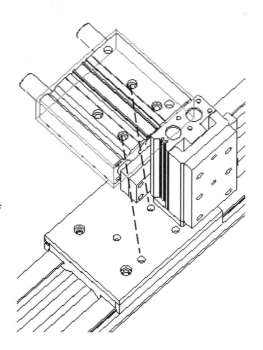

Insert a Concentric SmartMate.

54) Double-click the **top left Cbore cylindrical face** of the GUIDE-CYLINDER.

55) Click the **top left M8 Thru hole cylindrical face** of the PLATE-A part.

56) Click **OK** ✔.

Insert a Coincident SmartMate.

57) Double-click the **bottom face** of the GUIDE-CYLINDER.

58) Click the **top face** of PLATE-A. The 99-0221-3, 2AXIS-TRANSFER component is fully defined.

59) Click **OK** ✔.

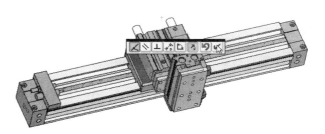

60) Click **OK** ✅ from the SmartMate PropertyManager.

Save the 99-022101, 3AXIS-TRANSFER assembly.

61) Click **Isometric** view.

62) Click **Save** from the Main menu.

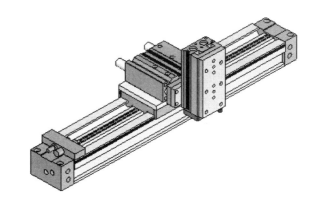

Display the ROTARY-GRIPPER assembly.
63)   Right-click **99-022104** from the FeatureManager.

64)   Click **Show**.

Move the ROTARY-GRIPPER component.
65)   Click and drag the **ROTARY-GRIPPER** component to the right of the 2AXIS-TRANSFER component.

66)   **Zoom in** on PLATE-C and the ROTARY assembly.

Insert three SmartMates.

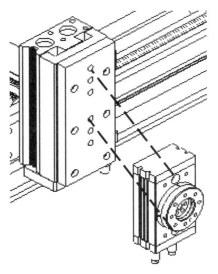

GRIPPER assembly hidden for clarity

Move

67)   Click **Move Component** Compo... from the Assembly toolbar.

68)   Click **SmartMate** ✎ from the Move Component PropertyManager.

Insert a Concentric SmartMate.
69)   Double-click the **top inside Cbore cylindrical face** of the ROTARY assembly.

70)   Click the **top M8.6 Thru Hole cylindrical face** of the PLATE-C part.

71)   Click **OK** ✔ .

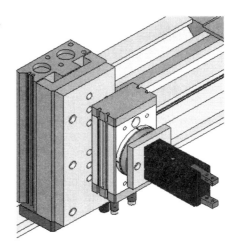

Insert a Concentric SmartMate.
72)   Double-click the **bottom inside Cbore cylindrical face** of the ROTARY assembly.

73)   Click the **fourth M8.6Thru Hole cylindrical face** of the PLATE-C part.

74)   Click **OK** ✔ .

Insert a Coincident SmartMate.
75)   Double-click the **bottom face** of the ROTARY assembly. Click the **top face** of the PLATE-C part.

76)   Click **OK** ✔ . Click **OK** ✅ from the SmartMate PropertyManager. The 99-022104 component is fully defined.

Save the 99-022101, 3AXIS-TRANSFER assembly.

77) Click **Isometric** view.

78) Click **Save**.

3AXIS-TRANSFER Design Table

A Design Table is the Excel spreadsheet used to create multiple configurations in a document. In Project 3 and Project 4, you inserted Design Tables into parts and assemblies and defined the parameters. Insert a new Design Table into the 99-022101, 3AXIS-TRANSFER assembly from an Excel spreadsheet 99-022101-DesignTable.XLS. Locate the Excel document in the Project5-2006\DeliveryStation-Project5 file folder.

The Excel spreadsheet 99-022101.XLS contains eight configurations for the 99-022101, 3AXIS-TRANSFER assembly. The names of the eight configurations are:

- Position1.
- Position2.
- Position3.
- Position4.
- Position5.
- Position6.
- Position7.
- Position8.

The Excel spreadsheet 99-022101-DesignTable.XLS combines the configurations of three sub-assemblies.

- 99-022102, LINEAR-TRANSFER assembly.
- 99-022103, 2AXIS-TRANSFER assembly.
- 99-022104, ROTARY-GRIPPER assembly.

Column A contains eight configuration names of the 3AXIS-TRANSFER assembly, Position1 through Position8.

	A	B	C	D
1		$Configuration@99-022102<1>	$Configuration@99-022103<1>	$Configuration@99-022104<1>
2	Position1	Normal	Normal-Normal	Vertical
3	Position2	Normal	Normal-Extended	Vertical
4	Position3	Normal	Extended-Normal	Vertical
5	Position4	Normal	Extended-Extended	Vertical
6	Position5	Extended	Normal-Normal	Horizontal
7	Position6	Extended	Normal-Extended	Horizontal
8	Position7	Extended	Extended-Normal	Horizontal
9	Position8	Extended	Extended-Extended	Horizontal

Column B contains two configuration names of the 99-022102, LINEAR-TRANSFER assembly: Extended and Normal.

Column C contains four configuration names of the 99-022103, 2AXIS-TRANSFER assembly: Normal-Normal, Normal-Extended, Extended-Normal, and Extended-Extended.

Column D contains two configuration names of the 99-022104, ROTARY-GRIPPER assembly: Vertical and Horizontal.

Activity: 3AXIS-TRANSFER Design Table

Insert a Design Table into the 99-022101, 3AXIS-TRANSFER assembly.
79)   Click **Insert**, **Design Table** from the Main toolbar.

80)   Click **From file**.

81)   Click **Browse**.

82)   Double-click **99-022101-DesignTable**.**XLS** from the PROJECT5-2006/DeliveryStation-Project5 folder.

83)   Click **OK** from the Design Table PropertyManager. The Design Table is displayed in the Graphics window

Create the configurations.
84)   Click a **position** in the SolidWorks Graphics window.

85)   Click **OK** to generate the new configurations.

Update the Design Table.
86)   Right-click **Design Table** from the FeatureManager.

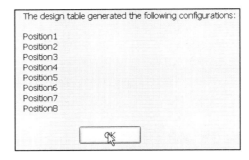

87)   Click **Edit Table**.

88)   Click **Default** from the Configurations box in the Add Rows and Columns dialog box.

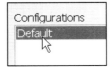

89) Click **OK**. The Design Table inserts the Default configuration name in Cell A10.

90) Click a **position** in the SolidWorks Graphics window.

Verify the configurations.
91) Double-click **Position1** through **Position8** from the ConfigurationManager.

	A	B	C	D
1		$Configuration@99-022102<1>	$Configuration@99-022103<1>	$Configuration@99-022104<1>
2	Position1	Normal	Normal-Normal	Vertical
3	Position2	Normal	Normal-Extended	Vertical
4	Position3	Normal	Extended-Normal	Vertical
5	Position4	Normal	Extended-Extended	Vertical
6	Position5	Extended	Normal-Normal	Horizontal
7	Position6	Extended	Normal-Extended	Horizontal
8	Position7	Extended	Extended-Normal	Horizontal
9	Position8	Extended	Extended-Extended	Horizontal
10	Default	Default	Default	Default

Return to the Default configuration.
92) Double-click **Default**.

Save the 99-022101, 3AXIS-TRANSFER assembly.
93) Click **Save**.

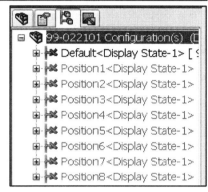

A summary of the configurations is as follows:

Position1:	Position2:	Position3:	Position4:
Position5:	Position6:	Position7:	Position8:

3AXIS-TRANSFER assembly drawing

Assembly drawings illustrate how to assemble components in manufacturing. Assembly drawings contain Section views to display internal details and Exploded Views with a Bill of Materials for item identification.

🔆 Utilize assembly drawings as working drawings. When you begin an assembly, in addition begin an assembly drawing. As the assembly develops, the drawing also develops. Assembly drawings determine potential problems between components early in the design process.

Develop the 99-022101, 3AXIS-TRANSFER assembly drawing. The 3AXIS-TRANSFER assembly drawing consists of three Sheets.

- Sheet1: Determines the critical overall dimensions of the assembly.

- Sheet2: Contains a Bill of Materials and an Exploded View.

- Sheet3: Contains a Section view.

ACTIVITY: 3AXIS-TRANSFER assembly drawing – Sheet1

Create a new 99-022101, 3AXIS-TRANSFER drawing.

94) Click **Make Drawing from Part/Assembly** 🔲 from the Standard toolbar.

95) Click the **MY-TEMPLATES** tab.

96) Double-click **A-ANSI-MM**. The Model View PropertyManager is displayed.

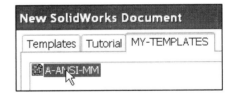

Insert a Front View.

97) Single View is selected by default. Front view is selected by default. Click **Hidden Lines Visible** for Display Style.

98) Click **Use custom scale**.

99) Select **User Defined**.

100) Enter **1:5** for Sheet Scale.

101) Click a **position** on the left side of Sheet1.

102) Click **OK** ✅ from the Projected View PropertyManager.

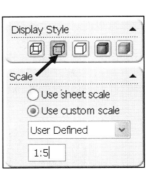

Expand the FeatureManager.

103) Expand **Drawing View1** from the FeatureManager.

104) Double-click **99-022101<1>**. The Default configurations are listed for the sub-assemblies 99-022102, 99-022103, and 99-022104.

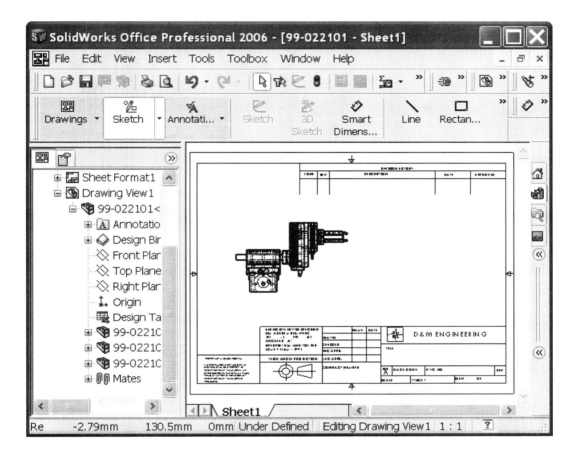

Select the Position2 configuration.

105) Right-click the **Front view** boundary.

106) Click **Properties**.

107) Select **Position2** from the Configuration information drop down list.

108) Click **OK**.

109) Click **Hidden Lines Removed** for Display

Style. Click **OK** from the Drawing View1 PropertyManager.

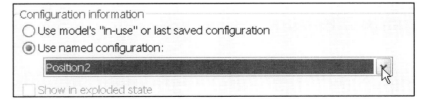

Utilize sketched centerlines to reference dimensions in drawing views. Sketched geometry in a drawing resides with the current view. A green view boundary indicates the current view.

Select the Drawing view.
110) Click the **Front view** boundary.

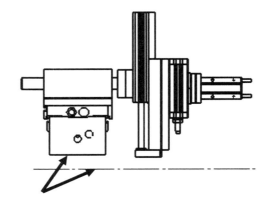

Sketch the first Centerline.

111) Click **Centerline** Centerl... from the Sketch toolbar.

112) Sketch a **horizontal centerline** below the profile lines.

113) Right-click **Select**.

Add a Collinear relation.
114) Click the **bottom horizontal line** of the LINEAR-TRANSFER assembly.

115) Hold the **Ctrl** key down.

116) Click the **horizontal centerline**.

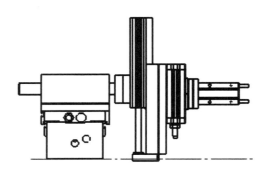

117) Release the **Ctrl** key.

118) Click **Collinear**. Click **OK** ✅ from the Properties PropertryManager .

Sketch the second Centerline.

119) Click **Centerline** Centerl... from the Sketch toolbar.

120) Sketch a **vertical centerline** on the right side of the LINEAR-TRANSFER assembly as illustrated.

121) Right-click **Select**.

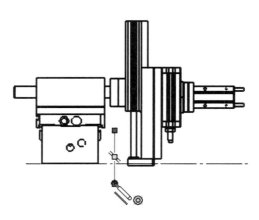

Activate Temporary Axis and Origins.
122) Click **View**, **Origins** from the Main menu.

123) Click **View**, **Temporary Axis** from the Main menu.

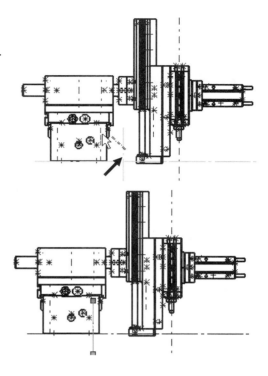

Add a Collinear relation.
124) Click the **Temporary Axis of the right Mounting Hole** of the LINEAR-TRANSFER assembly.

125) Hold the **Ctrl** key down.

126) Click the **vertical centerline**.

127) Release the **Ctrl** key.

128) Click **Collinear**.

129) Click **OK** ✅ from the Properties PropertyManager.

Deactivate the Temporary Axis.
130) Click **View**, uncheck **Temporarty Axis**.

Create the third Centerline.

131) Click **Centerline** Centerl... from the Sketch toolbar.

132) Sketch a **horizontal centerline** from the Origin of the ROTARY assembly to the right of the GRIPPER FINGERS part as illustrated.

133) Right-click **Select**.

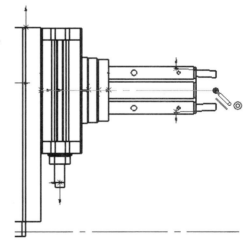

Add a Vertical relation.
134) Click the **right endpoint** of the centerline.

135) Hold the **Ctrl** key down.

136) Click the **end vertex** of the GRIPPER FINGER part.

137) Release the **Ctrl** key.

138) Click **Vertical**.

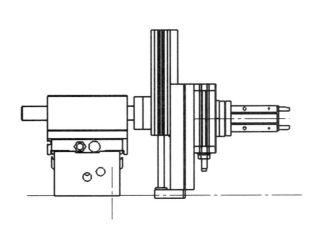

139) Click **OK** from the Properties PropertyManger.

140) Deactivate the **Origins**.

Three Driven Dimensions reference the three centerlines in the front view.

Driven Dimensions are dimensions controlled by other dimensions and conditions of a component. Driven dimensions can't be modified. Driven Dimensions created in the next steps utilize a sketched centerline and a vertex, origin or edge of a component.

Add dimensions.

141) Click **Smart Dimension** Dimens... from the Sketch toolbar.

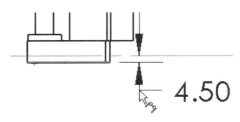

142) Click the **bottom horizontal centerline** and the **bottom edge** of the SLIDE-TABLE assembly.

143) Click a **position** below the horizontal centerline.

144) Check **Make this dimension diven**.

145) Click **OK**. The 4.50 Driven Dimension is displayed. Click **OK** .

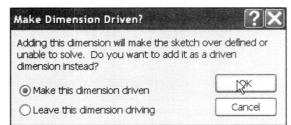

You encounter a design issue. There is an interference of 4.50mm between the MOUNTING-PLATE part and the SLIDE-TABLE assembly.

Do you raise the RODLESS-CYLINDER component? Answer: No. This option is too expensive. Do you design a new component? Answer: No.
This option will take too much time.

Do you modify the PLATE-A part? Answer: Yes. Increase the thickness of the PLATE-A part to raise the SLIDE-TABLE assembly.

The depth of the 45-6341, PLATE-A part is 15mm. You require a minimum of 4.5mm. Utilize 6.0mm for the new depth. Note: The PLATE-A part has not been released to Manufacturing. You do not need to modify the revision number.

Modify the PLATE-A part.
146) Click **45-63421** from the 99-022101, 3AXIS-TRANSFER drawing.

147) Right-click **Open Part**. The 45-63421, PLATE-A part is displayed in the Graphics window.

148) Double-click **Base-Extrude** from the FeatureManager.

149) Double-click **15**. Enter **21** for Depth.

150) Click **Rebuild**.

151) Click ✔.

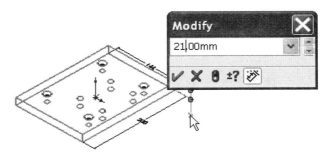

152) Click **OK** from the Dimension PropertyManager.

Save the 45-63421, PLATE-A part.
153) Click **Save**.

Close the 45-63421, PLATE-A part.
154) Return to the drawing. Click **File**, **Close** from the Main menu.

The PLATE-A design change from 15mm to 21mm affects other components in the assembly.

What components are affected? Answer: Review the following Design Change Task List table.

<table>
<tr><td colspan="2" align="center">**Design Change Task List:**</td></tr>
<tr><td>**Task:**</td><td>**Action:**</td></tr>
<tr><td>Identify the assembly and related components affected by the part.</td><td>PLATE-A is a component of the 99-022102, LINEAR-TRANSFER assembly.</td></tr>
<tr><td>Identify other assemblies that utilize the part.</td><td>PLATE-A is not used in any other assemblies.</td></tr>
<tr><td>Identify all the configurations that utilize this part.

Does the design change affect different configuration or suppressed components?</td><td>The Fastener configuration contains the hardware. Increase the fastener length to accommodate the increased PLATE-A thickness.</td></tr>
<tr><td>Review your company's Engineering Change Order (ECO) process.

Identify the parts, assemblies and drawings that require a revision change.</td><td>PLATE-A has not been released to manufacturing. No revision change is required.</td></tr>
</table>

Determine where the PLATE-A part is used in the 99-022102 assembly. Open SolidWorks Explorer.

155) Click **Tools**, **SolidWorks Explorer** from the Main menu.

156) Click **Browse**.

157) Double-click **45-63421**.

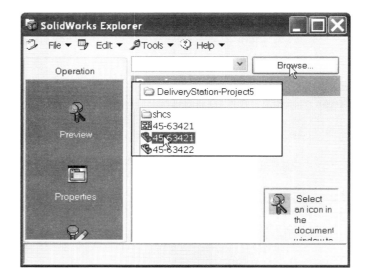

158) Click **Where Used**.

159) Click **Find Now**. The 99-022102.sldasm is displayed in the Used by window.

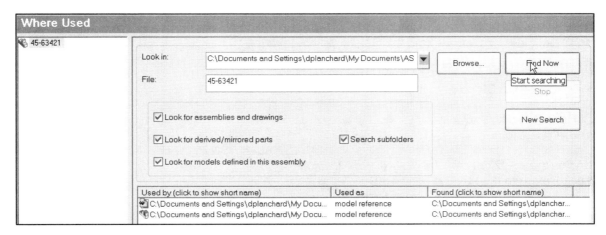

Note: Utilize Look In: to select different file folders.

Open the 99-022102, LINEAR-TRANSFER assembly.

160) Click the **99-022102.SLDASM** entry in SolidWorks Explorer.

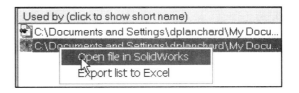

161) Right-click **Open file in SolidWorks**. You are in the 99-022102(Default) configuration.

Display the Fastener configuration.

162) From SolidWorks, double-click the **Fastener** configuration from the ConfigurationManager.

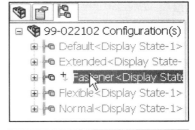

Display the 99-022102 (Fastener) FeatureManager.

163) Click the **FeatureManager** icon. The configuration contains the B18.3.1M-8x1.25x20 SHCS and the Derived LPattern1 in the Unsuppressed state.

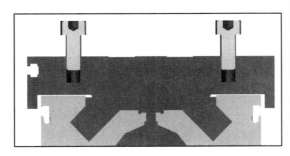

The M8x1.25x20 SHCSs are too short for the 21mm PLATE-A part. Utilize the Replace Components option located in the FeatureManager. Replace the SHCSs in the project exercises.

Return to the Default configuration.
164) Double-click **Default** from the ConfigurationManager.

Close the 99-022102, LINEAR-TRANSFER assembly.
165) Click **File**, **Close** from the Main menu.

Close SolidWorks Explorer.
166) Click **Close**.

Update the 99-022101, 3AXIS-TRANSFER drawing.
167) Return to the 99-022101, 3AXIS-TRANSFER drawing. Press **Ctrl-Tab**.

168) Update the 99-022101, 3AXIS-TRANSFER drawing with the modified 45-63421 PLATE-A part. Click **Rebuild**. The dimension displays 1.50. There is a 1.50mm clearance.

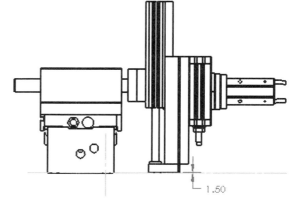

Activate the view.
169) Click the **Front view** boundary.

Add dimensions.

170) Click **Smart Dimension**
⬧
Smart
Dimens... from the Sketch
toolbar.

Add the second horizontal linear dimension.
171) Click the left **vertical centerline**.

172) Click the **bottom right vertex** of the GRIPPER FINGER part.

173) Click **Make this dimension driven.**

174) Click **OK**. Drag the **319.67 dimension** below the 1.50 text.

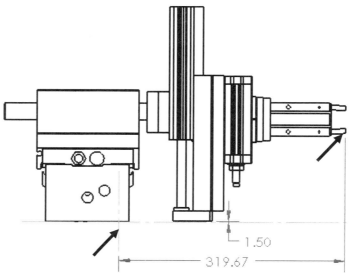

Add the first vertical linear dimension.

175) Click **View**, **Origins** from the Main menu.

176) Click the **bottom horizontal centerline**.

177) Click the **horizontal centerline** between the GRIPPER fingers as illustrated.

178) Click **Make this dimension driven**. Click **OK**.

179) Click **View**, uncheck **Origins** from the Main menu.

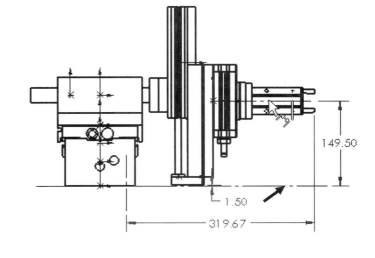

Add the second vertical linear dimension.

180) Click the **bottom horizontal centerline**.

181) Click the **right top vertex** of the SLIDE-TABLE assembly.

182) Click **Make this dimension driven**.

183) Click **OK**. Click **OK** from the Dimension PropertyManager.

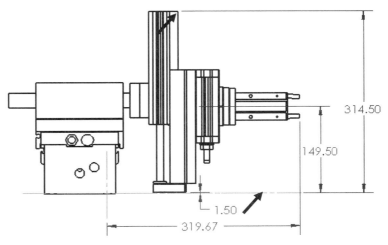

Copy the view.

184) Click **Drawing View1** from the FeatureManager. Press **Ctrl C**.

185) Click a **position** in the lower right corner of Sheet1. Press **Ctrl V**.

186) Right-click **Properties**.

187) Select **Position4** from the Configuration information box. Click

OK. Click **OK** .

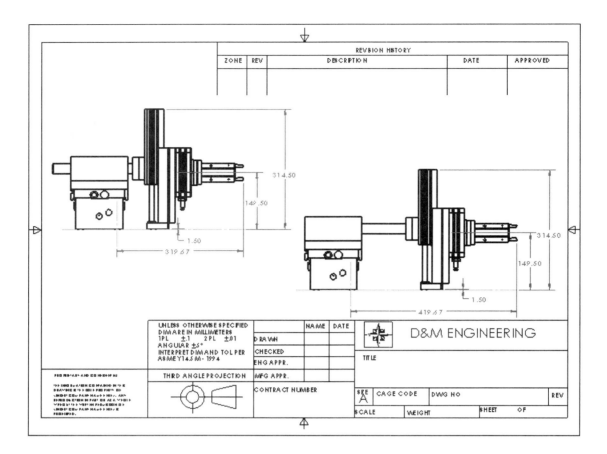

Note: If the dimension values remain unchanged, select Rebuild. If the dimension values are not correct after rebuild, return to the assembly and double-click the specific configuration. Return to the drawing and issue the Rebuild again.

You utilize Sheet1 as a working drawing to calculate interference and view potential issues between configurations. Display dimensions with 2-place decimal precision for calculations.

For a millimeter component drawing, remove the trailing zeros in accordance with ASME Y14.5 Types of Decimal Dimensions. Utilize the Tools, Options, Document Properties, ANSI Dimensioning standard. Select Trailing Zeros, Remove option.

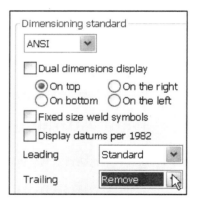

Review the types of decimal dimensions for millimeter and inch units:

TYPES of DECIMAL DIMENSIONS (ASME Y14.5M):			
Description:	Example: MM	Description:	Example: INCH
Dimension is less than 1mm. Zero precedes the decimal point.	0.9 0.95	Dimension is less than 1 inch. Zero is not used before the decimal point.	.5 .56
Dimension is a whole number. Display no decimal point. Display no zero after decimal point.	19	Express dimension to the same number of decimal places as its tolerance. Add zeros to the right of the decimal point.	1.750
Dimension exceeds a whole number by a decimal fraction of a millimeter. Display no zero to the right of the decimal.	11.5 11.51	If the tolerance is expressed to 3 places, then the dimension contains 3 places to the right of the decimal point.	

The Tolerance Display Inch and Metric table illustrates the rules for Unilateral, Bilateral and Limit Tolerance.

Tolerance Display for Inch and Metric DIMENSIONS (ASME Y14.5M)		
Display:	Metric:	Inch:
Unilateral Tolerance	$36^{\ 0}_{-0.5}$	$1.417^{+.005}_{-.000}$
Bilateral Tolerance	$36^{+0.25}_{-0.50}$	$1.417^{+.010}_{-.020}$
Limit Tolerance	14.50 11.50	.571 .463

Title block notes.

Edit the Title block information.
188) Right-click a **position** in the Graphics window. Click **Edit Sheet Format**.

189) **Zoom in** on the lower right hand corner of the Title block.

190) Double-click **<COMPANY NAME>**.

191) Enter your company name. Example: **D&M ENGINEERING**.

192) Click **OK** .

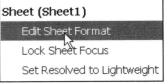

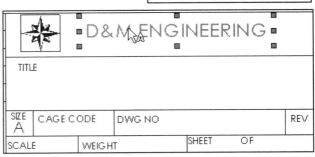

Enter a Note for the drawing name.

193) Click **Note**  from the Annotation toolbar.

194) Click a **position** in the TITLE Block as illustrated.

195) Select **16** for Font size.

196) Enter **3AXIS-TRANSFER ASSEMBLY**.

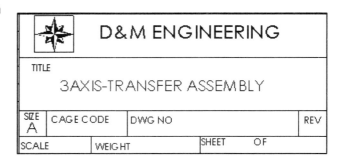

197) Click **OK** from the Note PropertyManager.

Create a Linked Note.

198) Click **Note** Note .

199) Click a **position** below the DWG NO. text.

200) Click **Link to Property** .

201) Select **SW-File Name** from the Link to Property drop down list.

202) Click **OK**.

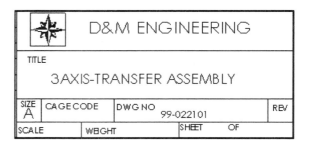

203) Click **OK** from the Note PropertyManager.

The drawing requires a revision letter. Control the revision letter with a Custom Property. Develop Custom Properties and Revision Tables later in this project.

Return to Sheet1.
204) Right-click **Edit Sheet**.

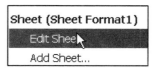

Save the 99-022101, 3AXIS-TRANSFER drawing.
205) Click **Save**.

Activity: 3AXIS-TRANSFER assembly drawing – Sheet2

Add Sheet2.
206) Right-click **Sheet1** tab.

207) Click **Add Sheet**.

Select the Sheet Format.
208) Click **Browse**.

209) Double-click MY-TEMPLATES/
a-format.slddrt.

210) Enter **1:5** for Scale.

211) Click **OK** from the Sheet Properties
box.

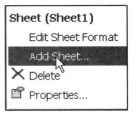

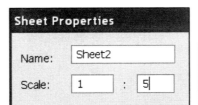

Insert an Isometric view.

212) Click **Model View** from the
Drawings toolbar.

213) Click **99-022101** for Part/Assembly to
Insert from the Open documents list.

214) Click **Next** from the Model View
PropertyManager.

215) If required, click *Isometric from the
Orientation list.

216) Click a **position** on the right side of
Sheet2.

217) Click **OK** from the Model View
PropertyManager.

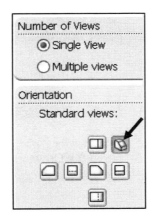

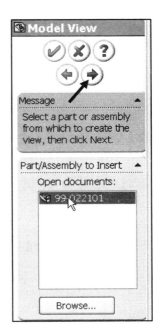

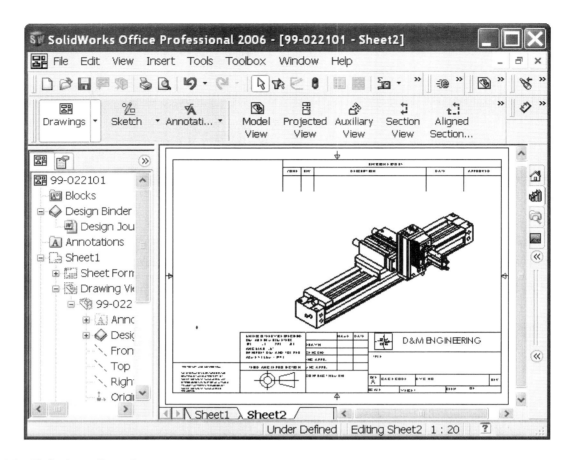

Select the Default configuration.
218) Right-click **Properties** from the Drawing View3 view boundary.

219) Select **Default** from the Used name configuration drop down list.

220) Click **OK**. Click **OK**  from the Drawing View3
PropertyManager.

Rename the Drawing View3.
221) Rename Drawing View3 to **BOM-VIEW**.

Bill of Materials – Part 1

The Bill of Materials (BOM) is a table that lists essential information on the components in an assembly. Insert a Bill of Materials (BOM) into 99-022101, 3AXIS-TRANSFER drawing, Sheet2.

The BOM is linked to the Custom Properties of the 99-022101, 3AXIS-TRANSFER components. There are two options to create a BOM in the drawing: the Table option and the Excel spreadsheet option. Investigate the Table option in this activity.

The first BOM Table inserted into the 99-022101, 3AXIS-TRANSFER drawing requires additional work.

Information is missing. Utilize Component Properties to define the majority of information located in the BOM.

The foundation for the BOM is the BOM Template. The Template contains the major column headings. The default BOM Template, bom-standard.sldbomtbt contains the following column headings:

- ITEM NO.
- PART NUMBER.
- DESCRIPTION.
- QTY (QUANTITY).

The SolidWorks\lang\<language> folder contains additional BOM Templates:

- bom-material.sldbomtbt.
- bom-stock-size.sldbomtbt.
- bom-vendor.sldbomtbt.
- bom-weight.sldbomtbt.
- bom-all.sldbomtbt.

The bom-all.sldbomtbt contains the all default column headings.

A BOM Template also contains User Defined Custom headings. The User Defined Custom headings link to Custom Properties in the part or assembly. Define Custom Properties with the ConfigurationManager and the Design Table.

The BOM Table Anchor point locates the BOM at a corner of the drawing. The BOM Table moves when the Attach to anchor option is unchecked.

The BOM Type contains three options:

- Top level only.
- Parts only.
- Indented assemblies.

BOM Type:

Utilize the <u>Top level only</u> option (for
assemblies that contain sub-assemblies) to
display the highest level components in the
FeatureManager.

ITEM NO.	PART NUMBER:
1	99-022102
2	99-022103
3	99-022104

Utilize the <u>Parts only</u> option to display the
parts in an assembly.

ITEM NO.	PART NUMBER:
6	50GF
7	50GR
8	45-63421
9	50M

Utilize the <u>Indented assemblies</u> option to
display lower level components indented in
the BOM.

ITEM NO.	PART NUMBER:
1	99-022102
	015081
	50
	50FL
	45-63421
2	99-022013
	015082

By default, the component
order in the assembly
determines its ITEM NO.
in the BOM.

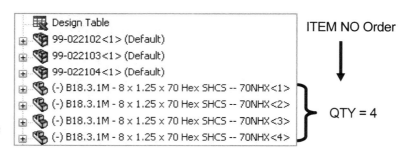

The occurrence of the
same component in an
assembly defines the value
in the QTY column.

The PART NUMBER column in the
BOM is the SolidWorks document name
entered in the File name box,

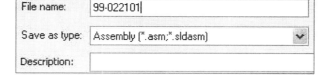

Example: 99-022101.

Utilize the document name for the Bill of
Materials PART NUMBER.

The DESCRIPTION column is the text entered in the Description box. The Description
box is blank for the Project 5 components. Define Description as a Custom Property in
the next section.

Create a Top level only Bill of Materials with the SolidWorks BOM Template, bom-material.sldbomtbt for Sheet2.

Add additional components and configurations to the assembly. Update the drawing. Modify the BOM to display other parameters in Sheet2.

Activity: Bill of Materials – Part 1

Insert the default Bill of Materials.
222) Click inside the **Isometric view boundary** of Sheet2.

223) Click **Insert**, **Tables**, **Bill of Materials** from the Main menu.

224) Double-click **bom-material.sldbomtbt** from the SolidWorks\lang\english folder.

225) Click **Top level only** for BOM Type.

226) Check **Default** in the Configurations box. Uncheck all other Configurations.

227) Click **OK**  from the Bill of Materials PropertyManager.

228) Click a **position** on the upper left corner of the sheet.

Save the drawing.
229) Click **Save**.

230) Modify the BOM-VIEW drawing **Scale to 1: 7**.

Information in the current BOM is incomplete. The Custom Properties in the components link to the DESCRIPTION and MATERIAL columns in the BOM. Create additional Custom Properties in the components to complete the BOM in the drawing.

ITEM NO.	PART NUMBER	DESCRIPTION	MATERIAL	Default/QTY.
1	99-022102			1
2	99-022103			1
3	99-022104			1

Fasteners

The 3AXIS-TRANSFER assembly requires two sets of SHCSs. The GUIDE-CYLINDER assembly requires four, M10x1.5x70 SHCSs. The ROTARY assembly requires two, M8 x 1.25 x 45 SHCSs. Utilize Custom Properties to add PART NUMBER and DESCRIPTION to the BOM.

The BOM updates to reflect the two components added at the top-level assembly. Modify the "Default" configuration name to a numeric part number. Insert MATERIAL as a Custom Property.

An interference issue exists between the GUIDE-CYLINDER and the M10 SHCSs. Modify the M10 x 1.5 x 70 Hex SHCSs to M8 x 1.25 x 70 Hex SHCSs. Utilize Replace Components to modify all four instances in one operation. The M8 x 1.25 x 70 Hex SHCS part is in a closed state in order to be utilized with Replace Components. The BOM updates to reflect the new component.

Changing four M10 x 1.5 x 70 Hex SHCSs to four M8 x 1.25 x 70 Hex SHCSs is an exercise in the Replace Components option. How could you have avoided inserting the wrong size fastener? Answer: Utilize Tools, Measure to determine the SHCS diameter.

Work between the part, assembly, drawing and BOM in the next activities.

Activity: Fasteners

Open the assembly.
231) Right-click **Open 99-022101.sldasm** from the Isometric drawing view.

232) Click the **Default** configuration.

Open the SHCS.
233) Click **File**, **Open** from the Main menu.

234) Double-click **DeliveryStation-Project5/ B18.3.1M-8 x 1.25 x 45 Hex SHCS**.

Display the models.
235) Click **Window**, **Tile Horizontally** from the Main menu.

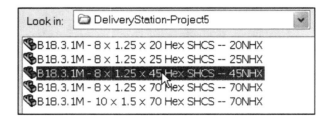

236) **Zoom in** on the circular edge of the SHCS.

237) **Zoom in** on the inside circular edge of the top Cbore of the ROTARY assembly.

Insert the first M8x1.25x45 Hex SHCS.
238) Click and drag the **SHCS circular edge** to the top ROTARY Cbore inside circular edge.

Insert the second M8x1.25x45 Hex SHCS.
239) Click and drag the **SHCS circular edge** to the bottom ROTARY Cbore inside circular edge.

Close the SHCS Graphics window.
240) Click **Close**.

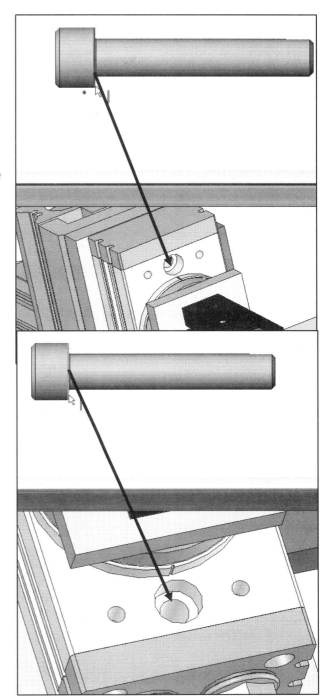

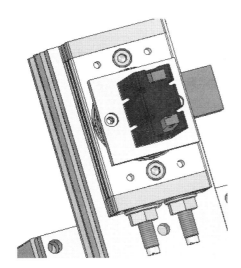

Open the SHCS.
241) Click **File**, **Open** from the Main
      menu.

242) Double-click **DeliveryStation-
      Project5/B18.3.1M-10 x 1.5 x 70**
      Hex SHCS.

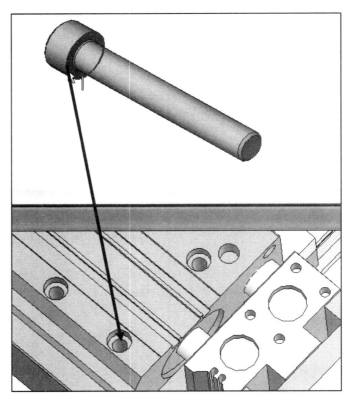

Display the models.
243) Click **Window**, **Tile Horizontally**.

244) **Zoom in** on the circular edge of
      the SHCS.

245) **Zoom in** on the circular edge of
      the front Cbore of the GUIDE-
      CYLINDER assembly.

Insert the first M10 x 1.5 x 70 Hex SHCS.
246) Click and drag the **SHCS circular
      edge** to the front, right GUIDE-
      CYLINDER Cbore inside circular
      edge.

247) Repeat the above process for the
      second, third, and forth
      **B18.3.1M-10 x 1.5 x 70 Hex
      SHCSs**.

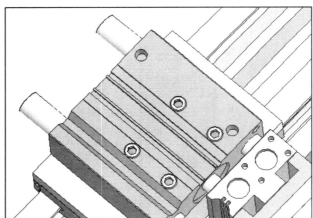

Close the SHCS.
248) Click **Close**.

Save the updates to 99-022101 assembly.
249) Click **Save**.

Update the Bill of Materials.
250) Return to the **99-022101 Drawing, Sheet2**. The Bill of
Materials is updated.

ITEM NO.	PART NUMBER	DESCRIPTION	MATERIAL	Default/QTY.
1	99-022102			1
2	99-022103			1
3	99-022104			1
4	Default	M8 x 1.25 x 45 Hex		2
5	Default	M10 x 1.5 x 70 Hex		4

Open the 99-022101 assembly.
251) Click **Window**, **99-022101** from the
Main menu.

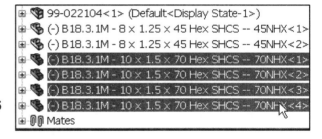

Select the components to replace.
252) Click the first **B18.3.1M-10 x 1.5 x 70
Hex SHCS** from the FeatureManager.

253) Hold the **Ctrl** down key.

254) Click the other **three B18.3.1M-10 x 1.5
x 70 Hex SHCS**.

255) Release the **Ctrl key**.

256) Right-click **Replace Components**.

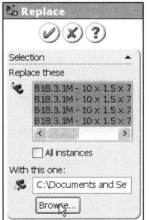

Select the replacing component.
257) Click **Browse**.

258) Double-click
**B18.3.1M-8 x 1.25 x
70 Hex SHCS**.

259) Click **OK** 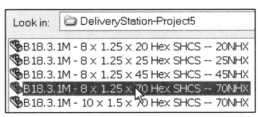 from
the Replace
PropertyManager.

260) Click **OK** 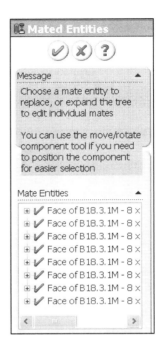 from the Mated Entities PropertyManager.

Save the assembly.
261) Click **Save**.

The FeatureManager contains the four new B18.3.1M-8 x 1.25 x 70 Hex SHCSs.

Update the Bill of Materials.
262) Press **Ctrl+Tab** to display the 99-022101-Sheet2.

ITEM NO.	PART NUMBER	DESCRIPTION	Default/QTY.
1	99-022102		1
2	99-022103		1
3	99-022104		1
4	Default	M8 x 1.25 x 45 Hex	2
5	Default		4

Modify the PART NUMBER, DESCRIPTION, and MATERIAL in the next activity.

Add Custom Properties to the M8x1.25x70 Hex SHCS.
263) Click the **M-8 x 1.25 x 70 Hex SHCS** from the 99-022101 FeatureManager.

264) Right-click **Open Part**.

265) Click the **ConfigurationManager**.

266) Right-click **Default**. Click **Properties**.

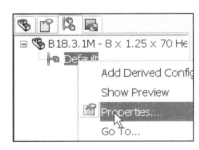

Enter the Bill of Materials Options.
267) Select **User Specified Name** from the drop down list.

268) Enter **SHC-90** for the Part number displayed when used in a bill of materials.

Enter the Custom Properties.
269) Click **Custom properties**.

Enter values in the Configuration Specific table.
270) Click the **Custom** tab.

271) Select **Description** for Property Name.

272) Enter **M8 x 1.25 x 70 Hex** for Value/Text Expression.

273) Select **Material** for Property Name.

274) Select **Material** for Value/Text Expression. No material was selected. In the next step, select Alloy Steel for material using the Materials Editor.

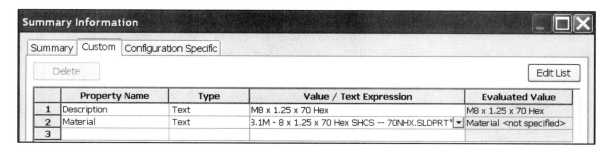

275) Click **OK** from the Summary Information box.

276) Click **OK** ✔ from the Configuration Properties PropertyManager.

277) Apply Alloy Steel to the **M-8 x 1.25 x 70 Hex SHCS** part.

Update the Bill of Materials.
278) Press **Ctrl+Tab** to display the 99-022101-Sheet2.

ITEM NO.	PART NUMBER	DESCRIPTION	MATERIAL	Default/QTY.
1	99-022102			1
2	99-022103			1
3	99-022104			1
4	Default	M8 x 1.25 x 45 Hex		2
5	SHC-90	M8 x 1.25 x 70 Hex	Alloy Steel	4

Add the User defined PART NUMBER and MATERIAL Custom Property to ITEM NO. 4, M8 x 1.25 x 45 Hex SHCS. Perform the above tasks.

ITEM NO.	PART NUMBER	DESCRIPTION	MATERIAL	Default/QTY.
1	99-022102			1
2	99-022103			1
3	99-022104			1
4	SHC-45	M8 x 1.25 x 45 Hex	Alloy Steel	2
5	SHC-90	M8 x 1.25 x 70 Hex	Alloy Steel	4

Return to the assembly.
279) Press **Ctrl+Tab** to display the 99-022101, 3AXIS-TRANSFER assembly.

Insert a new folder for the SHCSs.
280) Click the **first SHCS** from the FeatureManager.

281) Hold the **Ctrl+Shift** keys down.

282) Select the **last SHCS**.

283) Release the **Ctrl+Shift** keys.

284) Right-click **Add to New Folder**.

285) Rename **Folder1** to Hardware.

Save the 99-022101, 3AXIS-TRANSFER assembly.
286) Click **Save**.

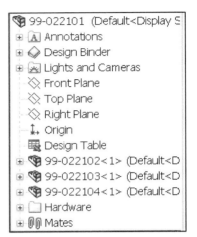

Fastener configuration

Develop a new configuration named Fastener in the 99-022101, 3AXIS-TRANSFER assembly. The Fastener configuration contains the six SHCSs. The $STATE parameter controls the suppressed or resolved value. The symbol, <*> affects all instances of the SHCS component.

	A	B	C	D	E $STATE@B18.3.1M - 8 x 1.25 x 70 Hex SHCS -- 70NHX<*>	F $STATE@B18.3.1M - 8 x 1.25 x 45 Hex SHCS -- 45NHX<*>
		$Configuration@99-022102<1>	$Configuration@99-022103<1>	$Configuration@99-022104<1>		
2	Position1	Normal	Normal-Normal	Vertical	S	S
3	Position2	Normal	Normal-Extended	Vertical	S	S
4	Position3	Normal	Extended-Normal	Vertical	S	S
5	Position4	Normal	Extended-Extended	Vertical	S	S
6	Position5	Extended	Normal-Normal	Horizontal	S	S
7	Position6	Extended	Normal-Extended	Horizontal	S	S
8	Position7	Extended	Extended-Normal	Horizontal	S	S
9	Position8	Extended	Extended-Extended	Horizontal	S	S
10	Default	Default	Default	Default	S	S
11	Fastener	Fastener	Fastener	Fastener	R	R

Activity: Fastener configuration

Insert the Fastener configuration.
287) Right-click **Design Table** from the FeatureManager.

288) Click **Edit Table**. Click **OK**.

289) Click Cell **A11**.

290) Enter **Fastener**.

291) Copy Fastener from Cell A11 to **Cells B11** through **D11**.

Copy the Component Name for the first SHCS.
292) Click **Cell E1**.

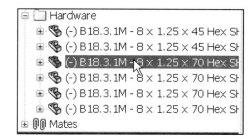

293) Click **M-8 x 1.25 x 70 Hex SHCS** from the FeatureManager.

294) Right-click **Component Properties**.

295) Select the **Component Name** box.

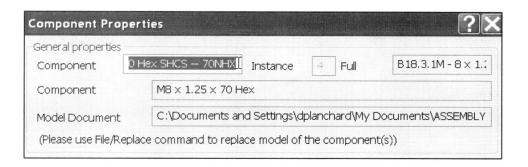

296) Press **Ctrl-C**.

297) Click **OK** from the Component Properties dialog box.

298) Click the **Formula Bar** for Cell E1.

299) Enter '**$STATE@**.

300) Press **Ctrl-V**.

301) Enter **<*>**.

302) Press the **Enter** key. ｆₓ '$STATE@B18.3.1M - 8 x 1.25 x 70 Hex SHCS -- 70NHX<*>

Enter the $STATE values.
303) Enter **S** in **Cell E2** through **Cell E10**.

304) Enter **R** in **Cell E11**.

Note: Spell entries correctly. Include spaces and underscore.
Example: '$STATE@B18.3.1M - 8 x 1.25 x 70 Hex SHCS --
70NHX<*>.

Copy the Component Name for the second SHCS.
305) Click **Cell F1**.

306) Click **M-8 x 1.25 x 45 Hex SHCS** from the FeatureManager.

307) Right-click **Component Properties**.

308) Select the **Component Name** box.

309) Press **Ctrl-C**.

310) Click **OK** from the Component Properties dialog
box.

311) Click the **Formula Bar** for Cell F1.

312) Enter **'$STATE@**.

313) Press **Ctrl-V**.

314) Enter **<*>**.

315) Press the **Enter** key.

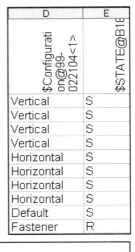

D	E
$Configuration@99-022104<1>	$STATE@B18
Vertical	S
Vertical	S
Vertical	S
Vertical	S
Horizontal	S
Horizontal	S
Horizontal	S
Horizontal	S
Default	S
Fastener	R

Hardware
  ⊞ (-) B18.3.1M - 8 x 1.25 x 45 Hex SH
  ⊞ (-) B18.3.1M - 8 x 1.25 x 45 Hex SH
  ⊞ (-) B18.3.1M - 8 x 1.25 x 70 Hex SH
  ⊞ (-) B18.3.1M - 8 x 1.25 x 70 Hex SH
  ⊞ (-) B18.3.1M - 8 x 1.25 x 70 Hex SH
  ⊞ (-) B18.3.1M - 8 x 1.25 x 70 Hex SH
⊞ Mates

_fx_ '$STATE@B18.3.1M - 8 x 1.25 x 45 Hex SHCS -- 45NHX<*>

Enter the $STATE values.
316) Enter **S** in **Cell F2** through **Cell F10**.

317) Enter **R** in **Cell F11**.

Create the Fastener configuration.
318) Click a **position** in the SolidWorks Graphics
window.

319) Click **OK** to generate the Fastener configuration.

E	F
$STATE@B18	$STATE@B18
S	S
S	S
S	S
S	S
S	S
S	S
S	S
S	S
S	S
R	R

View the configurations
320) Double click **Fastener** from the ConfigurationManager. View the SHCSs in the Graphics window.

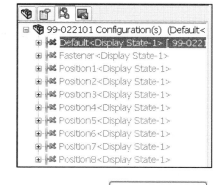

Return to the Default configuration.
321) Double-click **Default**.

Update the Bill of Materials.
322) Press the **Ctrl+Tab** keys to display the 99-022101- Sheet2.

Display the BOM PropertyManager.
323) Click the **Bill of Materials header**. The Cell PropertyManager is displayed. Click **Table Properties**.

Modify the configurations.
324) Check **Fastener** from the Configurations box.

325) Click **OK** ✓ from the Bill of Material PropertyManager.

ITEM NO.	PART NUMBER	DESCRIPTION	MATERIAL	Default/QTY.	Fastener/QTY.
1	99-022102			1	-
2	99-022103			1	-
3	99-022104			1	-
4	99-022102			-	1
5	99-022103			-	1
6	99-022104			-	1
7	SHC-45	M8 x 1.25 x 45 Hex	Alloy Steel	-	2
8	SHC-90	M8 x 1.25 x 70 Hex	Alloy Steel	-	4

Exploded View

The Exploded View illustrates how to assemble the components in an assembly. Create an Exploded View with multi-steps. Click and drag components in the Graphics window. Explode the CYLINDER assembly with a multi-step procedure.

The Manipulator icon ⊥ indicates the direction to explode. Select an alternate component edge for the explode direction. Drag the component in the Graphics window or enter an exact value in the Explode distance box. In this activity, manipulate the top-level components in the assembly. In the project exercises, create Exploded views for each sub-assembly and utilize the Re-use sub-assembly Explode ⊞ option in the top level assembly.

Access the Explode view option as follows:

- Right-click the configuration name in the ConfigurationManager.

- Select the Exploded View tool from the Assembly toolbar.

- Select Insert, Exploded View from the Main menu.

The Assembly Exploder utilizes a PropertyManager.

Components
of the
exploded step

Direction

Distance

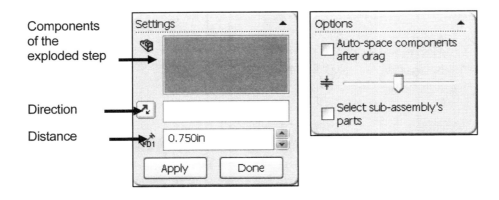

Activity: Exploded View

Insert an Exploded View.
326) Return to the **99-022101** assembly.

327) Double-click **Fastener** from the
ConfigurationManager.

328) Right-click **New Exploded View**. The Explode
PropertyManager is displayed.

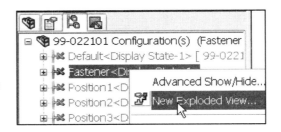

Create Explode Step 1.
329) Click the first **B18.3.1M-8x1.25x45 Hex** from the
FeatureManager.

330) Hold the **Ctrl** key.

331) Click the **second B18.3.1M-8x1.25x45 Hex**.

332) Release the **Ctrl** key.

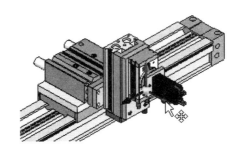

333) Click and drag the red **Manipulator** arrow to the
right as illustrated.

334) Click **Done**. Explode Step1 is created.

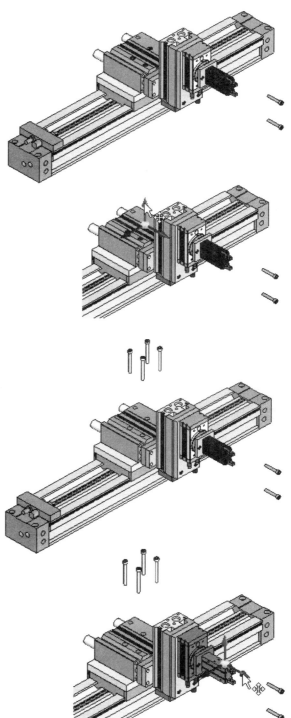

Create Explode Step 2.
335) Click the first **B18.3.1M-8x1.25x70 Hex SHCS** from the FeatureManager.

336) Hold the **Ctrl** key down.

337) Click the second, third and forth **B18.3.1M-8x1.25x70 Hex SHCSs**.

338) Release the **Ctrl** key.

339) Click and drag the green **Manipulator**.

arrow above the GUIDE-CYLINDER.

340) Click **Done**. Explode Step2 is created.

Create Explode Step3.
341) Click the **ROTARY-GRIPPER** assembly.

342) Click and drag the red **Manipulator** arrow to the right as illustrated.

343) Click **Done**. Explode Step3 is created.

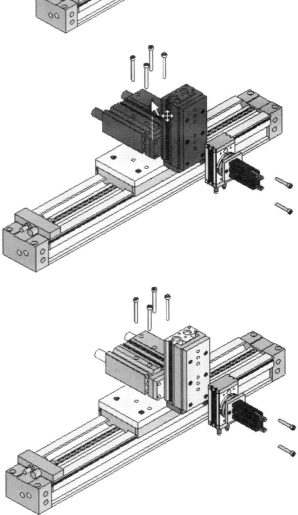

Create Step 4.
344) Click the **GUIDE-CYLINDER** assembly.

345) Click and drag the green **Manipulator** arrow above the LINEAR-TRANSFER assembly.

346) Click **Done**. Explode Step4 is created.

347) Click **OK** from the Explode PropertyManager.

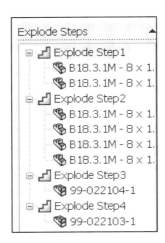

Collapse the Exploded View.

348) Expand **Fastener** configuration from the 99-022101 ConfigurationManager.

349) Right-click **ExplView1**.

350) Click **Collapse**.

Return to the 99-022101 [Default], 3AXIS-TRANSFER assembly.
351) Double-click **Default** from the ConfigurationManager.

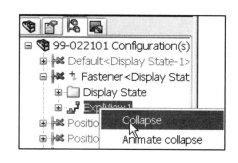

Save the 99-022101, 3AXIS-TRANSFER assembly.
352) Click **Save**.

Return to Sheet2.
353) Press **Ctrl+Tab**.

Display the Exploded View.
354) Click the **Isometric** view.

355) Right-click **Properties**.

356) Select **Fastener** from the Use named configuration drop down list.

357) Check **Show in exploded state** in the Configuration information text box.

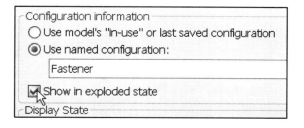

358) Click **OK**.

Modify the Scale.
359) Check **Use custom scale**.

360) Enter **1:10**. Reposition the BOM.

361) Drag the **BOM header** above the sheet boundary. Click **Table Properties**.

362) Uncheck **Default** from the Configurations box. The Fastener configuration remains checked.

363) Click **OK** ✅ from the Bill of Materials PropertyManager.

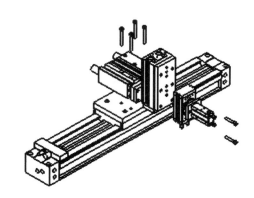

Balloons

The 99-022101-Sheet2 contains an Exploded Isometric view. Use Balloon annotations to label components in an assembly. The Balloon contains the Item Number listed in the Bill of Materials.

A Balloon displays different end conditions based on the arrowhead geometry reference. Drag the endpoint of the arrowhead to modify the attachment and the end condition.

There are three attachment types:

- Edge – arrowhead.
- Face – dot.
- No Reference – question mark.

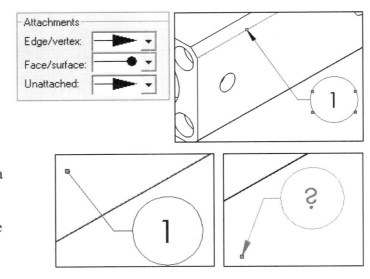

☀ View mouse pointer feedback to distinguish between a vertex in the model and the attachment point in a Balloon. The attachment point displays the Note ⛯ icon for a Balloon and the Point ⛯ icon for point geometry.

The Document Template, Document Properties, Balloons option defines the default arrow style and Balloons options.

The Balloons option controls the Single balloon, Stacked balloons, Balloon text, Bent leaders, and Auto Balloon Layout options.

The Auto Balloon Layout option determines the display of the Balloons. Square Layout is the default.

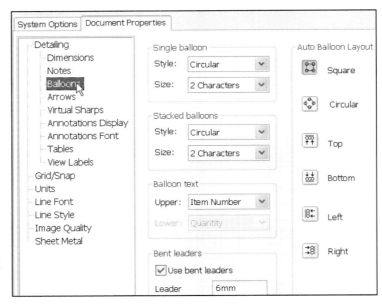

The Top Layout displays the Balloons horizontally aligned above the model. The Left Layout displays the Balloon vertically aligned to the left of the model.

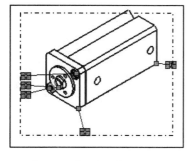

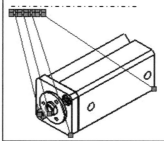

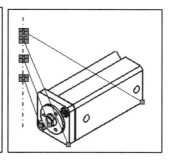

Square (Default)   Top Layout   Left Layout

Modify the selected Balloon with Balloon Properties. The Circular Split Line Style displays the Item Number in the Upper portion of the circle and the Quantity in the Lower portion of the circle.

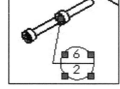

Select the Balloon option from the Annotations toolbar. Right-click Annotations in the Graphics window, or select Insert, Annotations from the Main menu.

The Balloon ⌀ option inserts a single item with a leader.

The Auto Balloon ⌀ option inserts Balloons based on the view boundary and the BOM type.

The Stacked Balloon ⚬⚬ option contains multiple item numbers with a single leader.

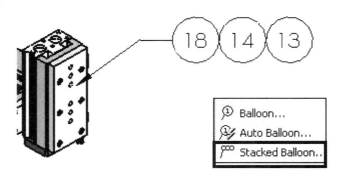

Activity: Balloons

Insert Balloons to Label each component.

364) Click **AutoBalloon** AutoBal... from the Annotations toolbar. Five Balloons appear in the Isometric view.

365) Click **OK** 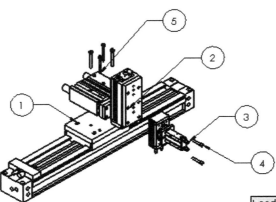 from the Auto Balloon PropertyManager.

Modify the Balloons.
366) Window-select the **five Balloons**. The Balloon PropertyManager is displayed.

367) Click **More Properties**.

368) Click **Bent Leader** from the Leader box.

Modify the font.
369) Uncheck **Use document's font**.

370) Click **Font**.

371) Enter **5** mm for font height.

372) Click **OK** from the Font dialog box.

Modify the arrowhead.
373) Click **Balloon 1**.

374) Drag the **arrowhead** to the middle edge of the PLATE-A.

375) Drag each **Balloon** into position. Leave space between Balloon numbers.

376) Click OK.

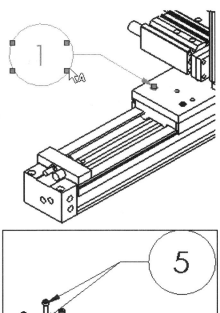

Create two leader lines.
377) Zoom in on the four CAP-SCREWS.

378) Hold the **Ctrl** key down.

379) Drag the **arrowhead** from the edge of the first CAP-SCREW to the edge of the back left CAP-SCREW.

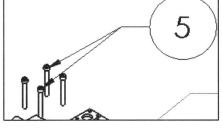

380) Release the **Ctrl** key. Click **OK** from the Balloon PropertyManager.

Save the 99-022101, 3AXIS-TRANSFER drawing.
381) Click **Save**.

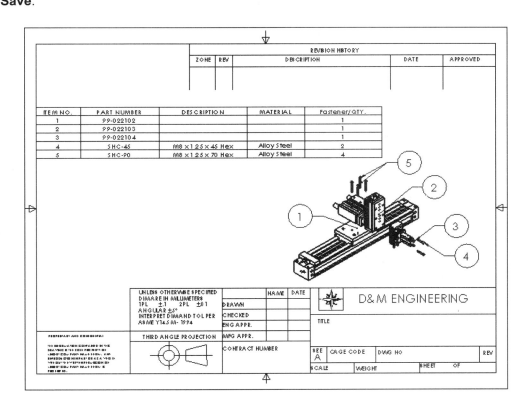

ITEM NO.	PART NUMBER	DESCRIPTION	MATERIAL	Fastener/QTY.
1	99-022102			1
2	99-022103			1
3	99-022104			1
4	SHC-45	M8 x 1.25 x 45 Hex	Alloy Steel	2
5	SHC-90	M8 x 1.25 x 70 Hex	Alloy Steel	4

Custom Properties

The Bill of Materials requires additional work. The assemblies: 99-022101, 99-022102, 99-022103, & 99-022104 contain a PART NUMBER. The assemblies do not contain a DESCRIPTION parameter.

Create the Custom Property, DESCRIPTION for assemblies:

1. 99-022101.

2. 99-022102.

3. 99-022103.

4. 99-022104.

Utilize the Custom tab. The Custom option assigns the same parameter and value to all configurations.

Minimize editing in the drawing Bill of Materials. Define all the parameters and values utilized in the BOM in the part or assembly. Spell values exactly. The parameter name matches the column heading in the BOM.

Update the Bill of Materials and insert a Linked Note into the Title block of the 99-022101, 3AXIS-TRANSFER drawing.

| **Activity: Custom Properties** |

Display the components in the drawing FeatureManager.
382) Expand **BOM-VIEW** from the FeatureManager in Sheet2.

383) Expand **99-022101** from the FeatureManager.

384) Click **99-022102**.

385) Right-click **Open Assembly**.

Add Custom Properties to the first sub-assembly: 99-022102, LINEAR-TRANSFER assembly.
386) Click the **Default** configuration from the ConfigurationManager.

387) Right-click **Properties**.

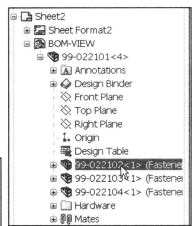

388) Click **Custom properties** Configuration Properties PropertyManager.

389) Click the **Custom** tab from the Summary Information box.

390) Select **Description** for Property Name.

391) Enter **LINEAR-TRANSFER** in the Value/Text Expression box.

392) Select **Cost** for Property Name.

393) Select **Number** for Type.

394) Enter **500** for Value.

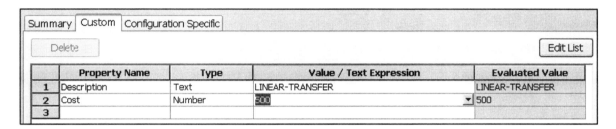

395) Click **OK** from the Summary Information box.

396) Click **OK** from the Configuration Properties PropertyManager.

Save the 99-022102, LINEAR-TRANSFER assembly.
397) Return to the **FeatureManager**.

398) Click **Isometric** view.

399) Click **Save**.

Close the 99-022102, LINEAR-TRANSFER assembly.
400) Click **File**, **Close** from the Main menu.

Display the components from the drawing 99-022101 FeatureManager.
401) Click **99-022103** from the FeatureManager.

402) Right-click **Open Assembly**.

Add Custom Properties to the second sub-assembly: 99-022103, 2AXIS-TRANSFER assembly.
403) Click the **Fastener** configuration.

404) Right-click **Properties**.

405) Click **Custom properties** from the Configuration Properties PropertyManager.

406) Click the **Custom** tab from the Summary Information box.

407) Select **Description** for Property Name.

408) Enter **2AXIS-TRANSFER** in the Value/Text Expression box.

409) Select **Cost** for Property Name. Select **Number** for Type.

410) Enter **600** for Value.

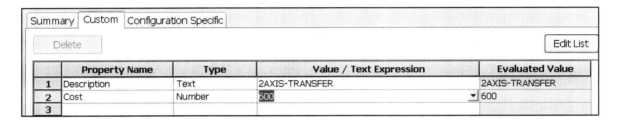

411) Click **OK** from the Summary Information box.

412) Click **OK** from the Configuration Properties PropertyManager.

Save the 99-022103, 2AXIS-TRANSFER assembly.
413) Return to the **FeatureManager**.

414) Click **Isometric** view.

415) Click **Save**.

Close the 99-022103, 2AXIS-TRANSFER assembly.
416) Click **File**, **Close** from the Main menu.

Display the components in the drawing 99-022101 FeatureManager.
417) Click **99-022104** from the FeatureManager.

418) Right-click **Open Assembly**.

Add Custom Properties to the third sub-assembly: 99-022104, ROTARY-GRIPPER assembly.
419) Click the **Default** configuration from the ConfigurationManager.

420) Right-click **Properties**.

421) Click **Custom properties** from the Configuration Properties PropertyManager.

422) Click the **Custom** tab from the Summary Information box.

423) Select **Description** for Property Name.

424) Enter **ROTARY-GRIPPER** in the Value/Text Expression box.

425) Select **Cost** for Property Name.

426) Select **Number** for Type.

427) Enter **450** for Value.

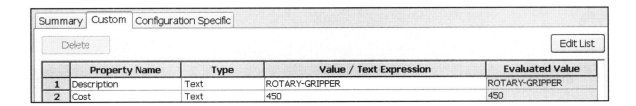

	Property Name	Type	Value / Text Expression	Evaluated Value
1	Description	Text	ROTARY-GRIPPER	ROTARY-GRIPPER
2	Cost	Text	450	450

428) Click **OK** from the Summary Information box.

429) Click **OK** from the Configuration Properties PropertyManager.

Save the 99-022104, ROTARY-GRIPPER assembly.
430) Return to the **FeatureManager**.

431) Click **Isometric** view.

432) Click **Save**.

Close the 99-022104, ROTARY-GRIPPER assembly.
433) Click **File**, **Close** from the Main menu.

Return to Sheet2, 99-022101 drawing.
434) Click **Window**, **99-022101-Sheet2**.

435) Click **Rebuild**. The three sub-assemblies in the Bill of Materials utilize the Description Custom Property. Utilize the Cost Custom Property later in this project.

ITEM NO.	PART NUMBER	DESCRIPTION	MATERIAL	Fastener/QTY.
1	99-022102	LINEAR-TRANSFER		1
2	99-022103	2AXIS-TRANSFER		1
3	99-022104	ROTARY-GRIPPER		1
4	SHC-45	M8 x 1.25 x 45 Hex	Alloy Steel	2
5	SHC-90	M8 x 1.25 x 70 Hex	Alloy Steel	4

Add Custom Properties to the 99-022101, 3AXIS-TRANSFER assembly.
436) Right-click a **position** in the Sheet2 Isometric view.

437) Click **Open 99-022101.sldasm**.

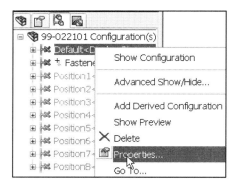

438) Click the **ConfigurationManager** .

439) Click **Default**. Right-click **Properties**.

440) Click **Custom properties** from the Configuration Properties PropertyManager.

441) Click the **Custom** tab in the Summary Information box.

442) Select **DESCRIPTION** for Property Name.

443) Enter **3AXIS-TRANSFER** in the Value/Text Expression box. Click **OK** from the Summary Information box.

444) Click **OK** from the Configuration Properties PropertyManager.

Save the 99-022101, 3AXIS-TRANSFER assembly.
445) Return to the **FeatureManager**.

446) Click **Isometric** view. Click **Save**.

Close the 99-022101, 3AXIS-TRANSFER assembly.
447) Click **File**, **Close** from the Main menu.

448) Display the **99-022101, 3AXIS-TRANSFER drawing**.

Add the Description Custom Property to the Title block, Sheet2.
449) Right-click **Edit Sheet Format**.

450) **Zoom in** on the lower right hand corner of the Title block.

Insert a Linked Note for Description.
451) Click **Note** Note from the Annotation toolbar.

452) Click a **position** to the right of TITLE text.

453) Click **Link to Property** .

454) Check **Model in view specified in sheet properties**.

455) Select **Description** from the drop down list.

456) Click **OK** from the Link to Properties box.

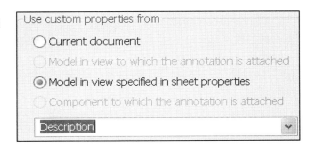

457) Enter **ASSEMBLY** text.

458) Click **OK** 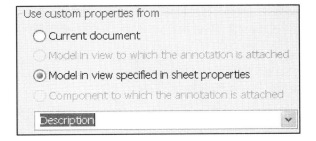 from the Note PropertyManger. The value, $PRPSHEET: "Description" ASSEMBLY is displayed in the Note.

TITLE

3AXIS-TRANSFER ASSEMBLY

Return to the drawing sheet.
459) Right-click in the **Graphics window**.

460) Click **Edit Sheet**.

The Model in view specified in sheet properties option populates parameters and values to Linked Notes. This option references Sheet Properties.

The Use custom property values from model shown option, is set to Default in the Sheet Properties dialog box.

Expand the drop down list to display the view names contained in Sheet1 and Sheet2.

Revision Table

The Revision Table lists the Engineering Change Order (ECO) in the top right section of the drawing. An ECO documents changes that occur to a component. The Engineering department maintains each ECO with a unique document number. In this project, the ECO 8531 releases the drawing to manufacturing.

The current Revision block on the drawing was imported from AutoCAD. Delete the current Revision block lines and text. Utilize the Insert, Tables, Revision option to create a Revision Table. The default columns are as follows: Zone, Rev, Description, Date, and Approved.

The Zone column utilizes the row letter and column number contained in the drawing border. Position the REV letter in the Zone area. Enter the Zone letter/number. Enter a Description that corresponds to the ECO number. Modify the date if required. Enter the initials/name of the engineering manager who approved the revision.

The REV. column in the Revision Table is a Sheet Property. Create a Linked Note in the Title block and utilize the Revision Sheet Property. The current Revision of the drawing corresponds to the letter in the last row of the Revision Table.

Activity: Revision Table

Activate Sheet1.
461) Click the **Sheet1** tab.

Edit the Sheet Format.
462) Right-click in the **Graphics window**.

463) Click **Edit Sheet Format**.

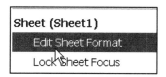

Delete the current Revision Table created in the Autocad format.
464) Zoom in on the upper right corner of the Sheet Format.

465) Window-select the **Revision Table**.

466) Press the **Delete** key.

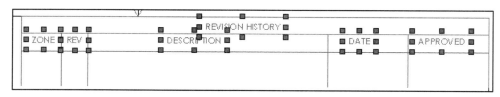

Return to the drawing sheet.
467) Right-click in the **Graphics window**.

468) Click **Edit Sheet**.

Fit the drawing to the Graphics window.
469) Press the **f** key.

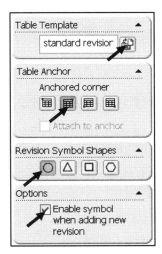

Insert a Revision Table.
470) Click **Insert**, **Tables**, **Revision Table** from the Main menu. The Revision Table PropertyManager is displayed.

471) Select the **standard revision** Table Template, **Top Right Anchor** corner, and **Circle Revision** Symbol Shape.

472) Check the **Enable symbol when adding new revision** option.

473) Click **OK** . The Revision Table is displayed in the upper right corner.

474) Drag the **Revision Table** downward to the inside upper right sheet boundary.

The Enable symbol when adding new revision option displays the Revision Symbol on the mouse pointer when you execute the Add Revision command. Position the revision symbol on the drawing that corresponds to the change.

Insert the first row.
475) Right-click the **Revision Table**.

476) Click **Revisions**, **Add Revision**. The Revision letter, A and the current date are displayed in the Revision Table.

Position the Revision Symbol.

477) The A Revision Symbol is displayed on the mouse pointer. Click a **position** in DrawingView2.

478) Click **OK** from the Revision Symbol PropertyManager.

Edit the Revision Table.
479) Double-click the **text box** under the Description column.

480) Enter **ECO 8531 RELEASED TO MANUFACTURING** for DESCRIPTION.

481) Click **OK** ✅ from the Note PropertyManager.

482) Double-click the **text box** under the APPROVED column.

483) Enter Documentation Control Manager's Initials, Example: **DCP**.

		REVISIONS		
ZONE	REV.	DESCRIPTION	DATE	APPROVED
	A	ECO 8531 RELEASED TO MANUFACTURING	3/20/2006	DCP

484) Click **OK** ✅ from the Note PropertyManager.

Edit the Sheet Format.
485) Right-click a **position** in the Sheet boundary.

486) Click **Edit Sheet Format**.

Insert a Linked Note for Revision.
487) Click **Note** Note .

488) Click a **position** below the REV text in the Title block.

489) Click **Link to Property** 📋 .

490) Select **Revision** from the drop down list.

491) Click **OK** from the Link to Property box. The value, $PRPSHEET: "Revision" is displayed in the Note.

492) Click **OK** ✅ from the Note PropertyManager.

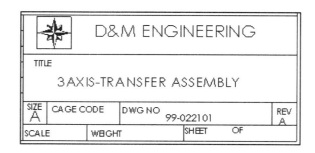

Return to the drawing sheet.
493) Right-click a **position** in the sheet boundary.

494) Click **Edit Sheet**.

Save the 99-022101, 3AXIS-TRANSFER drawing.
495) Click **Save**.

The File Properties button in the Link to Property box lists the Custom Properties of the sheet and their current values.

Insert the next revision in the Revision Table to increment the REV. text in the Title block. The Revision Table example shows how to control a REV. value through the drawing Sheet Properties.

Companies also control the REV. value by combining a Revision Custom Property in the part and a Linked Note in the drawing. PDM systems control document revisions based on the Revision rules in your company's engineering documentation practices.

Only Sheet1 displays the current REV. You will have to update the Title block in every sheet. Is there a more efficient method to control notes in the Title block? Answer: Yes. Develop a Sheet Format with Drawing Specific SolidWorks Properties and Custom Properties.

The default A-size SolidWorks Sheet Format contains Custom Properties defined in the Title block. Set Drawing Specific System Properties: SW-Sheet Name, SW-Sheet Scale SW-Sheet Format Size and SW-Template Size in the Sheet Properties dialog box.

The following Drawing Specific SolidWorks Properties exist only in a drawing:

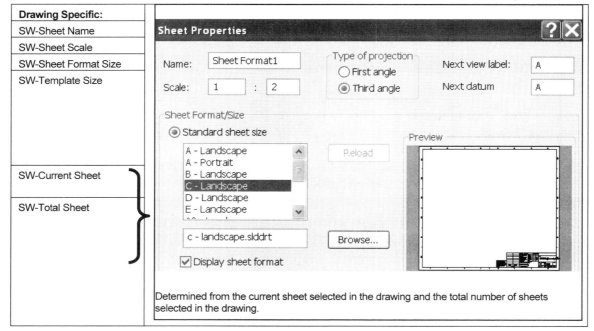

Creating customized Drawing Templates and Sheet Formats requires an understanding of SolidWorks Properties and Custom Properties. Customized Drawing Templates and Sheet Formats save you set-up time in every drawing and on every sheet.

Utilize Online help, customize, sheet formats for additional information.

Refer to **Drawing and Detailing with SolidWorks**, Project 1 for step-by-step instructions on creating Drawing Templates and Sheet Formats.

A .pdf file of Project 1 is available at the publisher's website, www.schroff.com.

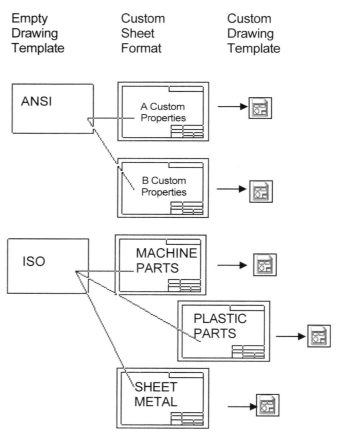

Bill of Materials – Part 2

The BOM requires additional changes. Right-click on a Cell in the BOM to display the four options:

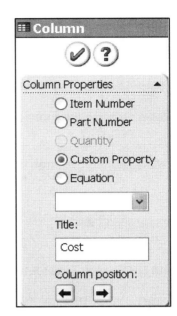

- Column Properties.

- Table Properties.

- Table Format.

- BOM Contents.

The Column Properties option inserts a Custom Property into the BOM column header. Utilize the Custom Property, Cost in the 99-022101, 3AXIS-TRANSFER BOM.

The Table Properties option returns you to the BOM PropertyManager.

The Table Format option modifies the BOM Title, Border, Text Format, Font and Layer. Enter a new Title for the 99-022101, 3AXIS-TRANSFER BOM.

Utilize the BOM Contents to modify the Item Number order, group, balloon state and visibility. The Pop-up menu contains additional tools to insert, delete and modify columns and rows, sort columns, split and merge the BOM table and Save as template.

Activity: Bill of Materials – Part 2

Insert the Cost column.
496) Click the **MATERIAL Cell** on Sheet2.

497) Right-click **Insert**.

498) Click **Column Right**.

499) Click the **top empty Cell**.

500) Click **Column Properties** from the Cell PropertyManager.

MATERIAL		Fastener/QTY.
		1
		1
		1
Alloy Steel		2
Alloy Steel		4

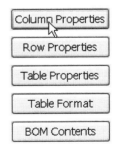

501) Select **Cost** from the Custom Property drop down list.

502) Enter **COST** in the Title box. All BOM column headings are in upper case letters.

503) Click **OK** from the Column PropertyManager.

504) Position the **mouse pointer** on the column line between COST and QTY.

505) Drag the **column grid line** to the left, to decrease the column size by half.

Insert the BOM Title.
506) Click a **Cell** in the BOM.

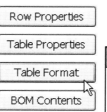

507) Click the **Table Format** button.

508) Check **Display title**.

509) Enter **3AXIS-TRANSFER 99-022101 BILL OF MATERIALS** for Title in the Header box.

510) Click **OK** from the Table PropertyManger.

Insert a bulk item in the BOM.
511) Right-click on the **Item No 5 Cell**, last row, first column.

512) Right-click **Insert**, **Row Below**.

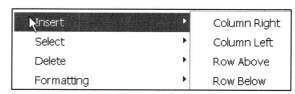

513) Double-click **inside** the Cell to the right of the Item No 6 cell.

514) Click **Yes** to the question, Continue editing the cell? Enter **INS-101** for the PART NUMBER.

515) Double-click **inside** the Cell to the right of INS-101.

516) Enter **INSTRUCTION SHEET** for DESCRIPTION.

517) Click **OK**.

Modify the Item Order.
518) Click a **Cell** in the BOM.

519) Click the **BOM Contents** button.

520) Click the **left most column Cell** to the left of the SHC-45 entry.

521) Click the Row **down** ⬇ icon until the current row is located below the part number SHC-45.

Note: Utilize the Row up ⬆ and Row down ⬇ icons to reposition the items in the BOM.

522) Click **OK**.

Column Properties
Row Properties
Table Properties
Table Format
BOM Contents

3 AXIS-TRANSFER 99-022101 BILL OF MATERIALS					
ITEM NO.	PART NUMBER	DESCRIPTION	MATERIAL	COST	Fastener/QTY.
1	99-022102	LINEAR-TRANSFER		500	1
2	99-022103	2 AXIS-TRANSFER		600	1
3	99-022104	ROTARY-GRIPPER		450	1
4	SHC-45	M8 x 1.25 x 45 Hex	Alloy Steel		2
5	SHC-90	M8 X 1.25 X 70 Hex	Alloy Steel		4
6	INS-101	INSTRUCTION SHEET			

523) Press the **f** key to fit the drawing to the screen. The Balloons update to reflect the new ITEM NO. order.

Modify the BOM Type.
524) Click the **BOM** table. Click the **Table Properties** button.

525) Check **Indented assemblies**. Click **Yes** to the message, Do you want to continue?

526) Select the **Fastener** configuration.

527) Click **OK** ✓.

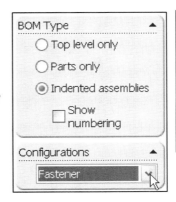

Format the Column text.

528) Select the **PART NUMBER** column header.

529) Click the **Table Format** button.

530) Click **Left Justify**.

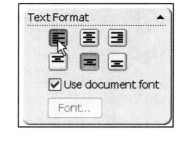

Modify the BOM Contents.

531) Click the **BOM Contents** button.

532) Click the **Toggle Row Visibility** 👆 icon for all components below the RODLESS-CYLINDER, 015801 without a Description value.

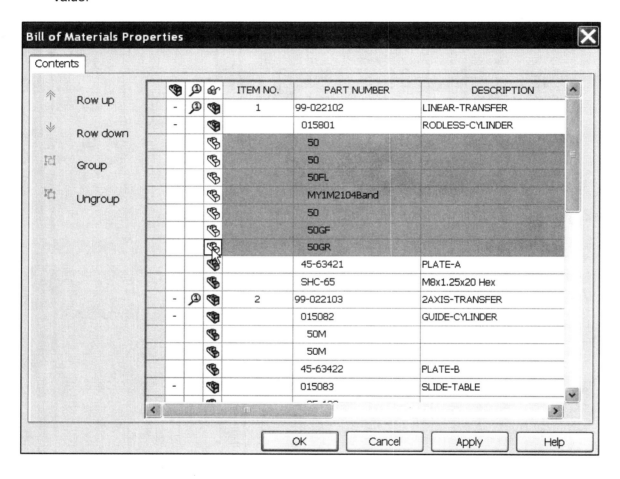

533) Repeat **Toggle Row Visibility** for all SMC purchased components.

534) Click **OK**.

Save the 99-022101 drawing.
535) Click **Save**.

3AXIS-TRANSFER 99-022101 BILL OF MATERIALS					
ITEM NO	PART NUMBER	DESCRIPTION	MATERIAL	COST	QTY.
1	99-022102	LINEAR-TRANSFER		500	1
	015801	RODLESS-CYLINDER			1
	45-63421	PLATE-A			1
	SHC-65	M8x1.25x20 Hex			4
2	99-022103	2AXIS-TRANSFER		600	1
	015082	GUIDE-CYLINDER			1
	45-63422	PLATE-B			1
	015083	SLIDE-TABLE			1
	45-63423	PLATE-C			1
	SHC-48	M6 x 1.0 x 20 Hex			8
	SHC-43	M6x1.0x50 Hex			2
3	99-022104	ROTARY-GRIPPER		450	1
	015084	ROTARY-ACTUATOR			1
	015085	GRIPPER			1
	45-63424	PLATE-D			1
	SHC-33	M - 5 x 0.8 x 12 Hex			2
	SHC-21	M4x0.7x16 Hex			2
4	SHC-45	M8 x 1.25 x 45 Hex	Alloy Steel		2
5	SHC-90	M8 X 1.25 X 70 Hex	Alloy Steel		4

Split the BOM.
536) Select **ITEM NO 3**. Right-click **Split**.

537) Click **Horizontally Above**.

Horizontally Above
Horizontally Below
Vertically Right

538) Click **OK** . Positon the Bill of Materials off of the Sheet.

3AXIS-TRANSFER 99-022101 BILL OF MATERIALS							3AXIS-TRANSFER 99-022101 BILL OF MATERIALS					
ITEM NO.	PART NUMBER	DESCRIPTION	MATERIAL	COST	QTY.		ITEM NO.	PART NUMBER	DESCRIPTION	MATERIAL	COST	QTY.
1	99-022102	LINEAR-TRANSFER		500	1		3	99-022104	ROTARY-GRIPPER		450	1
	015801	RODLESS-CYLINDER			1			015084	ROTARY-ACTUATOR			1
	45-63421	PLATE-A			1			015085	GRIPPER			1
	SHC-65	M8x1.25x20 Hex			4			45-63424	PLATE-D			1
2	99-022103	2AXIS-TRANSFER		600	1			SHC-33	M - 5 x 0.8 x 12 Hex			2
	015082	GUIDE-CYLINDER			1			SHC-21	M4x0.7x16 Hex			2
	45-63422	PLATE-B			1		4	SHC-45	M8 x 1.25 x 45 Hex	Alloy Steel		2
	015083	SLIDE-TABLE			1		5	SHC-90	M8 X 1.25 X 70 Hex	Alloy Steel		4
	45-63423	PLATE-C			1							
	SHC-48	M6 x 1.0 x 20 Hex			8							
	SHC-43	M6x1.0x50 Hex			2							

Save Sheet2.
539) Click **Save**.

Each section moves individually. To return the BOM to a single list, utilize the Merge option.

Drawing View Properties

The Drawing View Properties dialog box controls the display of edges and components. Utilize the Show/Hide option to display individual edges or components. Utilize the Drawing View Properties Show Hidden Edges and Hide/Show Components for efficient control.

Utilize a Design Table and the $Show@configuration<instance> parameter to Show/Hide a component. The values for the $Show parameter are Y for Show and N for Hide.

Activity: Drawing View Properties

Drawing View Properties – Show Hidden Edges.
540) Click the **Sheet1** tab.

541) Click **inside** DrawingView1.

542) Right-click **Properties**.

543) Click the **Show Hidden Edges** tab.

544) Click the **MGPRod** component from the Graphics window, as illustrated.

545) Click **Apply** from the Drawing View Properties box. The hidden edges of the MGPRod part inside the GUIDE-CYLINDER assembly are displayed.

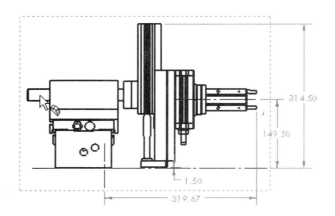

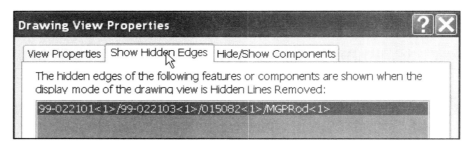

546) Click **OK** from the Drawing View Properties box.

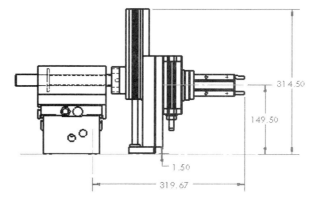

Hide two RBAshocks components.

547) Click **inside** DrawingView2, Position4.

548) Right-click **Properties**.

549) Click the **Hide/Show Components** tab.

550) Click the **RBAshocks<1>** component at the bottom of the ROTARY assembly as illustrated.

551) Click the **RBAshocks<2>** component from the FeatureManager.

552) Click **Apply**.

553) Click **OK**.

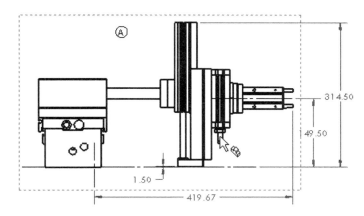

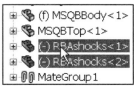

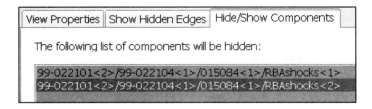

Note: If components are difficult to select, utilize the FeatureManager to select components for a specific drawing view.

Add Sheet3.
554) Click the **Sheet1** tab.

555) Right-click **Add Sheet**.

Select the Sheet Format.
556) Click **Browse**.

557) Double-click MY-TEMPLATES/**a-format.slddrt**.

558) Click **OK** from the Sheet Properties box. Sheet3 is added to the drawing.

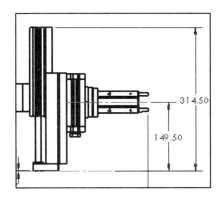

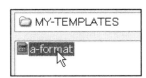

Copy DrawingView1 from Sheet1 to Sheet3.
559) Click the **DrawingView1** view boundary.

560) Press **Ctrl-C**.

Paste DrawingView1 from Sheet1.
561) Click a **position** on the left side of
Sheet3 inside the sheet boundary.

562) Press **Ctrl-V**. Drawing View4 is created.

Delete the dimensions.
563) Window-select the **dimensions** on
Sheet3.

564) Press the **Delete** key. Do not Window-
select the entire view or you will the
delete the view.

565) Click *Top for View Orientation.

566) Modify the scale to **1: 7**.

567) Drag the **view boundary** above the sheet
boundary.

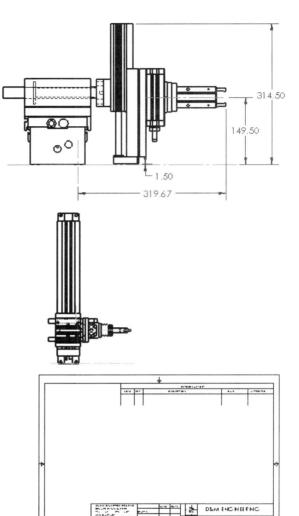

Insert a line.

568) The view boundary is selected. Click **Line** Line from the Sketch toolbar.

569) Sketch a **horizontal line** below the top view inside the view boundary.

570) Right-click **inside** the view boundary.

571) Click **Properties**.

572) Select **Position4** for use named configuration.

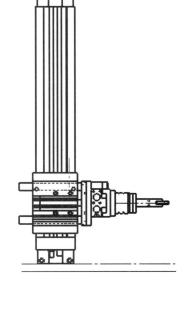

Add a Collinear relation.
573) Click **View**, **Temporary Axes** from the Main menu.

574) Click the **horizontal line**.

575) Hold the **Ctrl** key down.

576) Click the center **Temporary Axes**.

577) Release the **Ctrl** key.

578) Click **Collinear**.

579) Click **OK** from the Properties PropertyManager.

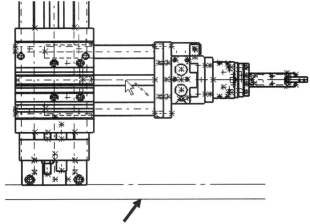

Hide the Temporary Axes.
580) Click **View**, uncheck **Temporary Axes**.

Insert the Section view.
581) Click the **horizontal** line.

Fit the drawing to the screen.
582) Press the **f** key.

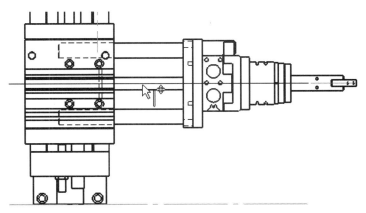

583) Click **Section View** View from the Drawing toolbar. Click **OK** to the message, Do you want this to be a partical section view. Flip direction if required.

584) Click **OK** from the Section Scope box.

585) Click a **position** below the Top view inside the sheet boundary.

586) Click **OK** from the Section View A-A PropertyManager.

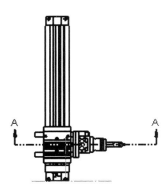

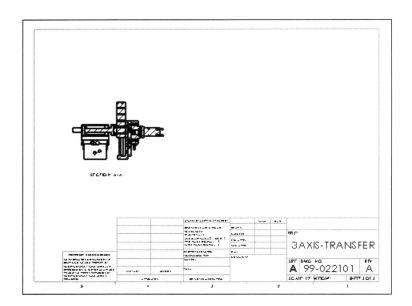

The Section Scope, Select Other option, toggles through components. The components displayed in the Section Scope box contain no section lines. Modify the Drawing View Properties, Section Scope to select the entire sub-assembly.

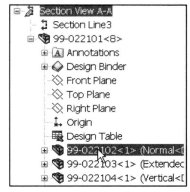

Modify the Section Properties.
587) Right-click **Properties** in the Section view boundary.

588) Click the **Section Scope** tab in the Drawing View Properties box.

589) Expand the **Section View A-A** in the FeatureManager.

590) Click **99-022102**, LINEAR-TRANSFER assembly.

591) Click **OK**.

Save the drawing.
592) Click **Save**.

The Auto hatching option causes the hatch lines to alternate between the mating components. The default hatch pattern is Steel.

Modify the hatch pattern in the assembly by assigning the Aluminum material in the part. Why return to the part when you can edit the hatch pattern in the drawing? Answer: You are required to create component drawings of the PLATE-A, PLATE-B, PLATE-C, and PLATE-D parts.

The component drawing and assembly drawing utilize the Material Property, Mass Property and hatch pattern in the Title block, Bill of Materials, and Drawing Views.

Engineering Change Orders and Revisions

An Engineering Change Order (ECO) documents changes that occur to a component. The Engineering department maintains each ECO with a unique document number, Example: 0845. The ECO describes the design change, the affected departments, implementation strategy and the required signoff signatures.

When Engineering issues an ECO that affects a drawing, the drawing revision, located in the Title block, is incremented. In a letter revision system, Revision A becomes Revision B. In a number revision system, Revision 1 becomes Revision 2. In a letter/number revision system A1 becomes A2.

In a manual system or automated 2D drafting application, the ECO process affected the drawing. In SolidWorks, the part, assembly and drawing share a common file structure. Your company requires copies of all modified documents on released products in manufacturing. You do not have a Product Data Management (PDM) system.

The 45-63421.sldprt, PLATE-A requires an etched number on the corner top face. The ECO documents the change to the PLATE-A part and PLATE-A drawing.

Use SolidWorks Explorer and the Revision Custom Property. Control the Revision Custom Property in the part.

The documentation control manager makes a decision not to "up-rev" the LINEAR-TRANSFER assembly. There are no 45-63421, PLATE-A parts in inventory. You do not have to address the assembly revision or parts in stock.

Note: The term up-rev means to increment the revision number or letter of a document. Companies up-rev under different conditions. Example: Company A chooses to up-rev a sub-assembly every time a change is made to a part contained within that assembly. Company B chooses not to up-rev the sub-assembly if the overall form, fit and function of the part does not change. Luckily, you work for Company B.

The automotive, aerospace, medical and many other industries are required by law to document all engineering changes. Keeping track of these changes is the responsibility of all engineers and designers.

Close all documents before utilizing SolidWorks Explorer. There are two activities to complete this task. The first activity utilizes SolidWorks Explorer to copy the original part and drawing. The second activity utilizes a new feature to modify the part and the drawing.

Activity: Engineering Change Orders and Revisions – SolidWorks Explorer

Close all documents.
593) Click **Windows**, **Close All** from the Main menu.

Locate the documents that contain the 45-63421.sldprt part.
594) Click **Tools**, **SolidWorks Explorer** from the Main menu.

595) Click **Browse**.

596) Double-click **45-63421.sldprt** from the DeliveryStation-Project5 folder.

597) Click **Where Used**.

598) Click the **Find Now** button. The 99-022101.sldasm and 45-53421.slddrw documents are displayed. The part and drawing require a revision. The assembly does not require a revision.

Used by (click to show long name)	Used as
45-63421.SLDDRW	model reference
99-022102.SLDASM	model reference

Copy the required documents. Append the current revision to the document name.
599) Right-click the part icon, **45-63421** in the SolidWorks Explorer window.

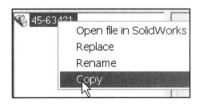

600) Click **Copy**. Check **Copy children** to display the Prefix/Suffix options.

601) Enter **–A** for Suffix.

602) Click **inside** the To: box.

603) Press the **End** key to display the filename, 45-63421-A.SLDPRT.

604) Check **Find where used**.

605) Click the **Find Now** button.

606) Uncheck the **99-022101.SLDASM** check box. The 99-022102.SLDASM, LINEAR-TRANSFER assembly is not updated.

607) Click the **New name** to display the short name, 45-63421-A.SLDDRW.

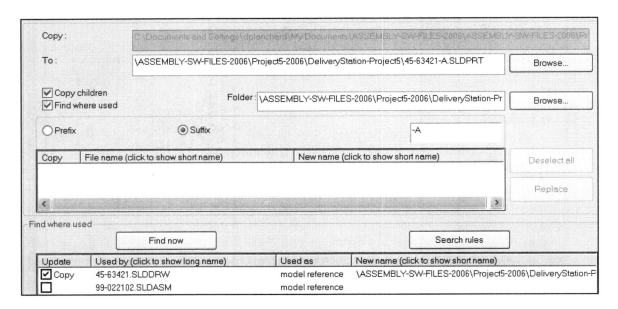

608) Click **Apply**.

SolidWorks Explorer copies the new part, 45-63421-A.sldprt and the new drawing, 45-63421-A.slddrw to the DeliveryStation-Project5 folder. The drawing, 45-63421-A.slddrw references the part, 45-63421-A.sldprt.

The original part, 45-63421.sldprt and original drawing, 45-63421.slddrw are modified to create Revision B.

Revision B is the current revision. The current revision contains no revision letter in the file name. As a result, the BOM requires no update since the part number does not change. The drawing, 45-63421.slddrw references the part, 45-63421.sldprt.

Add an Extruded Cut. Update the original part to Revision B. Update the drawing with a detailed view of the Extruded Cut. Add the ECO description to the Revision Table. Control the REV. letter in the Title block through the part Custom Properties.

When utilizing SolidWorks Explorer, utilize the Copy option to copy and save the original documents. Append the Revision letter or number to the copied file name. Make changes to the current parts, assemblies and drawings in your working folder. The copied original documents remains intact. Companies utilize an achive folder to maintain older revisions of documents.

Activity: Engineering Change Orders and Revisions – Part and Drawing

---

Open the 45-63421 part.
609) Click **45-63421.sldprt**.

610) Right-click **Open file in SolidWorks**.

611) Return to **SolidWorks**.

Add an Extruded Cut feature.
612) Click the **top face**.

613) Click **Sketch** Sketch .

614) Click **Centerline** Centerl... from the Sketch toolbar.

615) Sketch a **vertical centerline** in the lower left corner.

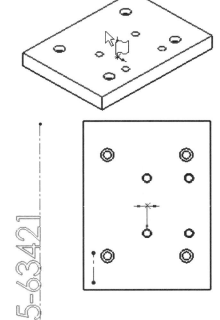

616) Click **Tools**, **Sketch Entities**, **Text** from the Main menu.

617) Enter **45-63421** in the text box. The text is sketched along the centerline.

Add Dimensions.

618) Click Smart Dimension Dimens... .

619) Click the **vertical edge**.

620) Click the **first point** of the sketched text.

621) Enter **10**. Click ✔ .

622) Click the **horizontal edge**.

623) Click the **first point** of the sketch text.

624) Enter **20**. Click ✔ .

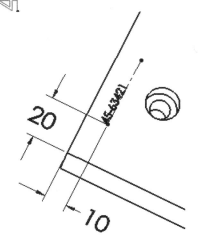

Insert an Extruded Cut

Extruded
625) Click **Extuded Cut** Cut from the Features toolbar.

626) Enter **0.5** for Depth.

627) Click **OK** from the PropertyManager.

Update the Revision Custom Property.
628) Click the **Default** configuration from the ConfigurationManager.

629) Right-click **Properties**.

630) Click **Custom properties**.

631) Click the **Custom** tab. The current REVISION Value is A.

632) Enter **B** for REVISION Value.

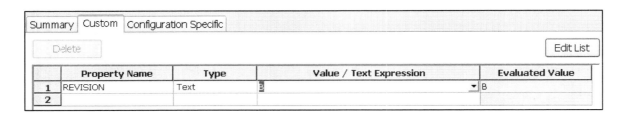

	Property Name	Type	Value / Text Expression	Evaluated Value
1	REVISION	Text	B	B
2				

633) Click **OK** from the Summary information box.

634) Click **OK** from the Configuration PropertyManager.

Save the 45-63421, PLATE-A part.
635) Click **Save**.

Insert a Detail view of the Extruded Cut.
636) As an exercise, create a Detail view of PLATE-A. Click **Detail** from the Drawing toolbar. Sketch a **circle** around the Extruded Cut text. Click a **position to the right** of the Right view to create the Detail view.

Save the 45-63421 drawing.
637) Click **Save**.

The Revision Table requires updating. The designer created the original drawing with SolidWorks 2003. SolidWorks introduced Revision Tables at SolidWorks 2004.

For every new release, SolidWorks documents additions and enhancements in the "What's New" .pdf file located in the Help menu.

You must decide what enhancements to incorporate into your engineering documentation practices.

Example: Option 1: You keep the old Revisions table and utilize Notes to enter text.

Example: Option 2: Delete the old Revisions table and utilize Insert, Table, Revision Table.

Companies have various methods for updating and documenting revisions in a drawing. Utilize the following Revision Procedure Task List to stimulate questions.

Revision Procedure Task List:
Obtain an understanding of how engineering, manufacturing, quality assurance, marketing, field service and the customer work with parts, assemblies, drawings and revisions in your company.
Develop an example assembly, not tied to a current product delivery schedule. Evaluate scenarios for: • A part revision. • An assembly revision. • A drawing revision. • A Bill of Material revision. • Addition/Deletion of a part. • Addition/Deletion of a sub-assembly. • Addition/Deletion of a configuration.
Create benchmark assemblies, parts and drawings to test new revisions of software.
Research PDM software applications.
Ask other users, either at a local meeting or online, about their revision procedures.

SolidWorks modifies the document structure with every major release. As a result, older versions of SolidWorks cannot open documents created in a newer version. When you open an assembly file in a newer release, SolidWorks updates the document structure in the assembly and the referenced components.

This process takes time. The Tools, Conversion Wizard option performs the task of converting older version files to new version files in bulk. Once you convert the assembly files and the related components, the documents cannot be opened at the older version.

Project Summary

In this project, you completed the 3AXIS-TRANSFER assembly with nine different configurations and a 3AXIS-TRANSFER drawing. The 3AXIS-TRANSFER drawing contained three sheets. Each Sheet displayed different configurations.

You added fasteners to the 3AXIS-TRANSFER assembly and created an Exploded View. Custom Properties controlled the values displayed in the Bill of Materials and in the drawing Title block.

The Bill of Materials contains multiple options to display Top level, Parts only or Indented. Determine the Bill of Material Type before you insert balloons or edit the BOM in the drawing. The more parameters and values you create in the part/assembly, the more time you will save in the BOM, Title block and other drawing views and annotations.

Revisions are an integral part of the engineering process. Engineering Change Orders track all revisions. Update all related documents when a change occurs. You explored a Revision Table and a Revision Custom Property in the part as two separate methods to control the REV letter in the drawing Title block.

In Project 5, you worked between multiple SolidWorks documents that simulated a concurrent engineering environment.

Review the exercises at the end of this project before moving on.

Questions:

1. Each component in an assembly has _____ degrees of freedom.

2. Identify a method to remove degrees of freedom in an assembly.

3. True or False. A Design Table is used to create multiple configurations in an assembly.

4. True or False. A Design Table is used to create multiple configurations in a part.

5. True or False. A Design Table is used to create multiple configurations in a drawing.

6. Describe the (f) symbol functionality in the FeatureManager.

7. Describe the procedure to create an Exploded View.

8. Describe the function of a Balloon annotation.

9. True or False. The PART NO. Property in the default Bill of Materials is determined by the file name.

10. The ITEM NO. order in the default Bill of Materials is determined by the component order in the Assembly FeatureManager. Explain the process to modify the order.

11. Describe the procedure to add additional Properties, such as DESCRIPTION, to the Bill of Materials.

12. Describe the procedure to add additional Properties, such as REV, to the Title Block of a drawing.

13. Describe the function of the $STATE variable in the Design Table.

14. A drawing can contain multiple configurations of a _____ and an _____.

15. Describe the consequence of an ECO on a SolidWorks drawing.

16. Identify the location of the Revision Table.

17. Identify the document that defines the part material.

Exercises

Exercise 5-1: PLATE-A design change

Modify the PLATE-A part from 21mm to 30mm. Modify the required SHCSs for the 99-022102, LINEAR-TRANSFER assembly.

Add the PART NUMBER and DESCRIPTION Custom Properties for the SHCSs contained in the 99-022102, LINEAR-TRANSFER assembly.

Update the 99-022101, 3AXIS-TRANSFER Bill of Materials to contain the new description for SHCSs.

Exercise 5-2: Section-Cut configuration

Create a new configuration named, Section-Cut for the 99-022104, ROTARY-GRIPPER assembly. Utilize the Assembly Cut feature. Sketch a rectangle on the Top Plane in the 99-022104, ROTARY-GRIPPER assembly. The endpoint of the rectangle is Coincident with the assembly Origin. The Assembly Cut feature is resolved for the Section-Cut configuration. The Assembly Cut feature is suppressed in all other configurations.

Insert the ROTARY-GRIPPER Section-Cut configuration and the 3AXIS-TRANSFER assembly on the same drawing sheet.

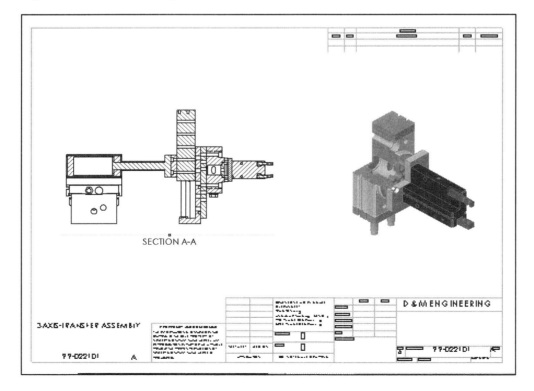

Exercise 5-3: Exploded Views and Bill of Materials

Create a drawing with a Bill of Materials and an Exploded View for the three sub-assemblies:

- 99-022102, LINEAR-TRANSFER assembly

- 99-022103, 2AXIS-TRANSFER assembly

- 99-022104, ROTARY-GRIPPER assembly

In the Bill of Materials, hide all sub-assemblies and parts contained below the top level of the SMC components.

Incorporate the sub-assembly Exploded Views into the 99-022101 [Fastener], 3AXIS-TRANSFER assembly in the project exercises.

Create the Exploded View steps in the order in which the physical component is disassembled.

Utilize Animate explode and Animate collapse options to document manufacturing procedures and assembly documentation.

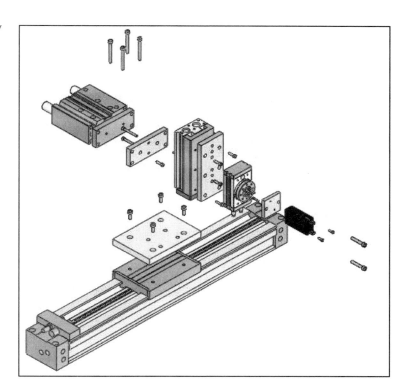

Exercise 5-4: PLATE-C design change.

Modify PLATE-C to 30mm thick. Redefine the 45-63423, PLATE-C part Linear Pattern of six Thru Holes to six Tapped Holes. Create a drawing of the 2AXIS-TRANSFER assembly. Modify the Bill of Materials to reflect the change.

Exercise 5-5: LINEAR-TRANSFER assembly and 2AXIS-TRANSFER assembly design change.

There is a design issue with mating components. You are required to utilize the four outside Mounting Holes of PLATE-B in the 99-022103, 2AXIS-TRANSFER assembly. Modify PLATE-A dimensions and/or the location of the SLIDE-TABLE assembly.

Modify the fasteners required for the PLATE-A part.

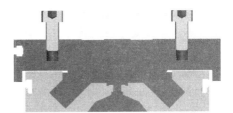

Note: There is more than one solution.

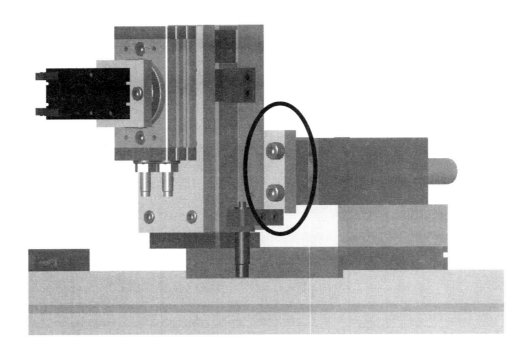

Exercise 5-6: Bill of Materials update.

Modify the Bill of Materials to display the
MASS column and values for PLATE-A
through PLATE-D. Utilize Aluminum for
the Material.

Exercise 5-7: Create a new drawing for the
3AXIS-TRANSFER assembly. The first
view explores the opening of GRIPPER
assembly in the Horizontal position.

The second view defines the endpoint of the
GRIPPER Finger part with respect to the
mounting holes of the RODLESS-
CYLINDER assembly.

Utilize these dimensions in Project 6.

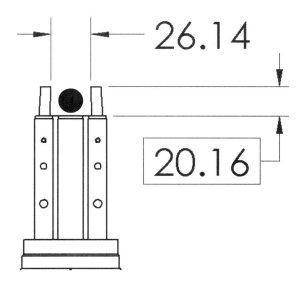

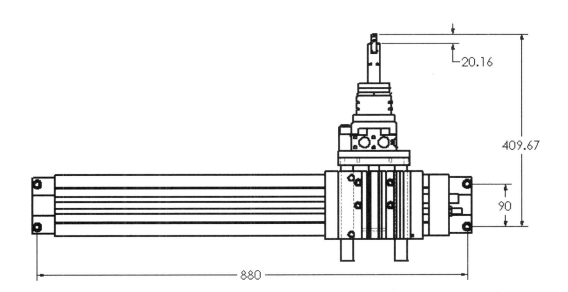

Notes:

Project 6

Top Down Design Assembly Modeling Techniques

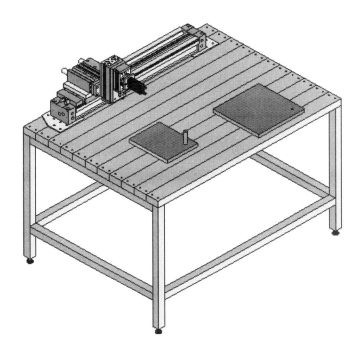

Below are the desired outcomes and usage competencies based on the completion of this Project 6.

Project Desired Outcomes:	Usage Competencies:
• DELIVERY-STATION assembly.	• Ability to create and modify a new Top Down assembly developed with a Layout sketch.
• OUTPUT-BASE-PLATE part. • INPUT-BASE-PLATE part.	• Knowledge to create and modify components developed In-Context of an assembly.
• INPUT assembly. • FRAME assembly.	• Ability to incorporate non-SolidWorks models into an assembly.

Notes:

Project 6 – Top Down Design Assembly Modeling Techniques

Project Objective

Create the DELIVERY-STATION assembly utilizing the Top Down design assembly modeling approach.

Create the OUTPUT-BASE-PLATE and the INPUT-BASE-PLATE parts with In-Context features.

Create the INPUT assembly.

Create the FRAME assembly utilizing imported 2D and 3D AutoCAD data.

On the completion of this project, you will be able to:

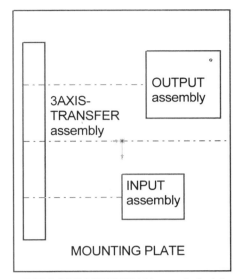

DELIVERY-STATION Layout sketch

- Apply a Layout sketch at the top-level assembly and sub-assembly.

- Define Link Values and Equations to control relationships in the Layout sketch.

- Utilize Convert Entities and build relationships from the Layout sketch to components developed in the context of the assembly.

- Recognize Edit Component while working in a multi-level environment between assembly, sub-assembly and part.

- Reorder components and dissolve sub-assemblies using the FeatureManager.

- Import AutoCAD 2D and 3D geometry to develop SolidWorks parts.

- Reuse component geometry with Component Pattern and Mirror Components.

- Insert and utilize an assembly reference envelope.

SolidWorks Tools and Commands

In Project 6, utilize the following SolidWorks tools and commands.

SolidWorks Tools and Commands:		
.dwg	Equations	Large Assembly Mode
Add/Edit Equation	Envelope	Mirror Components
Add relations	Features: Linear Pattern, HoleWizard	Reorder
Assembly Features	Form new sub-assembly here	Rename
Assembly Statistics	Import 2D sketch/3D curves	Reorganize components
Component Pattern	Insert Component	Save As, Save as copy
Dimension properties, name	Join/Split	Shortcut keys
Dissolve sub-assembly, pattern	Layout sketch	Sketch tools
Edit component, part, sub-assembly	Link Values	Simulation

Product Specification

You are on the final design phase of the DELIVERY-STATION assembly project. Your manager temporarily assigned your colleagues to a different project. You are required to keep the DELIVERY-STATION assembly project on track and to update the product specification. Review the preliminary product specification and utilize a Top Down design assembly modeling approach.

Major design requirements in the Top Down design assembly modeling approach translate into assemblies, sub-assemblies and components. You do not need all of the required component design details. Individual relationships are required. There are two methods to start a Top Down design assembly modeling approach:

- Method 1: Start with a Layout sketch in the assembly.

- Method 2: Start with a component in the assembly, (Recall Project 4).

Use Method 1 in this project.

Method 1 utilizes a Layout sketch in the top-level assembly. The DELIVERY-STATION assembly is the top-level assembly. Translate major design requirements into individual components and key relationships.

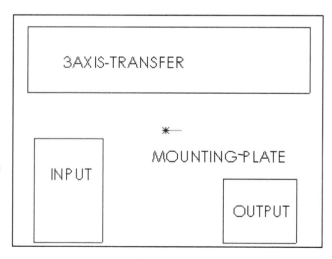

Delivery Station Layout Sketch

Consider the following questions in a preliminary design product specification:

- What are the major components in the design of the DELIVERY-STATION assembly?

    - 3AXIS-TRANSFER assembly.

    - INPUT assembly.

    - OUTPUT assembly.

    - MOUNTING-PLATE part.

- What are the key design constraints of the DELIVERY-STATION assembly?

    - INPUT assembly, BASE PLATE part: 250mm x 200mm x 20mm.

    - OUTPUT assembly, BASE PLATE part: 300mm x 200mm x 20mm.

    - Location of the GRIPPER fingers for the INPUT assembly.

    - Location of the GRIPPER fingers for the OUTPUT assembly.

    - Displacement between the INPUT pick point and the OUTPUT place point: 500mm in the x direction, 100mm in the y direction and 100mm in the z direction.

    - How does each part relate to the other parts? From past experience and discussions with the engineering department:

    - A 40mm minimum physical gap is required between the OUTPUT assembly and the outside edge of the MOUNTING PLATE part.

    - A 100mm x 400mm minimum area is required on both sides of the 3AXIS-TRANSFER assembly.

    - The 100mm x 400mm area is utilized to fasten switches and valves for the SMC components.

    - How will the customer use the product?

    - The customer does not disclose the specific usage of the DELIVERY-STATION assembly. The customer is in a very competitive market.

    - What is the most cost-effective material for the product?

    - Aluminum is the most cost-effective material. Aluminum is also strong, relatively easy to fabricate, corrosion resistant and is non-magnetic.

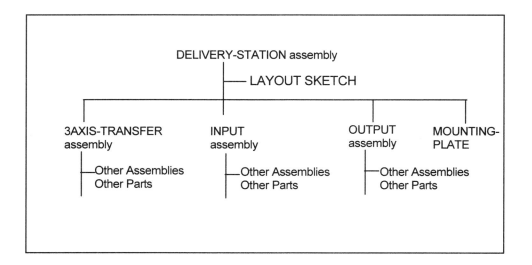

Incorporate the design specifications into the DELIVERY-STATION assembly. Use a Layout sketch. The Layout sketch represents components with sketched geometry, reference geometry and dimensions. Verify geometry relationships in the Layout sketch.

How do you know when an assembly requires a Layout sketch? How large is a large assembly that requires a Layout sketch? Answer: Although there is no direct answer, ask questions in the beginning of a design to determine if an assembly is a candidate for a Layout sketch. The follow table lists questions to ask at the beginning of the design process.

Assembly candidate for a Layout sketch:
Does the assembly contain new components that require modeling?
Does the assembly require design constraints between components to be determined?
Are major sub-assemblies modular?
Will sub-assemblies be developed in a team environment?
Does the top-level assembly require a majority of new models?
Are you working in a large assembly environment with hundreds of components?

Utilizing Top down design with a Layout sketch assists the engineer in planning and organization. Modeling takes less time when manipulating sketches, empty parts and empty assemblies compared to assemblies that contain hundreds of components with hundreds of features.

In reality, designers utilize a combination of Top down and Bottom up techniques.

DELIVERY-STATION
Assembly Overview

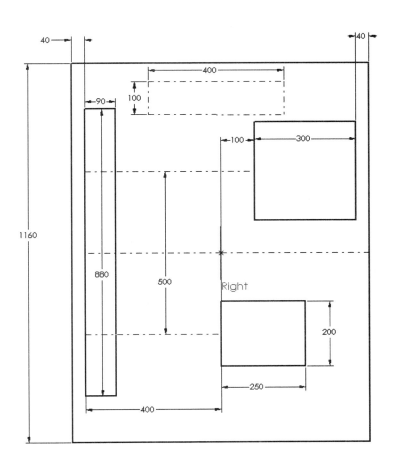

Create the Layout sketch in the DELIVERY-STATION assembly. Each sketched rectangle represents a different component in the top-level assembly.

Utilize relations and dimensions to constrain the Layout sketch. Insert Equations and Link Values to control geometry and relationships between components.

Insert a new part, OUTPUT-BASE-PLATE. Convert edges from the Layout sketch to develop the first sketch for the OUTPUT-BASE-PLATE part. The Extruded Base feature utilizes the first sketch.

Insert the INPUT-BASE-PLATE part as an empty part with three default reference planes.

Insert the INPUT-BASE-PLATE part into the DELIVERY-STATION assembly.

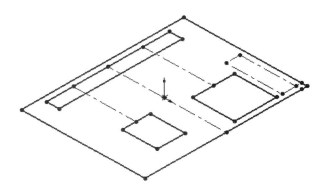

Develop the sketch for the INPUT-BASE-PLATE part. Convert the edges from the Layout sketch.

Review design options for the
MOUNTING-PLATE part.
Incorporate the MOUNTING-
PLATE part into the FRAME
assembly. The FRAME assembly
contains an imported 2D
AutoCAD part and an imported
3D AutoCAD solid assembly.

Utilize the Layout sketch to locate
the DELIVERY-STATION
components on the FRAME
assembly.

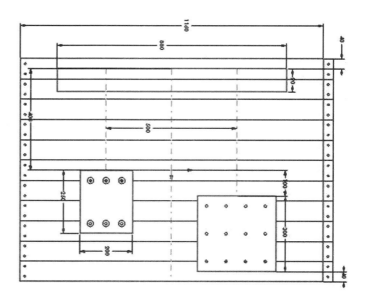

Layout Sketch

Utilize the Layout sketch to identify component space allocations and relations. A
Layout sketch is a sketch created at the Top level of the assembly. The Layout sketch
begins as a sketch in the assembly. Assemblies and parts reference the DELIVERY-
STATION Layout sketch. The first component in the Layout sketch is the 3AXIS-
TRANSFER assembly.

Find the hole locations to fasten the 3AXIS-TRANSFER assembly to the MOUNTING
PLATE part.

Represent the 3AXIS-TRANSFER hole locations with a 880mm x 90mm rectangle. The
endpoints of the rectangle are the center points of the mounting holes for the 3AXIS-
TRANSFER assembly.

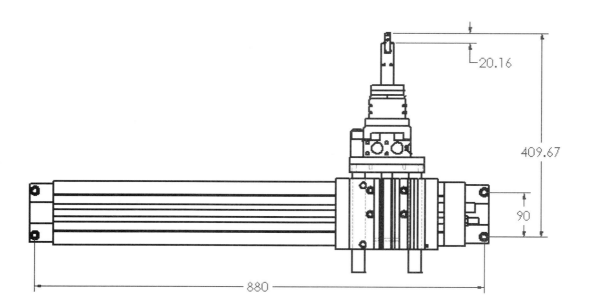

The Layout sketch provides two key
dimensions: 409.67mm & 20.16mm.

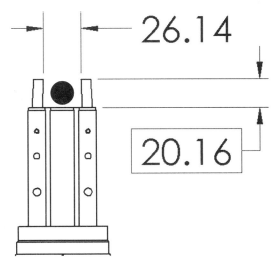

The 409.67mm dimension is the distance
between the back RODLESS-CYLINDER
assembly mounting holes and the GRIPPER
assembly.

The GRIPPER assembly contains two finger
parts. The GRIPPER fingers pick the object
from the INPUT assembly approximately at the
midpoint of each finger. The 20.16mm
dimension is the length of the GRIPPER finger.

The midpoint location of the Gripper finger is
20.16/2 = 10.08mm.

The INPUT assembly pick up point is (409.67mm – 10.08mm) = 399.59mm, (use
400mm) from the 3AXIS-TRANSFER assembly back mounting holes.

Note: The Top Down design – Layout sketch option also utilizes another technique that
begins with a part. Create a part that contains the Layout sketch. Insert the part as the
first component into the assembly. New components reference the Layout sketch
developed with a part.

Activity: Layout Sketch

Set the File Locations for the Document Templates, if required.
1)   Click **Tools**, **Options**, **System Options**.

2)   Click **File Locations**. Select **Document Templates**
     from the drop down list. Click **Add**.

3)   Select **ASSEMBLY-SW-FILES-2006\MY-TEMPLATES**.

4)   Click **OK**.

Copy the Project 6 folder.
5)   Copy the **Project6-2006** folder from the CD in the book
     to the ASSEMBLY-SW-FILES-2006 folder.

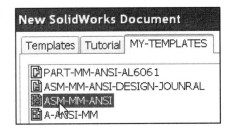

Create the DELIVERY-STATION assembly.
6)   Click **File**, **New** from the Main menu.

7)   Double-click **ASM-MM-ANSI**.

8) Click **Cancel**  from the Insert Component PropertyManager. Assem1 is displayed in the Graphics window.

Save the Assembly.
9) Click **Save**.

10) Select the **ASSEMBLY-SW-FILES-2006\Project6** file folder.

11) Enter **DELIVERY-STATION** for the assembly name.

12) Click **Save**. The DELIVERY-STATION FeatureManager is displayed.

Select the Sketch plane.
13) Click **Top Plane** from the FeatureManager.

14) Click **Sketch** Sketch .

Display a Top view.
15) Click **Top** view.

Sketch a horizontal centerline.
16) Click **Centerline** Centerl... from the Sketch toolbar.

17) Click the **Origin** for the first point.

18) Click a **position** to the left of the Origin for the second point as illustrated.

Dimension the centerline.

19) Click **Smart Dimension** Smart Dimens... from the Sketch toolbar.

20) Click the **horizontal centerline**.

21) Enter **400**.

22) Click ✔ .

Fit the model to the Graphics window.
23) Press the **f** key.

Create the first component sketch. The first component sketch vertices represent the 3AXIS-TRANSFER mounting holes.

Sketch the 3AXIS-TRANSFER mounting hole locations.

24) Click **Rectangle** Rectan... .

25) Click a **position** below the left point of the horizontal centerline for the first point.

26) Click a **position** above the centerline, to the right for the second point.

Add a Midpoint relation.
27) Right-click **Select**.

28) Click the **left point** of the horizontal centerline.

29) Hold the **Ctrl** key down. Click the left **vertical line** of the rectangle. Release the **Ctrl** key.

30) Click **Midpoint**. Click **OK** from the Properties PropertyManager.

Dimension the rectangle.

31) Click **Smart Dimension** Dimens... .

32) Enter **880** for the vertical dimension.

33) Enter **90** for the horizontal dimension. The black rectangle is fully defined.

The 3AXIS-TRANSFER assembly linearly translates 500mm. Create the second and third centerlines. The second and third centerlines are symmetrical about the first horizontal centerline. Sketch the centerlines 500mm apart.

The OUTPUT-BASE-PLATE part sketch is symmetrical about the second centerline. The INPUT-BASE-PLATE part sketch is symmetrically about the third centerline.

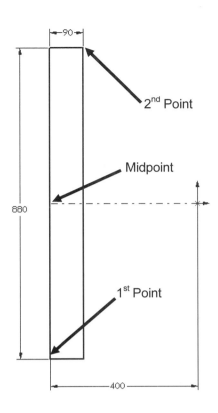

Add the second centerline.

34) Click **Centerline** Centerl....

35) Click the **first point** coincident with the left vertical line of the rectangle.

36) Click a **position** to the right of the Origin as illustrated.

Activate the Mirror Sketch tool.

37) Click **Mirror Entities** Mirror from the Sketch toolbar. The second centerline is listed in the Entities to mirror box.

38) Click a **position** inside the Mirror about box.

39) Click the **400mm horizontal** centerline.

40) Click **OK** from the Mirror PropertyManager to display the third centerline.

Dimension the centerline.

41) Click **Smart Dimension** Smart Dimens... .

42) Click the **second centerline**.

43) Click the **third centerline**.

44) Enter **500**.

45) Click **OK** from the Mirror PropertyManager.

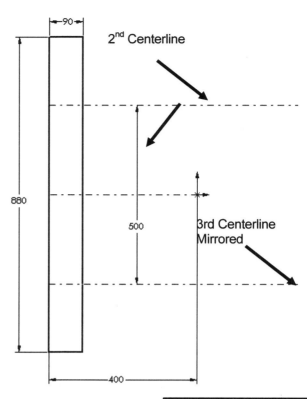

Create the second outline in the DELIVERY-STATION Layout sketch. The second component sketch represents the OUTPUT-BASE-PLATE part. The OUTPUT-BASE-PLATE part is 300mm x 300mm. The OUTPUT assembly place point is 100mm from the INPUT pick point.

The INPUT pick point is collinear with the DELIVERY-STATION Right Plane.

Sketch the profile of the OUTPUT-BASE-PLATE part.

46) Click **Rectangle** Rectan... from the Sketch toolbar. Sketch a **rectangle** to the right of the second centerline.

Add an Equal relation.
47) Right-click **Select**. Click the **vertical line** of the rectangle.

48) Hold the **Ctrl** key down. Click the **horizontal line** of the rectangle.

49) Release the **Ctrl** key. Click **Equal**.

50) Click **OK** from the Properties PropertyManager.

Add a Midpoint relation.
51) Click the **left vertical line** of the rectangle. Hold the **Ctrl** key down.

52) Click the **right endpoint** of the second centerline. Release the **Ctrl** key.

53) Click **Midpoint**.

54) Click **OK** from the Properties PropertyManager.

Dimension the rectangle.

55) Click **Smart Dimension** Smart Dimens... .

56) Enter **300** for the horizontal rectangular dimension.

57) Enter **100** for a horizontal dimension from the Origin to the left vertical line. The OUTPUT-BASE-PLATE black rectangle is fully defined.

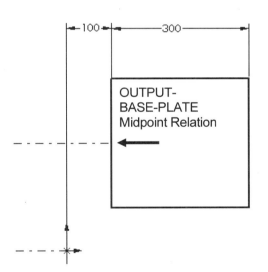

The third component in the DELIVERY-STATION Layout sketch is the INPUT-BASE-PLATE part. The INPUT-BASE-PLATE part is 250mm x 200mm.

The INPUT pick point is collinear with the
DELIVERY-STATION Right Plane. The
OUTPUT place point is 100mm from the INPUT
pick point.

Display the Right Plane of the DELIVERY-STATION
assembly.
58) Right-click **Right Plane** from the
FeatureManager.

59) Click **Show**.

Sketch the profile for the INPUT-BASE-PLATE part.
60) Click **Rectangle** Rectan.... The first point is
coincident with the Right plane, below the Origin.
The second point is to the right, below the third
centerline. Note: If required, add a Collinear
relation between the Right Plane and the left
vertical line of the rectangle.

61) Right-click **Select**.

Trim the centerline.
62) Click **Trim Entities** Trim .

63) Trim the third **centerline** to the right of the left
vertical profile line as illustrated.

64) Click **OK** from the Trim PropertyManager.

The Trim Entities sketch tool removes the right
segment of the centerline. The blue sketch is
under-defined.

Add a Midpoint relation.
65) Click the **left vertical line** of the rectangle. Hold
the **Ctrl key** down.

66) Click the **right end point** of the third centerline.

67) Release the **Ctrl key**.

68) Click **Midpoint**.

69) Click **OK** from the Properties
PropertyManager.

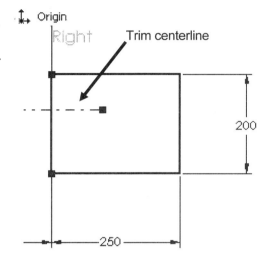

Trim centerline

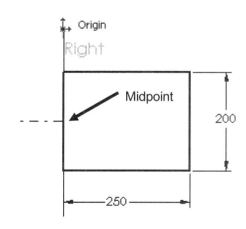

Midpoint

Dimension the rectangle.

70) Click **Smart Dimension** 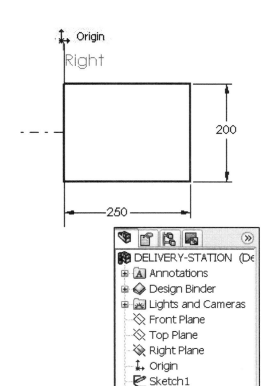 Smart Dimens....

71) Enter **250** for the horizontal dimension.

72) Enter **200** for the vertical dimension.

73) Click **OK** ✅ from the Dimension PropertyManager.

💡 Utilize centerlines for a Symmetric relation and their endpoints for a Midpoint relation. Build geometric relations into the profile and then insert dimensions.

The fourth rectangle in the Layout sketch defines the overall dimensions of the MOUNTING-PLATE part.

The MOUNTING-PLATE part defines the floor perimeter of the DELIVERY-STATION assembly. The INPUT, OUTPUT and 3AXIS-TRANSFER assemblies fasten to the MOUNTING-PLATE part.

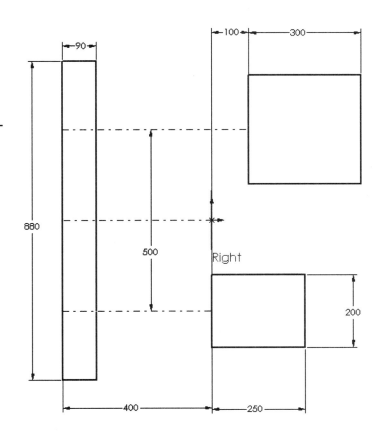

Sketch the profile for the MOUNTING-
PLATE part.

74) Click **Rectangle** Rectan… .

75) Click the **first point** to the left of the
narrow rectangle.

76) Click the **second point** to the right of
the top square.

77) Click **Centerline** Centerl… from the
Sketch toolbar.

78) Sketch a **horizontal centerline** from
the Origin to the right vertical line of
the rectangle.

Add a Midpoint relation.
79) Right-click **Select**.

80) Click the right **center point**.

81) Hold the **Ctrl** key down.

82) Click the **right vertical line** of the
large rectangle as illustrated.
Release the **Ctrl** key.

83) Click **Midpoint**.

84) Click **OK** from the Properties
PropertyManager.

Add dimensions.

85) Click **Smart Dimension** Dimens… .

86) Click the **right vertical line** of the large rectangle.

87) Click the **right vertical line** of the 300mm square.

88) Enter **40**. Click the **left vertical line** of the large rectangle.

89) Click the **left vertical line** of the narrow rectangle.

90) Enter **40**.

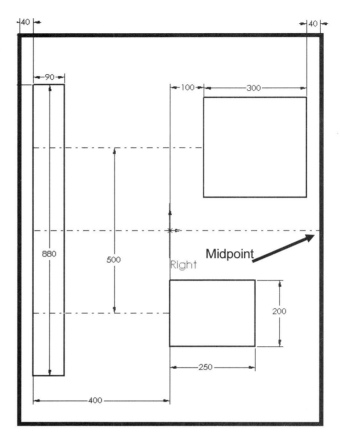

91) Click the **left vertical line** of the large rectangle.

92) Enter **1160**. Note: (880 + 2x(40+100)) = 1160.

93) Click **OK** 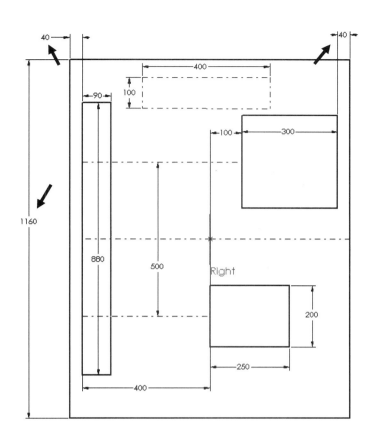 from the PropertyManager. The black sketch if fully defined.

A 40mm gap is required. The 100mm dimension is based on the additional space required for the CONTROLLER assembly.

Sketch a profile for the CONTROLLER sub-assembly.

94) Click **Rectangle** Rectan... from the Sketch toolbar.

95) Sketch a **rectangle** above the OUTPUT rectangle as illustrated.

96) Right-click **Select**.

97) Window-select the **rectangle**.

98) Check the **For construction** box.

99) Click **OK** 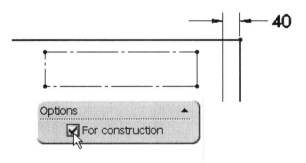 from the Properties PropertyManager.

Insert Centerlines.

100) Click **Centerline** Centerl... from the Sketch toolbar.

101) Sketch a **horizontal centerline** from the upper right corner to the right most vertical line.

102) Sketch a **vertical centerline** from the upper right corner to the top most horizontal line.

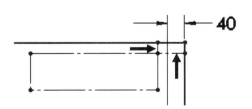

Add an Equal relation.
103) Click the **horizontal centerline**.

104) Hold the **Ctrl** key down.

105) Click the **vertical centerline**.
Release the **Ctrl** key.

106) Click **Equal**. Click **OK** .

Add an Collinear relation.
107) Click the **vertical centerline**.

108) Hold the **Ctrl** key down. Click the **300mm OUTPUT vertical line**. Release the **Ctrl** key.

109) Click **Collinear**. Click **OK** .

Insert dimensions.

110) Click **Smart Dimension** Smart Dimens...

111) Click the **horizontal** line.

112) Enter **400**.

113) Click the **vertical** line.

114) Enter **100**.

115) Click **OK**  from the Dimension PropertyManager.

Save and Exit the Layout sketch.

116) Click **Exit Sketch** Exit Sketch .

Save the DELIVERY-STATION assembly.
117) Click **Save**.

Construction lines are sketched lines not utilized by SolidWorks features. The 400mm x 100mm construction line sketch indicates that there is sufficient room for the CONTROLLER assembly.

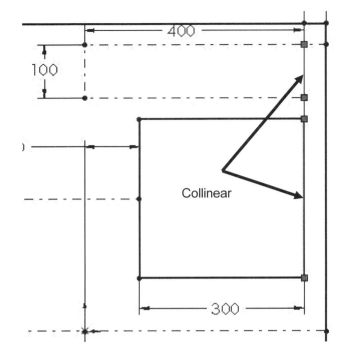

Collinear

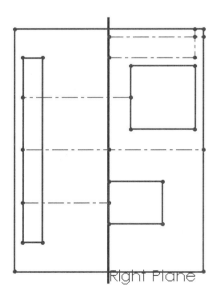

The MOUNTING-PLATE part width, 880mm is determined by the component requirements; (400mm + 100mm + 300mm + 2x(40mm)) = 880mm.

The dimensions of the MOUNTING-PLATE part, 880mm x 1160mm represent the minimum material required. Increase the height dimension of the MOUNTING-PLATE part from 1160mm to 1200mm.

The Layout sketch is complete. The Layout sketch provides information on how each component interacts with the other. Utilize the Layout sketch to extract information and to build new parts in the DELIVERY-STATION assembly.

Insure that the DELIVERY-STATION maintains the required minimum 40mm spatial gap between the internal components and the MOUNTING-PLATE part outside edges. How do you design for future revisions?

Answer: Through Link Values and Equations.

Link Values and Equations

Define equal relations between dimensions with Link Values. A Link Value requires a shared parameter name.

Mathematical expressions that define relationships between parameters and/or dimensions are called Equations. Equations use shared names to control dimensions. Use Equations to connect values from sketches, features, patterns and various parts in an assembly. Use Link Values within the same part. Use Equations in different parts and assemblies.

Activity: Link Values and Equations

Display the Dimensions.
118) Right-click **Annotations** from the FeatureManager.

119) Click **Show Feature Dimensions**.

Create Link Values.
120) Right-click on the top right horizontal dimension **40**.

121) Click **Link Values**.

122) Enter **gap** for Name in the Shared Values box.

123) Click **OK** from the Shared Values box.

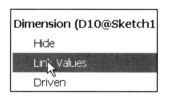

124) Right click on the left horizontal dimension **40**.

125) Click **Link Values**.

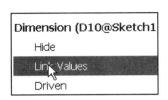

126) Click the **drop down arrow** from the Name text box.

127) Select **gap**. Click **OK**.

Verify the Link Values.
128) Double-click the left **40** dimension.

129) Enter **50**.

130) Click **Rebuild** in the Modify dialog box. The two Link Values change. Return to the original value.

131) Enter **40**. Click ✔ . All Link Values are equal to 40.

Each dimension has a unique parameter name. Utilize the parameter names as Equation variables. The default parameter names display the sketch, feature or part. Rename parameters for clarity when creating numerous equations.

Edit the dimension name in the Layout sketch.
132) Rename **Sketch1** to **Layout**.

Edit the dimension name for hole spacing.
133) Right-click the vertical dimension, **880**.

134) Click **Properties**.

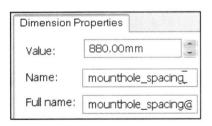

135) Enter **mounthole_spacing** in the Name text box.

136) Click **OK**. The Full name box displays mounthole_spacing@Layout.

Edit the dimension Name for the height.
137) Right-click the vertical dimension, **1160**.

138) Click **Properties**.

139) Enter **mountplate_height** in the Name text box.

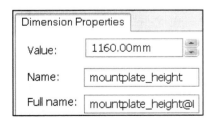

140) Click **OK**. The Full name box displays mountplate_height@Layout.

141) Click **OK**  from the Dimension PropertyManager.

Display the dimension Name.
142) Position the **mouse pointer** over
the 1160 dimension and the 880
dimension to display the full name.

Add an Equation for the Layout sketch.
143) Click **Equations** from the
FeatureManager.

144) Right-click **Add Equation**.

Create the first half of Equation1.
145) Click the mountplate_height
dimension, **1160**. The variable
"mountplate_height@Layout" is
added to the equation text box.

Create the second half of Equation1.

146) Enter **Equals** $\boxed{=}$ from the
keypad. Click
mounthole_spacing dimension,
880. The variable
"mounthole_spacing@Layout" is
added to the equation text box.

147) Enter $\boxed{+}$ $\boxed{2}$ $\boxed{*}$ $\boxed{(}$ from
the keypad.

148) Click gap, **40**. The variable
"gap@Layout" is added to the
equation text box.

149) Enter $\boxed{+}$ $\boxed{1}$ $\boxed{0}$ $\boxed{0}$ $\boxed{)}$
from the keypad.

Display Equation1.
150) Click **OK** from the Add Equation
box. The Equations –
DELIVERY-STATION dialog box
contains the complete equation.

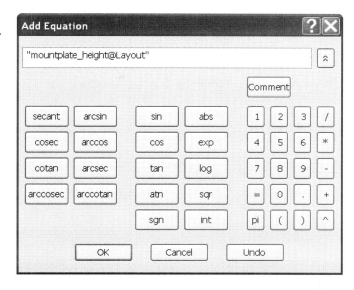

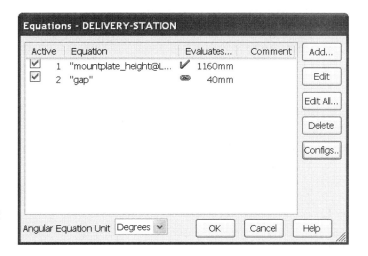

Note: A large green check mark ✔ indicates that the Equation is solved. The chain link symbol indicates a Link Value ∞ .

Return to the DELIVERY-STATION assembly.
151) Click **OK** from the Equations box.

Modify Equation1.
152) Double-click the **880** mounthole_spacing dimension.

153) Enter **980**.

154) Click **Rebuild**. Double click the gap dimension, **40**.

155) Enter **50**. Click **Rebuild**.

Return to the original dimensions.
156) Enter **40** for Gap. Click **Rebuild**. Enter **880** for the mounthole_spacing.

157) Click **Rebuild**. Click **OK** .

The Equation maintains the design intent of the DELIVERY-STATION assembly.

💡 Dimensions driven by an Equation are preceded with the red Equation symbol n. Link Values are preceded with the red Link ∞ symbol.

Display the Isometric view and hide all dimensions.
158) Click the **Isometric** view.

Hide all dimensions.
159) Right-click **Annotations** from the FeatureManager. Uncheck **Show Feature Dimensions**. Right-click **Right Plane** from the FeatureManager. Click **Hide**.

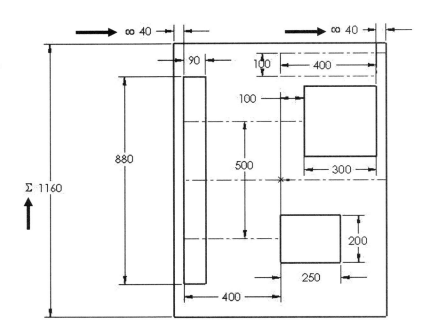

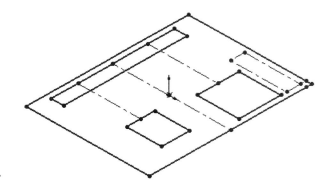

Save the DELIVERY-STATION assembly.
160) Click **Save**. The Layout sketch is complete.

🔆 Find the file references. Save both the assembly and the referenced components when you exit SolidWorks. When components reference the Layout sketch, open the assembly before opening individual components in a new session of SolidWorks.

Create the OUTPUT-BASE-PLATE part

Create the OUTPUT-BASE-PLATE part In-Context of the DELIVERY-STATION assembly. Utilize the Insert, Component, New Part option. Create the OUTPUT-BASE-PLATE Extruded Base feature utilizing existing geometry from the Layout sketch.

Components added In-Context of the assembly automatically receive an InPlace Mate within Mates entry in the FeatureManager. The system automatically selects Edit
Component ᴱᵈⁱᵗ Compo.... The OUTPUT-BASE-PLATE text appears in the FeatureManager.

The blue OUTPUT-BASE-PLATE entry indicates the active part. The current Sketch plane is the Top Plane. The current sketch name is Sketch1. SolidWorks automatically selects Sketch Sketch .

Activity: Create the OUTPUT-BASE-PLATE part

Display the Layout sketch in an Isometric view.
161) Click **Isometric** view.

Insert the OUTPUT-BASE-PLATE component.
162) Click **Insert, Component, New Part** from the Main menu. Double-click **PART-MM-ANSI-AL6061**.

Save the part.
163) Click **Save**. Select the **ASSEMBLY-SW-FILES-2006\Project6-2006** file folder.

164) Enter the **OUTPUT-BASE-PLATE** for part name. Click

• **Save**. The Component Pointer 👆◇ is displayed on the mouse pointer. The OUTPUT-BASE-PLATE component requires a sketch plane.

165) Click **Top Plane** from the DELIVERY-STATION FeatureManager.

SolidWorks inserts an InPlace Mate between the Top Plane of the OUTPUT-BASE-PLATE component and the Top Plane of the DELIVERY-STATION assembly. Sketch1 is the active sketch.

Convert existing outside edges from the Layout sketch.

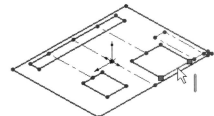

166) Click the **right vertical line** of the 300mm square.

167) Click **Convert Entities** Convert. The Resolve Ambiguity box is displayed.

168) Click **closed contour**. Click **OK**. The outside perimeter of the Layout sketch is the current Sketch.

Insert the Extruded Base for the OUTPUT-BASE-PLATE part.

169) Click **Extruded Boss/Base** Boss/B... from the Features toolbar. Enter **20** for Depth. The direction arrow points upward.

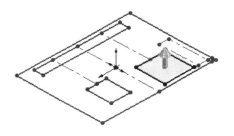

170) Click **OK** from the Extrude PropertyManager.

The OUTPUT-BASE-PLATE entry in the FeatureManager is displayed in blue. You are editing the part In-Context of the DELIVERY-STATION assembly.

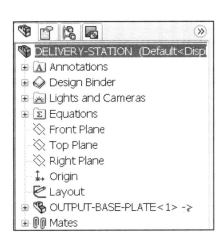

Display the Extruded-Base feature.

171) Expand **OUTPUT-BASE-PLATE** from the FeatureManager. Extrude1 is the first feature.

Return to the DELIVERY-STATION assembly.

172) Click **Edit Component** Compo... from the Assembly toolbar. The OUTPUT-BASE-PLATE entry is displayed in black.

Save the DELIVERY-STATION assembly.
173) Click **Save**.

The OUTPUT-BASE-PLATE part requires additional features that do not reference the Layout sketch or other components in the DELIVERY-STATION assembly. Open the OUTPUT-BASE-PLATE part.

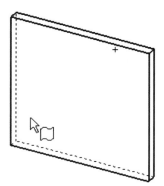

☼ Work in the part to save rebuild time and avoid unwanted External references. The part produces:

- Faster rebuild times.

- A simplified FeatureManager.

- No External references outside the part geometry.

Create the M10 Thru Hole for the OUTPUT-BASE-PLATE part.
174) Right-click **OUTPUT-BASE-PLATE** from the FeatureManager.

175) Click **Open Part**.

Fit the model to the Graphics window.
176) Press the **f** key.

177) Click the **front face**.

178) Click **Hole Wizard** Wizard from the Features toolbar.

179) Click the **Hole** tab.

180) Click **Ansi Metric** for Standard.

181) Click **Drill sizes** for Type.

182) Click **10.0** for Size.

183) Select **Through All** for End Condition.

184) Click the **Positions** tab.

185) Right-Click **Select**.

Display a Front view.
186) Click **Front** view.

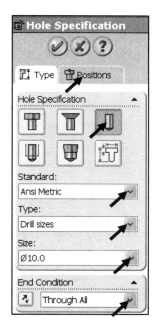

Add dimensions.

187) Click **Smart Dimension** Dimens….

188) Click the center of the **hole**. Click the **horizontal** line.
Enter **40**. Click ✔ .

189) Click the center of the **hole**. Click the **vertical line.**
Enter **40**. Click ✔ .

190) Click **OK** ✅ from the Dimension PropertyManager.

191) Click **OK** ✅ from the Hole Position PropertyManager.

192) Click **Isometric** view.

Return to the DELIVERY-STATION assembly.
193) Press **Ctrl-Tab**. The M10 hole is
displayed in the upper right corner of
the DELIVERY-STATION assembly.

🔆 Verify the position of additional
component features in the assembly.
The InPlace Mate in the assembly
determines the Origin of the part.

Save the DELIVERY-STATION assembly.
194) Click **Save**.

Explore additional OUTPUT-BASE-
PLATE features in exercises at the end
of this project.

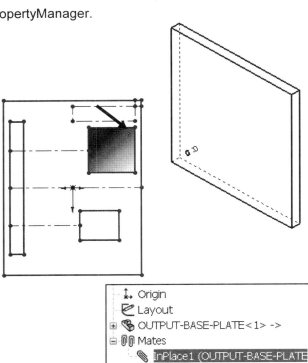

INPUT-BASE-PLATE part

Create the INPUT-BASE-PLATE as an empty part. Assemble the three INPUT-BASE-
PLATE reference planes, Top, Front and Right to the three reference planes of the
DELIVERY-STATION assembly. The Layout sketch, 250mm x 200mm rectangle
defines the first sketch of the INPUT-BASE-PLATE part.

Activity: INPUT-BASE-PLATE part

Create the INPUT-BASE-PLATE part.
195) Click **File**, **New** from the Main menu.

196) Double-click **PART-MM-ANSI-AL6061**.

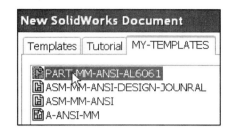

Save the part.
197) Click **Save**.

198) Select the **ASSEMBLY-SW-FILES-2006\Project6-2006** file folder.

199) Enter **INPUT-BASE-PLATE** for part name.

200) Click **Save**.

Display the Planes.
201) Click **Front Plane** from the FeatureManager.

202) Hold the **Ctrl** key down. Click **Top Plane** & **Right Plane**.

203) Release the **Ctrl key**.

204) Right-click **Show**.

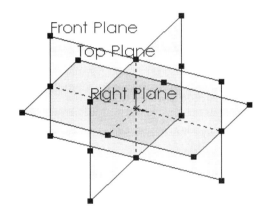

Assemble the INPUT-BASE-PLATE part to the DELIVERY-STATION assembly.
205) Click **Tile**, **Horizontally** from the Main menu.

206) Click and drag the **INPUT-BASE-PLATE** icon into the DELIVERY-STATION Graphics window.

207) Click a **position** on the front left side of the Layout sketch.

208) Maximize **DELIVERY-STATION.**

209) Click **View**, **Planes** from the Main menu.

Fit the model to the Graphics window.
210) Press the **f** key.

Insert a Coincident mate.
211) Click the **front centerline** that passes through the Midpoint of the DELIVERY-STATION assembly.

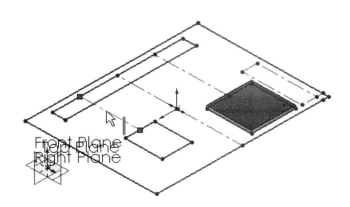

212) Click **Mate** .

213) Click **Front Plane** of the INPUT-BASE-PLATE from the FeatureManager. Coincident is selected by default.

214) Click ✔.

Insert a Coincident mate.
215) Click **Top Plane** of the INPUT-BASE-PLATE from the FeatureManager.

216) Click **Top Plane** of the DELIVERY-STATION from the FeatureManager. Coincident is selected by default.

217) Click ✔.

Insert a Coincident mate.
218) Click the **Right Plane** from the INPUT-BASE-PLATE part.

219) Click the **Right Plane** of the DELIVERY-STATION assembly. Coincident is selected by default.

220) Click ✔. Click **OK** from the Mate PropertyManager.

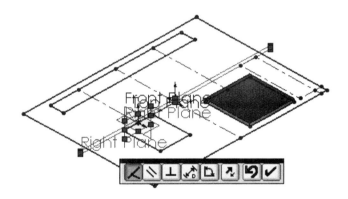

Edit the INPUT-BASE-PLATE.
221) Right-click **INPUT-BASE-PLATE** from the FeatureManager.

222) Click **Edit Part**. The INPUT-BASE-PLATE text is displayed in blue.

Insert a Sketch.
223) Click the INPUT-BASE-PLATE **Top Plane** from the FeatureManager.

224) Click **Sketch** Sketch.

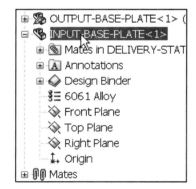

Convert existing outside edges from the Layout sketch.

225) Click a **line segment** from the 200mm x 250mm rectangle as illustrated.

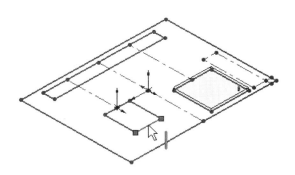

226) Click **Convert Entities**  . The Resolve Ambiguity box is displayed.

227) Click **closed contour**.

228) Click **OK**. The current Sketch is the outside perimeter of the small left box from the Layout.

Extrude the sketch.

229) Click **Extruded Boss/Base**  from the Features toolbar. Enter **20** for Depth. The Extrude direction is upward.

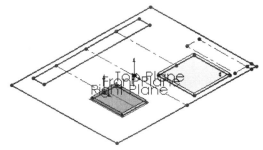

230) Click **OK** from the Extrude PropertyManager.

231) Click **View**, uncheck **Planes** from the Main menu.

Return to the DELIVERY-STATION assembly.

232) Click **Edit Component**  . The INPUT-BASE-PLATE text is displayed in black.

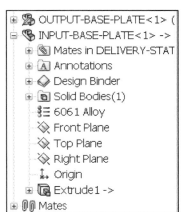

Save the DELIVERY-STATION assembly.

233) Click **Save**. Click **Yes** to rebuild the assembly and save the referenced models.

Create the M10 Thru Hole for the INPUT-BASE-PLATE part.

234) Right-click **INPUT-BASE-PLATE** from the FeatureManager.

235) Click **Open Part**.

Display an Isometric view.

236) Click **Isometric** view.

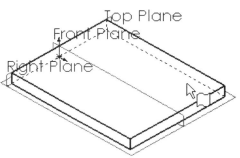

237) Click the **top face** in the top right corner as illustrated.

238) Click **Hole Wizard** 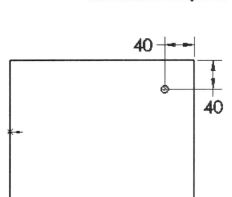 .

239) Click the **Hole** tab.

240) Click **Ansi Metric** for Standard.

241) Click **Drill sizes** for Type.

242) Click **10.0** for Size.

243) Select **Through All** for End Condition.

244) Click the **Positions** tab.

245) Right-Click **Select**.

Display a Top view.
246) Click **Top** view.

Add dimensions.

247) Click **Smart Dimension** .

248) Click the center of the **hole**. Click the **horizontal** line. Enter **40**. Click ✔ .

249) Click the center of the **hole**. Click the **vertical** line. Enter **40**. Click ✔ . Click **OK** ✅ from the Dimension PropertyManager. Click **OK** ✅ from the Hole Position PropertyManager.

250) Click **Isometric** view.

Return to the DELIVERY-STATION assembly.
251) Press **Ctrl-Tab**. The M10 hole is displayed in the upper right corner.

Save the DELIVERY-STATION assembly.
252) Click **Save**.

253) Click **View**. Uncheck **Planes** from the Main menu.

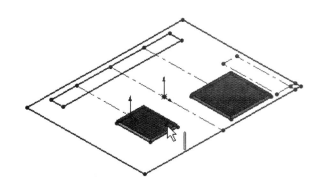

Input assembly, Reordering components, and Dissolve Sub-assembly

The INPUT assembly contains the INPUT-BASE-PLATE part. The DELIVERY-STATION assembly contains the INPUT assembly.

Create the INPUT assembly In-Context of the DELIVERY-STATION assembly. Reorder the INPUT-BASE-PLATE part. Move the INPUT-BASE-PLATE part into the INPUT assembly. The INPUT-BASE-PLATE part moves down one level in the DELIVERY-STATION assembly.

Reordering assemblies and parts removes InPlace Mates. Reordering creates both over defined and under defined Mates.

Determine component location in the assembly early in the design process to avoid problems. Create empty parts and sub-assemblies to determine and organize the assembly layout structure.

Avoid future Mate issues. Test the Mates for all related components and assembly features that you reorder.

Reordering components in an assembly can be confusing. Evaluate the reordering procedure for the INPUT assembly.

Add the INPUT assembly to the DELIVERY-STATION assembly.

The OUTPUT-BASE-PLATE part, INPUT-BASE-PLATE part and the INPUT assembly reside in the first level of the DELIVERY-STATION assembly.

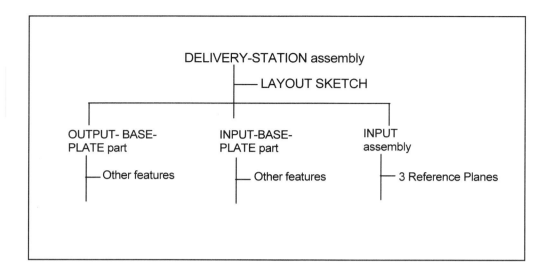

Reorder the INPUT-BASE-PLATE part from the DELIVERY-STATION assembly to the INPUT assembly. The INPUT-BASE-PLATE part is at the second level.

Drag the component to a new location to reorder the component in the FeatureManager. Utilize Tools, Reorganize Components when reordering multiple components in one operation.

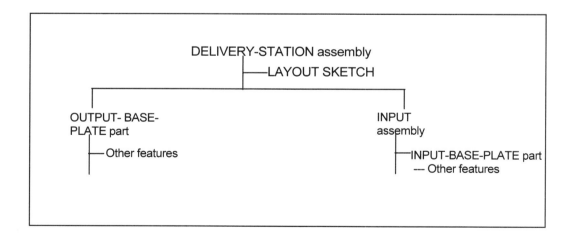

The Dissolve Sub-assembly command moves components up one level in an assembly structure through the FeatureManager. Utilize a Local Pattern to create a copy of the INPUT assembly.

Dissolve the Local Pattern to create the INPUT <2> assembly. Utilize the Dissolve Sub-assembly command.

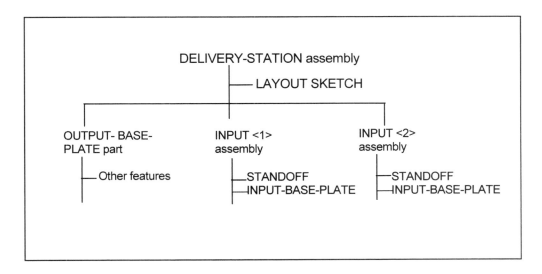

The INPUT<2> components move up one level in the assembly hierarchy. SolidWorks deletes the INPUT<2> assembly.

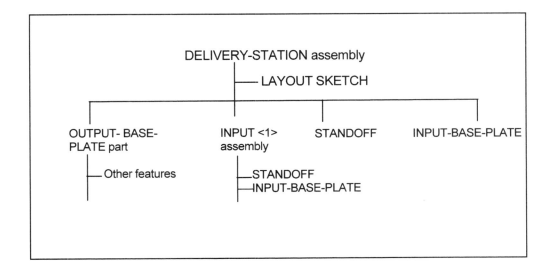

Create the INPUT assembly in the context of the DELIVERY-STATION assembly. Reorder the INPUT-BASE-PLATE part into the INPUT assembly. Create the new part, STANDOFF in the INPUT assembly.

Activity: Input assembly, Reordering components, and Dissolve Sub-assembly

Insert a new assembly, INPUT.
254) Click **Insert**, **Component**, **New Assembly** from the Main menu.

255) Double-click **ASM-MM-ANSI**.

256) Select the **ASSEMBLY-SW-FILES-2006\Project6-2006** file folder.

257) Enter **INPUT** for assembly name.

258) Click **Save**. The DELIVERY-STATION FeatureManager displays the INPUT assembly. The INPUT assembly is under-defined.

Reorder the INPUT-BASE-PLATE part.
259) Click the **INPUT-BASE-PLATE** icon.

260) Drag the **INPUT-BASE-PLATE** icon to the INPUT assembly icon. The mouse pointer displays the Reorder icon.

261) Expand the **INPUT** assembly.

The Reorder command modifies the three Coincident mates reference components from the INPUT-BASE-PLATE part to the INPUT assembly. The INPUT assembly is fully defined. The INPUT-BASE-PLATE part is under defined.

Open the INPUT assembly.
262) Right-click **INPUT** from the FeatureManager.

263) Click **Open Assembly**. You are working in the INPUT assembly.

264) Click **View**, **Planes** from the Main menu.

Display an Isometric view.
265) Click **Isometric** view.

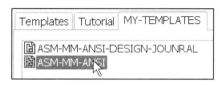

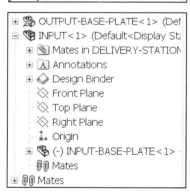

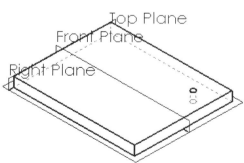

Fix the INPUT-BASE-PLATE.

266) Right-click **INPUT-BASE-PLATE** from the
FeatureManager.

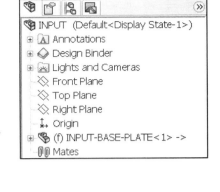

267) Click **Fix** to locate the INPUT-BASE-PLATE part with
respect to the INPUT assembly Origin.

Insert a new component In-Context of the INPUT assembly.

268) Click **Insert**, **Component**, **New Part** from the Main menu.

269) Double-click **PART-MM-ANSI-AL6061**.

270) Select the **ASSEMBLY-SW-FILES-2006\Project6-2006**
file folder.

271) Enter **STANDOFF** for the part name.

272) Click **Save**.

Insert the Sketch.

273) Click the **top face** of the INPUT-BASE-PLATE.

274) Click the **M10 circular edge**.

275) Click **Convert Entities** Convert .

276) Click **Circle** Circle from the Sketch
toolbar.

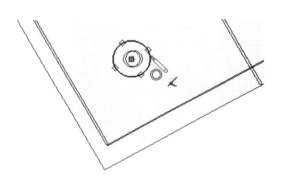

277) Sketch a **circle** centered on the M10
hole. Right-click **Select.**

Add a dimension.

278) Click **Smart Dimension** Dimens..., from
the Sketch toolbar.

279) Click the **circle**.

280) Enter **20**.

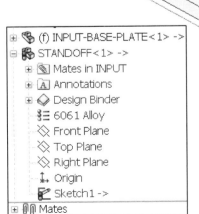

281) Click **OK** . The
two-circle sketch is
fully defined.

Extrude the Sketch.

282) Click **Extruded Boss/Base** 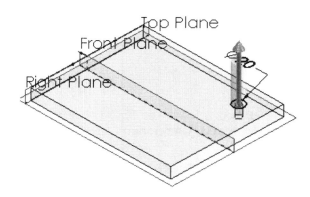 Boss/B... .

283) Enter **70** for Depth. The Arrow point upward

284) Click **OK** ✅ from the Extrude PropertyManager.

Return to the INPUT assembly.

285) Click **Edit Component** Compo... .

Save the STANDOFF part.
286) Click **Save**.

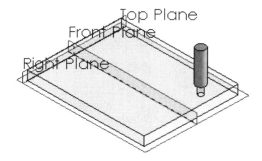

Return to the DELIVERY-STATION assembly.
287) Press **Ctrl-Tab**.

288) Expand the **INPUT** assembly from the DELIVERY-STATION FeatureManager. The INPUT-BASE-PLATE part and STANDOFF part are contained in the INPUT assembly.

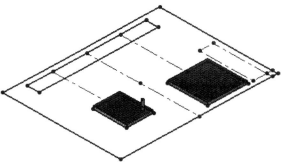

Save the DELIVERY-STATION assembly.
289) Click **Save**.

Note: In the following steps, utilize the Fix option to constrain components in the assembly. Usually the Fix option is not a good mating practice. The Fix option expedites the Mates in this activity in order to focus on the Dissolve Sub-assembly option, Insert New Sub-assembly and the Dissolve Pattern options.

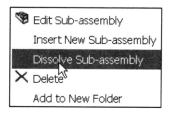

Insert a Linear Pattern for the INPUT sub-assembly.
290) Click **INPUT** from the FeatureManager.

291) Click **Insert**, **Component Pattern**, **Linear Pattern** from the Main menu. The Linear Pattern PropertyManager is displayed.

292) Click the Layout Sketch **right line** for Direction1. The Direction arrow points towards the left as illustrated.

293) Enter **225** for Spacing.

294) Enter **2** for Number of Instances.

295) Click **OK** 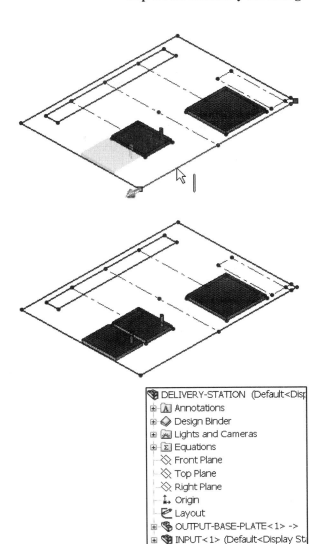 from the Linear Pattern PropertyManager.

Dissolve the Local Linear Pattern.
296) Click **LocalLPattern1** from the FeatureManager.

297) Right-click **Dissolve Pattern**. INPUT<2> is displayed in the DELIVERY-STATION FeatureManager. The DELIVERY-STATION assembly contains two instances of the INPUT component. INPUT<2> contains the INPUT-BASE-PLATE<1> part and the STANDOFF<1> part.

Dissolve the INPUT<2> assembly.
298) Click **INPUT<2>** from the FeatureManager.

299) Right-click **Dissolve Sub-assembly**.

Review the Assembly Structure Editing dialog box.
300) Click **Move**.

Dissolving the INPUT assembly and moving the INPUT-BASE-PLATE and STANDOFF parts to the DELIVERY-STATION assembly results in a warning message.

SolidWorks deletes the InPlace1 Mate and the STANDOFF\Sketch1 external reference.

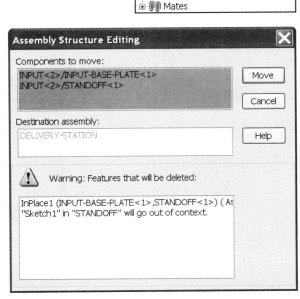

☀ When you dissolve an assembly, keep track of the Warning message component entries. The InPlace1 Mate lists the under defined components. Example: INPUT-BASE-PLATE and STANDOFF. These components require Mates in the DELIVERY-STATION assembly level. The features and sketches listed out of context require new references. Example: STANDOFF\Sketch1 requires a Sketch plane and an inside diameter dimension.

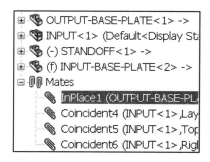

Review the FeatureManager. The STANDOFF part is under defined and free to move. Define the STANDOFF part with the Fix option. The INPUT-BASE-PLATE<2> is fixed.

☀ Define components in the assembly before utilizing the Edit Component tool. Editing an under defined component in the context of an assembly produces unpredictable results.

Fix the STANDOFF.
301) Click **STANDOFF** from the FeatureManager. Right-click **Fix**.

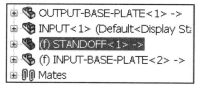

Create a new assembly in the FeatureManager.
302) Click **STANDOFF<1>**. Hold the **Ctrl** key down.

303) Click **INPUT-BASE-PLATE<2>**.

304) Release the **Ctrl** key.

305) Right-click **Form New Sub-assembly Here**.

306) Double-click **ASM-MM-ANSI**.

307) Enter **INPUT-R2** for assembly name.

308) Click **Save**.

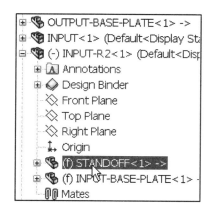

Edit the sub-assembly In-Context of the DELIVERY-STATION assembly.
309) Click **INPUT-R2** from the FeatureManager.

310) Right-click **Edit Sub-assembly**. The INPUT-R2 entry is displayed in blue.

Insert a Linear Pattern.
311) Click **STANDOFF** from the FeatureManager.

312) Click **Insert**, **Component Pattern**, **Linear Pattern** from the Main menu.

313) Click the INPUT-BASE-PLATE **front edge** for Direction 1. The Direction arrow points towards the left.

314) Enter **50** for Distance.

315) Enter **4** for Number of Instances.

316) Click **OK** from the Linear Pattern PropertyManager.

Return to the DELIVERY-STATION assembly.

317) Click **Edit Component** .

Delete the INPUT-R2 assembly.
318) Click **INPUT-R2** from the FeatureManager.

319) Right-click **Delete**.

320) Click **Yes** to confirm.

Add additional features to the INPUT assembly, OUTPUT assembly and the OUTPUT-BASE-PLATE part in the exercises at the end of this project.

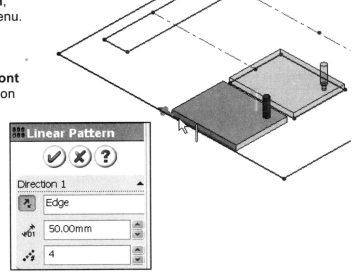

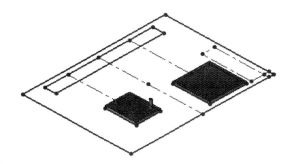

Assembly Modeling Techniques with AutoCAD 2D and 3D Components

Create the MOUNTING-PLATE part. Fasten the 3AXIS-TRANSFER, INPUT, and OUTPUT assemblies to the MOUNTING-PLATE part. What type of MOUNTING-PLATE part and supporting frame will you design? You explore two options.

Option 1: Construct a MOUNTING-PLATE part from 5mm aluminum plate supported by a welded tubular steel frame. After a discussion with your teammates, you decide that this is not a good option. A custom steel frame lead-time is too long to meet the delivery schedule and the large MOUNTING-PLATE part is difficult to assemble and ship.

Option 2: Assemble a modular T-slotted aluminum framing system. The vendor, 80/20, Inc. (8020.net) manufactures this type of support framing system. Large vendors sell through smaller distributors. Example: Air, Inc. (airinc.net), sells, supports and maintains 80/20's products. Work with an Air, Inc. Application engineer who suggests incorporating the MOUNTING-PLATE part directly into the FRAME assembly. The FRAME assembly eliminates the need for the MOUNTING-PLATE part. The DELIVERY-STATION components fasten directly to the aluminum FRAME assembly members. This saves time and reduces overall cost of the project.

The Application engineer suggests a design change to increase the FRAME assembly width from 1160mm to 1200mm. This will allow the FRAME assembly to contain an even number of standard members. Note: The width increase is within the customer's specification. The distance from the floor to the top of the FRAME assembly is 790mm. The Application engineer recommends leveling feet to adjust for any factory floor discrepancies.

The Application engineer provides a drawing, Bill of Materials, quotation and an electronic copy of the part file. The AutoCAD Solids file, Q52423.dwg is contained in the ASSEMBLY-SW-FILES-2006\Project6-2006 file folder.

Your Purchasing department orders the individual frame members, JOINING-PLATEs and hardware required based on the Bill of Materials. Your Field Service engineer assembles the items at the customer site. This action saves delivery cost and time.

Vendors utilize a variety of CAD systems. Open AutoCAD files directly into SolidWorks as a part or drawing. Open the AutoCAD file, Q52423.dwg as an imported SolidWorks part.

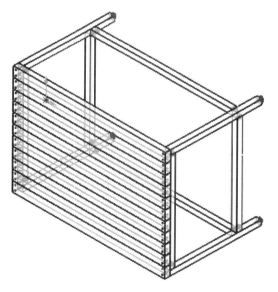

The SolidWorks Q52423 part produces 21 imported surfaces and 28 imported curves from the AutoCAD file. The part is not oriented on the correct plane. Modify the Q52423 part orientation in the new FRAME assembly.

The FRAME assembly contains the aluminum framing components. The FRAME assembly supports the 3AXIS-TRANSFER, INPUT, and OUTPUT assemblies.

Activity: Assembly Modeling Techniques with AutoCAD 2D and 3D Components

Create a new reference plane, Floor Plane.

321) Click the DELIVERY-STATION assembly **Top Plane** from the FeatureManager.

322) Right-click **Show**. Hold the **Ctrl** key down.

323) Click and drag the **Top Plane** downward from the Graphics window. The Plane PropertyManager is displayed.

324) Release the **Ctrl** key.

325) Enter **790** for Distance.

326) Click OK 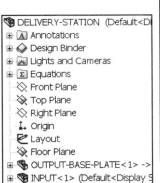 from the Plane PropertyManager.

327) Rename **Plane1** to **Floor Plane**.

Create a new FRAME assembly from within the DELIVERY-STATION assembly.

328) Right-click **DELIVERY-STATION** from the FeatureManager.

329) Click **Insert, New Sub-assembly**.

330) Double-click **ASM-MM-ANSI**.

331) Enter **FRAME** for File name.

332) Click **Save**.

333) Expand **FRAME** assembly from the FeatureManager.

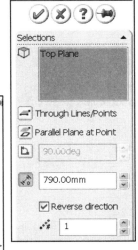

SolidWorks inserts the FRAME assembly into the DELIVERY-STATION FeatureManager. The FRAME assembly is under defined. Create three Coincident Mates to fully defined the FRAME assembly.

Assemble the FRAME assembly to the DELIVERY-STATION assembly. Insert a Coincident mate.

334) Click **Front Plane** from the FRAME FeatureManager.

335) Click **Mate** Mate .

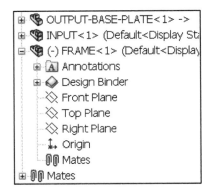

336) Click **Front Plane** from the DELIVERY-
STATION Feature Manager. Coincident is
selected by default.

337) Click ✔ .

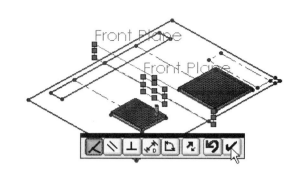

Insert a Coincident mate.
338) Click the **Top Plane** from the FRAME
FeatureManager.

339) Click **Top Plane** from the DELIVERY-
STATION FeatureManager. Coincident
is selected by default.

340) Click ✔ .

Insert a Coincident mate.
341) Click **Right Plane** from the FRAME
FeatureManager.

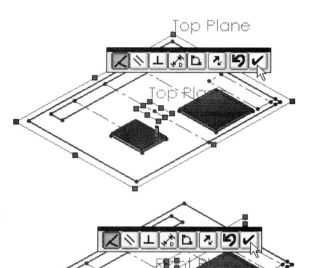

342) Click **Right Plane** from the DELIVERY-
STATION FeatureManager. Coincident is
selected by default.

343) Click ✔ .

344) Click **OK** ✅ from the Mate
PropertyManager.

345) Expand **Mates** from the FeatureManager.
Three Coincident Mates are added to the
DELIVERY-STATION FeatureManager.
The FRAME assembly is fully defined.

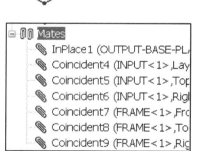

The FRAME assembly requires geometric information
from the Layout sketch. Create a new sketch, named
MountingPlate-Sketch, in the context of the DELIVERY-
STATION assembly. Utilize the MountingPlate-Sketch to
develop the components for the FRAME assembly.

Insert the MountingPlate-Sketch.
346) Right-click **FRAME** from the FeatureManager. Click **Edit
Sub-assembly**. The FRAME entry in the FeatureManager
is displayed in blue.

347) Click the FRAME **Top Plane** from the FeatureManager.

348) Click **Sketch** Sketch from the Sketch toolbar.

349) Click the **outside line segment** of the Layout sketch.

350) Click **Convert Entities** Convert .

351) Click **close contour**. Click **OK**.

352) Click the narrow rectangular sketch **line segment**.

353) Click **Convert Entities** Convert .

354) Click **close contour**. Click **OK**.

355) Click **Exit Sketch** Exit Sketch .

356) Rename **Sketch1** to **MountingPlate-Sketch**.

357) Click **Edit Component** Edit Compo... from the Assembly toolbar to return to the DELIVERY-STATION assembly.

Open the FRAME assembly.
358) Right-click **FRAME** from the DELIVERY-STATION FeatureManager.

359) Click **Open Assembly**.

Display an Isometric view.
360) Click **Isometric** view.

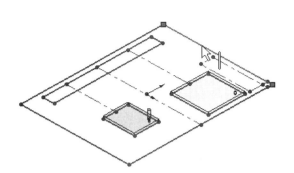

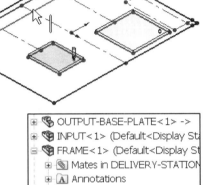

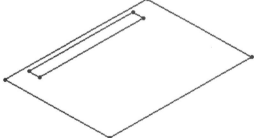

The AutoCAD Solid file consists of twenty-one different parts. SolidWorks converts each part into imported surfaces and requires a temporary Part Template. Set the Default Part Template to avoid being prompted.

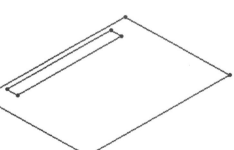

The AutoCAD Solid file contains four leveling feet parts. The leveling feet parts were created as an AutoCAD sweep. SolidWorks imports the leveling feet parts as curves. Utilize the imported curves to create a new SolidWorks part, LEVELING-FOOT. Create the LEVELING-FOOT part in the project exercises.

Set the default template using the Tools, Options, System Options, Default Template option before opening other file types such as .dwg (AutoCAD) or STEP.

Set the Default Part Template.
361) Click **Tools**, **Options** from the Main menu.

362) Click **Default Templates**.

363) Click **Browse** for Parts.

364) Select **ASSEMBLY-SW-FILES-2006/MY-TEMPLATES/PART-MM-ANSIAL6061**.

365) Click **Always use these default document templates option**.

366) Click **OK**.

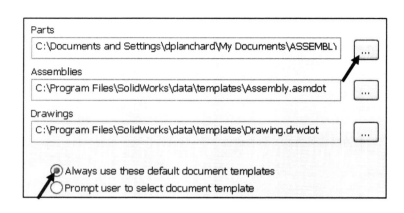

Open the AutoCAD file.
367) Click **File**, **Open** from the Main menu.

368) Select the **ASSEMBLY-SW-FILES-2006\PROJECT6-2006** folder.

369) Select **DWG Files (*.dwg)** from the Files of type box.

370) Double-click **Q52423**.

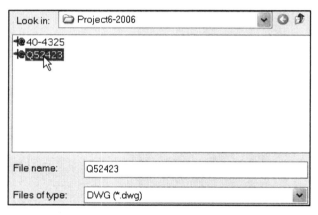

371) Click **Import to a new part** from the DXF/DWG Import box.

372) Click **Next>**.

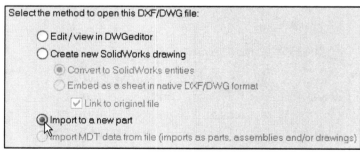

373) Click **White background**.

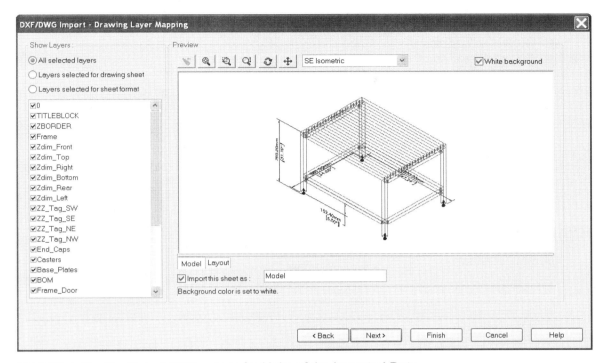

374) Click **Next>**. Select **Millimeters** for Units of the Imported Data.

375) Click **as 3D curves/model**. Click the **Model** tab.

376) Click **Finish**.

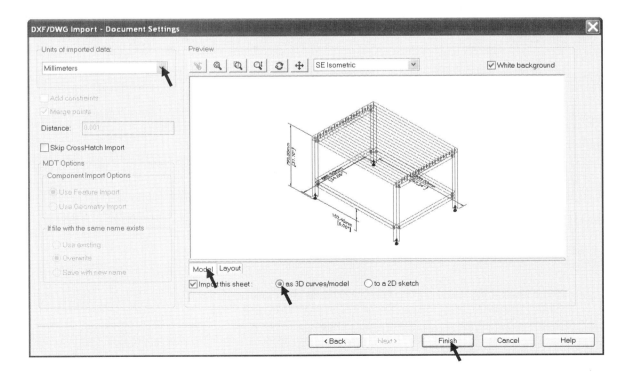

Wait approximately 30 seconds. SolidWorks converts each AutoCAD part into an imported surface. Twenty-one new parts open and close in the Graphics window. The new part, PartX.sldprt, displays the imported surfaces and curves.

Display the PartX.
377) Click **Isometric** view.

378) **Zoom in** on the leveling-foot curves to view the imported curves.

379) Press the **f** key to fit the model to the Graphics window.

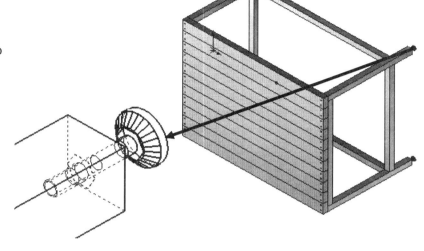

Save the imported part.
380) Click **Save**.

381) Enter **80-20-Q52423** for part name.

382) Click **Save**.

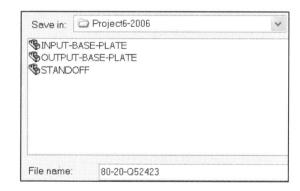

Insert the imported 80-20-Q52423 part into the FRAME assembly.
383) Press **Ctrl-Tab** to display the FRAME assembly.

Insert

384) Click **Insert Component** Compo... from the Assembly toolbar.

385) Click **80-20-Q52423**.

386) Click a **position** to the right of the MountingPlate-Sketch.

Display the profile of the LEVELING-FOOT.
387) Click **View**, **Curves** from the Main menu.

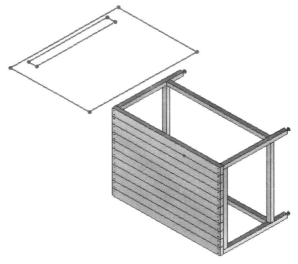

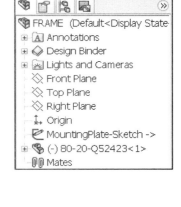

💡 Display sketches and curves from imported geometry. By default, sketches and curves are not displayed in the assembly. Utilize View, Sketch to display sketches. Utilize View, Curves to display curves. Create Shortcut keys for these two options.

Move and Rotate the 80-20-Q52423 part.
388) Click **80-20-Q52423** from the FeatureManager. Note: Float the part if required.

Rotate
389) Click **Rotate Component** Compo... .

390) Rotate the **component** until the top frame members are approximately parallel with the MountingPlate-Sketch as illustrated.

391) Click **OK** from the Rotate Component PropertyManager.

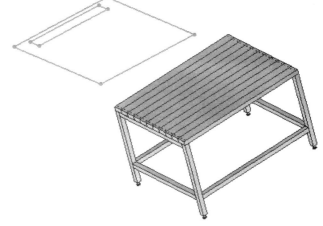

Assemble the 80-20-Q52423 part to the MountingPlate-Sketch.

392) Click the **top left edge** of the 80-20-Q52423 part.

393) Click **Mate**  .

394) Click the **left edge** of the MountingPlate-Sketch. Coincident is selected by default.

395) Click ✔.

396) Click the **top front edge** of the 80-20-Q52423 part.

397) Click the **front edge** of the MountingPlate-Sketch. Coincident is selected by default.

398) Click ✔. The 80-20-Q52423 part is fully defined with two Coincident Mates.

399) Click **OK** 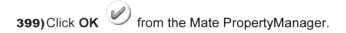 from the Mate PropertyManager.

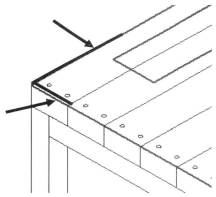

Modify the MountingPlate-Sketch to correspond to the 80-20-Q52423 part dimensions modified by the design change.

The MountingPlate-Sketch references geometry in the DELIVERY-STATION assembly. Edit the MountingPlate-Sketch in the context of the DELIVERY-STATION assembly.

Modify the MountingPlate-Sketch.

400) Right-click **MountingPlate-Sketch** from the FRAME FeatureManager.

401) Click **Edit In Context**. You are in the DELIVERY-STATION assembly.

Display the dimensions.

402) Double-click the **Layout** sketch from the DELIVERY-STATION FeatureManager.

Display a Top view.

403) Click **Top** view.

The mountplate_height value is 1160mm. Equation1 drives the value. Edit Equation1.

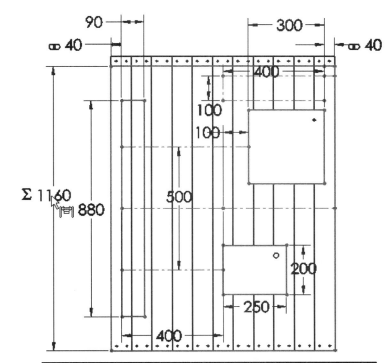

Edit Equations.

404) Right-click **Equations** from the DELIVERY-STATION assembly FeatureManager.

405) Click **Edit Equation**.

Modify Equation1.

406) Click **Equation1** from the Equations box.

407) Click **Edit**.

408) Delete **100** in the Edit Equation box.

409) Enter **120**.

410) Click **OK** from the Edit Equation box. The mountplate_ height is 1200mm. The value is displayed in the Equations dialog box.

411) Click **OK** from the Equations box.

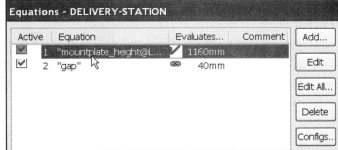

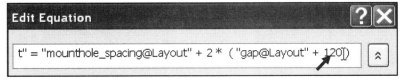

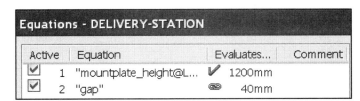

Update the assembly.
412) Click **Rebuild**.

Display an Isometric view.
413) Click **Isometric** view.

414) Double-click **Layout** sketch from the FeatureManager. View the updated dimension.

Save the DELIVERY-STATION assembly.
415) Click **Save**.

Return to the FRAME assembly.
416) Return to the **FRAME** assembly.

417) Click **Save**.

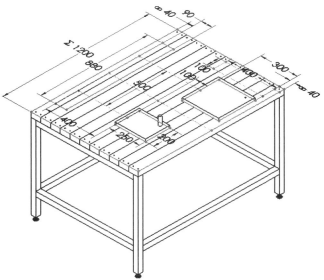

FRAME (Default<Display State·
- ⊞ A Annotations
- ⊞ ◇ Design Binder
- ⊞ ⛯ Lights and Cameras
- ◇ Front Plane
- ◇ Top Plane
- ◇ Right Plane
- ⤷ Origin
- ⧉ MountingPlate-Sketch ->
- ⊞ ⛃ 80-20-Q52423<1>
- ⊞ ❘❘❘ Mates

Working with AutoCAD geometry

Two JOINING-PLATES parts are required between the FRAME assembly and the 99-22101, 3AXIS-TRANSFER assembly. The MountingPlate-Sketch locates the center point of the M14 Tapped Holes.

The FRAME assembly utilizes a simplified rectangular cross section to display its structural members. The simplified cross section creates an assembly that is quicker to modify and to rebuild.

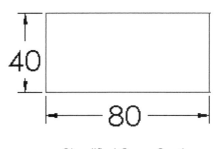

Simplified Cross Section

Actual Cross Section

☀ Utilize additional configurations to create a simplified part or assembly for a quicker rebuild time.

🔆 Import AutoCAD profiles with the Import to a new part as sketch option to save time in SolidWorks. Utilize existing .dwg and dxf profiles. Add relations to constrain the sketch profile with respect to the part Origin. To modify the sketch plane, utilize Edit Sketch Plane in the FeatureManager. SolidWorks DWGEditor edits and saves .dwg and .dxf files in their native file format.

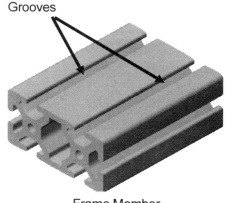

Grooves

Frame Member
Grooves 40mm on center

The company 80/20, Inc. produces JOINING-PLATEs. The 40-4325 JOINING-PLATE is available in AutoCAD .dxf or .dwg 2D format.

The holes of the JOINING-PLATE are located 40mm on center. Fasten the JOINING-PLATEs to the FRAME assembly. Each FRAME member contains two grooves located 40mm on center.

The 3AXIS-TRANSFER assembly requires two additional M14 Tapped holes. Insert the M14 Tapped holes 90mm apart in the center of the JOINING-PLATE.

Import the 40-4325.dwg file. Utilize the front profile and create a SolidWorks part file. Work with your 80/20 distributors to obtain cost, lead-time, availability and any other required options.

Select the .dwg format. The .dwg format file size is smaller than the .dxf format.

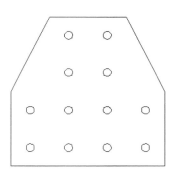

40-4325 Standard

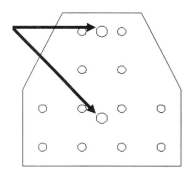

2-M14 Tapped Holes (Custom)

Activity: Working with AutoCAD geometry

Import the 40-4325 JOINING-PLATE part.
418) Click **File**, **Open** from the Main menu.

419) Select the **ASSEMBLY-SW-FILES-2006/PROJECT6-2006** folder.

420) Select **DWG (*.dwg)** from Files of type.

421) Double-click **40-4325**.

422) Click **Import to a new part**.

423) Click **Next>**.

424) Click **White background**.

425) Click **Next>**.

426) Select **Millimeters** for Units for the Imported data.

427) Click the **to a 2D sketch** option.

428) Click **Finish**.

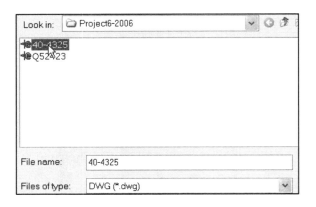

The current sketch displays the Top, Front, and Right views. SolidWorks displays Part2 and the 2D to 3D toolbar in the Graphics window. The Front view and Right view are required to extrude the sketch. Delete the Top view.

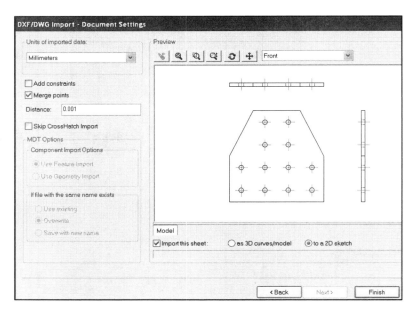

Extract the Sketches.
429) Window Select the **Top view** of Sketch1.

430) Click **Delete**.

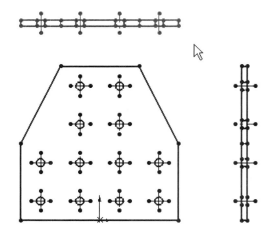

Set the Front view.
431) Click the **Origin** from the FeatureManager.

432) Hold the **Ctrl** key down. Click the **horizontal** line.

433) Release the **Ctrl** key.

434) Click **Midpoint**.

435) Click **OK** 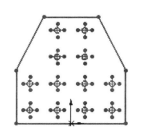 from the Properties
PropertyManager.

436) Window-select the **Front profile**.

437) Click **Fix** from the Properties box.

438) Click **OK** 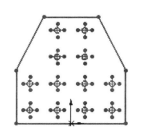 from the Properties
PropertyManager.

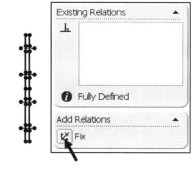

439) Window-select the **Front profile**.

440) Click **Front** view from the 2D to
3D toolbar. The view icons highlight in the 2D
to 3D toolbar.

Set the Right profile.
441) Window-select the **Right profile**.

442) Click **Right** view from the 2D to 3D toolbar.
The Right view moves and rotates.

Display an Isometric view.
443) Click **Isometric** view.

Align the sketches.
444) Click the **Front edge** of the Right profile.

445) Hold the **Ctrl** key down. Click the **Right edge**
of the Front profile. Release the **Ctrl** key.

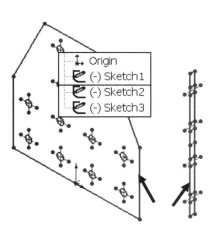

446) Click **Align Sketch** from the 2D to 3D
toolbar.

447) Click **Exit Sketch** . Sketch2 and
Sketch3 are displayed in the FeatureManager.

Extrude the Sketch.
448) Click **Sketch2** from the FeatureManager.

449) Click **Extrude** from the 2D to 3D toolbar.

450) Click the **top back point** on the Right profile of Sketch3.

451) Click **OK** from the Extrude PropertyManager.

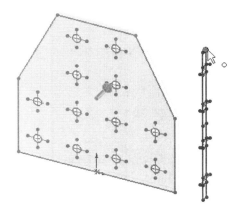

Save the part.
452) Click **Save**.

453) Enter **40-4325** for part name.

Save the current part to a new part name.
454) Click **File**, **Save As** from the Main menu.

455) Enter **40-4325-14MM-HOLES** for part name. The 40-4325-14MM-HOLES part is displayed in the FeatureManager.

456) Click **Save**.

457) Hide **Sketch3** from the FeatureManager.

Note: The Save As option displays the new part name in the Graphics window. The Save as copy option copies the current document to a new file name. The current document remains open in the Graphics window.

Add additional Hole features to the 40-4325-14MM-HOLES part. The RODLESS-CYLINDER assembly determines the M14x2.0 Tapped Hole size.

Insert two M14x2.0 Tapped Holes.
458) Click the **front face** below the top two holes as illustrated.

459) Click **Hole Wizard** Hole Wizard from the Features toolbar.

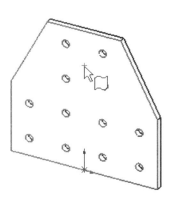

460) Click **Hole** for Hole Specification.

461) Click **Ansi Metric** for Standard.

462) Click **Drill sizes** for Type.

463) Click **14** for Size.

464) Select **Through All** for End Condition.

465) Click the **Positions** tab.

Display a Front view.
466) Click **Front** view.

467) Click a **position** for the second hole below the first hole.

468) Right-click **Select**.

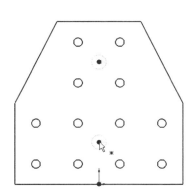

Add a Vertical relation.
469) Click the **Origin**. Hold the **Ctrl** key down. Click the **first point** and **second point**.

470) Release the **Ctrl** key.

471) Click **Vertical**. Click **OK** 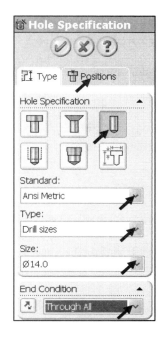 from the Properties Property Manager.

Add a dimension.

472) Click **Smart Dimension** Dimens... .

473) Click the **first hole** and the **second hole**.

474) Enter **90**. Click ✔.

475) Click the **second hole** and the **Origin**.

476) Enter **120**. Click ✔. Click **OK** from the Dimension PropertyManager.

477) Click **OK** from the Hole Position PropertyManager.

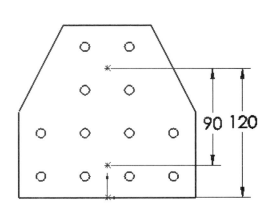

Save the 40-4325-14MM-HOLES part.
478) Click **Save**.

Insert the first 40-4325-14MM-HOLES part into the FRAME assembly.
479) Open the **FRAME** assembly.

Insert the 40-4325-14MM-HOLES part into the FRAME Graphics window.

480) Click **Insert Component** Compo… .

481) Click **40-4325-14MM-HOLE**.

482) Click a **position** to the left of the FRAME assembly.

483) Position the part with **Rotate Component** and **Move Component commands** as illustrated.

Display the Temporary Axes.
484) Click **View**, **Temporary Axes** from the Main menu.

Mate the 40-4325-14MM-HOLES part to the FRAME assembly.
485) Click the **bottom face** of the 40-4325-14MM-HOLES part.

486) Click **Mate** Mate .

487) Click the **top face** of the 80-20-Q52423 part. Coincident is selected by default.

488) Click ✔ .

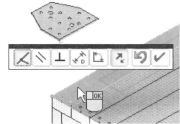

•

489) Click the **M14 Tapped Hole left axis**.

490) Click the **left vertex** of the MountingPlate-Sketch. Coincident is selected by default.

491) Click ✔ .

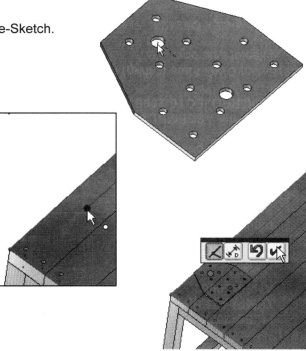

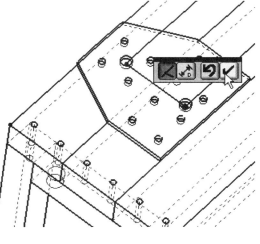

492) Click the **M14 Tapped Hole right axis**.

493) Click the **right vertex** of the MountingPlate-Sketch. Coincident is selected by default.

494) Click ✔ .

495) Click **OK** ✅ from the Mate PropertyManager. The 40-4325-14MM-HOLES part is fully defined.

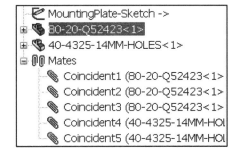

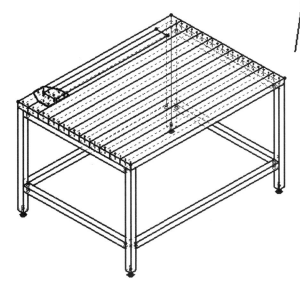

Insert the second 40-4325-14MM-HOLES part.

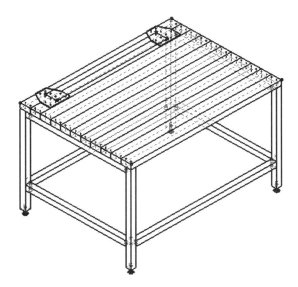

496) Click **Insert Component** Compo... .

497) Click and Drag the second **40-4325-14MM-HOLES** part into the FRAME assembly as illustrated.

Mate the second 40-4325-14MM-HOLES to the FRAME assembly.

498) **Repeat** the previous process of mating the first 40-4325-14MM-HOLES part to the FRAME assembly. Note: Three Coincident mates are needed for the second part using the right vertices.

Deactivate Temporary Axes.

499) Click **View**, uncheck **Temporary Axes** from the Main menu.

Save the FRAME assembly.

500) Click **Save**.

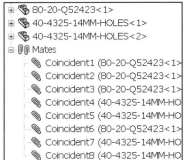

Reusing Components: Component Pattern and Mirror Component

In the previous activity, you created a second instance of the 40-4325-14MM-HOLES part. If you change the part, both instances update.

What other commands are available to copy components?

Answer: Component Pattern and Mirror Components.

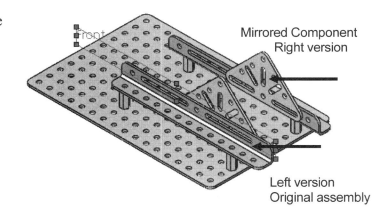

Example of Mirrored component has left/right version option.

Component Pattern consists of three options:

- Linear Pattern.

- Circular Pattern.

- Feature Driven Pattern.

You utilized the Linear Pattern (Local) and Feature Driven Pattern (Derived) options in the 3AXIS-TRANSFER assembly.

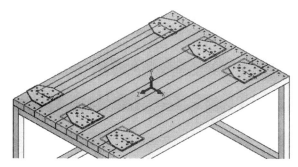

Example of a Component Pattern, Linear Pattern option

The Mirror Components option also reuses existing parts and assemblies. There are two options for Mirror Components:

- Mirrored component has left/right version option.

- Instanced component is used on both sides option.

Utilize the second option in the next activity.

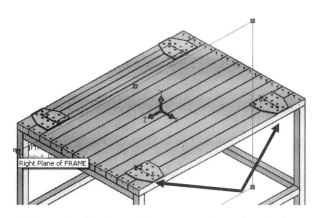

Example of Instanced component, used on both sides.

The Selections box requires a mirror plane.

The Components to Mirror box lists a check box before the component name.

When the box is checked, the mirrored component has a left/right version. When the box is unchecked, SolidWorks creates an instanced component.

The mirrored components are free to translate and rotate. To fully define a mirror component, insert Mates between the components and the assembly.

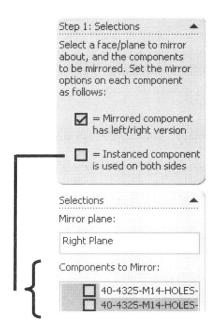

Activity: Reusing Components: Mirror Component

Mirror the two 40-4325-14MM-HOLES parts.
501) Click **40-4325-14MM-HOLES<1>** from the FeatureManager

502) Hold the **Ctrl** key down.

503) Click the **40-4325-14MM-HOLES<2>** from the FeatureManager.

504) Release the **Ctrl** key. Click **Insert, Mirror Components** from the Main menu.

505) Click **Right Plane** from the FeatureManager.

506) Click **Next** 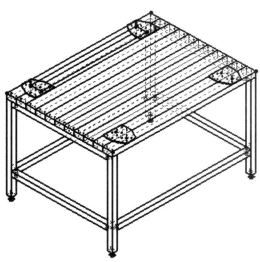 from the Mirror Components PropertyManager. Click **OK** from the Mirror Components PropertyManager.

Two additional instances are mirrored and added to the FeatureManager. The components 40-4325-14MM-HOLES<3> and 40-4325-14MM-HOLES<4> require additional Coincident Mates. Inserting Mates is an additional exercise. For now, suppress the two instances.

A quick mating technique is to utilize the Fix option for the components listed in the Components to Mirror box. Why is the Fix option not a good modeling technique in this project?

Answer: The FRAME sub-assembly and top level DELIVERY-STATION assembly utilize Layout sketches. If the Layout dimensions change, the position of the mirrored components remains the same.

Suppress the mirror components.
507) Click **40-4325-14MM-HOLES<3>**.

508) Hold the **Ctrl** key down.

509) Click **40-4325-14MM-HOLES<4>**. Release the Ctrl key.

510) Right-click **Suppress**.

Save the FRAME assembly.
511) Click **Save**.

Close all models.
512) Click **Window**, **Close All** from the Main menu.

Inserting the DELIVERY-STATION assembly

You are now at the last step of the project. Insert the 99-022101, 3AXIS-TRANSFER
assembly into the DELIVERY-STATION assembly. Mate the Tapped Holes. Save
memory. Load the 99-022101, 3AXIS-TRANSFER assembly in Lightweight mode.
Resolve the 99-022102, LINEAR-TRANSFER assembly to obtain the Mate references
from the Cbore mounting holes.

The 3AXIS-TRANSFER assembly fastens to the JOINING-PLATE part. The 99-
022101/99-022013/015801/MY1M2104HeadCover part contains the Cbore Hole features
required to assemble the JOINING-PLATE.

Activity: Inserting the DELIVERY-STATION assembly

Open the DELIVERY-STATION assembly.
513) Click **File**, **Open** from the Main menu.

514) Double-click **DELIVERY-STATION**.

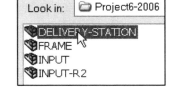

Insert the 99-022101, 3AXIS-TRANSFER assembly.

Insert
515) Click **Insert Component** Compo...

516) Click **Browse**.

517) Click **99-022101.sldasm**
from the DeliveryStation-
Project5 folder.

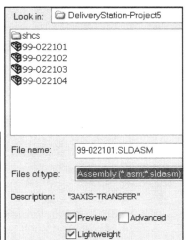

518) Click the **Lightweight**
check box.

519) Click the **Position1**
configuration.

520) Click **Open**.

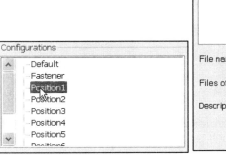

521) Click a **position** above the
DELIVERY-STATION.

Know your level in the assembly and the component that makes sense for mating. The MY1M2104 HeadCover contains the holes to fasten to the JOINING-PLATE parts.

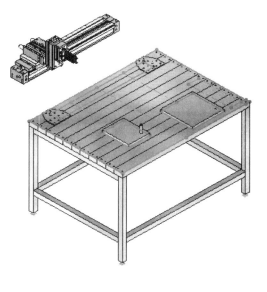

The MY1M2104 HeadCover is four levels down from the top-level DELIVERY-STATION assembly.

Locate the MY1M2104 HeadCover<1> part.
522) Expand **99-022101**, 3AXIS-TRANSFER assembly.

523) Expand **99-022102**, LINEAR-TRANSFER assembly.

524) Expand **015801**, RODLESS-CYLINDER assembly.

525) Expand **MY1M2104HeadCover<1>**.

526) Double-click **Mount_CBore** from the FeatureManager. The Cbore diameter is 17mm.

Assemble the 99-022101, 3AXIS-TRANSFER assembly to the DELIVERY-STATION assembly. Insert a Coincident SmartMate.
527) Hold the **Alt key** down.

528) Click the **left CBore face** of the 99-022101/ 99-022013/015801/ MY1M2104HeadCover.

529) Drag the left CBore face to the **left face** of the 40-4325-14MM-HOLES part M14 Tapped Hole. Coincident is selected by default.

530) Release the **Alt** key

531) Click ✔ .

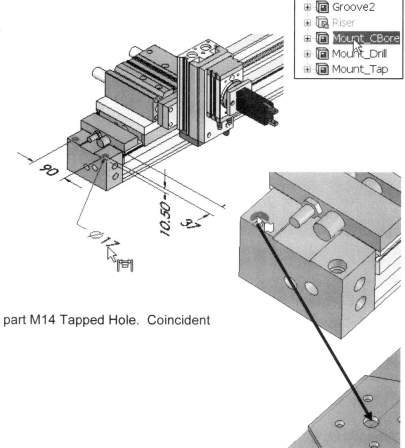

532) Hold the **Alt key** down.

533) Click the **right Cbore face** of the 99-022101/
99-022013/015801/MY1M2104HeadCover
part.

534) Drag the right CBore face to the **right face** of
the 40-4325-14MM-HOLES part M14
Tapped Hole. Concentric is selected by
default.

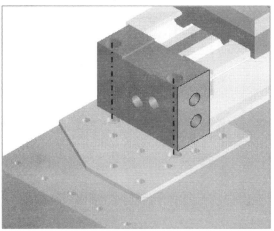

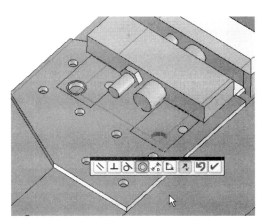

535) Click ✔ .

536) Hold the **Alt key** down.

537) Click the **bottom face** of the 99-022101/99-022102/
015801/MY1M2104HeadCover part.

538) Drag the bottom face downward to the **top face** of
the 40-4325-14MM-HOLES part. Coincident is
selected by default.

539) Click ✔ .

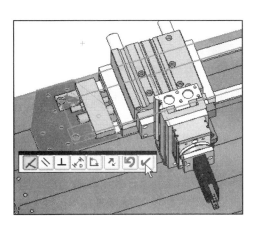

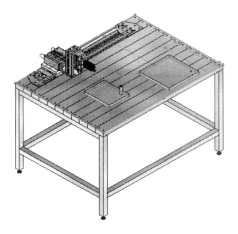

Display the Assembly Statistics.

540) Click **Tools**, **Assembly Statistics** from the Main menu. All Fasteners are suppressed. Note: Fasteners, and components created in the project exercises are not included in the Assembly Statistics. Click **OK**.

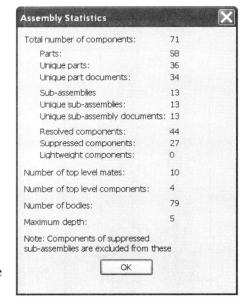

What modeling techniques does this Assembly Statistics report illustrate?

Answer:

- Unnecessary components are suppressed. Twenty-five fasteners are not loaded into memory.

- Parts are reused. Twenty parts out of fifty-six are copied through multiple instances and patterns.

- Top level mates and top level components are minimized. Only four components are inserted at the top-level.

You have completed your tasks for the DELIVERY-STATION assembly. The completion of the project depends on your colleagues to design additional assemblies. It is time to move to another project. But wait. Remember, the next engineer who works on the DELIVERY-STATION assembly will handle the INPUT and OUTPUT assemblies and load hundreds of components into memory.

How can you assist your colleagues to select and show components in the assembly? Answer: Insert an assembly envelope into the DELIVERY-STATION assembly.

Envelopes

An assembly envelope is an assembly component that utilizes its volume to determine the position of other components in the assembly.

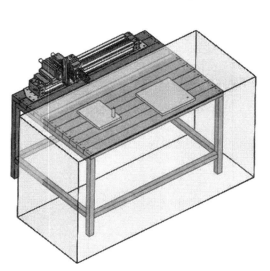

Utilize an envelope to modify the visibility of assembly components and to select components for suppress, copy resolve, delete and other editing operations.

As a solid reference component, an envelope plays no role in the Bill of Materials, Mass Properties or other global assembly operations.

SolidWorks displays envelope components in a light blue transparent color in Shaded view mode.

The FeatureManager contains the envelope entry that defines its geometry. The CommandManager contains the envelope configuration that defines selection criteria.

Activity: Envelopes

Insert an envelope.
541) Click **Insert**, **Envelope**, **New** from the Main menu.

542) Enter **ENVELOPE-DELIVERY-STATION** for name.

543) Click **Save**.

544) Click the DELIVERY-STATION **FRONT Plane** from the FeatureManager.

Display the Front view.
545) Click **Front** view.

Sketch the profile.

546) Click **Rectangle** Rectan... from the Sketch toolbar.

547) Sketch a **Rectangle** in the Front view as illustrated. The left edge of the rectangle is to the left of the Origin. The INPUT rack profile and the right half of the FRAME assembly are enclosed by the rectangle.

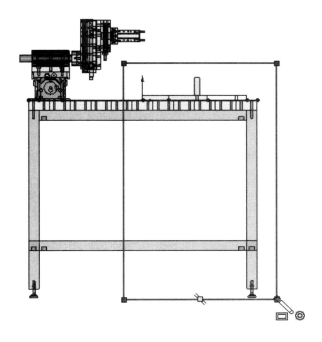

Extrude the profile.

548) Click **Extruded Boss/Base** Boss/B... from the Features toolbar.

549) Click **Mid Plane** for Direction1.

550) Enter **1600** for Depth. Click **OK** ✔ from the Extrude PropertyManager.

551) Click **Edit Component** Compo... to return to the DELIVERY-STATION assembly. The FeatureManager displays the Envelope1 entry.

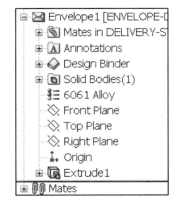

Utilize the Envelope reference component.
552) Click the **ConfigurationManager**.

553) Click the **Envelope1** configuration.

554) Right-click **Show/hide Using envelope**.

555) Check **Show part component** in the Apply Envelope box.

556) Check **Inside envelope** for Criteria. The 3AXIS-TRANSFER assembly is located outside the envelope.

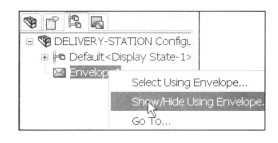

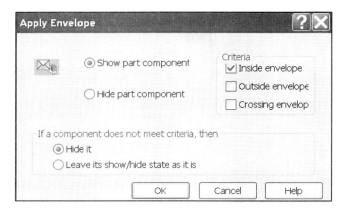

557) Click **OK** from the Apply Envelope box.

Display the Outside envelope part components.
558) Click the **Envelope1** configuration.

559) Right-click **Show/hide** using envelope.

560) Uncheck **Inside envelope**. Click **Outside envelope**.

561) Click **OK** from the Apply Envelope box.

Display all components.
562) Right-click **Show/hide** using envelope.

563) Check **Inside envelope**.

564) Check **Outside envelope**.

565) Click **OK** from the Apply Envelope box.

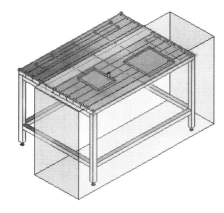

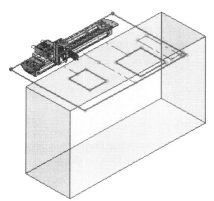

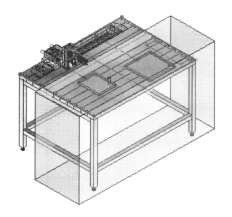

The Select using envelope option
provides the ability to select components
at the top assembly level based on their
position in relationship to the envelope.

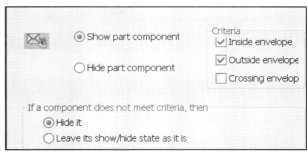

Return to the FeatureManager. Suppress the
FRAME assembly.

566) Right-click **FRAME** from the
FeatureManager.

567) Click **Suppress**.

568) Right-click **Envolope1** from the FeatureManager.

569) Click **Hide**.

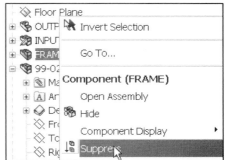

570) Click **View**, uncheck **Sketches** from the Main menu.

Save the DELIVERY-STATION assembly.

571) Click **Save**.

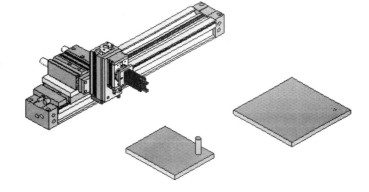

Before you hand off the assembly
to a colleague or save the assembly
at the end of the day, perform the
following tasks.

End of the day Save Task List:
• Suppress components not required for initial loading.
• Minimize all entries in the FeatureManager for easier viewing.
• Display an Isometric view for a clear thumbnail.
• Review the Rebuild status. If red flags exist, address the mate issues.
• Follow your company's back up procedure.

Additional Assembly Modeling tools: Join, Split, and Explode Line Sketch

The following assembly modeling tools are for information only, they are not related to the DELIVERY-STATION project. Additional assembly modeling information is available in Online help and the SolidWorks Reference Guide. The SolidWorks Reference Guide is a 1,000 page .pdf document that is available to subscription users from the SolidWorks web site.

Join Feature.

The Join feature combines multiple components in an assembly into a single part. Utilize the Join feature with casting and plastic applications. Explore the Join feature with the COSMOSXpress analysis tool.

Approximate an analysis with COSMOSXpress by combining parts in an assembly with the Join feature. This method is a good first analysis approach if the components utilize the same material.

To perform the analysis, execute the Join feature in the context of the CRANK-ORG assembly. Combine the BASE part and the HANDLE part to create the JOIN-CRANK part. Analyze the JOIN-CRANK part with COSMOSXpress.

The COSMOSXpress 🔌 command is located in the Tools menu or the Tools drop down list in the Standards toolbar. The COSMOSXpress tool is visible in the part document.

Note: The components in this section are available in the Project6-AdditionalModels-2006 on the CD in the book. Copy the folder to Project6-AdditionalModels-2006.

Activity: Join Feature and COSMOSXpress

Copy the Project6-AdditionalModels folder.
572) Select **Project6-AdditionalModels2006** from the CD contained in the book.

573) Copy the **folder** to Project6-Additional-Models-2006.

Open the CRANK-ORG assembly.
574) Click **File**, **Open** from the Main menu.

575) Double-click the **Project6-AdditionalModels2006\CRANK-ORG** assembly. The CRANK-ORG assembly contains the BASE part and the HANDLE part. The HANDLE part is free to rotate around the vertical axis of the BASE part.

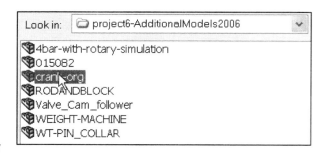

Insert a new part into the CRANK-ORG assembly.
576) Click **Insert, Component, New Part** from the Main menu.

577) Enter **JOIN-CRANK** for Part name.

578) Click **Save**.

579) Click **Front Plane** from the FeatureManager.

Exit

580) Click **Exit Sketch** Sketch . The Edit Component mode icon is selected. The JOIN-CRANK text is displayed in blue.

Insert the Join feature into the JOIN-CRANK part.
581) Click **Insert**, **Features**, **Join** from the Main menu.

582) Click **BASE** from the CRANK-ORG FeatureManager.

583) Click **HANDLE** from the CRANK-ORG FeatureManager.

584) Check the **Hide parts** option.

585) Click **OK** from the Join Property Manager.

Return to the CRANK-ORG assembly.
Edit
586) Click **Edit Component** Compo... .

Open the **JOIN-CRANK** part.
587) Right-click **JOIN-CRANK** from the FeatureManager.

588) Click **Open Part**.

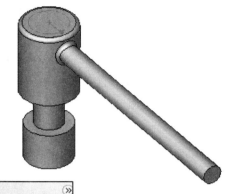

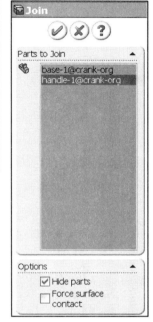

Run a COSMOSXpress Analysis.

589) Click the **COSMOSXpress Analysis Wizard** from the Standard toolbar. The Welcome tab is displayed.

590) Click **Next>**.

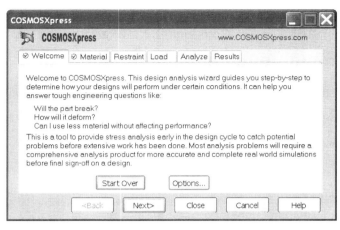

591) Select **Alloy Steel** from the Material list. Click **Apply**.

592) Click **Next>**. View the Restraint screen.

593) Click **Next>**.

594) Click the BASE **bottom circular face** for the Restraint. Face<1> is displayed.

595) Click **Next>**.

596) Click **Next>**. The Load tab is displayed.

597) Click **Next>**.

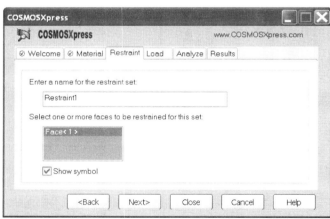

598) Click **Force**.

599) Click **Next>**.

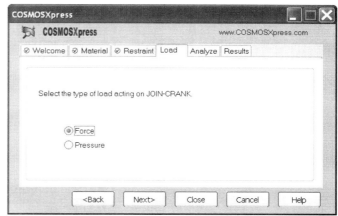

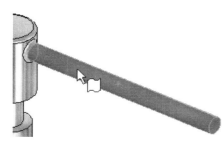

600) Click the **HANDLE circular face** to apply a load.

601) Click **Next>**.

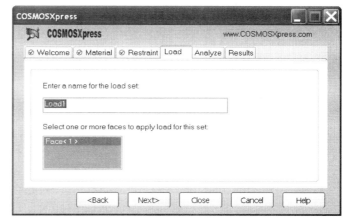

602) Enter **100 N** for the vertical force.

603) Click **Top Plane** from the FeatureManager for the **Normal to a reference plane**.

604) Click **Next>**. Click **Next>**.

605) Click **Next>**. Run the first Analysis.

606) Click **Run** from the Analyze tab to review the FOS. The FOS is 7.56. Click **Next>**. Click **Show Stress distribution**.

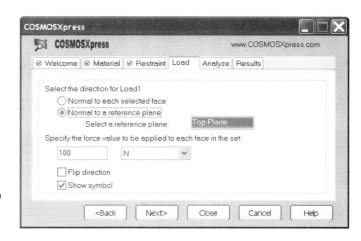

607) Click **Next>**. Review the stress distribution.

608) Click **Close**. Click **Yes** to save data.

As an exercise, modify the force on the Handle part to obtain a FOS between 3 and 6.
Rerun COSMOSXpress.

609) Click **COSMOSXpress Analysis Wizard** 🔊 from the Standard toolbar.

610) Click **Update** from the Analyze tab.

Refer to the COSMOSXpress Online tutorial or **Engineering Design with SolidWorks 2006** for additional examples.

☼ Tips on performing analysis. You are dealing with thousands or millions of equations. Every analysis situation is unique.

- Utilize symmetry. If a part is symmetric about a plane, one half of the model is required for analysis. If a part is symmetric about two planes, one fourth of the model is required for analysis.

- Suppress small fillets and detailed features in the part.

- Avoid parts that have aspect ratios over 100.

- Utilize consistent units.

- Estimate an intuitive solution based on the fundamentals of stress analysis techniques.

- Factor of Safety is a guideline for the designer. The designer is responsible for the safety of the part.

Split feature.

The Split feature is utilized to break a single solid body into multiple bodies. To create a Split feature perform the following steps:

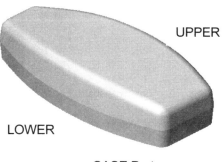

UPPER

LOWER

CASE Part

1. Select the Split feature.

2. Select a plane or curve for the Trim Tool.

3. Select the bodies to form individual parts.

4. Name the parts.

Create Assembly tool.

The Create Assembly tool builds a new assembly from the parts developed in the Split feature. To utilize the Create Assembly tool perform the following steps:

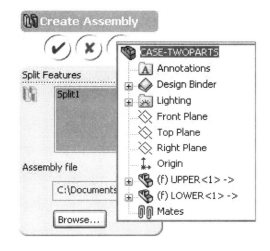

1. Select Insert, Features, Create Assembly.

2. Select the Split feature.

3. Enter a new assembly file name.

The assembly contains the parts developed with the Split feature.

The CASE part is available in the Project6-AdditionalModels folder. The Split feature and Create Assembly feature are an additional exercise.

Exploded Line Sketch.

The Exploded Line Sketch tool is a 3D sketch added to an Exploded View in an assembly. The explode lines indicate the relationship between components in the assembly.

Insert an Exploded View. Add the Exploded Line Sketch between components.

The 4BAR-WITH-ROTARY-SIMULATION assembly contains five components - three links and two joints. Utilize an Exploded Line Sketch to specify how to assemble the three links.

Activity: Exploded Line Sketch

Create an Exploded View.
611) Click **File**, **Open** from the Main menu.

612) Double-click the **4BAR-WITH-ROTARY-SIMULATION** assembly.

613) Click **Exploded View** from the Assembly toolbar.

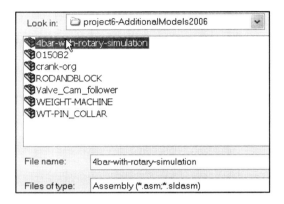

Create Exploded Step1.
614) Click the **lower joint** part as illustrated.

615) Drag the **blue arrow** to the right.

616) Click **Done**.

Create Exploded Step2.
617) Click the **upper link** part as illustrated.

618) Drag the **blue arrow** to the left.

619) Click **Done**.

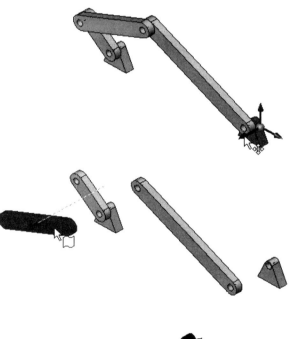

Create Exploded Step3.
620) Click the **upper joint** part as illustrated.

621) Drag the **blue arrow** to the right.

622) Click **Done**.

623) Click **OK** from the Explode PropertyManager.

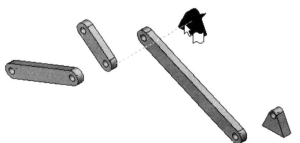

Insert the Explode Line Sketch.

624) Click **Explode Line Sketch** from the Assembly toolbar.

625) **Zoom in** on the first link-english part and joint-english part.

626) Click the **axis** from the link-english right hole.

627) Click the **axis** from the joint-english hole. The direction arrow points towards the back.

628) Click **OK** from the Route Line PropertyManager.

629) Repeat the **Explode Line Sketch** three times between the remaining components.

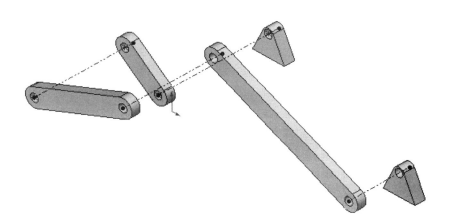

630) Right-click **Collapse** from the ConfigurationManager.

631) Return to the **FeatureManager**.

632) Click **Isometric** view.

633) Click **Save**.

634) Click **Window**, **Close All** from the Main menu.

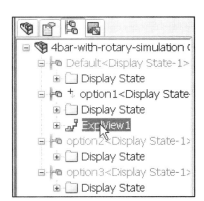

The 3DExplode1 feature is displayed as the first entry in the ExplView1. To edit an Exploded Line Sketch, right-click Edit Sketch.

Project Summary

There are Top-Down and Bottom-Up assembly modeling techniques. In this project, you utilized the Top-Down Layout sketch controlled by design constraints and equations. You created parts and assemblies in the context of the Layout sketch. You also developed the empty parts that contained multiple features and empty assemblies that contained multiple components.

Working with assemblies required you to import components of different files types and manipulate their geometry. Utilizing other 2D and 3D data saved time in the design process. Consulting with Application engineers from your supplier early in the project produced faster lead times for purchased components and an understanding of design options.

A Top-Down design assembly model is well organized and reduces errors as you developed new components. You reviewed all model dependencies. The DELIVERY-STATION Layout sketch populated with parts and assemblies. The FRAME sub-assembly contained a second Layout sketch with parts and assemblies.

You reviewed Component Pattern and Mirrored Components options to reuse geometry in an assembly. The envelope component provided a method to view and select geometry inside/outside a known volume.

The Explode Line Sketch, Join feature, and Split feature were explored as additional assembly modeling tools.

Engineers and designers study hard, work diligently and gain knowledge from their experiences. Parts, assemblies and drawings are only a portion of this project. In an engineering environment, you must also work with your engineering colleagues, other departments and the customer to complete a successful project.

Questions

1. Describe the Top Down design approach to assembly modeling.

2. Describe two methods to create a Top Down design assembly.

3. Describe a Layout sketch.

4. True or False. Centerlines cannot exist in a Layout sketch.

5. True or False. A Layout sketch exists only in a part.

6. How do you create a new part in the context of an assembly?

7. Explain the differences between a Link Value and an Equation.

8. Explain the procedure to edit an Equation.

9. Identify the location in the assembly to position the Layout sketch.

10. True or False. Only AutoCAD 2D geometry can be imported into SolidWorks.

11. Why set the Default Part template before importing an AutoCAD Solids assembly?

12. Why does the FRAME assembly utilize a simplified rectangular cross section?

13. Describe the types of Component Patterns you can create in an assembly.

14. Identify the two major options available in Mirror Component.

15. True of False. A Mirror Component creates a component that is fully defined in the assembly.

16. Define an envelope. Why would you utilize an envelope in a large assembly?

17. Identify two locations to activate Large Assembly Mode.

18. How does the Assembly Statistics tool assist you when you are creating an assembly?

19. Identify the procedure to create a new sub-assembly by utilizing components in the FeatureManager.

20. Describe how Assembly Features differ from features developed in a part.

21. An Explode View contains an _____ to indicate how components are assembled together.

Exercises

Note: All dimensions have not been provided for exercises 6.1 through 6.3. There is more than one answer.

Exercise 6.1: Create a new OUTPUT assembly. Reorder the OUTPUT-BASE-PLATE part into the OUTPUT assembly.

Exercise 6.2a: Add a Linear Pattern of Cbore Holes to the bottom face of the INPUT-BASE-PLATE part. Utilize the STANDOFF part to create a Derived Component Patten in the INPUT assembly. Add SHCSs to complete the INPUT assembly.

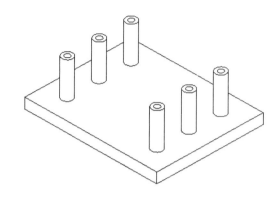

Exercise 6.2b. Add a Linear Pattern of Holes to the OUTPUT-BASE-PLATE part. Create a Design Table for the STANDOFF part. Add configurations to represent lengths of STANDOFFs: 70, 100, 200 and 300.

Insert the STANDOFF(100) configuration into the OUTPUT assembly. Create a Derived Component Pattern with the STANDOFF(100) part.

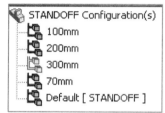

Create a Design Table for the OUTPUT-BASE-PLATE Rack. Utilize the Design Table to control the OUTPUT-BASE-PLATE thickness and Linear Pattern of Hole locations.

Assemble the GUIDE-CYLINDER-12MM assembly from Project1 to the OUTPUT assembly.

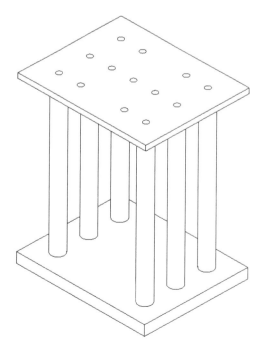

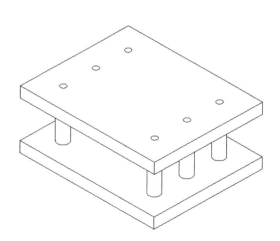

Exercise 6.3: Industry Collaborative Exercise.

Automatic Systems, Inc. Kansas City, MO, USA (www.asi.com) designs, manufactures, and installs quality material handling systems.

a) Utilize the World Wide Web to investigate the types of industries that require material handling systems.

b) Utilize 3DContentCentral to investigate the suppliers of Gearmotors, Bearings and Air Cylinders. Utilize the SolidWorks Manufacturer's Partner Network to determine machine shops and sheet metal shops in your geographical area.

c) ASI engineers evaluate their customer's requirements and propose an innovative and cost effective material handling solution. Identify the types of questions you would propose to a potential customer that requires a material handling system.

Model of a High Lift Fork Transfer
Courtesy of Automatic Systems, Inc.
Kansas City, MO USA
www.asi.com

Exercise 6.4: Project Data Management (PDM).

The DELIVERY-STATION assembly now contains thousands of components. Numerous engineers and designers worked on the assembly. How do you manage the parts, drawings and assemblies? Note: PDM/Works is a project data management software application that runs inside SolidWorks.

The application is comprised of four major components:

- Automated Revision Control.

- Check In/Check Out of Vaulted Area for Security.

- Support of Concurrent Engineering Activities.

- Maintaining a History of Design Activities.

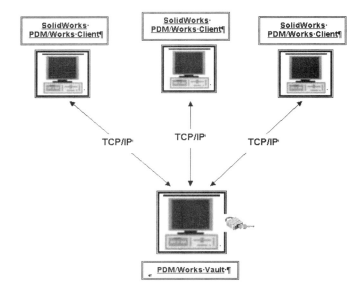

How would PDM be used in a concurrent engineering application with the DELIVERY-STATION assembly? Identify other departments in a company that could utilize a PDM system.

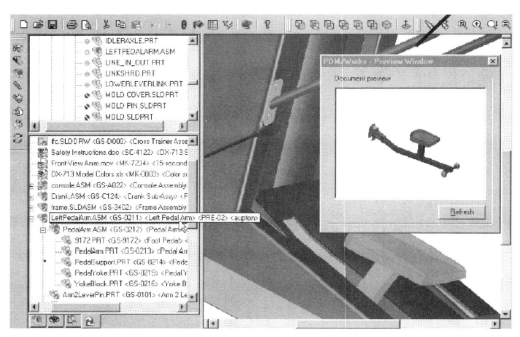

Exercise 6.5: Leveling Foot.

a) Create the Leveling Foot with Extrude, Loft and or Revolve features. Utilize the imported curves from the AutoCAD assembly.

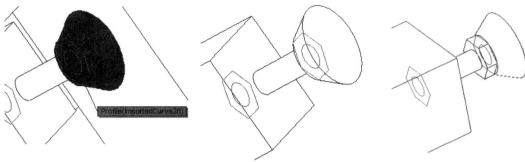

b) The Leveling Foot assembly is manufactured by 80-20, Inc. How would you obtain the information required to recreate the Leveling Foot as a SolidWorks assembly?

Exercise 6.6: Importing Geometry in .IGES format.

A 1″ diameter Shaft and Pillow Block Bearing support a 60-tooth Change Gear. Boston Gear modeled the Pillow Block Bearing and Change Gear in .IGES format.

Locate the PILLOW-BLOCK.IGS and GD60B-ENG.IGS files in the Exercise/ Exercise-Project6 file folder on the enclosed CD.

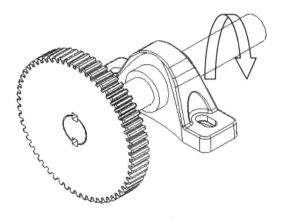

Models Courtesy of Boston Gear, Quincy, MA USA

Import the IGES files. Save the SolidWorks parts. Create a reference axis between the two reference planes for the PILLOW-BLOCK part and the GD60B-ENG part.

Create the SHAFT part. The SHAFT part is 6″ long. The SHAFT's double keyways are the same size as the GD60B-ENG keyways.

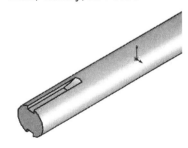

Create the BEARING-GEAR assembly. The PILLOW-BLOCK bearing is the first component in the assembly. The SHAFT is free to rotate in the PILLOW-BLOCK bearing.

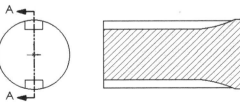

Exercise 6.6: Industry Collaborative Exercise.

Create a quality inspection CHECKING STATION assembly. Work with the team of manufacturing engineers. The quality inspection CHECKING STATION is comprised of four aluminum COREPLATE parts. Each COREPLATE measures 20in. x 14in., (508mm x 355.6mm).

The COREPLATE parts are clamped to a large steel TABLETOP 60in. x 36in., (1524mm x 914.4mm) during the checking process.

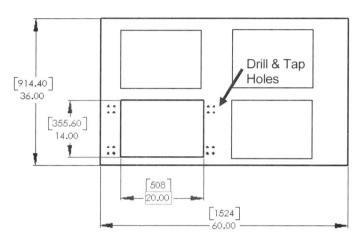

You require four holding CLAMPs mounted at the corners of the COREPLATE part. Each compact CLAMP assembly allows the quality control inspector to operate in a tight area. The TABLETOP part contains drilled and tapped holes for the CLAMP assembly. Fasten the CLAMP assembly to the TABLETOP part.

The senior manufacturing engineering on your team presents you with a few initial calculations. The CLAMP requires a minimum holding capacity of 500 lb (340 daN). Select the Horizontal Hold Down Clamp, part number 309-U manufactured by DE-STA-CO Industries: Madison Heights, MI USA. Visit the DE-STA-CO web site (www.destaco.com).

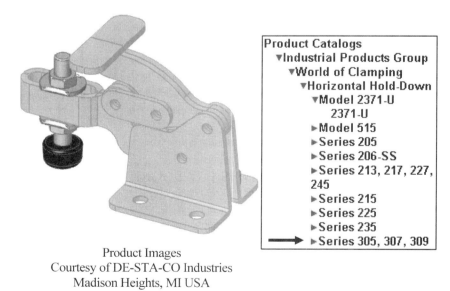

Product Images
Courtesy of DE-STA-CO Industries
Madison Heights, MI USA

Product Catalogs
▼Industrial Products Group
  ▼World of Clamping
    ▼Horizontal Hold-Down
      ▼Model 2371-U
        2371-U
      ►Model 515
      ►Series 205
      ►Series 206-SS
      ►Series 213, 217, 227, 245
      ►Series 215
      ►Series 225
      ►Series 235
  →   ►Series 305, 307, 309

Click the Product Catalogs button. Click Industrial Products Group, World of Clamping, Horizontal Hold-Down, Series 305, 307, 309. The Model No. 309-U row contains a Flanged Washer and a Spindle assembly part numbers.

Record the part numbers and hole dimensions.

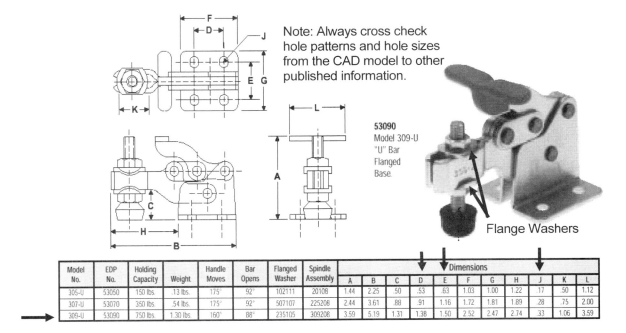

Note: Always cross check hole patterns and hole sizes from the CAD model to other published information.

53090
Model 309-U
"U" Bar
Flanged
Base.

Flange Washers

Model No.	EDP No.	Holding Capacity	Weight	Handle Moves	Bar Opens	Flanged Washer	Spindle Assembly	Dimensions										
								A	B	C	D	E	F	G	H	J	K	L
305-U	53050	150 lbs.	.13 lbs.	175°	92°	102111	20108	1.44	2.25	.50	.53	.63	1.03	1.00	1.22	.17	.50	1.12
307-U	53070	350 lbs.	.54 lbs.	175°	92°	507107	225208	2.44	3.61	.88	.91	1.16	1.72	1.81	1.89	.28	.75	2.00
309-U	53090	750 lbs.	1.30 lbs.	160°	88°	235105	309208	3.59	5.19	1.31	1.38	1.50	2.52	2.47	2.74	.33	1.06	3.59

Download the components required to create the CLAMP-WASHER-SPINDLE sub assembly.

Use the On-line Help to review the commands: Linear Pattern, Mirror, Mirror All, Component Pattern and Mirror Component.

Manually sketch a plan of the CHECKING STATION assembly. Develop a Layout sketch in the CHECKING STATION assembly. Create the components TABLETOP and COREPLATE from the Layout sketch. Add the CLAMP-WASHER-SPINDLE sub assembly.

Product Images
Courtesy of DE-STA-CO Industries
Madison Heights, MI USA

Insert four fasteners for each CLAMP.

Create an assembly drawing and a Bill of Materials for the CHECKING STATION assembly.

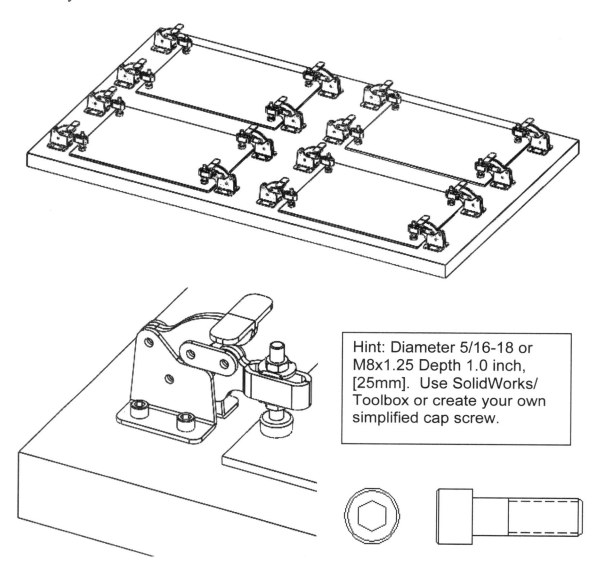

Hint: Diameter 5/16-18 or M8x1.25 Depth 1.0 inch, [25mm]. Use SolidWorks/ Toolbox or create your own simplified cap screw.

Exercise 6.7: Industry Collaborative Exercise.

Create a new SolidWorks part from imported 2D geometry.

In Project 6, you created profiles from the company 80/20, Inc. (www.8020.net). Hundreds of .dwg (AutoCAD Drawing) and .dxf files (Drawing Exchange Format) exist on their web site. Many companies support .dwg or .dxf file format.

Download the 2D .dxf library from www.8020.net (8Mb).

Open the part, 4140-2d.dxf. Click Open. Select .dxf for File type. Import the geometry as a Part and Import to a 2D Sketch. Utilize the 2D to 3D Tools. Create two new sketches. Extrude the profile.

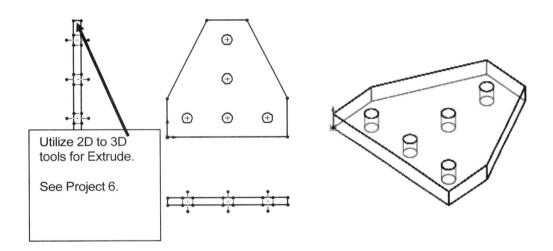

Model Courtesy of 80/20, Inc., Columbia City, IN USA

Notes:

Appendix

Engineering Changer Order (ECO)

D&M	Engineering Change Order		ECO # _____
			Page 1 of __

		Author
☐ Hardware		Date
☐ Software		Authorized Mgr.
Product Line ☐ Quality		Date
☐ Tech Pubs		

Change Tested By

Reason for ECO(Describe the existing problem, symptom and impact on field)

D&M Part No.	Rev From/To	Part Description	Description	Owner

ECO Implementation/Class		Departments	Approvals	Date	
All in Field	☐	Engineering			
All in Test	☐	Manufacturing			
All in Assembly	☐	Technical Support			
All in Stock	☐	Marketing			
All on Order	☐	DOC Control			
All Future	☐				
Material Disposition		ECO Cost			
Rework	☐	DO NOT WRITE BELOW THIS LINE (ECO BOARD ONLY)			
Scrap	☐	Effective Date			
Use as is	☐	Incorporated Date			
None	☐	Board Approval			
See Attached	☐	Board Date			

This text follows the ASME Y14 Engineering Drawing and Related Documentation Practices for drawings. Display of dimensions and tolerances are as follows:

TYPES of DECIMAL DIMENSIONS (ASME Y14.5M)			
Description:	**UNITS:** **MM**	**Description:**	**UNITS:** **INCH**
Dimension is less than 1mm. Zero precedes the decimal point.	0.9 0.95	Dimension is less than 1 inch. Zero is not used before the decimal point.	.5 .56
Dimension is a whole number. Display no decimal point. Display no zero after decimal point.	19	Express dimension to the same number of decimal places as its tolerance. Add zeros to the right of the decimal point. If the tolerance is expressed to 3 places, then the dimension contains 3 places to the right of the decimal point.	1.750
Dimension exceeds a whole number by a decimal fraction of a millimeter. Display no zero to the right of the decimal.	11.5 11.51		

TABLE 1 TOLERANCE DISPLAY FOR INCH AND METRIC DIMENSIONS (ASME Y14.5M)		
DISPLAY:	**UNITS:** **INCH:**	**UNITS:** **METRIC:**
Dimensions less than 1	.5	0.5
Unilateral Tolerance	$1.417^{+.005}_{-.000}$	$36^{0}_{-0.5}$
Bilateral Tolerance	$1.417^{+.010}_{-.020}$	$36^{+0.25}_{-0.50}$
Limit Tolerance	.571 .463	14.50 11.50

Cursor Feedback

Cursor Feedback provides information about SolidWorks geometry. The following tables summarize cursor feedback. The tables were developed by support engineers from Computer Aided Products, Inc. Peabody, MA. Used with permission.

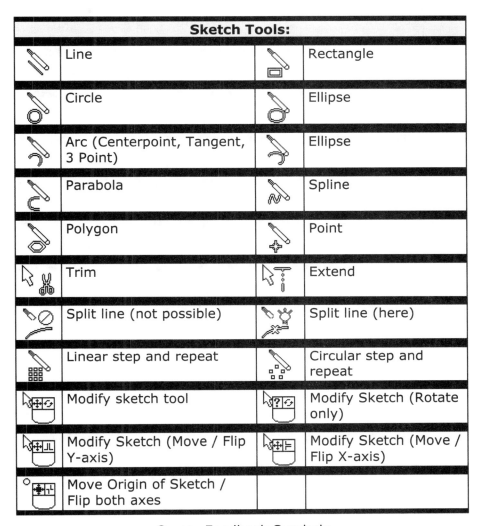

Sketch Tools:			
	Line		Rectangle
	Circle		Ellipse
	Arc (Centerpoint, Tangent, 3 Point)		Ellipse
	Parabola		Spline
	Polygon		Point
	Trim		Extend
	Split line (not possible)		Split line (here)
	Linear step and repeat		Circular step and repeat
	Modify sketch tool		Modify Sketch (Rotate only)
	Modify Sketch (Move / Flip Y-axis)		Modify Sketch (Move / Flip X-axis)
	Move Origin of Sketch / Flip both axes		

Cursor Feedback Symbols

Courtesy of Computer Aided Products, Inc. Peabody, MA USA

Sketching relationships:			
	Horizontal		Vertical
	Parallel		Perpendicular
	Tangent		Intersection
	Coincident to axis		Midpoint
	Quarter arc		Half arc
	3 quarter arc		Quadrant of arc
	Wake up line/edge		Wake up point
	Coincident to line/edge		Coincident to point
	3D sketch		3D sketch
	3D sketch		3D sketch
	3D sketch		3D sketch

Dimensions:			
	Dimension		Radial or diameter dimension
	Horizontal dimension		Vertical dimension
	Vertical ordinate dimension		Ordinate dimensioning
	Horizontal ordinate dimension		Baseline dimensioning

Cursor Feedback Symbols

Courtesy of Computer Aided Products, Inc. Peabody, MA USA

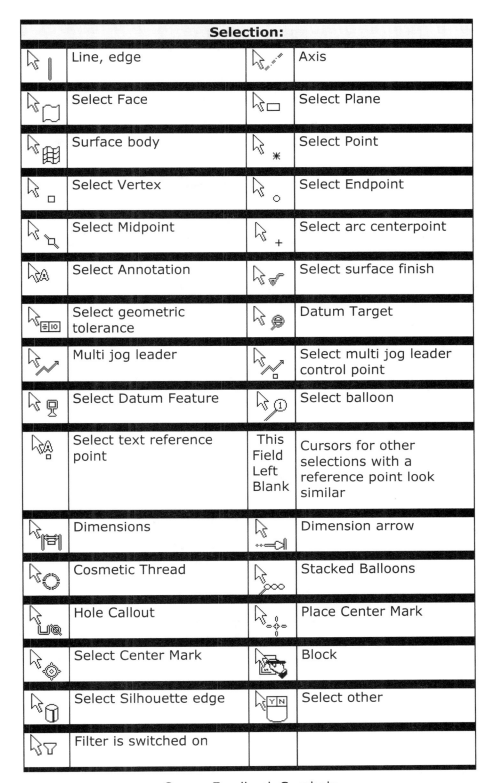

Selection:			
↖‖	Line, edge	↖ ⋰	Axis
↖⚐	Select Face	↖▭	Select Plane
↖▦	Surface body	↖ ✳	Select Point
↖ □	Select Vertex	↖ ○	Select Endpoint
↖◿	Select Midpoint	↖ +	Select arc centerpoint
↖Ⓐ	Select Annotation	↖⌙	Select surface finish
↖⊟⋈	Select geometric tolerance	↖⊕	Datum Target
↖↗	Multi jog leader	↖↗□	Select multi jog leader control point
↖⎓	Select Datum Feature	↖①	Select balloon
↖Ⓐ□	Select text reference point	This Field Left Blank	Cursors for other selections with a reference point look similar
↖⊨	Dimensions	↖⊶◁	Dimension arrow
↖○	Cosmetic Thread	↖∞	Stacked Balloons
↖⊔⊕	Hole Callout	↖⊹	Place Center Mark
↖✲	Select Center Mark	↖▨	Block
↖⊍	Select Silhouette edge	↖ Y N	Select other
↖▽	Filter is switched on		

Cursor Feedback Symbols

Courtesy of Computer Aided Products, Inc. Peabody, MA USA

Assemblies:			
	Choose reference plane (insert new component/envelope)		Insert Component from File
	Insert Component (fixed to origin)		Insert Component to Feature Manager
	Lightweight component		Rotate component
	Move component / Smartmate select mode		Select 2nd component for smartmate
	Simulation mode running		

Cursor feedback with Smartmates:			
	Mate - Coincident Linear Edges		Mate - Coincident Planar Faces
	Mate - Concentric Axes/Conical Faces		Mate - Coincident Vertices
	Mate - Coincident/Concentric Circular Edges or Conical Faces		

Feature manager:			
	Move component or feature in tree		Copy component or feature in tree
	Move feature below a folder in tree		Move/copy not permitted
	Invalid location for item		Move component in/out of sub assembly

Cursor Feedback Symbols

Courtesy of Computer Aided Products, Inc. Peabody, MA USA

Drawings:		
Drawing sheet		Drawing view
Move drawing view		Auxiliary view arrow
Change view size horizontally		Change view size vertically
Change view size diagonally		Change view size diagonally
Align Drawing View		Select detail circle
Block		Select Datum Feature Symbol
Insert/Select Weld Symbol		Select Center Mark
Select Section View		Section view and points of section arrow
Select Silhouette edge		Hide/Show Dimensions

Standard Tools:		
Selection tool		Please wait (thinking)
Rotate view		Pan view
Invalid selection/location		Measure tool
Zoom to area		Zoom in/out
Accept option		

Cursor Feedback Symbols

Courtesy of Computer Aided Products, Inc. Peabody, MA USA

Helpful On-Line Information

The SolidWorks URL: http://www.solidworks.com contains information on local resellers, Partners and SolidWorks users groups.

The SolidWorks URL: http://www.3DContentCentral.com contains additional engineering electronic catalog information.

The SolidWorks web site provides links to sample designs, frequently asked questions, an independent News Group (comp.cad.solidworks) and Users Groups.

Helpful on-line SolidWorks information is available from the following URLs:

- http://www.mechengineer.com/snug/

  News group access and local user group information.

- http://www.nhcad.com

  Configuration information and other tips and tricks.

- http://www.solidworktips.com

  Helpful tips, tricks on SolidWorks and API.

- http://www.topica.com/lists/SW/

  Independent News Group for SolidWorks discussions, questions and answers.

Certified SolidWorks Professionals (CSWP) URLs provide additional helpful on-line information.

- http://www.scottjbaugh.com   Scott J. Baugh

- http://www.3-ddesignsolutions.com   Devon Sowell

- http://www.zxys.com   Paul Salvador

- http://www.mikejwilson.com   Mike J. Wilson

- http://www.frontiernet.net/~mlombard   Matt Lombard

- http://www.dimontegroup.com   Gene Dimonte & Ed Eaton

On-line tutorials are for educational purposes only. Tutorials are copyrighted by their respective owners.

INDEX

D

S

Notes:

Notes:

Notes:

Notes:

Notes: